PUBLISHER'S NOTE

No contest on Earth is more crucial, more exciting or more important than the election process by which a free nation chooses its leaders.

We at Berkley are proud to take part in presenting this in-depth analysis and complete book-of-record of the 1980 Presidential campaign.

Our intention is to help provide the information and analysis essential to an informed electorate in a democracy; our hope is that this book will thus become part of the process it describes so vividly and so well.

November 1980

WASHINGTON POST/BERKLEY BOOKS

THE PURSUIT OF THE PRESIDENCY 1980
GUYANA MASSACRE: THE EYEWITNESS ACCOUNT

THE PURSUIT OF THE PRESIDENCY 1980

DAVID BRODER ★ LOU CANNON ★ HAYNES JOHNSON
MARTIN SCHRAM ★ RICHARD HARWOOD
and the staff of

The Washington Post

edited by RICHARD HARWOOD

A WASHINGTON POST/BERKLEY BOOK
published by
BERKLEY BOOKS, NEW YORK

E8
875
P87

THE PURSUIT OF THE PRESIDENCY 1980

A Berkley Book / published by arrangement with
The Washington Post Company

PRINTING HISTORY
Washington Post/Berkley edition / December 1980

ISBN: 0-425-04703-2

Acknowledgments

We are grateful to a number of people for assistance on this book:

To Benjamin C. Bradlee and Howard Simons for cooperation and encouragement; to Lucila George Woodard for continuing and excellent editorial assistance; to Valarie Thomas, Bridget Roeber and Chris Colford for research assistance; to Victor Temkin and the editors at Berkley Books; to William Dickinson of The Washington Post Writers' Group and to Esther Newberg, our literary agent.

A special acknowledgment is owed Barry Sussman, The *Washington Post*'s polling director, whose public opinion research provided a conceptual basis and substantial materials for the book; and to Maralee Schwartz for invaluable research assistance during the entire political campaign.

For Laurence M. Stern
1929–1979
Colleague and friend
who conceived this book
and missed the last chapter

CONTENTS

★ Foreword ★
by Benjamin C. Bradlee

THE DISTINGUISHED American novelist, E.L. Doctorow, once compared writing fiction to driving at night: you know your destination, you know the way, but headlights clarify only the road immediately in front of you.

Reporting a presidential election in America today offers similar challenges, similar difficulties. The destination is a calendar given: Election Day. The route gets longer and longer every four years, but it, too, is known: the arduous path from caucus to primary to whistle-stop in one state after another—up, down and across the American landmass.

The danger for readers, who after all are the voters, is that we journalists will see only what lies before our headlights—the trees down across the highways, if you will—and not what we can't see, just off the highway.

The trees across the highway were easy enough to spot:

- The first one, all the way back in October, 1979, in Florida caucuses, straw votes and conventions.
- In November, 1979, a full year before the election, there were the hostages in Iran, the Kennedy candidacy, and the Kennedy interview on CBS with Roger Mudd.
- The Iowa caucuses in January, 1980.
- The New Hampshire primary in February. (On one day that month no less than nine *Washington Post* reporters were falling all over each other in the Granite State.)
- In Illinois in March, Ronald Reagan all but sewed up the Republican nomination, and Jimmy Carter all but put Teddy Kennedy away.
- The Anderson candidacy became a reality in April.

- In May and June, Kennedy and George Bush made final and futile last gasps.
- The conventions came in July and August. And the *mano a mano* battle began.

Those were basically the easy stories for newspaper reporters to write . . . straightforward and hard to trivialize.

But what was going on out there, I ask myself today only a few days after the election, that we didn't see, that the pollsters missed, that even the winners still find hard to believe?

What role did we ourselves play? Candidates run against the media nowadays, and voters love it, charging us with the bias that is opposite to their own. We are generally felt to be pro-Democrat and anti-Republican, when the fact of this campaign is that reporters covering Carter found it hard to like him personally, and reporters covering Reagan found it comfortable to like him.

The answers to these questions won't be available for months to come. The daily stories are the "first rough draft of history," as Philip L. Graham once said succinctly. This book is a new draft, answering some of the questions that we didn't know when we started, but leaving many still unanswered, waiting for more information.

For the *Washington Post*, the hard-core political team all the way consisted of the dean of American political journalists, David Broder, with the inimitable Lou Cannon covering Reagan, plus Dick Harwood, Haynes Johnson, Bob Kaiser, Bill Peterson, T. R. Reid, Marty Schram, Barry Sussman, Nicholas Lemann and Ed Walsh. Directing them were Bill Greider, our national editor, and Dan Balz, political editor. Assisting them with grace and ability was Maralee Schwartz.

This book is the product of their work. We are proud of that work and we commend it to you.

★ Prologue ★

ON THE first Sunday in November, in the last year of the 1970s, before dawn, delivery trucks carrying the final editions of the bulky morning papers were moving through the deserted streets of Washington. There were the usual distant alarms—small wars in Africa, a coup in Latin America, fear of local famines in Asia. But America, in the new jargon, was into itself. Joggers loped along trails and city streets. The professional football season was well underway with 80 million television fans every Sunday. President Carter, as usual, attended church services.

He had need of spiritual solace that Sunday. His standing in the Gallup Poll was one of the lowest ever recorded. Across the nation, he was seen as a decent, well-meaning man who simply was not up to the job. Things were not going right at home. He had done little about the energy crisis. The federal government he had promised to overhaul was as ungainly and profligate as in the past. His foreign policy initiatives had come to little. And overshadowing all that was the state of the economy. Americans were hurting in their pocketbooks. The consumer price index was rising at a rate of 13 percent a year. It took $223.70 to buy what you could buy for $100 in 1967. A recession and higher unemployment were forecast for 1980.

He appeared so politically vulnerable that it was difficult to keep count of the Republicans who wanted to run against him. There were new entries every week—Ronald Reagan, George Bush, Lowell Weicker, Philip Crane, Robert Dole, John Anderson, Howard Baker, John Connally and maybe even Gerald Ford.

The longest shadow, however, was cast by Edward M.

Kennedy, the last of the brothers whose lives and deaths had affected and then altered American politics for a generation. His candidacy for the Democratic nomination for president would be announced in 48 hours in Boston.

News of Kennedy dominated the newspapers. He was, in a sense, the leading political figure in the country. Year after year he had topped the political popularity readings. In political and journalistic circles he was regarded as a virtually invincible candidate, despite Carter's earlier brave promise to "whip his ass." In three previous election years the presidential nomination might have been his for the asking. Each time he refused to run. But now, at the age of 47, after 17 years in the Senate, he was ready. He was the heir to a legendary political dynasty. Beyond that, he was regarded as the family's best politician, as one of the great orators in public life. The opinion polls reflected his political stature. Democrats preferred him over Carter in 1980 by a margin of more than 2 to 1.

The first test between these men, so different in style and background and philosophy, would come in just 79 days in Iowa. Iowa had propelled Carter from obscurity to "front-runner" status in 1976. Now, it was widely said, Iowa could write Carter's finish. The latest statewide poll available that November weekend showed Kennedy winning 49 to 26 percent.

While Carter prayed that morning and Kennedy prepared for a national television interview that night, plans 10,000 miles and nine time zones away had been set in motion that would profoundly affect the fortunes of both men and become one of the great "hinge events" of the election of 1980.

At the lunch hour, Washington time, the first bulletins were received. Iranian militants had seized the American embassy in Tehran and had taken its occupants hostage. The timing reminded some people of Pearl Harbor—the disruption of a peaceful Sunday. There were no bombs this time, merely chanting mobs, screaming "Death to the Shah," "Death to Carter." They massed outside the embassy's ten-foot wall and metal gates on Taleghani Street. Using powerful shears, they cut the chain securing the gates and surged into the compound. In less than two hours, without a struggle, they had captured the American personnel and paraded them blindfolded and bound onto the embassy grounds.

In the hours that followed, television screens in America were filled with the taunting images of American captives dragged and driven along by the mob: "Death to America." American flags were burned for the television audiences. Carter was burned in effigy. At home, Americans responded in kind: a flash of anger and a surge of patriotism unmatched since the beginning of World War II.

All the presumed logic of the 1980 presidential campaign had been altered. A baffling and extraordinary political year had begun.

★ I ★

On the Eve

Richard Harwood
Haynes Johnson
Nicholas Lemann

★ Americans—1980 ★

by Richard Harwood

THE STARTING point for this book is a carton of yellow questionnaires collected in national opinion polls by Barry Sussman of our staff. As we read through them at the beginning of 1980, we were struck by the simplicity and clarity of America's social and political agenda. People of all ages, races and conditions would settle happily for peace, prosperity and good health. They had no imperialistic designs on the world. They harbored few radical or revolutionary impulses. They had no delusions about the course of their own lives or what was attainable. They were realists.

Let them speak for themselves:

Jackie, a 20-year-old unmarried woman, dreams of "a nice house, not too big; a few kids who will not have as many problems as we have now." Her fears are "a broken home, no money, and being in debt."

Ronnie, a 26-year-old oil field worker from the Southwest, a born-again Baptist with a high school education, wants this for himself: "A loving family, a good Christian home and world peace."

Tony, a wealthy young Jewish lawyer in the Midwest, single and college-educated:

"1. I want a family. 2. Have a job I enjoy. 3. To have good health."

Todd, a 28-year-old airplane pilot, earning more than $30,000 a year, Catholic and single, hopes for: "Happy home life, a good job, friends." He fears: "Miserable life, unsatisfactory job, to be alone."

To be alone—those are dreadful words to most Americans,

3

expressed repeatedly in this era supposedly dedicated to self. "I'd like to get married or live with someone," said Palma, a 22-year-old black sales clerk. Celia, a 36-year-old auditor, Hispanic and college-educated, wants: "To marry the guy I'm engaged to." Her fear: "Living alone."

These are single people, mostly. For parents, the hopes and fears are more likely to focus on the health of family members, on their children's prospects for education and good jobs and happy lives.

Vivian, a mother and teacher, a Southerner and born-again Christian, expressed it this way: "I would say (I hope for) continued health and cohesiveness of my family. A future that is dependable enough where my children would be happy and well and a world of peace." Her fears: "Probably the world is running out of things. No leadership, no oil, et cetera. If it continues it will be much more difficult for my children to have what I have. Also the immorality of our citizens affects the future of everything."

Beverly, a 37-year-old rural Catholic housewife, who is separated from her husband: "I would want my family always to be together and happy. I hope that I could find someone who would love me for who I am. I would like to see peace and the end of poverty and war."

They are real people, not statistics—the American electorate of 1980. There were 220 million of them—give or take a few million—scattered from the Arctic Circle to the Caribbean; 160 million were old enough to vote; 2.5 million would die before the year was out. They represented, in one sense, a marketing nightmare for the politicians who sought the presidency. Their diversity was remarkable—Eskimo hunters, fishermen on Pacific Islands, Spanish-speaking farm workers, Italian and Polish and Anglo-Saxon mill hands, bankers and coal miners, Asian refugees, expatriates from the Middle East, Jews, Germans, East Europeans, blacks, Indians and Melanesians. They nurtured regional, racial and ethnic prejudices, passions and self-interests. They quarreled and lobbied and staged demonstrations over their shares of the nation's wealth, over abortion, homosexuality, gun control, military service, the place of women in the sun.

There were fewer young children in the population and far more people over 65 than in 1970. The median age in a single decade had risen from 28 to over 30.

Great population shifts were occurring. Millions were leaving cities and suburbs for small towns and rural areas. Millions were leaving the northeast and north central states for the South and the West. Families were smaller. Marriages were coming at a later age.

The people were full of pathologies: each year, 20,000 murders, 25,000 suicides, 55,000 rapes, 1 million violent assaults and robberies, 10 million thefts. There were millions of alcoholics and drug addicts; 2.5 million were in prisons, mental hospitals, homes for the aged and dependent; 25 million were handicapped.

But on the whole, they could only be described as optimistic, stable, faithful, caring, tolerant and moral. They did not whine or complain about "fate." They believed, overwhelmingly, that they have had their share of good breaks and that life has treated them fairly. They believed, overwhelmingly, that they were better off financially than their parents at the same age and they believed, overwhelmingly, that their children would fare better than themselves. They lived close-knit family lives; nearly three quarters had family dinners every day. Work and religion were as important to them as to their parents. They expressed, in a variety of ways, a deep sense of patriotism and national pride.

Our portrait of that electorate, reinforced by other polls and by the reporting and interviewing of our staff, impressed us as both accurate and unexceptional.

But it was a substantially different portrait than the one painted only a few months earlier by the President of the United States, Jimmy Carter.

Frustrated and despondent in the summer of 1979, he went into seclusion at Camp David and prepared a "crisis of confidence" speech which he delivered to the nation in July. His assessment of his countrymen was grim and despairing.

America, he declared, suffers from a "crisis that strikes at the very heart and soul of our national will. We can see this crisis in the growing doubt about the meaning of our own lives and in the loss of a unity of purpose for our nation.

"The erosion of our confidence in the future is threatening to destroy the social and political fabric of America.

"Two thirds of our people do not even vote. The productivity of American workers is actually dropping and the willingness of Americans to save for the future has fallen below that of all other people in the Western world.

"... There is growing disrespect for government and for churches and for schools, the news media and other institutions. This is not a message of happiness or reassurance, but it is the truth and it is a warning."

The differences in the President's reading of America as another election neared and in our own reading was more than an academic debate between his polltakers and ours. Those differing visions of the country were, in fact, central to the coming campaign and to the fortunes of the President and those who wished to replace him.

In the President's formulation, the American "crisis" was essentially a "spiritual" failing, the product of a popular "malaise" rooted in the selfishness, narcissism and alienation of the American people, in short, in *their* failures as citizens.

Three years earlier, as a candidate for president, Carter had taken the opposite view. What America needed then, he said, was simply a "government as good as its people." If the problem now was the people and not the government, his own record as president—and the government's record over nearly two decades—was not a real political issue. The governing class, in other words, could not be held responsible or accountable for the state of domestic or international affairs.

Our own studies and conclusions as the election contest began were at total variance with that judgment. We found "a nation proud of hard work, strong families, close-knit communities, and ... faith in God." We also found a nation disillusioned and even cynical about the *performance* of its political leaders and institutions. And those attitudes had been building for a long time.

A century ago, three-quarters of the electorate participated in the choosing of their presidents. That was long before the spread of education in the land, long before the instant communications miracles of the 20th century. As recently as 1960, we recorded a turnout of nearly two-thirds of registered voters. Since then, it has been all downhill. Barely 50 percent of the electorate took part in the 1976 presidential election; 70 million potential voters engaged in what amounted to a boycott. Thus, Jimmy Carter's "mandate" four years ago was provided by only 27 percent of the whole electorate.

The following year the governor of New Jersey was elected by 15 percent of the people, the mayor of New York by 12 percent. The 1978 congressional elections were ignored by 100 million potential voters—roughly two-thirds of those with the franchise. In the South that year, the turnout was barely 25 percent. No other democratic society in the world was so turned off by the processes of self-government. In Britain and Western Europe voter participation ranged up to 95 percent. Only in America was indifference or cynicism the norm.

On January 6, 1980, in the midst of the Iranian and Afghanistan troubles, President Carter bought 30 minutes of national television time to tell people why he should be reelected. Only 4 percent of his countrymen tuned in. Two weeks later, the President and his chief rival, Edward Kennedy, spent 30 minutes on the national networks, talking issues, seeking votes. Their combined audience was 10 million people. Hours later that day, 105 million people watched the Super Bowl football game.

Maryland Senator Charles Mathias has told a story about contemporary political inattentiveness. In seeking reelection he bought hours of television time to explain his position on the great issues of the day. Occasionally, he used a brief TV spot showing his family walking along the banks of the Potomac River with their dog. As the commercial ended, the dog jumped into the river for a swim.

"As I went through the campaign," he said later, "nobody ever asked me about the issues. All they asked me was 'How's your dog?'"

This inattentiveness, cynicism and disillusionment about the *performance* of government is confirmed in innumerable public opinion studies as well as in the voting and non-voting behavior of the American people. The University of Michigan Institute for Social Research has been charting the electorate's "trust in government" since 1958. In that year, with Dwight Eisenhower in office, with the country at peace although the economy was faltering, three out of five Americans—60 percent—expressed "trusting" opinions about the government; only 11 percent were classified as "cynical." The downward curve began in 1964 and has continued. By 1978 only 19 percent of the people were "trusting" in their attitudes toward government; 52 percent were "cynical."

A year later a Yankelovich, Skelly and White opinion survey found 67 percent of the people persuaded that America was in "deep and serious trouble." The Roper Organization reported that 65 percent of the people thought the country was "on the wrong track." Another poll found only 28 percent of the people with "a lot of confidence that in a few years . . . our country will be strong and prosperous." Following Carter's "crisis of confidence" speech in July, 1979, 86 percent of all Americans agreed that the country suffered a "crisis of confidence". Nearly 70 percent thought "things are going . . . badly."

Disillusionment with the national government was endemic. People believed the government wasted money, that it was run for big interests, that it could not be trusted to do what was right, that it was run by people who didn't know what they were doing. Fewer than 20 percent of us had substantial confidence in the Congress or the executive branch of government, in the leaders of major corporations or the labor unions or in organized religion. The number of pessimists about America's future outnumbered the optimists by 3 to 1.

All this—the lack of voter participation, the dissatisfaction with large institutions, doubts about the future, and the "growing sense of trouble" in the land—would seem to confirm Carter's dismal analysis of the American "malaise."

Our reading of our own public opinion polls (and those of others) and our reporters' soundings of the American mind and mood as the 1980 election season began showed nothing of the sort.

The American people were not aberrational, defeatist, ungenerous or lacking in any of the qualities of citizenship, patriotism or humanity on which they have prided themselves throughout history. Their own morale was high. Their hopes were modest, their fears were rational. The disillusionment and suspicion about the performance of the great institutions of their society were well-founded.

They had gone through many traumas since 1964 when the erosion of national "confidence" set in. They were promised a utopian "Great Society" that was not achieved. They were taken into a war in Southeast Asia and gave up 57,000 of their sons to no end. They placed their trust in presidents who lied and engaged in criminal behavior. They witnessed the conviction and imprisonment of many of the highest officials of their government. They endured an oil embargo, gas lines and "stagflation." Their incomes and livelihoods were eroded and threatened by inflation and foreign competition growing out of government policies. Their tax burdens soared—to uncertain ends.

They had reason, as the 1980 election campaigns began, to question the competence of the institutions that affected their lives. The annual inflation rate was approaching 20 percent. They were warned incessantly that western civilization was imperiled by an energy crisis. They were threatened—rhetorically, at least—with lowered standards of living. Their leaders held out the spectre of World War III while confessing military inferiority to the Soviet Union. Their diplomats were murdered with impunity in distant lands; in Iran, an entire embassy was held hostage by a mob. Leading members of the American Congress faced prison terms for seeking or accepting bribes. Industrial giants—steel and rubber companies, automakers, textile and shoe manufacturers—were tottering from foreign competition. The American dollar was in serious trouble as an international currency. The whole concept of America as the world's leading power was dissolving.

As evidence of the American malaise—he called it "gloom" and others would call it a lack of "confidence"—the pollster, Louis Harris, reported at the end of October, 1979:

"66 percent of Americans . . . expect that the cost of living will be going up as fast or faster in the months ahead than it is now.

". . . A 54 percent majority also expects that voluntary price and wage controls will be increasingly violated.

". . . Only 26 percent think it is very likely that Congress will pass a new law requiring mandatory price and wage controls."

But this was no evidence of irrational "gloom" rooted in some narcissistic despondency. It was an accurate and realistic reading of what, in fact, happened.

And it was this clear-eyed realism that lay behind the "erosion of confidence in the future" which Carter decried in July, 1979. He arrived at that judgment on the American people largely on the basis of a memorandum written for him by Patrick Caddell of Cambridge Research, Inc., the President's polling company. Caddell subsequently defended with great eloquence his own conclusions about the American "malaise." He wrote in *Public Opinion* magazine: "One argument that has been raised against the 'crisis of confidence' thesis is that people may have become more pessimistic about the state of the nation but they have remained optimistic about the state of their own personal lives. In other words, any pessimism can be written off as political rather than truly personal." That is what we have concluded from our own surveys. But Caddell dissents:

"This argument rests upon only a thin reed of truth—there are, indeed, more optimists than pessimists when people talk about their personal lives—but in my view, the argument collapses when one looks at the entire range of evidence....

"...The average American still thinks his personal life is better than five years ago and that it will be better still five years from now, but the degree of optimism about the future has clearly fallen over the past two decades....

"The issue is not ...that people have lost faith in our basic system of government or the free enterprise system. They most certainly have not. What they are losing faith in is the ability of our institutions or their leaders either to be responsive or to solve their problems.... So long as people do not have faith to support solutions, it is difficult to imagine that problems of energy, inflation or others can be effectively solved.... The evidence is abundant that a strong public will is not prevalent. Whatever the cause—poor leadership, failure of government, persistent inflation, economic stagnation—the problem remains. It is real and it is serious."

We began this book with our carton of questionnaires because, whatever their mood or attitudes, the people of America are sovereign in the choice of their political leaders. Their perceptions and prejudices and values *are* decisive. All the rest—the attempted manipulation of public opinion, the strategies and promises of candidates, the "issues," the political alliances, the endorsements and non-endorsements—are meaningless without an understanding of ourselves.

Major opinion surveys usually focus on political attitudes—the alienation and malaise themes, the response to "issues." Our own polls at the start of the 1980 election year concentrated more on personal perceptions, the family values and traditional faith which are presumed to be the bedrock of American vitality. These values—in some respects—have changed dramatically over the last generation and a significant minority feel uncomfortable with those changes—the aspirations of women and blacks and other minorities, the open sexuality, the emphasis on leisure as well as work in one's life. The majority of people, however, are less upset by such issues as pornography or homosexuality or marijuana than they were a decade ago. We interpret that not as decadence but as tolerance.

The American family is changing too, but that should not obscure its stability and permanence in people's lives. Men are taking more responsibility for household work, a clear signal of feminism's impact over the last decade. But, as we have noted, most families still eat dinner together today and family "togetherness" remains a widely held value.

If one looks at the broad and stable middle ground of American opinion, the nation looks a lot more contented and optimistic than it does on the margins, which Patrick Caddell has described. The popular political notion that Americans have lost faith in the American Dream—the idea of upward-and-onward from one generation to the next—is simply wrong. They haven't.

Indeed, that creed of "progress" is shared so widely in this nation, by rich and poor, white and black, that social critics sometimes dismiss it as too obvious to mention.

In our opinion surveys we asked a simple question: Do you feel that you are better off financially than your parents were at the same age? The answer was yes—resoundingly yes—with 81 percent of the citizens declaring themselves better off than their parents. Only 9 percent feel worse off.

This feeling, even if it is subjective, cuts across every group in the society, every region, the wealthy and the impoverished, white citizens and racial minorities. When the same people are asked if they expect their children to be better off than themselves, 60 percent answer yes; only 11 percent expect their children to be worse off.

This faith in onward-and-upward is strongest among black Americans—80 percent of black men believe their children will rise above them and so do 70 percent of black women.

Professional and managerial types, people who have already made it to the top, understandably are slightly less convinced that their children will climb still higher. But most families who are lower in the wage ladder, even very poor families, believe their children will move upward in economic status.

Of all the people in our surveys, 85 percent chose this mellow perspective: "All in all, I've had my share of good breaks."

hese conclusions about the morale and the mental state of American people were derived "scientifically," which means that they came out of national opinion polls conducted by our Barry Sussman according to the scientific rules of the game: a "true" mathematical sample of the whole population.

Robert Kaiser of our staff and Jon Lowell of our sister publication, *Newsweek*, went about it in a different way. They spent many months in extended conversations with 200 "Middle Americans" and produced a book which they called *Great American Dream*. They summarized for us their findings:

> For most of its history America has been a country of strugglers, have-nots working hard to have. But in recent years the have-nots have shrunk to a minority. The country is now dominated by a new class, a literal "Middle America" bunched around the middle of the social and economic scale.
>
> We are talking about a middle class that excludes the wealthiest 5 percent and the poorest third. These exclusions leave a "typical" enough collection of Americans, but a thoroughly unrepresentative one, too—richer, whiter, less vulnerable to unemployment and other social ills than the population as a whole.
>
> These are the 110 million or so people for whom America works. They repay their America with fierce loyalty and patriotism, with faith in the American Dream.
>
> These Middle Americans pay more these days for a car than many of their parents paid for a house. Not long ago Father and his lunch pail rode to work on a trolley car; now husband and wife may leave for separate jobs in separate cars. In a culture whose truck drivers can earn more than bank vice presidents, whose coal miners' wages exceed $20,000 a year, the traditional social categories no longer make sense. From auto worker's blue collar to dentist's white jacket, we have created a two-car, boat-in-the-garage, cabin-at-the-lake class that defies old measures of social rank.
>
> These Americans define the popular culture of our time. Their preferences produced urban sprawl, the highway culture and the decline of the old central cities. They sustain the national mania for sports, fast-food chains, Ford and GM. They made millionaires of the

*makers of CB radios and striped tennis sneakers. To a
degree that may be unfashionable to acknowledge, these
Americans seem to be having a hell of a time.*

*. . . Gross national statistics on income are virtually
meaningless if one wants to understand how many
Americans are living "well." One set of local statistics
makes the point: the average family buying a first home
in San Francisco in 1977 had an income of $26,000 and
paid $72,000 for the house. A comparable family in
Portland, Oregon, earned about $16,900 and paid
$35,000 for the house. Yet both families surely shared
the same economic status in their communities, and both
are demonstrably members of the middle class.*

*At the beginning of 1979, the median income for an
average American family (about 3.35 persons) was approximately $18,500. If that family existed, which it
doesn't, we might say it would be doing fine in Portland,
but scraping by in San Francisco. In fact, Portland is
more typical of the communities in which most people
live.*

*After playing with the official figures and consulting
numerous experts, we concluded that it was safe to es-
timate that 50 to 60 percent of the American population
now has an indisputably middle class standard of living.
These Americans have a substantial amount of what the
economists call discretionary income, and they can
amass thousands of dollars in consumer credit.*

*There are statistics that support this conclusion, be-
ginning with that median income figure. Another statistic
suggests that the average income of families that include
at least one adult who holds a full-time, year-round job
was about $24,000 at the beginning of this year. Why
is that figure so much higher than the median income?
Because families aren't what we might think. The most
common size for an American family today is two persons. A substantial majority of Americans live in families
consisting of three or fewer persons.*

*. . . President Carter told us that "for the first time
in the history of our country the majority of our people
believe that the next five years will be worse than the
past five years." This is a pollster's finding and it may
be profoundly misleading.*

Polltakers arrive at front doors—or call on the tele-

*phone—with solemn questions about a family's prefer-
ences in tooth paste and/or the state of the nation.
Americans don't like to appear foolish or ignorant; when
asked questions, most give answers. History shows that
whenever the general drift of "the news" is bad, polls
of the kind Carter mentioned show increased pessimism.
That, however, hardly reflects the true emotions around
the family dinner table.*

*In interviews with hundreds of Americans about what
concerned them, about their own agendas . . . we found
that pollsters' agendas are generally irrelevant. We also
found that Americans still tend to be deeply optimistic
and extraordinarily happy.*

*This idea that a large proportion of Americans think
their lives are pretty terrific is a missing element in most
contemporary social or political analysis, but it is a fact.
An important fact, too, if one is to understand American
society and American politics. Politicians and pundits
who find "conservatism" in the electorate are often pro-
jecting their own interests and thoughts onto people who
generally don't share them. Americans are not much
taken with politics; any honest reading of who votes
(barely half the voting population in 1976, barely one
third in 1978) confirms that.*

*Middle America doesn't need new programs, new
government activism—or it doesn't perceive such a need.
Middle Americans enjoy being left to their own devices.
The "conservatism" so many politicians claim to see is
really something much simpler than politics; it is con-
tentment with the way things have been going and reluctance to allow much change.*

We have asserted that another current was running in America
at the end of the 1970s, a "clear-eyed realism" about the way
institutions worked or failed to work. The American people
believed strongly in their way of life and in the institutions
they had created. But they expected competence from their
leaders and that, in the summer of 1979, was the source of
President Carter's political problem; that was the "crisis of
confidence" that shook him. The electorate was passing judgment on him and it was harsh.

Americans wanted peace, prosperity and good health. It was obvious to them in mid-1979 that their prosperity was at risk. Inflation spread inexorably through the economy. The government, simultaneously, was warning of an impending recession and a loss of jobs. There was fear and confusion over energy supplies, compounded by gasoline shortages and the total absence of any government plan or solution. The popular verdict was clear and simple: Carter was not up to the job.

His countrymen rated his effectiveness approximately on a par with an earlier president—Richard Nixon—at the nadir of Nixon's term. Carter's morality and decency were not the issue. The issue was leadership, competence, effectiveness. People who called themselves Democrats rejected him, intellectually, as a candidate for reelection; by a margin of more than 2 to 1, they preferred Edward Kennedy as their presidential nominee in 1980. Among the whole electorate in July, 1979, both Gerald Ford and Ronald Reagan were preferred to Carter. The President, by any measure, was in desperate political trouble.

There is an old political bromide which holds that 24 hours is a long time in the life of an American politician. It recognizes the role of chance and unforeseen events in the fortunes of politicians. The unforeseen event in Edward Kennedy's political life occurred on July 18, 1969, at Chappaquiddick Island in Massachusetts. The unforeseen event in Jimmy Carter's fortunes occurred on November 4, 1979, when Iranian terrorists, supported by their government, seized the American embassy in Tehran and made hostages of 53 American citizens. That action, a close associate of the president said a few weeks later, was a "hinge event" that transformed attitudes and political calculations. It offered, he said, a "bridge back to credibility" for the President, a chance for Carter to disprove the verdict of his countrymen that he was weak and incompetent. A second "hinge event" occurred a few weeks later, at Christmastime, when the Soviet Union invaded Afghanistan, creating what the President called "the greatest threat to peace since World War II."

Now, it was not only prosperity that was at risk. Peace in the world was at risk. The spectre of war was raised, a spectre of armies in conflict, mass death and destruction—Armageddon. The prosperity issue was overshadowed and set aside, just as the 1980 nominating contests began.

As they have always done, the American people rallied to

their president. His support in the polls rose incredibly and incredibly fast, reaching sixty percent in the first weeks of the new year. And, as they have always done in such times, the people turned their attention to the *character* of the president and his rivals. The columnist Joseph Kraft later remarked on this turn of affairs in the *Washington Post*:

"... Baffling national troubles have further emphasized the exaggerated weight attached to personal qualities—especially trust—in choosing a leader. The rub is that the private virtues are currently at odds with the qualities necessary to master public problems...

"Television, especially the recent surge, which has reduced most of the rest of us to boutique journalism, also figures importantly. The camera gives intense focus to personal traits. Toward institutions and ideas it turns a blind eye...

"Confusion, laced with suspicion of chicanery by government, the oil companies or other supposed authorities, is the normal reaction to the new difficulties. Thus cut adrift from their normal moorings, voters instinctively turn to traditional standards—especially personal confidence.

"Jimmy Carter measured up in every way. He is a moral man who believes in his God, cherishes his family and saves his money."

In their classic study of the 1960 election, Angus Campbell and Warren Miller described a woman in Chicago who was torn between Kennedy and Nixon and finally made her decision after watching one of the televised debates. She chose Kennedy, she said, because of Nixon's eyes, especially the left eye. Something about his eyes disturbed her.

This is the "orneriness" factor in American politics, a symbol of the unpredictable and maverick character of the electorate.

That character would be asserted time and again in the campaigns of 1980, despite the best efforts of the American political industry to predetermine the outcome. This industry of advertisers, journalists, marketing experts, demographers, image-makers and pollsters had arisen in the 1960s and 1970s to usurp and replace traditional functions of the withering political parties. It "packaged" the candidates, created television personalities for them, sold them in "prime time" in "major media markets" and raised their money with slick fundraising techniques.

But the orneriness factor remained. The most ingenious television commercial could not obscure or erase the profound and disturbing questions Americans were asking about the state of the nation. We have described the steady loss since the mid-60s of confidence in public and private institutions, the popular disaffection with politicians and politics, the fears for the nation's future in a disorderly world.

These attitudes were reinforced by the realities of 1980, which were so at variance with memories of the American past. Throughout our history, optimism, progress, growth, opportunity and triumph had been the operative words in the American experience: onward and upward. But at the beginning of this new decade, another vocabulary was entering the public dialogue—lower living standards, limits of growth, exhaustion of resources, military helplessness, stagflation. A Harvard professor published a book in 1979 that seemed to be a vision of things to come. It was called *Japan As Number One*.

The most troublesome idea in the popular consciousness was the idea of impotence, the notion that we were becoming the victims of historical forces that were out of control. Barry Sussman's polls picked this up late in 1979 when a substantial number of people held the President blameless for the inflationary firestorm. There was nothing a president could do, they said.

James Sundquist, one of the resident scholars at the Brookings Institution in Washington, discussed this "malaise" in *SETTING NATIONAL PRIORITIES*, a book timed for the 1980 campaign.

"After what has happened," he wrote, "the day of exaggerated expectations about what government can accomplish may have passed, and fortunately so. Yet, if people are to take the trouble to vote, they must expect *something* from the leaders they choose. . . . At a minimum, I suggest, the people expect this much: First, that a candidate for president have a program to address the central problems that concern the people—not necessarily one with all the answers, but at least a philosophy and an approach that give promise of succeeding; second, that the winning candidate then proceed to accomplish this program—again, not in every detail or all at once, but with enough actual achievement to give the public a sense of progress toward the goals that were projected in the campaign."

The candidates of 1980 knew perfectly well what the American people wanted—peace, prosperity and good health. They wanted a president with "character." They wanted a president to meet Sundquist's definition of "competence."

The task of the political industry as the campaign unfolded was to link those hopes with the fortunes of a particular man; to create, in short, a hero for our times.

★ Industry ★

by Nicholas Lemann

ON A fine springlike day in early March of 1980, a clutch of reporters gathered outside a townhouse on Lafayette Square in Washington, just across Pennsylvania Avenue from the White House. They had assembled for one of those events in the presidential campaign that was, in retrospect, of no importance, but seemed absolutely crucial at the time. Inside the townhouse was Gerald Ford, who had come to Washington to meet with the men who would help him decide whether or not to enter the race.

One by one the men arrived, smiling and waving to the reporters, showing their credentials to the Secret Service men at the door, saying nothing. Their names, for the record, were John Marsh, Robert Teeter, Stuart Spencer, Richard Cheney, Thomas Reed, Douglas Bailey, and John Deardourff—not household words. In fact, here was a man, Ford, who had been an elected official in the Republican Party from 1946 to 1977 and a loyal party man for all that time, deciding whether to seek his party's nomination and gathering around him for advice a group that included only two people who had ever run for office. Marsh was a former obscure congressman from Virginia, and Cheney was in his first term in the House.

The other members of the group were not political leaders. They controlled no votes, and headed no constituencies. Most of them—Teeter, Spencer, Bailey, and Deardourff—were political consultants. They made their living by hiring themselves out to Republican campaigns. They were completely uninvolved in the processes of government. But they knew, presumably, how to persuade large numbers of people to vote for a political candidate, and thus they were better able than anyone else in American politics—including all elected officials and heads of organizations—to deliver votes. Ford was certainly better off talking to them than to anyone who could be called a political boss, if indeed there were any "bosses" left in America.

19

Just twelve years earlier Hubert Humphrey had entered the presidential race even later than Ford's flirtation and won the nomination easily. "Humphrey had entered no primaries," Theodore H. White wrote at the time, ". . . but the AFL/CIO structures had delivered to him almost all of Pennsylvania, Maryland, Michigan, and Ohio; Democratic governors and mayors, who had found Humphrey the man in the Johnson administration most sensitive to their problems, could deliver hundreds more delegates from New Jersey to Washington."

By 1980, winning the nomination that way was out of the question. Not only that, all the people Humphrey used were almost completely useless to a presidential candidate. In 1976 Jimmy Carter had won the Democratic nomination without any organized support, but when Mayor Richard Daley of Chicago endorsed him after it was clear he would be nominated, it was seen as at least a symbol that Carter had it locked up. Four years later, Daley was dead and the Mayor of Chicago, Jane Byrne, endorsed Edward Kennedy, who then lost the Illinois primary to Carter. Conversely, Mayor Edward Koch of New York endorsed Carter, who then lost the New York primary to Kennedy. Carter generally ignored the political establishment in planning his reelection campaign, relying instead on a detailed strategy prepared in January by his chief aide and in-house political consultant, Hamilton Jordan. The way to win the presidency now was to go directly to the voters, and the people who understood how to do that were the political consultants. They were the new machine, translating the hopes and fears of the electorate into actual victories.

The political industry is fairly small, consisting of perhaps a thousand people across the country, most of them upper middle class and well-educated. They spent 1980 scurrying around from state to state in a traveling circus. They included bored young lawyers seeking fame, fortune, and adventure carrying candidates' bags; press secretaries, advance men, script girls; assistant professors cranking out position papers, college students manning phone banks, fund-raising specialists, even an occasional precinct captain. They performed a variety of jobs—mailing, filmmaking, polling, telephoning, writing, organizing, strategizing. Their tasks were as general as running entire campaigns, and as specific as that of Ruth Jones, a woman in New York universally referred to as a genius (hyperbole is the mother's milk of 1980s politics), whose sole job it was to buy time on television for campaign commercials. They came from all over but lived, to a greater extent than the generation that preceded them, in a circumscribed world. They gossiped together, fought, got married, got divorced, and compared notes on airports and in Holiday Inns. They ended up changing the country to some degree, but they were in a way not deeply rooted in it. The old bosses had controlled turf, and had to be paid homage by presidential candidates; the political consultants, no matter how powerful, were replaceable by other specialists with similar skills. Ronald Reagan fired his chief strategist, John Sears, midway through the campaign, with no ill effects. Nobody could have fired Mayor Daley, except the voters.

The consultants' most important function—the job of the people at the top of the field, and the centerpiece of modern American political campaigning—was taking public opinion polls and then designing television advertising based on the results. To put it more generally, what they did was try to determine what it was that would make people vote for a candidate, and then find a way to present that argument directly to the voters it was meant to sway. They were self-confident people who believed that through the techniques of research, targeting, and contact they could persuade virtually anyone to do virtually anything, as if they understood better than anyone else the true rhythms and forces of our age. Sixty years ago Sherwood Anderson, describing the boom days of the Ohio Valley in the late 19th century, wrote, "The youth and optimistic spirit of the country led it to take hold of the hand of the giant, industrialism, and lead him laughing into the land." The leaders of the political industry believed that industrialism was dead, and that the new giant that controlled the nation was communications.

In harnessing the giant it was considered much more important to understand what the voters wanted than what the candidates were like, with the caveat that a presidential candidate could not be successfully presented as something substantially different from what he really was. One of the elder statesmen of the political industry, an advertising man named Tony Schwartz from New York, had articulated the basic theory of the industry better than anyone else, in a book called *The Responsive Chord*. Schwartz, an eccentric man who lived a hermetic existence in a home and office in Hell's Kitchen, surrounded by tapes, yelling at his aging blonde secretary who retaliated by yelling at her aging gray poodle, argued that the point of political advertising is not to sell a candidate to voters but to appeal to feelings the voters already have, making them think the candidate fits those feelings. "I'm attaching to what's inside people," he said, "bringing it out, and restructuring it. I'm trying to connect candidates to *your* feelings."

Working on that basis, with polls as their raw material, most of the consultants in the 1980 presidential campaign started by assuming that the responsive chord in the voters was the competence chord. When prosperity but not peace seemed imperiled, they saw the candidates' ability to accomplish things—and Jimmy Carter's inability in that regard—as the point to emphasize. Their favorite word, in the fall of 1979, was "leadership." Then came Iran and Afghanistan and a widespread perception that the nation was in danger; in the early primaries, when concern about peace was at its height, leadership didn't seem to be working as an appeal. People were voting for character, not competence. Finally, as the crises in Iran and Afghanistan dragged on and seemed to pose less of a hazard than they once had, attention—and advertisements— began to focus once again on domestic prosperity and on the issue of competence. The see-sawing between Carter and Kennedy could be seen as a vacillation on the part of the voters between character and competence; to some extent, the same could be said about Ronald Reagan and George Bush. Certainly there were strong echoes of that tension in the fall campaign. A *Newsweek* poll taken during the summer showed voters perceiving Carter as by far the most calm, compassionate, ethical, intelligent candidate, but Reagan as the man of competence, the one who would be forceful and get things done.

Whatever its message, the political industry in 1980 was essential to the fortunes of every major candidate. In Iowa, where only Jimmy Carter had campaigned hard in 1976, there were six major television advertising campaigns. In New Hampshire, for the first time ever, all the major presidential candidates bought time on Boston television stations to reach the southern part of the state. Because every candidate relied heavily on the industry, it was difficult to factor out its specific effects; the best indication of the industry's power was the universal homage paid to it by the candidates.

As candidates began to drop out of the race, their consultants went about other business. Bush's adman worked in the Kansas Senate campaign of Bush's onetime opponent in the presidential race, Bob Dole. Edward Kennedy's pollster took on 15 statewide races across the country. Even the consultants to the winners would take on other clients, and even if their man landed in the White House they would be, at most, a kitchen cabinet for political strategy, as men like Patrick Caddell and Gerald Rafshoon were for Carter. Government was not their concern, although, as Carter's first term shows, heavy reliance on the political industry does have a strong indirect effect on the presidency that follows.

Carter took office without, as he liked to point out, owing anything to anybody. Nobody owed anything to him either. Having gone directly to the people (via consultants) to get elected, he continued to go directly to the people when he was in trouble, through the old campaign technique of public opinion polling followed by appearances on television (which were now free, of course). Carter had a great deal of trouble using the traditional mechanisms of politics that presidents once used to govern as well as to get elected—the members of Congress from his own party, the governors, the mayors, and the major interest groups. He was hamstrung by single-issue groups. He didn't have a party in the traditional sense because the parties have died and been replaced by political consultants. A political party that works is a way of getting a majority of people to agree to work out overall goals that transcend their many specific interests. In that way, old-fashioned politics made it possible to govern; but old-fashioned politics requires an elaborate series of deals made, jobs given, and coalitions formed that have become unnecessary with the rise to preeminence of television advertising in politics.

The most common view of the political industry was that it sold candidates on the basis of concocted "images," whereas in the good old days people had voted on the basis of the "real issues." It was true that the rise of the advertising campaign paralleled the end of one of the most ideological periods in American politics, but otherwise the common view was largely nonsense. Throughout American history, the times in which presidential elections were referenda on policy and ideology have been fairly rare. Franklin Roosevelt and Abraham Lincoln may have won election for ideological reasons, but many other presidents, great (Washington, Jackson) and not (William Henry Harrison, Zachary Taylor, Herbert Hoover), won because they personally were presented as the embodiment of what Americans held most dear about their country.

Also, there has always been a political industry of some sort—a small group of people who held disproportionate power in the selection of our political leaders. For the first half of this century, the industry was made up mainly of bosses. Now it's made up mainly of communications and opinion research specialists. What this latter group really changed was not the *content* of politics (images versus issues) but its *form*. Through their direct appeals to targeted market segments, they eliminated the middleman from politics—the party, the coalition.

The background for the rise of the present industry was a series of demographic changes occurring mainly in the two decades following World War II. Then, in the ten years after that, some changes in the election and nominating laws and a few influential campaigns brought the communications specialists to their present powerful status.

Most of the old bosses were products of a large, cohesive class of poor or blue-collar people in big cities or rural areas. The city bosses, especially, were based in neighborhoods where they knew everyone. They could go for a walk and see their constituency. Often, they *were* their constituency. They intimately knew their concerns. After the war, the old neighborhoods lost their cohesiveness as the people in them began to do better financially. The passage of the G.I. Bill and the opening of the first Levittown started a mass migration to the suburbs, a huge increase in the education level of the population, and, ultimately, marked increases in the median family income too. These changes meant, first, that people were now out where their old precinct captains couldn't reach them; second, that they were more inclined to decide who to vote for on their own; and third, that they had less need for the kind of help from their local government that was the traditional quid pro quo for votes. Not only were Americans on the whole better off financially; those who were needy were increasingly looking to the Federal government rather than local officials for munificence. From 1960 to 1976 public social welfare expenditures increased from $52.3 billion to $331.4 billion, making a turkey from the local boss at Christmastime or a low-paying job with the sheriff's office far less alluring.

At the same time that these traditional conduits from politicians to voters were eroding, a new conduit, television, was emerging. In 1950, 9 percent of American households had televisions; in 1960, 87 percent; in 1970, 95 percent. More than anything else, television was the great national shared experience. In 1948, the national political conventions were televised for the first time. In 1953, Eisenhower became the first presidential candidate to hire a television adviser, the actor Robert Montgomery. By 1956, both major candidates were running professionally produced television advertising as part of their campaigns.

Eisenhower had also used direct mail as a way of fundraising, and a series of longshot candidates a decade later—Barry Goldwater, George Wallace, George McGovern—brought direct mail to maturity as a political tool. Polling was also becoming more often used and more sophisticated technically through the '50s and '60s, with Louis Harris's work for John F. Kennedy in 1960 being the most prominent breakthrough there.

In the meantime, television advertising was spreading throughout American politics. Charles Guggenheim, who made Adlai Stevenson's ads in 1956, produced and directed a half-hour film in 1958 for an unsuccessful gubernatorial campaign in Arkansas. In 1962 Guggenheim made a half-hour film for the successful outsider Senate campaign of George McGovern. In 1964 he made a third half-hour film, for Robert Kennedy's Senate race in New York, and won again. The next year, David Garth made his dramatic entry into the business by engineering John V. Lindsay's television-based New York City mayoral campaign. In 1966 an unknown, anti-machine Democrat, Milton Shapp, came out of nowhere to win the Democratic nomination for governor of Pennsylvania, again largely on the strength of a Guggenheim half-hour film, which Shapp himself had never even seen.

Pretty soon, television advertising was killing off established politicians who thought they had safe seats. In 1968 Richard Schweiker used television to upset Senator Joseph Clark of Pennsylvania. The same year, Mike Gravel took away Ernest Gruening's Alaska Senate seat by using a film by Shelby Storke called "Man From Alaska." On the weekend during the primary campaign when the film was shown, Gravel went from 30 points behind in the polls to 10 points ahead. In 1970 Governor James Rhodes of Ohio refused to use television advertising in his Senate race, and lost; in 1974 he recaptured the governorship by spending 90 percent of his campaign budget on television. By 1978 even old Senator Jennings Randolph of West Virginia, a member of Congress since 1933, was calling on David Garth to run a media campaign for him.

Two changes in the political rules also helped the present industry rise to power. First, a series of reforms in the party nominating processes in the seventies eliminated the ability of bosses to deliver votes at the conventions and made the primaries the controlling factors in winning party nomination. That meant that to be nominated, presidential candidates had to turn away from leaders of organizations, and toward pollsters and admen. Second, campaign finance laws passed throughout the seventies severely limited the size of contributions, which meant that political money, like votes, would come more through direct appeals to people and less through the support of big shots. At the same time, the laws allowed corporations' and labor unions' political action committees to act as large-scale conduits of political funds and thus become, in effect, multiple mini-parties. "Corporate people move a lot," one PAC (Political Action Committee) manager in Washington explained. "Christ, it takes them two years to figure out how to get to work. They don't get into the community much. They feel they should be doing something, and the corporate PAC is there. Probably they're involved in that instead of a party."

It was only natural that the experts in polling and advertising would reap the maximum financial advantage from their new influence by forming independent consulting firms. The first political consulting firm on record was Campaigns, Inc., founded in 1933 by a husband and wife, Clem Whitaker and Leonee Baxter, in California, fertile ground for the industry because of its weak party system and heavy suburban population. Stuart Spencer, an influential strategist, started his consulting business in Newport Beach, California, in the early sixties and helped mastermind Ronald Reagan's rise to power.

By 1980, the consulting business had so proliferated that, as one old pro, Clifton White, put it, "when a guy wants to run for office, the first thing he does is hire a political consultant." The major statewide races pitted consultant against consultant, so while the stock of the industry stayed high the stocks of its members rose and fell as their candidates won and lost. A consultant who was hot could lend instant legitimacy to a campaign, bringing the candidate who had hired him the serious attention of the press and the PACs. The dozen or so leading figures in the political industry, operating mostly out of New York, Washington, and Los Angeles and working mostly for candidates of one party, had helped elect at least half of the senators, governors, and big city mayors in the country, not to mention the presidents of Venezuela, the Philippines, and France. In short, they had put more important politicians into power than Boss Tweed or Mayor Daley ever dreamed of.

Because the leading consultants had succeeded in doing what the old bosses never could—extending their operations across state and regional lines—they had helped create a national political culture that dominates local politics. To watch campaign ads is to see a country where Biloxi is not much different from Pittsburgh. It is possible to detect some difference between ads in the Northeast, which are more argumentative, and ads from the West, which emphasize music and scenery and the candidate's heroic aspects more. Also there are differences between the styles of individual consultants. But overriding all that is a consensus that the American people like candidates who are informal, who have seemingly happy marriages and healthy children, who are against crime and corruption and high taxes while remaining deeply concerned about the needy and the elderly (the latter being the group with the highest voter turnout).

For the political industry, the 1980 campaign began as a mating ritual between the leading candidates and the leading consultants.

President Carter was the only candidate whose team of consultants was in place from the start. His chief of staff, Hamilton Jordan, was in effect an in-house consultant on political strategy. His pollster and advertising consultant were the two men who had engineered his election in 1976, Patrick Caddell and Gerald Rafshoon. Caddell, 30, had made his name as George McGovern's pollster in 1972 and then worked for Carter in

1976. Most people in the industry frowned on spending any time with a candidate after his election; Caddell was intimately involved in the affairs of his major client, sometimes to the detriment of the smaller fry that he worked for. Rafshoon, a little-known Atlanta advertising agency executive and friend of Carter, designed for the 1976 campaign a folksy series of ads that used a country-rock theme song. After the election, he was suddenly a hot political consultant, but his stock went down fairly quickly following his work in the unsuccessful New York mayoral campaign of Mario Cuomo in 1977. But Carter stuck by him.

In the fall of 1979 Caddell and Rafshoon brought in temporarily a third consultant, a filmmaker named Robert Squier. Squier, 42, deeply tanned and deeply blue-eyed, had been making political ads since the 1968 Humphrey Campaign, but 1979 had been by far his biggest year; he had taken to victory three longshot gubernatorial candidates in the South, Robert Graham of Florida, John Y. Brown Jr. of Kentucky, and William Winter of Mississippi. For Graham, Squier concocted the idea of having him work a hundred days in a hundred different jobs across the state, with the cameras grinding away, of course. Brown, new to politics, rich, resident mostly in New York, and recently married to Phyllis George, the former Miss America and television personality, ran the splashiest media campaign of 1979, which was designed to capitalize on his and his wife's glamour inferentially, while insisting for the record that they were just folks. "Everybody thinks I'm a big city slicker just 'cause I got lucky," said Brown in one of Squier's ads. "That's not me. I got the same friends I did 25 years ago."

Squier's job in the Carter campaign was to make a half-hour film. He produced a reverent day-in-the-life documentary called "The President," which showed Carter meeting with his advisers, expressing concern on the major issues of the day, greeting the Pope, and helping his daughter Amy with her homework. He then left the campaign. "In a presidential campaign," he said, "you've got too many cooks. I couldn't see any way I could work parallel to Rafshoon, so I opted out."

But in designing Carter's spot-advertisement campaign, Rafshoon largely used segments of Squier's footage. Here a curious thing happened. The assumption behind Squier's film was that leadership would be the major theme of the campaign—in other words, that the people wanted competence.

Thus, the decision to advertise Carter by emphasizing his hard, forceful work in the White House. But as October gave way to November and December and Squier's film was transformed by Rafshoon into ads, Carter's character began to emerge as the strongest theme of his campaign. One ad showed Carter with his family, and ended with the words, "Husband. Father. President. He's done these three jobs with distinction." Another said, "You may not always agree with President Carter, but you'll never find yourself worrying if he's telling you the truth." Rafshoon's general slogan for the campaign was "A Solid Man In a Sensitive Job." All this served to take attention away from Carter's weakest point, his ability to get things done, and to assure people that, at a time of grave national peril, there was a sane, trustworthy man at the helm.

It was also a fairly unsubtle dig at Carter's chief Democratic rival, Kennedy, whose own camp sensed strongly at the beginning that it was competence that was their strong point and character where they were weak. No one save perhaps John Connally talked more about leadership as the campaign began than Kennedy. Because Carter was so weak early in the fall, and because he had never lost an election before, Kennedy was far more loath than his rival to use the political industry fully— a reluctance that would hurt him badly. For all of the period during which the modern techniques of the American political campaign had been developed—to wit, mainly, using opinion research to concoct an advertising campaign—Kennedy had held a safe seat in the Senate. So despite his and his family's reputation as political wizards of the media age, most of the latest developments had passed him by. It wasn't until weeks after he announced that Kennedy put together his team from the political industry, and it wasn't until weeks later that the team put together a workable strategy.

From what can be pieced together, Kennedy apparently turned first to David Garth, 46, of New York City, a mostly Democratic all-around strategist and media consultant. Garth was accustomed to more control over a campaign than any other consultant, and certainly more than he was likely to get in the Kennedy campaign. He ordinarily planned a candidate's strategy, produced the ads, wrote the speeches, developed the issues, and hired the pollsters. His clients, more than the others', were deemed his creations, and by the fall of 1979 he had created the mayor of New York City, the governor of New

Jersey, the governor of New York, and the governor of Connecticut. He hadn't had as many winners as some of the others, but the winners he did have were concentrated enough around New York to give him a more boss-like aura than the others. In the sixties, Garth had been in the forefront of the movement toward personality-based campaigns, but in 1970 he renounced his earlier style and, a few years later, started using "supers," superimposed printed facts that gave his ads a newsy, combative style that was particularly well-suited to New York. Still, he was not beyond image-making; as he put it, "You use issues to describe an image."

Besides the degree of control he would have, there was one other point on which, apparently, Garth and Kennedy could not agree; Chappaquiddick. "I said to Kennedy," Garth said later, with the benefit of hindsight, "'Get out with Chappaquiddick and get out with issues.' If he's had eight positions on the issues, then Chappaquiddick would have been a question, but it would have been just one part of the panoply. You have to take positions. The electorate is into facts. There's 20 percent inflation. You have to not be mealymouthed. You have to have the goddam guts."

Over Thanksgiving weekend, Garth having said no, the Kennedy campaign turned to Bobby Kennedy's adman, Charles Guggenheim. By this time the hostages had been taken in Iran and Carter, on the basis of the crisis and of his character, was shooting up in the polls. Guggenheim first produced a series of ads showing Kennedy speaking to the camera. They were shown in Iowa, where Kennedy lost badly, and Guggenheim decided to try a new tack—what he called a "personalization campaign" based on Kennedy the man, which, in retrospect, was precisely his weakest point. The ads came out of the tradition of Kennedy myth-making in which Guggenheim had played such an important part over the years. They showed Kennedy looking forceful in Senate hearings, Kennedy walking through ecstatic crowds, Kennedy frolicking with his family at Hyannisport. One of the ads introduced the subject of Chappaquiddick by having an announcer say, "He was the last survivor of four brothers and tragedy had followed him much of his life." Another showed Ethel Kennedy in a tennis dress talking ramblingly about her love for her brother-in-law. The ads did not go over, either among the professionals who follow such things or, apparently, among the voters; the state where they ran the most, Illinois, was Kennedy's biggest loss.

After Illinois, the Kennedy campaign woke up to the true nature of Kennedy's appeal—namely, the public's doubts about Carter's competence. To focus the campaign on either Kennedy himself or on the issue of character generally was to play into Carter's hands. In the same way, as long as Iran was at the forefront of the public's consciousness it was good for Carter, while when domestic problems, particularly inflation, were at the forefront it was good for Kennedy. Guggenheim began a slow fade from the Kennedy campaign, and David Sawyer, an urbane 45-year-old New Yorker, became the campaign's chief adman in time to design a new sales pitch for the New York primary in late March.

"We found what worked is if you don't say necessarily it was a positive vote for Kennedy," Sawyer said later. "He himself is not perceived as a leader capable of leading the American people. They wanted to say, 'Who's most qualified to lead?' For Christ's sake, don't raise the question that way. Your research tells you that. You're constantly shifting to your weakest, weakest attribute." To shift back again, Sawyer went on the attack against Carter. The centerpiece of his campaign was an ad that didn't show Kennedy at all—it had Carroll O'Connor, the actor who plays Archie Bunker on television, talking derisively about Carter and ending with the line, "Let's fight back, folks." Sawyer's ads began running the weekend before the New York primary, which Kennedy surprised all the experts by winning. By the time of the Pennsylvania primary in April, which Kennedy won narrowly, the candidates had almost succeeded in neutralizing each others' positive sides. Kennedy was continuing to run Sawyer's anti-Carter ads. He won in California on the strength of an even more nasty series of advertising attacks on Carter. Carter's camp, as the Iran crisis dragged on and seemed to be becoming more a way of life than a temporary threat, found that their character appeal was losing its force, and Rafshoon began running ads that showed people on the street complaining about Kennedy. So by the end of the Democratic campaign, Carter's strongest point was that he wasn't Kennedy and Kennedy's strongest point was that he wasn't Carter.

Among the Republicans, to use the same terminology, Ronald Reagan appeared to be the candidate of character and a variety of challengers—George Bush, John Connally, Howard

Baker—represented competence. It's worth noting, too, that Reagan's opponents ran their campaigns absolutely by the book, which is to say that they hired the best-known political consultants and largely did their bidding, while Reagan seemed much less comfortable with the political industry. His pollster, Richard Wirthlin of Santa Ana, California, was one of the best in the business; but his adman, Elliott Curson of Philadelphia, was a relative unknown and not much liked because of his brash style and his habit of working for anyone who would hire him rather than just for candidates of one party. Reagan even fired his campaign manager, John Sears, a strategist who was well respected in the industry and widely assumed to be Reagan's Svengali, midway in the campaign and immediately started doing better.

To draw the conclusion, however, that Reagan was just a lucky amateur would be all wrong. He understood modern politics perfectly well. His entire career lay outside the realm of the party system; his rise had been through the mechanisms of television and celebrityhood and the direct appeal to voters. He was careful to present himself more clearly than anyone else as the candidate of the disaffected taxpayer who was fed up with the way things were going. And he had, over a period of nearly 20 years, built up a substantial national constituency that was loyal only to him. Hundreds of thousands of people all across the country were waiting to vote for Ronald Reagan. The chord he had to touch was already well established, and Curson wisely kept his ads simple and direct. "This is the greatest country in the world," said Reagan in one ad, speaking against a plain background, looking directly into the camera. "We have the talent, we have the drive, we have the imagination. Now all we need is the leadership."

George Bush took the opposite approach and hired Robert Goodman, a conservative Republican political adman from outside Baltimore. Goodman would have been a figure out of the nightmares of a League of Women Voters or Common Cause member. He was an unabashed and irrepressible master of the extremist techniques of political image-mongering. He had gotten an English-bred native New Yorker named Malcolm Wallop elected to the Senate from Wyoming via a series of ads showing cowboys saddling up and galloping across the range as an announcer said, "Ride with us, Wyoming." He had filmed Senator Harrison Schmit, a former astronaut, walking around in a Western shirt as a voice-over told the voters of New Mexico, "He walks among the people . . . he speaks . . . he listens." He had put Senator Rudy Boschwitz in a plaid shirt in a Minnesota country store, looking up from chatting with the storekeeper and saying to the audience, "People like Arnie here need a friend in Washington. I really wanna be that friend."

For Bush, Goodman designed a jazzy series of ads that tried to capitalize on his man's experience while at the same time creating a somewhat forced aura of excitement around him. In one ad (for which Goodman had even hired actors to pose as Secret Service men to make Bush appear more big-time), as the crowds swirled around him and the music swelled in the background, Bush said he would move America "into a position of strength. We're gonna be strong, we're gonna lead, and we're gonna win!" Goodman explained that he had decided that "I would reach into the heroism I felt in George. That became the word for me, heroism. I dubbed him the American eagle."

Howard Baker hired perhaps the most respected political consulting firm in the country, John Deardourff and Douglas Bailey of Washington. Bailey and Deardourff had helped elect ten of the 16 Republican governors and most of the liberal Republican senators. Their most highly regarded campaign was a losing one, Gerald Ford's in 1976; their ads were given much of the credit for Ford's surge in the polls at the end of the campaign. Both men were Ph.D.s and former assistant professors, but their ads were emotional, full of music and frequent references to America. "I want my product to be thought of in a way that relates to you," said Bailey. "That's why America. That's why family. I'm trying to connect up with you. I think, frankly, that music is more important than talk. It can communicate. It plays on your mindframe." For Baker, Bailey and Deardourff designed a low-key series of ads that showed Baker in a plaid shirt speaking softly about his vision of America, interspersed with folksy photographs that Baker himself had taken. However, as Bailey put it, "in the tumultuous volatility of this race that is not going to send people running to the polling place." So he and Deardourff made a new campaign ad built around Baker's angry put down of an Iranian student who had asked him a hostile question. Those who follow such things loved the ads, but Baker himself went nowhere.

   John Connally, who had gotten on the competence bandwagon earlier than anyone by adopting the slogan "Leadership
for America" in mid-1979, was then faced with the problem
that his polls showed voters didn't like him as a person. So
his adman, Roger Ailes, a veteran of the 1968 Nixon campaign,
designed a curiously listless series of ads meant to prove Connally was a nice guy. They showed him with his wife, dressed
like a subdued Roy Rogers and Dale Evans, strolling around
their ranch in south Texas talking about their devotion to the
land, to their children, and to one another. In December, 1979,
Connally and Ailes had a parting of the ways.
   Connally also had a brief flirtation with Richard Viguerie,
the king of direct mail and an ultraconservative ideologue.
Viguerie had computerized mailing lists containing five million
names, to whom he frequently sent pleas for funds or votes
for a variety of causes—candidates, the restoration of school
prayer, the defeat of the Panama Canal treaties, a constitutional
amendment banning abortions. He pioneered the use of the
computerized postcard campaign, in which a voter would get
in the mail a pre-addressed, pre-written postcard to an official
that he had only to sign, stamp, and slip into the mail; he once
generated 720,000 postcards to President Ford about a common
situs picketing bill. Viguerie had been involved with George
Wallace's presidential campaigns and in 1979 he had joined
forces with Philip Crane and then when it appeared that Crane
was going nowhere had jumped to Connally. After Connally
dropped out of the race, Viguerie complained that he had fool-
ishly insisted on talking about economic issues, when what the
voters had wanted was "values."
   The candidate who made by far the best use of direct mail
was John Anderson. His mail specialists, Roger Craver and
Thomas Mathews, two former members of the staff of Common
Cause, sent out a mailing of 50,000 letters in January, at a cost
of $18,000, and got back $108,000 in contributions, which
was matched by the federal government. Two weeks later they
sent out 400,000 letters, grossing $970,000 after the matching
funds came in, and then a third mailing of a million letters.
They planned to mail five million letters by November.
"There's been a growing body of unattached freefloating anxious people in the U.S.," said Mathews, "who want a man
they can believe and trust and who'll give them a renewed
feeling about the politics of integrity." The letter that elicited

all that money played strongly on voters' feelings of personal alienation, in a way that managed at the same time to flatter them:

"You may be a well-informed, intelligent, courageous, fair-minded citizen, but you don't count.

"The reason they think you don't count is simple. They believe that Presidential candidates are selected by fools, by citizens who believe lies, evasions, half truths, and soft soap."

Anderson was really another character candidate, in an indirect way. By taking strong positions, he seemed to be campaigning on the basis of issues. But it wasn't what he said— that there should be a 50-cent tax on gasoline, for instance— that was popular; it was that his saying it seemed to prove that he was a man of courage and integrity. In the words of David Garth, he used issues to describe an image. In April, just as Anderson was deciding to leave the Republican primary campaign and run as an independent, Garth joined forces with him.

★

People in the political industry like to talk about campaigns as if they were works of art, and to argue about which one was the most *perfect*. Presidential campaigns were never perfect because the politicians and especially the press played too large a role but a gubernatorial or Senate race could come very close to the industry's platonic ideal.

There was, for instance, William Winter's gubernatorial campaign in Mississippi in 1978, in which Robert Squier had teamed up with Peter Hart, a leading Democratic pollster. Winter was a career moderate politician in Mississippi who had served one term as lieutenant governor and run for governor and lost in 1967 and 1975. In 1979 he was widely considered a loser.

Hart's polling showed that of Winter's three main opponents in the Democratic primary, the strongest was Evelyn Gandy, the lieutenant governor. It further showed that Gandy had two weak points: she was identified with the administration of the unpopular incumbent governor, Cliff Finch, and she was a woman. Winter, therefore, would be the candidate of change and of masculinity.

Hart dealt with the change theme in several ways. He wrote out a brief announcement statement for Winter that said, "As

I begin this race for governor, I tell you that it is time to put an end to the status quo government of special interest, and to begin to tackle the problems that have been neglected for too many years. The other candidates offer more of the same, and I say that is unacceptable." He also designed a series of newspaper ads explaining Winter's 52 new ideas for state government.

Squier, meanwhile, came up with the answer to the masculinity issue. He produced an ad showing Winter standing on a dusty military base amidst tanks, guns, and soldiers. "The governor is commander in chief of the National Guard," he says, "and the National Guard is the first line of national defense." Squier recalled proudly that "nobody ever used the Guard as an issue before. We tried to imply that there are parts of the job that she can't handle."

The only problem with the ad was that it worked too well; Hart's polls showed Gandy dropping precipitously and the two other men in the race gaining. Knowing they had a way to beat Gandy and so wanting to face her in the runoff, they pulled the Guard ad; then they started running it again in the Winter-Gandy runoff campaign and won the Democratic second primary by 14 percentage points.

In the general election campaign against Gil Carmichael, another problem developed: Hart's polls showed that it was now Carmichael, not Winter, who was perceived as the candidate of change. Winter, then, would become the candidate of permanence. The newspaper ads with the 52 new ideas for state government were immediately cancelled. Squier made an ad accusing Carmichael of wanting to destroy Mississippi's precious county system, keystone of the state's traditional way of life. Hart wrote a new speech for Winter to use in the final weeks of the campaign, which began, "The time has come to put a little order and stability into our state government." In November, Winter won by 21 points.

Hart and Squier, Winter says now, "meant the obvious difference between winning and losing." Was their support more important than that of anyone in Mississippi? "Absolutely. Sure. We did not seek any organized support, we did not want any, and we did not have any."

There is no evidence that William Winter is anything but a fine governor of Mississippi; that isn't the point of this story. The point is how successful the political industry can be at finding out what the voters want and then giving it to them, even when that means changing course in major ways midway through a campaign.

In the 1980 presidential campaign, such absolute dexterity would be impossible, but the techniques were the same. All the candidates were investing heavily in polling and television advertising. None of them were paying much attention to the political parties, or to organized groups at all. The campaign ran completely on the principle of trying to reach voters directly, rather than through intermediaries.

So midway through the year, there was a curious state of affairs in American politics. On one hand, we had now a perfectly democratic system, tuned to catch the smallest whims of public opinion. On the other hand, the nation seemed to be falling apart. Inflation was high, unemployment was rising, the spirit of business innovation seemed to have gone elsewhere, and in Tehran the charred remains of American boys were being put on public display largely for the benefit of American television audiences. It was impossible not to feel that we needed to be brought together, to regain a sense of common national purpose. But the mechanics of the political campaign then underway, presumably our best chance to do that worked to the opposite effect. The political industry had so targeted and segmented us, and was so good at appealing to whatever our feelings of the moment were, that for the new president to take office with a strong, durable coalition and consensus whose support he could count on and to whose wishes he would respond, seemed to be a total impossibility.

★ Media ★

by Haynes Johnson

The dominance of the media over our politics has now led to the creation of a monstrosity that presents a grave danger to what is left of democracy in the United States. We are now in the midst of a deep, intractable crisis of consciousness, and hence of institutional structure. This, if anything, is the meaning of the 1980 presidential campaign. . . . Now the functions of parties have been taken over largely by media organizations. These ad hoc groupings apply precisely the same kinds of mass-merchandising techniques to the electoral market that are used to sell soap, deodorant, and pain-killers in the economic market. From a structural point of view, this leads directly to a deflation if not to a collapse of power as constitutional fragmentation does its work. From a democratic point of view, it leads to an irresponsible politics and a debased currency of political ideas.

—PROF. WALTER DEAN BURNHAM
Massachusetts Institute of Technology

BY THE advent of the 1980 campaign television had become a powerful and pervasive fixture in American life. Some 99 percent of all American homes had at least one TV set, and it was estimated that adult Americans spent nearly six hours daily before the tube. (By middle age an average American would have spent the equivalent of nearly 11 *years* before the set, one government survey estimated.) Television's influence on personal attitudes and values was both incalculable and profound, but nowhere was its power more vividly displayed

38

than in its impact on the political process.

All national campaign events were scheduled with television in mind. All presidential candidates structured their appearances to try and gain maximum network exposure on the morning and evening news programs. All campaign financial planning, all strategy sessions begin with television.

It was the "Media Age," in the words of Professor James David Barber of Duke University. It was an age, it was argued, in which the media had taken over the old functions of the political parties—the shaping of national opinion and national political debate, the choice of nominees and, through the techniques of campaign coverage, the ultimate decision on who would occupy the White House.

That is an extreme statement of the case. But it was a truism among all the political pros, that television had a special influence on our political processes. They could cite examples: John Kennedy's impressive performance in the 1960 television debates with Richard Nixon; the portrait of the Democrats as a helpless and strife-ridden party captured by the cameras at the riotous 1968 Chicago convention; the "weakness" and therefore presidential unfitness of Edmund Muskie as he was shown shedding tears of rage in New Hampshire in 1972; the doubts about Gerald Ford's competence engendered by a misstatement on Poland during a 1976 television debate with Jimmy Carter.

In each of these cases, impressions were created that may have had no relation to reality. But in the age of television the impression imparted—and the media's interpretation of it—could become decisive realities.

That truth was demonstrated powerfully on the eve of the 1980 campaign. Consider the events of November 4, 1979, exactly one year before the first presidential election of the new decade. All of the politics of 1980 were shaped by perceptions that began to form that day through the medium of the television screen.

★

The TV choice that Sunday evening was among a movie about a monster shark, a megalomaniacal military hero, and a documentary about a politician. Americans were still predictable. They chose escape over politics. It was *Jaws* or *MacArthur* by a wide margin over the documentary, "Teddy." Still, enough people out of the total national viewing audience of 100 million switched on their television sets to an hour-long report about Edward Moore Kennedy.

Kennedy then stood at the peak. Within two days he planned to announce his candidacy in Boston. Already the press was describing him as a certain winner; the latest surveys in the papers that Sunday showed him widening his already commanding lead over President Jimmy Carter. The President's political people were apprehensive about the TV program and angry at CBS. Technically, Kennedy was not yet a candidate. Thus CBS's recent decision to move up the Kennedy show to prime time Sunday night before his presidential announcement meant the network would not be compelled to grant air time to other candidates under the equal-time law governing political broadcasts. Gerald Rafshoon, Carter's advertising specialist, saw the CBS decision as part of a pro-Kennedy bias on the part of the media: all three networks had refused his request to sell a half-hour of time for a Carter political broadcast later in the week, he complained to reporters that weekend. Now CBS was giving Kennedy free, superb national exposure. It was unfair. Adding to the Carter camp's disquiet was another concern: the belief Kennedy would receive gentle treatment. Roger Mudd, the CBS correspondent who wrote the script and conducted the interviews for the Kennedy program, had been a friend of the Kennedy family for years.

The opening scenes reinforced the Carter fears. Across the screen came the familiar face of Ted Kennedy. The senator, a study in confidence, was speaking to a group of Massachusetts voters. Their cheers and shouts ("We want Ted!") drowned out his last lines. In quick succession two other Kennedys filled the screen. John, slim and exuberant and smiling, was speaking as President: "Ladies and gentlemen, I will introduce myself. I am Teddy Kennedy's brother." The President joined in the laughter his words drew from the crowd. Robert, whose accent and vocal timber eerily matched those of his brothers, was smiling widely to the accompaniment of more cheers and laughter: "Well, I'm very pleased to come here and accept your nomination. There's one person I hope you don't tell, and that's my younger brother."

The evocation of the past, stirring the memories of national heartbreak and tragedy, was powerful. As a vehicle for a projection of the Kennedy mystique—a political drama whose last act had yet to be written—it was compelling.

Roger Mudd and Kennedy were seen talking, in a relaxed outdoor setting, at the senator's Cape Cod home. Their initial conversation was amiable, with Kennedy responding easily to expressions of public concern that his presidential candidacy might take the country through the trauma of another assassination. "One does what one feels one must do," he said. Mudd turned to the way the press had treated Kennedy and his family. How fair had it been? Fair enough, Kennedy said: "I have always felt that they have been reasonable and fair to myself and to the family." Mudd followed up. What sort of separation should the press maintain between the senator's private and public life. "I think there is a natural inquisitiveness of people about all aspects of people's lives," Kennedy said. "I mean I understand that."

Until that point, Kennedy appeared completely at ease. Then, suddenly, the interview took a sharp turn and both Kennedy's demeanor—and his poise—were shattered.

"What's the present state of your marriage, Senator?" Mudd asked.

A look of discomfort crossed Kennedy's face. His reply was halting.

"Well, I think that it's a . . . we've had some difficult times, but I think we have . . . we, I think, have been able to make some very good progress and it's . . . I would say that it's, it's, it's . . . delighted that we're able to, to share the time and the relationship that we, that we do share."

What followed in the next long painful minutes of exposure before the nation was more than the disintegration of a personality; it was the destruction of a political myth, a myth years in the making, a myth of Kennedy invincibility, of strength and competence, of eloquence and articulateness, of the keeper of the family flame restoring the lost days of glory. The Kennedy who spoke now was faltering, inarticulate, incapable of addressing the questions Mudd proceeded to raise—questions about his personal life; questions about the accident 10 years before at Chappaquiddick Island off Martha's Vineyard in which a young campaign worker, Mary Jo Kopechne, drowned inside the car the senator was driving when it plunged off a bridge late at night; questions even about why he wanted to be president.

Mudd's summaries, interspersed after the various segments, were unsparing.

"It is obvious now," he said, after concluding his examination of the accident, "that Kennedy and his advisers plan to volunteer nothing more on Chappaquiddick, or make any attempt to clear away the lingering contradictions. So the American voter is left with three choices: One, that Kennedy's account of a tragic accident is believable, and is therefore of no political consequence. Two, that Kennedy's account is not believable, but that knowing any other account could have ruined a career which, since Chappaquiddick, has become substantial, makes it an acceptable defect. Three, that Kennedy's account not only is a fabrication, but it is also a major flaw that disqualifies him from the presidency."

To those watching Kennedy that night, it was evident he was even less able to answer basic questions about his political beliefs than he was to resolve doubts about his personal life. His response to the simple question of why he wanted to be president brought a meandering, vague reply composed of the broadest generalities: "Were I to make the announcement and to run, the reasons that I would run is (sic) because I have a great belief in this country, that it is—there's more natural resources than any nation of the world; there's the greatest educated population in the world; greatest technology of any country in the world; and the greatest political system in the world."

A more disturbing impression was created when Mudd asked what Kennedy would do differently from Carter as president. In what particular areas? Kennedy asked. Leadership, Mudd said. Kennedy's exact reply was:

"Well, it's um, you know you have to come to grips with the different issues that, ah, that, ah, we're facing—I mean we can, we have to deal with each of the various questions that we're talking about whether it's a question of the economy, whether it's in the area of energy."

Kennedy was severely damaged. Whether he could have recovered from such a dismal start never will be known, for on that same day fate intervened in extraordinary fashion to alter all the presumed logic of the presidential year that was just beginning. Again, television became the vital instrument of political change.

Americans already had become accustomed, in the previous

months, to watching the Iranian revolution played out, live and in color, before their eyes. They had seen the frenzied crowds emotionally greeting Iran's new leader, the Ayatollah Ruhollah Khomeini, when he returned to his native land in triumph after 15 years in exile upon the Shah's overthrow. They listened to the public abuse the ayatollah directed at the U.S. in speeches and appearances before the masses. They reacted as the ayatollah—an old man garbed in black robes, his stern, unsmiling features framed by a long snow-white beard—became increasingly strident and his revolution ever more violent. But Iran remained distant.

With the taking of the hostages the same day as the Kennedy telecast, all that changed. Iran became the most intensively covered television story in years, with the full energies of the U.S. electronic media centering on that Middle Eastern land. Americans awoke in the morning to see the menacing figure of the ayatollah breathing hatred and preaching holy war against "pagans" and "heathens." They went to bed at night after seeing mobs of Iranian demonstrators marching before the occupied U.S. Embassy, waving their fists, shouting defiant slogans, burning the American flag and effigies of Uncle Sam and Jimmy Carter.

Morning after morning, evening after evening, the TV networks showed those same scenes. Through TV, the Iranian crisis became institutionalized and a part of American daily life: the networks began and ended their daily telecasts by numbering each day the Americans had been seized. Reminders of Iran were constant—and, to the TV viewer, inescapable. TV programs were broadcast under such running titles as "Americans Held Hostage." News telecasts, national as well as local, ended with shots of the American flag and the tolling of the Liberty Bell. The result was to make the Iranian story the focus of unprecedented national attention. As the networks continued to highlight the hostage story, the country became unified in opposition to Iran as it had rarely been on a single issue in the past generation. The networks discovered something else—their Iranian broadcasts were attracting enormous new audiences. Iranian coverage, and competition for new angles of it, intensified. The political impact was immense. Attacks on Carter personally by Iranian leaders prominently reported via TV to Americans at home, gave the President a stature he had failed to achieve in three years in office. Carter became the personification of the nation, the symbol of American resolve, the rallying point for Americans at home to respond to insults from abroad.

Carter was quick to capitalize on the situation. He cancelled all his planned political campaign appearances, including a TV debate with Kennedy. Immediately, he began to rise dramatically in the opinion polls. Kennedy, left to campaign alone after the debacle of the Mudd interview, suddenly found the spotlight of the political press shining solely—and critically—on him.

Later, after Carter's and Kennedy's public ratings became exactly reversed in the most stunning turnabout since the creation of modern public opinion polling techniques in 1932, certain critics blamed a biased press for Kennedy's fall.

"The press gang-up on Kennedy has been a herd attack, an obscene feast," wrote Ronnie Dugger, publisher of *The Texas Observer*, in the *Nation*. "Whoever thought of the metaphor first,* it's true: reporters are like crows perched on a power line. When one of them flies down to investigate something, the flock follows. When one of them moves to another spot, the others follow. And when one returns to the power line to wait, so do the rest."

In Dugger's view, "the job on Kennedy began with Roger Mudd's CBS special on him last fall." And, he added:

"CBS News made Chappaquiddick *the* issue. Though this was CBS News's definitive presentation on 'Teddy,' there was no real discussion of Kennedy's 8,500 votes on the record over 17 years in the Senate. Here, in the leading liberal candidate's record, was abundant grist for a full review of the serious domestic and foreign policy issues of our times, along, of course, with Chappaquiddick, too. Instead we were given Chappaquiddick with a vengeance and very little but Chappaquiddick."

The complaint about press abuse and press bias was familiar. It was stated—and restated—each presidential election year. Obviously, the charge contained some truth. In every campaign there were instances of unfair, inaccurate, and distorted (sometimes deliberately so) reporting. But these were not the real problems, nor did they address larger questions concerning the

---

* It was Eugene McCarthy, commenting on press performance during his 1968 presidential race.

role of the media in the electoral process and how it had changed by 1980.

Lyndon Johnson once boasted to reporters covering him that he would enhance their careers. "If you play along with me, I'll play along with you," he said, during a private session not long after he became president. "I'll make big men of you. If you want to play it the other way, I know how to play it both ways, too, and I know how to cut off the flow of news except in handouts."

His attempt to strike a bargain with the press shocked some of his listeners. They thought it smacked of bribery. But LBJ was only expressing out loud in cruder fashion, what most politicians felt: they knew their press relationships were crucial, and they sought to do all they could to manipulate them to their political advantage. As Johnson's press secretary, George Reedy, recalled of his chief:

"He regarded newspapers and newscasts as partisan arenas in which contending politicians struggled for an advantage. . . . He was convinced that every news story (with the possible exception of the weather) was printed because it had been inspired by a public relations counsel. He could not believe that anything was set up in type just because it happened. . . . His view of journalism led him to treat journalists as people who had to be bamboozled, cajoled, or bribed with entertainment. He could not comprehend any business relationship in which he accepted them for what they were and they accepted him for what he was. He thought his attitude toward the press was entirely ethical because in his mind it was what every other political leader was doing and he was merely reacting in self-defense."

When Johnson spoke of the press he didn't mean the 2,000 correspondents accredited to cover the White House. It was the so-called "national press" that he—and virtually all presidential hopefuls—courted. What they sought was exposure over the three TV networks, CBS, NBC, and ABC; the national news magazines, *Time* and *Newsweek;* the pages of such papers as the *New York Times* and the *Washington Post,* read regularly by members of Washington's political industry and whose stories circulated throughout the country via their respective 24-hour news wire services; and the major syndicated political columnists. Leading Washington correspondents for influential newspapers—the *Wall Street Journal,* the *Washington Star,* the *Chicago Tribune,* the *Boston Globe,* the *Detroit News,* the *St. Louis Post-Dispatch,* the *Christian Science Monitor*—plus the newspaper chains, Knight-Ridder, Cox, Gannett and the wire services, the Associated Press and United Press International, comprised the rest of the national press network.

In numbers they were small, in political power great.

The power was not conspiratorial, part of the liberal bias of the national media so often fought to exist. It was the power of influence that counted. Collectively, these correspondents could determine which politician became a "serious" presidential prospect. Through their coverage they could make known the politican across the nation—on the network newscasts, on the newsmagazine covers, on the front pages of the *Times* and the *Post.* If the judgment took hold that a certain candidate appeared a winner, or at least a "front-runner," that perception guaranteed additional national exposure. The line between perception and reality was thin; the greater the press coverage the more chance the collective judgment would become a self-fulfilling prophecy.

One of Senator Henry Jackson's advisers, demographer Ben Wattenberg, observed after the 1972 campaign:

"When you try to work the press on behalf of a candidate, you find that the way to get the video coverage that you want is to get the print coverage that you want. In other words, video people take their cue from what the commentators, the reporters, the guys traveling write—whether Jackson is a conservative or a liberal, whether Humphrey is an old politician or a new politician, whether McGovern is the wave of the future or the wave of the past. It is very difficult to work the TV network guys themselves because so many of the decisions are made by some faceless people up in New York. Whereas you can get to Dave Broder by picking up the phone. It's a different process really."

A McGovern campaign official, in his own retrospective on 1972, made this comment:

"I would guess that we subscribed daily to 80 or 90 newspapers from around the country, and these were our main sources of information about what was happening. What the candidate said in Seattle or . . . in Portland was probably more determined by newspapers than any other single set of information we were receiving, other than the advice of our local campaign managers."

There was nothing sinister about this, nor should it be surprising. By the 1980 campaign, the relative handful of national political correspondents who exert influence over the race had become more critical in the process of choosing a president. Journalism had entered a new period and in the age of television its own practitioners often took on celebrity status. What Walter Cronkite chose to report over CBS every night had great impact on shaping American attitudes about public life and politicians, while he himself was accorded a respect from citizens everywhere not even granted to the president. Journalists were better paid (some at princely salaries equalling the highest corporate officials), better educated, and their national reach extended far wider. A few of the reporters had become influential in both electronic and print journalism. They covered the daily grist of the political race for their newspapers and also served as political commentators on national television and wrote nationally syndicated political columns.

The press had become an integral part of the political industry. Perhaps, in truth, it was *the* integral part. Its leading members, mainly stationed in Washington, associated daily, professionally and socially, with the key pollsters, political managers, and media consultants who had become so significant in shaping the way candidates wage their campaigns. They attended the same "background" breakfasts, lunches, and dinners that were a staple of political Washington. They exchanged views, read each other's stories, traveled together to the dreary political events—a governor's conference, a political party mini-convention—that filled the time for the three years when presidential elective politics lay essentially fallow. And once the long primary process began, they instantly became the presumed source of political wisdom. They were the experts. What they reported, whom they chose to cover, and how, had a major role in the fortunes of the candidates.

As Wattenberg noted, if a David S. Broder of the *Washington Post* or a Jack Germond of the *Washington Star* wrote that a particular candidate was doing well—or poorly—their views were certain to bear directly on how those politicians were assessed and covered by the networks.

Press critics, wary of the increasing power they saw the journalists wielding on the presidential campaign, expressed alarm—and often without a sense of historical perspective.

The argument of press power out of control was not new. Every chief executive starting with George Washington had railed against its excesses and its presidentially perceived offenses.

Before he became president, Washington complained bitterly about the damage being done his Continental Army by the press. "It is much to be wished," he wrote in 1777 at the height of the Revolutionary War operations, "that our Printers were discreet in many of their publications. We see almost in every paper, proclamations or accounts transmitted by the enemy, of an injurious nature."

His successors also often expressed their belief that the press was aiding the enemy of the moment, and even those founding father apostles of liberty—John Adams and Thomas Jefferson—came to hold doleful views about the press during their White House terms. "If there is ever to be an amelioration of the condition of mankind," Adams wrote, as President, "philosophers, theologians, legislators, politicians and moralists will find that the regulation of the press is the most difficult, dangerous and important problem they have to resolve. Mankind cannot now be governed without it, nor at present with it."

And Jefferson, whom the pooh-bahs of the press never cease quoting approvingly for saying, "Were it left to me to decide whether we should have a government without newspapers, or newspapers without a government, I should not hesitate a moment to prefer the latter," had a quite different view of the press once he became president. "The abuses of the freedom of the press here have been carried to a length never before known or borne by any civilized nation," he said at one point. And while still president:

> "During the course of this administration, and in order to disturb it, the artillery of the press has been leveled against us, charged with whatsoever its licentiousness could devise or dare. These abuses of an institution so important to freedom and science are deeply to be regretted, inasmuch as they tend to lessen its usefulness and to sap its safety; they might, indeed, have been corrected by the wholesome punishments reserved and provided by the laws of the several states against false-

hood and defamation, but public duties more urgent press upon the time of public servants, and the offenders have therefore been left to find their punishment in the public indignation."

Throughout much of American history the relationship between press and government was contentious. But as the nation's power and influence expanded around the world, the press had become far more comfortable as handmaiden to the mighty. In Washington particularly, where correspondents dealt so closely on a daily basis with the leaders of the government from president down, and therefore shaped much of national public opinion about them through their reports, a club atmosphere had developed. The press filtered out what it deemed unsuited for public consumption—presidential illicit romances, for example, as in the cases of Warren Harding, Franklin Roosevelt, and John Kennedy—and printed news that more often than not supported the government's official viewpoint. The press was not, despite its reputation for fierce independence, much of a boat rocker.

The condition of the Washington press corps that Arthur Krock described privately to his publisher when he assumed control over the *New York Times'* prestigious Washington Bureau in 1932 prevailed for decades: "It is a sub-calibre group—lazy, sycophantic, the ways of local room forgotten, often stupid, devoted to the 'huddle' instead of original research in the quest for news, intent on radio appearances and Gridiron dinners . . . no breadth of outlook . . . this newspaper world folds upon itself and most of its members look inward."

This insular, inward-looking world was shaken badly by long years of Vietnam and Watergate. Vietnam was the longest, most divisive war in American history, and the first where the press openly came into conflict with the policy of the government. Before it was over, the war had engendered bitter recrimination: step by step, statement by statement, the government's official explanations for its involvement in Vietnam led to even harsher disputes with the press. Accusations of lying and news management—and of news distortion—tore apart the layers of mutual respect fashioned over the years between journalists and officials. In the poisonous climate that existed, a series of events brought the press itself under attack by the government. In the Pentagon Papers case of 1971 the U.S.

government, for the first time since the founding of the Republic, succeeded (if only briefly) in imposing the doctrine of prior restraint on the press and halting publication of current news of vital public importance. And in a growing number of legal cases, the courts upheld the issuance of subpoenas served on the news media and rejected protests that such subpoenas constituted a violation of the First Amendment guarantees of freedom of the press.

Watergate intensified the difficulties. The legacy of both those historic episodes had significant bearing on the way presidential politics was covered. No longer was the word of the President accepted at face value by the press. No longer would the candidates for that office escape with the cursory press examination of their private lives, as well as their public records, as had been the past practice. And no longer could they take the press for granted as a passive factor in the race. The ending of the war in Vietnam and the toppling of the President at Watergate had given impressive evidence of the power of the press. Every candidate and every political media manager knew it. So did members of the press.

For the army of journalists who set out to cover the 1980 campaign, the criticism of their role by scholars, citizens, and public officials alike was, at best, academic. They were heading into the longest presidential campaign in American history, and by far the costliest. Their organizations had budgeted, conservatively, $100 million for their effort. And whatever fears were being expressed about the role of the press in politics, the press proceeded on the assumption that its part in the process would be more influential than ever. In that, the press was correct. Never had its sheer presence been so overpowering.

★

In 1980, the path to press glory was not overseas but at home. For the press corps, the most prized assignment was covering the political battlegrounds across America, and the pinnacle of success was to be the top correspondent on the presidential trail. The boys and girls of the press clamored to board the campaign bus, wearing their Burberrys as badges of entry to the national election wars. And, in fact, they covered the election much like a war—a contest involving grand strategy, opening skirmishes and quick assaults and flanking maneuvers, with bitter defeats and long forced marches, and finally, for one among all the gladiators, victory. Even their terminology—The Campaign—evoked a military image.

Several factors distinguished press coverage of the 1980 campaign—the length of the process, the reliance on polls, and the more critical cast of mind of the reporters, especially the younger journalists.

Of these, the most significant involved the primaries. The proliferation of the presidential primaries coincided with the rise of television and further disintegration of the political parties.

Each four years the number of primaries had increased, rising from 13 in 1960 to 34 in 1980. The primaries themselves had become binding on the delegates selected. That, too, was a change. In 1952, Senator Estes Kefauver swept the Democratic primaries but was denied the nomination when the party chiefs, operating in the old way, picked Adlai Stevenson. Now the primaries had become the only way to win. They dictated the strategy—get recognized immediately, gain the attention of the nation through the press by an early victory, project the image of an unstoppable "front-runner," and roll on to victory.

The press—and, again, television—was critical. The increase in the number of primaries meant the race began earlier each four years, and the struggle for press coverage became more intense. With a primary a week, the power of the national political press corps in assessing who was on top became all the more important. And by 1980, the ability of the state political caucuses to begin the convention delegation selection process added to that press power. Jimmy Carter, every presidential candidate knew well, had catapulted ahead of the pack when the press certified him in the 1976 Iowa Democratic caucuses "the man to beat."

Carter had gained that position by campaigning hard in Iowa for more than a year before the election year itself. In 1980, everyone followed that lead. And the national press set up shop in Iowa as if the convention were to be held there and nominees selected.

Early in January, while flying back to Des Moines, a political reporter for the *Washington Post* came to a startling realization: the 1980 presidential trip had already been going on for more than a year, and this was his eleventh trip to Iowa.

Most of his trips had been lonely, frustrating forays, attempts to find meaning—and space in his paper—out of basically minor political developments—a straw poll, a party gathering, a presidential steamboat trip down the Mississippi. They had seemed surreal, he thought, like running a marathon on a treadmill. You ran hard, but you stayed in the same place; you never got anywhere.

But that changed when he boarded his flight in Chicago the day after New Year's and headed for Des Moines. Aboard were young Kennedy volunteers and Carter White House political operatives, and members of the national press. Politics was in the air. The reporter felt exhilarated. Now, the campaign really had begun. When he called his newspaper office from Des Moines, his spirits soared higher. Politics was back "in," he was told. There would be space—lots—for his stories.

Des Moines was ready for the invasion of press and politicians. Indeed, it welcomed it. The campaign brought a boom-time atmosphere. Money flowed, most of it expended by the press. Business prospered. At the Fort Des Moines Hotel, the Republican quarters, NBC occupied several floors. At the Savery Hotel, the Democratic establishment, workmen were hurriedly completing a new bar and the charge for local phone calls from rooms had jumped to 50 cents a call. The city's new Civic Center, a white elephant teetering on financial disaster, was rescued temporarily by CBS. The network leased the entire center for the whole month. It would serve as the backdrop for the elaborate—and expensive—political set from which Walter Cronkite, the national press guru, would broadcast.

All that attention for only one event—the prospect of a Kennedy-Carter debate in Des Moines. ABC alone had booked 130 rooms to cover the debate. When the President, citing Iran and the hostages as a reason, withdrew from the debate, ABC reduced its force for the Republican presidential debate from 130 to a mere 30.

But the influx of journalists into Iowa continued. By the night of the caucus balloting, Des Moines resembled an occupied city. The citizens were ecstatic over having such notables as Cronkite, John Chancellor of NBC and other national press luminaries in their midst. The Democrats even capitalized on the press craze—election night, they sold tickets, at $10 a head, to people who wanted to watch the press at work reporting the returns from the Savery Hotel.

Iowa was instructive in another sense. Its emphasized campaign established the greater role of the polls in the 1980 political race, and their impact on press coverage.

By the 1980s polls had become a barometer of national life. Politicians lived or died by them. The media managers commissioned the leading polling organizations to work for them exclusively. Polls dictated campaign strategy and defined stands the candidates would take. They pinpointed themes, issues, and positions. They gave legitimacy to candidates who began to move up in their ratings. And they became a vehicle for the press to interpret the strength of the candidates.

Polls were not new—the first had been taken in Wilmington, Delaware, by a newspaper, The *Harrisburg Pennsylvanian* in 1824—and politicians had come to rely on them increasingly. Franklin Roosevelt, typically, had become fascinated by them when he was given the first memo on the state of public opinion about him ("What the American People Think About President Roosevelt") early in his first term. What was different, in 1980, was the way they were being utilized by the press.

Now the newspapers were commissioning their own polls and giving their results wide display. In Iowa, for instance, the state's leading newspaper, The *Des Moines Register,* influenced reporting of the national press by its polls during the caucus campaign period (and it also had sponsored the GOP debate in the state capital). Many other newspapers, the *Washington Post* and the *New York Daily News* among them, had their own polling operations. The TV networks were now combining their own extensive resources and polling capabilities with other news organizations: the *New York Times* and CBS and NBC and the Associated Press had their own major polls on the political campaign year. The results guaranteed heavy coverage in these news organizations. And in 1980 all the networks provided so-called "exit polls" on the day of each caucus or primary balloting. These were polls taken of voters after they cast their ballots, and they came to be relied on by the press as a source of wisdom about the candidates. (They were also used to project the winners, with the results often leaked to the writing press by midafternoon of a primary day.)

Like the primaries, the polls had proliferated. Never had so many been taken, never had their results been so widely disseminated, never had the press used them to such effect. The primaries gave the press an opportunity to declare a winner a week in the presidential sweepstakes. Intense press competition put pressure on the reporters to be first in detecting the trends of the victors and vanquished. For them, the polls were a convenient crutch to certify the instant analysis after each primary day's balloting. Who was ahead, who was slipping, who had momentum—these became the weekly wisdom, as pronounced by the press, thanks to results of the polls.

The nature of the polls themselves had a special influence. In the exit polls conducted throughout the primary season, the pollsters expanded the range of their questions far beyond the simple who was ahead or whom did the voter prefer. They were asking a series of highly subjective questions about national moods and attitudes and impressions; the results, in turn, were widely publicized as being the essence of what America thinks—and what America wants in a president or a presidential candidate. These findings, dubious or otherwise, became part of the press's presumed wisdom. Thus, by the sheer publicity they received—often page one in such papers as the *Post* and the *Times*—and the repetition of them in a wave of press analyses and commentary, they became the "truth."

How one network handled its exit polls provided an example of all. On that first weekend in November, 1979, when the hostages were seized and the Kennedy TV program aired, ABC phone interviewers operating out of Radner, Pennsylvania, already were busy asking Americans about whom they wanted for president a year in advance of the election.

Results of that first poll sample were illuminating: a full third of the people questioned said they didn't know. In the pollsters' parlance, they were "undecided." Of those who expressed a preference, 29 percent chose Kennedy, 17 percent Carter, and 9 percent Ronald Reagan.

Those first polls' results bore no resemblance to the way the final sampling came out seven months later, when the primary season ended in June. Nor did that first poll provide a clue to the kinds of success—and subsequent press attention—two major political players in 1980 would have. The names of John Anderson and George Bush were mentioned by less than 1 percent of the November sample. Howard Baker and John Connally easily outscored them then.

As Jeffrey D. Alderman, ABC's exit poll manager, commented later: "Not only do the results of that poll show that public opinion is fragile, they also illustrate—at least on the GOP side—that public opinion is not the only key to political success."

But the exit polls delved into other areas and, by emphasizing them, had a power of their own. Questions about Chappaquiddick, for example, were asked from the very first samplings. When the initial findings showed that about a third of the population still had doubts about that incident, these results became more grist for more Chappaquiddick stories—even though such stories had run repeatedly and prominently for more than a decade in the press.

Halfway through the primary process, ABC news began asking voters a different sort of question. They wanted to know whether a president—any president—could be effective in solving the nation's problems. That question stemmed in part from President Carter's celebrated "malaise of the spirit" speech in July, 1979, Carter described national American life as one of reduced expectations and lack of confidence in government institutions, including the presidency itself.

Carter voters, ABC found, were buying the president's line that the presidency no longer could be very effective. Kennedy voters disagreed. But since the initial primary season was dominated by Carter victories in smaller Midwest, New England and Southern states, those findings served to reinforce the impression of Carter strength with the voters. They became more sources of wisdom for the press.

One result was to place further emphasis on the press's tendency to cover the campaign as a horse race, with the major members of the trade cast in the position of handicappers. Merely to be judged a front-runner by an important pundit had a power of its own. The very naming could become a self-fulfilling prophecy, particularly if sufficient numbers of the press proclaimed it so.

Not that the press was always right—or even right most of the time. On the morning after the Iowa caucus voting, the event that formally opened the 1980 presidential campaign, an NBC political correspondent gave millions of watching Americans his interpretation of what it all meant. Based on how the citizens of Iowa had voted, he announced, Ronald Reagan was on the verge of political death. It was not the first, nor would it be the last of false forecasts from the press in 1980. The incident underscored an old truth about America's press. The corps has always been better at reporting the battle instead of the war.

Generals are said always to fight the battles of the last war, no matter how changed the circumstances of the present one. So, too, the press. Lessons of the last campaign are always dutifully put into practice—and—print—in the next: that the race for the presidency is a noble adventure, one that stirs mythic chords in the populace (*The Making of the President, 1960*) . . . that image makers merchandise the candidates, and are out to manipulate the innocent press (*The Selling of the President, 1968*) . . . that politicians—and even presidents—are ignoble creatures not above indulging in a lie or outright corruption in their pursuit of victory (*The Presidential Transcripts, 1972*). But the tome that struck home most directly for the press was a wry analysis of the press itself on the presidential trail (*The Boys on the Bus, 1972*).

After that unstinting critique of press behavior, pack journalism, with its celebration of group think, its tribal jealousies and sophomoric antics, was, supposedly, a vestige of the past. Yet 1980 saw the pack out in greater numbers and hotter pursuit.

Journalism, operates under a certain clubhouse atmosphere. The way presidential campaigns are waged, particularly in the television age, intensifies that natural trait: reporters covering the candidate are strapped together in aluminum tubes and hurtled across vast distances each day, their jet travels cutting them off from reality and political perspective. For the writing press particularly, the reporters become appendages of the TV apparatus designed by the media managers and utilized by the TV networks. At each step they wait while the candidate tapes a TV interview, conducts a TV press conference, or speaks at a session aimed to attract TV attention. Small wonder they feel isolated, and fall back into their own group for reinforcement. They trade ideas, rumors, and theories; they rely on the polls, in part because they have no other way of determining how voters feel; they raise expectations—or lower them—by measuring how well their candidate does in the face of the presumed wisdom; they worry about their careers and fear making mistakes. A collective sense of what's important often becomes easier—and safer—than risking an individual judgment. And try as they do to deal with "serious" subjects and issues, the nature of the campaign process forces them into daily trivia. Critics correctly say the press fails to examine the major issues. But the reality of the campaign caravan virtually precludes it. The pressure to meet a deadline, to catalogue the travels of the candidate, to watch for a supposedly newsworthy event—a slip of the tongue, a new strategy, a new campaign technique— dominates the daily effort.

It is no way to run a presidential campaign, but that is how it is run. The press remains as much a hostage to the campaign apparatus as, in some respects, the candidates are to his campaign advisers and media managers.

The 1980 campaign witnessed all these tendencies and, because of special circumstances, saw them become magnified.

Edward Kennedy's candidacy alone assured unusual press attention. Kennedy's first campaign foray after announcing in Boston received more press coverage than trips of many presidents: two full plane loads of press personnel followed the senator as he campaigned from New England into the Midwest and then South and back to Washington. The Kennedy coverage, too, was certain to be judged with abnormal criticism. The charge that the so-called liberal press had favored the two older Kennedy brothers, John and Robert, at the expense of conservative candidates was a factor in the way the press reported on the last Kennedy and his campaign. Initial coverage of Ted Kennedy, especially the repeated emphasis on Chappaquiddick, was as harsh as in any presidential campaign in memory.

Compounding Kennedy's problem of severe press examination was Iran and its dramatic impact on the campaign. Since Carter had cancelled all his campaign appearances, Kennedy bore almost total press scrutiny.

An internal memo, written at the end of January by a *Washington Post* reporter assigned to Kennedy, captured the situation. He wrote:

> "I often get the feeling that this election campaign is being run of, by, and for the TV networks, and so it was fitting that it was a TV show that perfectly crystallized Ted Kennedy's dilemma. The show was the January 20

edition of ABC's 'Issues and Answers,' on which Kennedy appeared only after he was turned down in an effort to worm his way onto 'Meet the Press' for a joint appearance with Carter. (Must note here the utterly brazen arrogance of Carter in agreeing to go on that show one day before the Iowa caucuses after he had said in writing that he would have to forego personal appearances until the Tehran hostages were freed.) Kennedy's whole campaign has been upstaged by Carter's handling of the Mideast situation, and sure enough, his appearance on 'Issues and Answers' was interrupted twice by news bulletins reporting what Carter was saying at the same time on 'Meet the Press.' Then, toward the end of the show, ABC's Bob Clark asked Kennedy a complicated question about domestic policy, and Kennedy launched into what might have been a fairly thoughtful answer. He was halfway through when Clark interrupted and said 'people might think we were derelict if we don't get one Chappaquiddick question into this show.' Clark then asked his question and by the time he finished Kennedy had 40 seconds left to try to answer.

"The Chappaquiddick plague hit Kennedy again two days later, on a day when he got two key labor endorsements and picked up ten points on Carter in the CBS/New York Times poll. The big news that day turned out to be neither endorsements nor polls but rather Kennedy's effort to explain some arcana about tide tables in the waters off Cape Cod. The tidal issue had come up in two new articles that purportedly proved again that Kennedy was lying about Chappaquiddick."

Jimmy Carter's use of the press in 1980 provided perhaps the most brilliant example of the power of a chief executive to dominate the news to his own advantage. Carter adopted what came to be called "The Rose Garden Strategy." For half the year he stayed within the confines of the White House, never straying beyond his Rose Garden, and let the press carry his campaign message for him. It was not the first instance of a president seemingly being above the tumult of a campaign—Franklin Roosevelt during World War II and Richard Nixon in 1972 deliberately stressed the rigors of their jobs as requiring them to refrain from political forays. But Carter's was by far the most successful. By using Iran as an excuse not to expose himself to the campaign trail, he remained sealed inside the White House—and saw his popularity soar as the press focused on Iran and on Kennedy's failures.

The great irony was that Carter's insulation in the White House and subsequent dramatic reversal of his previously dismal poll ratings was based on little more than his failure to develop a foreign policy. And while he said publicly that events in Iran were too critical for him to engage in partisan politics, he spent dozens of hours telephoning supporters in the primary states from his White House command post. And he dispatched Vice President Mondale, his wife, Rosalynn, and, it seemed, half the federal government's top hierarchy into the field in his behalf.

As the primary weeks rolled by, the White House press corps remained immobilized. Each primary date brought a similar approach to the press there: word would filter back from such Carter operatives in the primary states as Greg Schneiders and Tim Smith that the reporters should not expect the President to do well, or even win. This strategy of "lowered expectations" was intended to make the resulting Carter victory seem all the grander in the press analyses that followed—a point White House Press Secretary Jody Powell would stress while making the round of TV studios to give the Carter victory statements on the scene in the primary state. (Powell would leave Washington just before the primary to be present for the vote counting and available for the inevitable press interviews.)

The rest of the press corps was left behind with Carter, whom they seldom saw, and when they did, it was almost always in a highly controlled situation—a talk to one group or another in the East Room—where the press was reduced to the role of spectators instead of questioners.

For the correspondents, the situation bred frustration. They knew there would be recriminations against them if Carter gained renomination and was reelected in the fall. Political critics were certain to charge Carter won because he got a "free ride" from the press. But other than writing about "The Rose Garden Strategy," they were powerless to do anything else. The President commanded the media. When he wanted to make news at a desirable political moment, he always did so. Merely summoning the reporters to his office, as he did on the morning of the important Wisconsin primary to give positive news about the hostages (which turned out to be false), meant he was guaranteed vital access to TV viewers across the nation via the morning network news programs.

The ironies were overwhelming. Four years before, members of the White House press corps heard the bitter complaints from the Carter camp about their performance. Then, the Carter people denounced the White House regulars for allowing Gerald Ford to escape hard scrutiny or press criticism. By 1980 the tables were turned with a vengeance. Now it was the Carter people who wrapped themselves in the flag and presidential office and held the press at an unprecedented arm's length—and all to their advantage.

Weeks of relative inactivity at the White House took their toll on the press corps. A sense of ennui developed. Even the most aggressive reporters began to show signs of weariness at the routine of attempting to question Powell or other officials, who more often than not were unavailable, but seldom receiving answers. John Osborne, the veteran president-watcher who writes for *The New Republic*, called the press corps the most passive he had seen. Privately, and with increasing frustration, many of the reporters agreed.

A sure sign of the tedium that spread through the White House press room came in the rise of the card-playing phenomenon. In place of getting more news, as the campaign continued the reporters took to organizing tournaments. The first annual White House Press Corps Gin Rummy Tournament was followed by the second annual tournament. It attracted even more participants than the first.

While the press corps passed the time playing cards, the White House political operatives were busy trying to gain still more favorable news treatment for the President. A favorite device was the "backgrounder"—a briefing by an unnamed official at which information is given to make the administration look good without being held accountable for supplying the material. Two glimpses of the backgrounder in full swing:

Just before Christmas, Robert Strauss, the President's campaign manager, called in four reporters from major papers, the *Washington Post*, the *New York Times*, the *Wall Street Journal*, and the *Los Angeles Times*. The purpose of the exercise was to show the newsmen that Carter was actually hurting himself politically by being such a stickler on political ethics. Yes, the President was using the power of his office to full advantage,

Strauss conceded; but in many respects he was doing himself more harm than good by his insistence on the highest political standards.

Strauss offered a personal example. He had a direct line to the President on which they would talk politics. But Carter recently had the line pulled: he didn't want to give even the appearance of engaging in partisan politics from his office while the hostage crisis continued. Why, Strauss went on, when the President did make political phone calls from the White House to backers around the country, he insisted on charging them to a campaign credit card. As they left, Strauss gave the reporters documents setting forth campaign committee guidelines on how to make sure the campaign was run cleanly. He was carefully laying the groundwork to refute the inevitable charges that Carter was abusing his position as the incumbent for political advantage—charges which soon began to surface.

A few weeks after Christmas the President showed himself to be no less adept at making news in his interest through a backgrounder. He invited a small group of columnists and TV commentators for breakfast upstairs in the family quarters at the White House. Under the rules imposed by the White House, the President was not to be identified as the source of any stories—but what he said that morning made news around the world, even though the material was unattributed to him. The stories said the President was prepared to take any action, including war, to block Soviet aggression in the Mideast after the invasion of Afghanistan; that he would cancel U.S. participation in the Summer Olympic games scheduled for Moscow, and that he was planning a new, tough speech to the nation outlining a "Carter doctrine" for the Mideast.

The stories were a trial balloon for Carter, and they made him appear strong just at a time when the first critical primary contests with Kennedy loomed.

In theory, individual reporters and editors and television producers control the material at hand. They are not, in theory, obliged to co-operate in the launching of trial balloons for a president or for any lesser mortal.

But theory and reality are at odds. The media industry and the political industry need each other. Competitive pressures are at work in both camps. The necessity for "access" is at work in both camps. Without "access" to the men and women of politics, the journalist is hobbled. Without access to the journalists, the politician is hobbled.

There is another factor at work here that has a particular influence on the television news producers. Their demand for "news" often exceeds the supply. This is seen most clearly at national political conventions when gavel to gavel coverage—many hours of prime time—leaves the networks with a desperate problem: what to put on the air when nothing transpires?

This supply and demand problem becomes more acute as the hours of television time devoted to "news" and "news specials" expands. The expanding void must be filled and the political industry is eager and willing to fill it.

So the two camps live off one another, satisfying mutual needs. That is the ultimate reality in the media politics of the 1980s.

★ II ★

Scramble:
The Primaries

T.R. Reid
Martin Schram
Lou Cannon
William Peterson

★ Kennedy ★
by T.R. Reid

BY SEPTEMBER, they had to wait in line.

By September of 1979, President Jimmy Carter's political liabilities seemed so clear to so many leaders of his own party that Democratic VIPs from all over the country were literally lining up behind one another in the high-ceilinged anteroom outside office 2241 of the Dirksen Senate Office Building on Capitol Hill. Almost every day you could see two or three prominent Democrats there, waiting to speak to the inhabitant of that office, waiting to ask him to come to the aid of the party by offering himself as the Democratic candidate for president in 1980.

Among those making that plea as the hot summer of 1979 turned into fall were Democratic senators like John Culver of Iowa, Birch Bayh of Indiana and George McGovern of South Dakota, all facing reelection challenges in 1980 and all sorely worried about running on a ticket headed by Jimmy Carter. There were senior Democrats like Sen. Henry M. (Scoop) Jackson of Washington and Reps. Paul Simon of Illinois and Morris Udall of Arizona, who felt less personal jeopardy but feared a general Republican landslide if Carter were the Democratic nominee again. There were state officials from the East (Gov. Hugh Carey of New York, for example), from the Midwest (Secretary of State Joan Growe of Minnesota, a protege of Walter F. Mondale) and from the West (Lieutenant Gov. Robert Mondragon of New Mexico). There were labor leaders—men like Fred Kroll, of the Railway and Airline Clerks, George Hardy, of the Service Employees, and William Wimpisinger, of the Machinists—who had backed Carter in 1976 but were scared now that he would lead the Democrats to defeat in 1980. There were black leaders—Ronald Brown, vice president of the National Urban League, was one of the most outspoken—and Jewish leaders and Greek-American leaders and feminist leaders. There were, in short, representatives from nearly every traditional Democratic constituency, recruiting a challenger to take on the incumbent Democratic president.

The man they wanted to see, Edward M. Kennedy, the 47-year-old senior senator from Massachusetts, had heard it all before. As the last member of the party's most successful family, Ted Kennedy had been most Democrats' idea of a dream candidate for the better part of ten years. In 1972, and again in 1976, he had heard and rejected various pleas for him to enter the race. But in 1980, a series of considerations—the urging of his colleagues, Carter's drastic plunge in the opinion polls, his own distaste for Carter's talk about "malaise," and his intuitive sense that he had waited long enough—prompted Kennedy to say, yes, the time had finally come. By the first week in October he had firmly decided to run; by the first week in November, in a gala ceremony at Boston's Faneuil Hall, he had formally launched his race for the White House.

And by the first week in February, that race was effectively over. With his precipitous drop in the polls and his big loss in the Iowa caucuses, it quickly became evident that Kennedy's campaign was a lost cause. Now the Democratic VIPs, even old friends like House Speaker Thomas P. (Tip) O'Neill Jr., started dropping hints that Kennedy should withdraw. His own campaign manager (and brother-in-law) Stephen Smith suggested late in January that Kennedy should call it quits. With the tenacity that became a hallmark of his campaign, the candidate rebuffed all these suggestions. But he could not brush off the basic point. In three months' time, the youngest Kennedy had gone from shoo-in to sure loser. One of the longest-lived bubbles in American politics—the image of Edward Kennedy as a political superman—had been burst, quite possibly beyond repair.

★

Looking back now, it is hard to recall how far and how fast Kennedy fell. In fact, though, Jimmy Carter's long string of lopsided victories in the Democratic caucuses and primaries constitutes the most striking upset of the 1980 campaign. When the contest for the Democratic nomination began, Kennedy was the first choice among Democrats in every opinion poll—as he had been in virtually every survey of Democrats since 1970. He led the President decisively in every region but the South—and was not far behind there. Carter, meanwhile, had a lower approval rating than Richard Nixon at his nadir. The polls did show that Kennedy had a "character" problem; the public had not forgotten Chappaquiddick. But this seemed minor compared to the problems facing Carter. In a CBS/New York Times poll taken a week before Kennedy declared his candidacy, Carter's "negative" rating was twice as high as Kennedy's.

To a degree, these polls reflected a feeling shared by many Democrats that Kennedy's rise to the top was more or less inevitable. He was not, after all, Ted Smith or Ted Jones; he had been born into a family where politics was virtually in the blood. From the day of his birth, on February 22, 1932, when family legend holds that patriarch Joseph P. Kennedy was on the telephone raising campaign funds for Franklin D. Roosevelt when word arrived that the ninth Kennedy child had arrived safely, the last Kennedy found himself enveloped in Democratic politics. Though his childhood was marked by constant movement—the boy lived in four states and attended a dozen schools before following his brothers to Harvard—there was one fixed star in the family horizon: the parents' political ambitions for their sons.

Edward Kennedy learned from his father early on that Kennedy boys were meant to get involved in politics, right up to the presidency—and they were meant to win. The youngest son's first job, after he graduated from the University of Virginia Law School in 1959, was recruiting delegates in the Rocky Mountain states for John F. Kennedy's presidential campaign. Three years later, at the urging of his father and over the objection of his brother, the President, Edward M. Kennedy launched his own political career. His race for the Senate sparked critics to complain that the Kennedys were trying to build an American "dynasty." The objection failed to take hold in Massachusetts, partly because a lot of voters there were quite willing to see the Kennedys start a dynasty, and partly because both of Ted's opponents that year—Edward McCormack in the Democratic primary, and George Cabot Lodge in the general election—were themselves products of political dynasties.

Kennedy won the 1962 race with ease, and went on to win every election he entered thereafter. His only political defeat came in 1971, when his fellow Democrats in the Senate refused to vote him a second term as majority whip. The voters of Massachusetts stayed with him through four primary and four general elections, and Democrats around the country made him the "winner" in poll after presidential poll.

And then came 1980—when Ted Kennedy emerged as the year's champion loser. Because he stayed in the Democratic race right to the end, Kennedy ended up losing more elections during the year than any other candidate. He entered all 34 primaries, and lost 24 of them. He contested all 25 state and territorial caucuses, and lost 20 of them.

Some people say that Kennedy effectively lost the 1980 race in July of 1969, when his conduct on Chappaquiddick Island— "incomprehensible and completely inexcusable" was Kennedy's own description—left a young woman dead and the nation shocked. There is no question that, for many voters, that incident rendered Kennedy permanently ineligible for the nation's highest office. Any pollster could find scores of people who said they felt to vote for Kennedy was to reward immorality.

But Chappaquidick was a central part of American political lore all those ten years that Edward Kennedy's name stood at the top of the opinion polls. And Chappaquiddick was hardly a forgotten subject among the professional politicians who agreed—before Kennedy took himself out of the contest—that the 1976 Democratic nomination was his for the asking. And so in 1980 Chappaquiddick and the other incidents that added up to Kennedy's "character" problem cannot alone explain Kennedy's failure.

For candidate Kennedy had to deal with other substantial problems. He was still an old-line liberal, a true believer in big government's ability to solve people's problems—a belief that was not shared by many of his countrymen. He was challenging the President just when Americans felt a patriotic duty to rally 'round their leader. He was an erratic, often inarticulate campaigner who could not live up to the superhuman ideal that Democrats associated with the name "Kennedy."

This last revelation was the first big surprise of the Kennedy campaign. His reputation as a tough, articulate campaigner dissipated with remarkable speed. The process began, in fact, a few days before he formally launched his campaign—in the nationally-televised and heavily-ballyhooed interview with Roger Mudd of CBS News.

Kennedy had not wanted to do the Mudd program. He was not ready, he said, to discuss his candidacy in detail, and anyway, he wasn't sure it would do him any good. But his press secretary, Tom Southwick, pressed hard and convinced the Senator that the nationwide broadcast could be a golden opportunity.

The result—a stumbling, vacuous performance that showed Kennedy as a man with no coherent explanation for Chappaquiddick and no clear reason for seeking the presidency—was a disaster from which the campaign never recovered. Southwick never did either. The dedicated young aide took personal blame for the Mudd fiasco, grew increasingly morose as the campaign sputtered, and eventually quit his job and went off to New Mexico to try to forget.

Kennedy's stump campaigning—scrutinized with unusual intensity by the national press—did little to offset the image Mudd's interview created. For the first month of the campaign—when Kennedy asked for support from "every fam farmily in Iowa"—to the last—when he declared "I am an uphill battle"—his effort was plagued by flubs and slips of the tongue. Sometimes Kennedy did rise to the compelling rhetorical heights he was known for—and then he turned out to be too forceful. He was, the media experts said, too "hot" for the "cool" medium of television, which was most voters' window onto the campaign. His shouted speeches may have inspired the people who came out to hear him in person, but they tended to frighten the remaining millions who stayed home and watched snatches on the TV news.

Candidate Kennedy seemed much of the time to be afflicted with a fundamental inability to get his points across. "I guess Bobby never gave him no speaking lessons," observed a union man in Des Moines after hearing Kennedy's verbose, tangled, and occasionally incomprehensible answers to voters' questions. The problem was crystalized at a joint appearance in

Milwaukee with Walter Fauntroy, the District of Columbia's delegate in Congress. Kennedy opened the session with a vague and hard-to-follow indictment of Carter's latest budget proposals. Then Fauntroy stepped up to the microphone and clipped off a half-dozen specific decisions Carter had made, explaining why each one was a mistake. The contrast with Kennedy's meandering performance was clear to everyone present—including Kennedy. "Well," the Senator said sheepishly after Fauntroy had finished, "I guess I just say 'Amen' to everything Walter just said."

If Kennedy often seemed unable to say things clearly, it also seemed, in the first weeks, that he had almost nothing to say. This resulted from an initial strategic decision that Kennedy later admitted was dead wrong.

With the challenger far ahead of the incumbent in the polls his campaign manager, Smith, and his top political thinker, Paul Kirk, decided at the start that it would be safest for Kennedy to tone down his liberal rhetoric so as not to alarm a skeptical electorate. The result was a bland stump speech that was heavy on abstractions—"hope," "leadership," "the American spirit"—but devoid of specific reasons for Democrats to abandon their incumbent president.

The most serious blow to Kennedy's hopes, though, came on November 4, 1979—about twelve hours before the Mudd broadcast—when Iranian militants seized the U.S. embassy in Tehran and took 63 Americans hostage. Almost overnight the nation's attention was diverted from economic problems at home to the military and diplomatic crisis overseas. And overnight there developed a conviction among the American people that a time of international conflict was a time to rally behind the President—no matter how unpopular that president had been a month before.

Like all the other candidates seeking Carter's job, Kennedy was sorely frustrated by the Iranian crisis. He, too, supported the President's efforts to free the hostages—he said so, in those first few weeks, in every speech. But he still wanted to talk about Carter's economic policies, energy policies, foreign policy. And now nobody wanted to listen.

Kennedy's frustration finally boiled over on December 2, at the end of a tiring 14-hour campaign day, in an interview with San Francisco's KRON-TV. Asked to respond to Ronald Reagan's defense of the Shah of Iran, Kennedy disagreed angrily. The Shah had run "one of the most violent regimes in the history of mankind," he said, and had "stolen . . . umpteen billions of dollars" from the Iranian people.

The producers at KRON saw nothing particularly striking about Kennedy's remarks on the Shah, and thus left them on the cutting room floor that night when brief passages of the interview were broadcast on the late news. Kennedy's traveling press corps, after watching the news broadcast, concluded that this had been just one more uneventful interview and turned in for the night. If nothing else had happened before Kennedy and the press corps left San Francisco early the next morning, the KRON interview would probably have vanished without a trace. But the reporter from United Press International couldn't sleep that night; he wandered down to the press room and found a transcript of the entire KRON interview. In the pre-dawn quiet of the news rooms of the major eastern newspapers, warning bells began to ring on the UPI teletypes—the signal that "urgent" news was on the way. The first major furor of the 1980 campaign had been born.

In a time when most other candidates had effectively taken a vow of silence on Iran, Kennedy's eruption became big news. Now the questions people already had about his character and his political views had to make way for doubts about his judgment.

There were a good many Americans, of course, who had no doubts about Kennedy—they knew quite clearly that they hated him. As with his brothers, there was something about him and his background that stirred intense dislike among a variety of constituencies. As a result, Kennedy tended to make enemies even when he took the same stand his opponents did.

There was almost no difference between Kennedy and Carter on abortion, for example, but the anti-abortion movement, which disliked both, focussed its ire on Kennedy. Anti-abortion demonstrators became a fixture of Kennedy campaign stops, while Carter's surrogates were generally left alone. "It's obvious the anti-abortionists want bogeyman Ted not just down but out before they start blasting Carter's lousy abortion record," reported the anti-abortion newsletter "Lifeletter." One reason might have been a feeling—as articulated by a "pro-life" demonstrator outside a Kennedy fund-raiser in New Hampshire—that "he's a Catholic and he ought to know better."

Similarly, gun owners' groups spent heavily on advertising and bumper stickers ("If Kennedy Wins—YOU LOSE!") attacking Kennedy, even though his position—he favored banning the sale of certain handguns—was precisely the same as Carter's. A businessman from Columbus, Ohio, spent $7,500 from his own pocket to form an organization called "s.t.o.p." (stop Teddy on presidency). "I don't trust any politician, but mainly Kennedy," he explained.

Whether Kennedy's campaign staff was a help or hindrance in overcoming these problems is a question the political professionals will probably debate for years. Some top figures in the political consulting industry (miffed, perhaps, because Kennedy relied on them so little) called his advertising ineffectual and his failure to use regular opinion surveys inexcusable. Low-level staffers at the campaign headquarters in Washington never stopped complaining about Smith, the brother-in-law and campaign manager; he was, they said, too slow to recognize the campaign's early trouble and too quick to call for surrender when the message sunk in.

But every losing campaign generates that kind of criticism. In this case, it is probably safe to say that the 200-plus men and women who worked full-time for the Kennedy campaign did as good a job as anyone could have under the circumstances.

The Kennedy staff was an amalgam drawn from three main categories: the old Kennedy hands, such as strategist Paul Kirk, press secretary Dick Drayne, and Peter Edelman, a veteran of Robert Kennedy's staff who signed on to run the younger brother's issues research; the candidate's Senate staff, including Southwick, speechwriter Carey Parker, and political adviser Carl Wagner; and veterans of the McGovern '72 campaign, including speechwriter Robert Shrum, chief scheduler Steve Robbins, and financial experts Morris Dees and Martin Katz. Except for Stephen Smith, there was no one who ranked as the candidate's peer in age or status; while old friends like Washington lawyers John Douglas and John Reilly were called on for advice and consultation now and then, Kennedy never had a close political adviser to help him respond to each day's developments on the trail.

The Kennedy campaign staff made some definite mistakes. At the outset, Robbins and the advance team he recruited, mainly from his colleagues in the 1972 campaign, designed a frenetic, three-media-market-per-day schedule that might have been useful for a relative unknown like George McGovern but was a waste of energy and funds for a figure as familiar as Ted Kennedy. The campaign never settled on a surrogate spokesman to answer the opposition's barbs; that meant Kennedy sometimes used up all his time on the evening news responding to a verbal zinger from an underling in the Carter campaign. On the other hand, Kennedy's financial people somehow kept the money coming in—about $150,000 per week, right to the end—long after the campaign was clearly hopeless. Shrum, Parker, and their back-up staff turned out a body of campaign speeches of consistently high quality, including two major addresses—at Georgetown University, and at the Democratic National Convention—that could arguably stand as the two best speeches of the political year.

With the staff Kennedy assembled, with his solid knowledge of a wide range of issues, and with the priceless Kennedy assets of good looks, personal charm and universal name recognition, another politician might have gone very far in 1980. But Kennedy, faced with all the unexpected problems he ran into, and burdened by the onus of "character," hardly went anywhere.

"I always knew," Kennedy said when his campaign was over, "that there would be questions about, about the incident and about my family, but I had really expected they would not persist the way they did."

As it happened, news stories and questions about Chappaquiddick, about the candidate's personal life, about the wife who lived apart from him, and about the general subject of "character" did persist right to the end. As late as June 2, the last campaign day of the primary season, Kennedy was still answering questions—in a local television interview in San Jose—about "the Kopechne incident."

But if Chappaquiddick and "character" posed the biggest barrier to his success, the enduring irony of the 1980 Kennedy campaign was that the candidate who lost for lack of character demonstrated a rare degree of tenacity, decency, and inner strength. He showed himself, in short, to be a man of considerable character.

Through all the reverses he experienced, Kennedy absolutely refused to cry or complain; he kept plugging resolutely away. The political story of the 1980 Kennedy campaign was that the "winner" in ten years worth of opinion polls turned out, in the primaries, to be a loser. The human story is that he was a gutsy and gracious loser.

That first became clear on the night of January 21, when the returns from the Iowa caucuses showed that Carter, in the opening contest of the campaign, had won 59 percent of the vote to Kennedy's 31 percent—a margin considered astounding then, but one that became ordinary as the primary season wore on. It was the first time in Kennedy's 18-year political career that he had lost at the polls. He took it in stride. "We congratulate the President on his victory in Iowa," Kennedy said, and when it was suggested that Carter's big win meant Kennedy ought to quit the race, the loser managed to laugh. "Of course we intend to go on," he said. "Thirty-one percent of the people in Iowa can't be wrong."

Kennedy did go on, shrugging off fatigue and frustration and bouncing back with a striking resilience after each new Tuesday night calamity. By the last weeks of his exhausting struggle, he seemed satisfied, even proud, in his role as an underdog spokesman for the liberal cause.

One reason for this equanimity was that the candidate never lost his sense of humor. He could laugh at himself and the sometimes ludicrous rituals involved in traversing the country with an entourage of 150 staffers, security agents, reporters, and camera crew members in pursuit of votes. At one point Kennedy got himself involved in a peripheral but still vehement argument with the Carter camp as to whether the President had made a deal with Congress over Navy shipbuilding plans. In a television interview, Kennedy declared sternly that the transaction had all the characteristics of a political deal, and "If it looks like a duck, walks like a duck, and quacks like a duck, it's a duck." With that the interview ended, and the lights and microphones were turned off. The senior senator from Massachusetts then turned to the reporter, flapped his wings in a duck-like manner, and quacked three times.

A modern political campaign, at least that of a candidate deemed "serious" by the media, has the general configuration of a comet, with the candidate at the head and the entourage tailing raggedly along for a long distance behind. The Kennedy campaign never learned the trick of controlling the tail, of splitting it off so the candidate could deal directly with the voters. As a result, the candidate was regularly overwhelmed by his entourage. When Kennedy rode the subway on the morning before the New York primary, he was followed onto the train by a shoving, cursing, jostling throng of reporters and photographers, cameras and cables. By the time everybody was settled, there wasn't an inch left on the car for real-life commuters; the candidate rode to the next stop making small talk with the Secret Service. When he toured a roller-skate factory in New Hampshire, each worker looked up from her machine to see Ted Kennedy—and a swarm of five dozen reporters right behind him. After Kennedy shook hands and asked quietly for "a little help on election day," the press corps would dive in to ask questions of its own: "Ma'am, what do you think about Chappaquiddick?"

Kennedy, with a finely honed sense of the absurd, put up with all that, and with the 20-hour days and red-eye flights and long, bumpy bus trips that left him literally bent over in pain from his old back injury. He put up with the constant hi-jinks of a press corps that created its own radio station (broadcast over the campaign plane's PA system) to mock his speeches and replay tape recordings of his most embarrassing verbal flubs. At one point, with the campaign low on funds, he traveled the country in an ancient two-engine prop plane chartered from Air New England, with the pilot informing his passengers before each approach that this would be his first landing at the airport in Wichita, or Charleston, or wherever. Although he had once been seriously injured in the crash of a small plane, Kennedy managed to laugh on bumpy, storm-tossed flights when the reporters began playing "The High and the Mighty" on kazoos.

The toughest test of Kennedy's unfailing spirit came on a raw, blustery Friday in New York. Three days before, he had been decimated in Illinois; four days ahead loomed the New York and Connecticut primaries, and the public polls all suggested that he would be clobbered again. Still, Kennedy was able to laugh his way through an unrelenting Day of Ignominy, a day filled with political slights and botched schedules and small, tepid crowds. The crowning blow came in Syracuse, when the candidate and his bedraggled entourage trooped out of their plane into a chilly downpour for the day's TV "visual"—Kennedy was to be endorsed by the local Congressman, James Hanley. For 20 minutes Hanley shouted generalities into the rain; finally a reporter broke in to ask, "Congressman, are you going to vote for Senator Kennedy?" Hanley spluttered, coughed, cleared his throat: "I would have to say that I will keep that private," he finally said. Kennedy cracked up with everybody else. Then he sauntered over, put his arm around Hanley's shoulders, and pointed to the waiting reporters. "C'mon, Jim, you can tell these guys," Kennedy said. "They won't tell anybody."

For all that, Kennedy went on the next Tuesday to score big victories in both New York and Connecticut, giving him his biggest night of the primary season. But Kennedy's big night came too late; the winning momentum Carter had begun to build in Iowa had given the President such a healthy margin in the delegate count that it was all but impossible for Kennedy to catch up. "To some degree Iowa was probably the most significant one," Kennedy noted at the end of his campaign. "After that, the chances for our success were, were remote."

But in a curious way, that thumping loss in Iowa was the best thing that happened to candidate Kennedy all year.

For one thing, his steadfast reaction to defeat made him, if not quite a sympathetic figure, at least one whom many people could admire, regardless of political views. The new image—which became the standard stuff of media reports on Kennedy as the campaign wore on—of a stalwart fighter moving ahead against terrible odds, might help counter the "character" problem in any future Kennedy campaign. The political packager David Garth observed that the most striking development of the Kennedy campaign was the emergence of a new image—"gallant Teddy"—to replace the old "playboy Teddy" idea.

More important, Iowa liberated Kennedy. In a long strategy session after the voting there, Kennedy told his advisers that he might as well go back to the clear advocacy of the liberal cause that had been his political trademark. This was partly strategic: the mushy, middle-of-the-road stance he had taken in the campaign so far had obviously not worked, and the polls showed that people thought of Kennedy as a liberal no matter what he said. But the shift reflected as well Kennedy's personal distress with the conservative economic thinking and the harsh anti-Soviet rhetoric in the State of the Union message Carter delivered two days after the Iowa caucuses. To Kennedy, that speech was a clear sign that Carter was moving right to counter the Republican challenge in the fall. Kennedy was determined to keep up the pressure from the left.

The result, six days after Iowa, was the Georgetown University speech. "I have only just begun to fight," Kennedy declared before a whooping, cheering audience of supporters, and the new weapons he took up—specific proposals for wage-price controls and immediate gasoline rationing, together with strong criticism of Carter's "helter-skelter militarism," finally gave him a distinctive message to carry to his party. Whether or not columnist William Safire was right when he said the Georgetown address "revived the art of the political speech, which has been dormant for a decade," it did revive the liberal spirit of the candidate and his campaign workers.

Kennedy seemed comfortable with his distinctive new message, but it was one that most voters did not seem ready to accept. The candidate would get furiously fired up before a crowd somewhere about food stamps or job programs or the idea he loved most of all, the need for a comprehensive federally funded health insurance program. Then the questions would start. "Won't that cost a lot of money?" "Won't that just mean more bureaucracy?"

Coupled with the public's distrust of government programs was a widespread belief—nurtured, perhaps, by Carter's speeches about the limits of presidential power—that the government's work would not change much no matter who was elected president. This idea, the notion that the election didn't matter much, was the thing that annoyed Kennedy most of all.

"Mr. Carter says there isn't much a president can do about these problems," Kennedy would shout at his campaign stops, his voice laced with scorn. "Well, I *reject* that idea. It is alien to everything I stand for and my family has stood for." Then he would run through a litany of activist presidents, from Franklin D. Roosevelt to John F. Kennedy and Lyndon B. Johnson, who had "proved that a president can make things happen in this country."

The voters, though, indicated they had a less expansive view of presidential power. In primary votes and opinion surveys, they made it clear they did not hold the President accountable for the nation's troubles.

For almost three months at the height of the primary season, inflation and interest rates both hovered near 20 percent while economists predicted daily that recession was on the way. Jimmy Carter responded that "these problems are not simple"— and he kept on winning, week after week. Just before the Indiana primary, Kennedy spent the better part of a weekend in Anderson, Indiana, an auto-industry town where high interest rates the Carter Administration had helped impose had shut the two largest factories and caused a city-wide unemployment rate of 25 percent. Kennedy won enormous cheers at a campaign rally in a union hall, had a quiet, poignant conversation with a group of unemployed auto workers, and spent the night at the home of a union man who had just lost the job he had held for 22 years. It all got heavy coverage in the local media, and Kennedy was pointed in placing the blame for the city's problems on Jimmy Carter's doorstep. On primary day, Carter carried every precinct in Anderson.

Kennedy's traditional liberalism clearly had its appeal to some Democrats, and there was evidence that the whole party still found the Kennedy formulae attractive, at least in the abstract. The outpouring of emotion—an uproarious mixture of cheers, tears, laughter, and roars of affection—that greeted his forthright statement of liberal doctrine at the Democratic convention would seem to indicate that Kennedy's view still had a place in the party's heart. But if this is true, the party did not vote its heart in the primaries of 1980. Jimmy Carter got 51 percent of all the Democratic votes cast; Kennedy got 38 percent.

Edward M. Kennedy was not the only Democrat in 1980 who tried and failed to turn the nation's difficulties into votes against Jimmy Carter. The third contender, Edmund G. (Jerry) Brown Jr., the governor of California, started the race with impressive credentials, but somehow never became a factor in the Democratic contest.

On paper, the angular, intense young governor had a lot going for him. He had won two imposing electoral victories in the nation's most populous state. As a late-starting presidential hopeful in 1976, he had beaten Jimmy Carter in five of the six primaries he had entered. That performance was not enough to keep Carter from gaining the nomination, but it was sufficient to focus national attention on the upstart challenger, a politician of delightful unpredictability who refused to adhere to traditional political rules and sometimes refused to acknowledge political reality. On the third night of the 1976 Democratic convention, with Carter holding a 2,000-delegate lead over his nearest rival, Brown had walked into the convention hall insisting that he had not given up. "My strategy is still evolving," Brown had said with a straight face.

The strategy that evolved for Brown's 1980 campaign was to nurture that same image—to convey the impression that this youthful-looking, 40-year-old ex-Jesuit was in fact something totally new. And so Brown entered the race—on November 8, 1979, four days after Kennedy's formal announcement—with a brief speech (ten short paragraphs that barely filled a single page) which dealt with issues no other candidate was talking about. "My principles are simple," Brown announced. "Protect the earth, serve the people, and explore the universe." His discussion of the third goal offered a nice example of Brownspeak: "I see a future where we reach out into space itself and bring with us other nations, so that at last we begin to sense our unity in the Spirit of this small speck of universal time."

To say that the Democratic party was not ready for Brown's self-described "insurgent movement" would be an understatement. Struggle as he might—and he worked extremely hard—Brown never managed to get reporters, contributors, or voters to take him seriously. He spent the first two months of his campaign fighting just for a seat at the *Des Moines Register*'s Kennedy-Carter debate; the newspaper finally gave in (after Brown diverted precious campaign funds for two Iowa trips) but then Carter dropped out of the debate and Brown was out of luck.

If Brown had gotten the attention he wanted, however, it is not clear that he would have profited. Although the grand sweep of his ideas was exciting, candidate Brown turned out to be extremely weak on the details. His campaign was riddled with errors and overstatements that evidenced either carelessness or a basic ignorance about the government and the country.

At a campaign stop in Maine, for example, Brown told a press conference that balancing the federal budget would be "easy." "You just cut all the programs, across the board," he snapped. "There's no magic to it." When the reporters asked the inevitable follow-up question—Did that across-the-board cut include a cut in Social Security payments?—Brown had to back down: "Well, there would be some exceptions." When the reporters told him that he had just "excepted" the largest single line-item in the federal budget, the candidate seemed incredulous. "No way," he said. "It's not the biggest single item." In fact, Social Security has been the biggest line-item in the federal budget for nearly a decade.

Politically, Brown's best chance all year came in the Maine caucuses, where cheap media and the presence of an active anti-nuclear movement offered him a genuine opportunity. (Carter's supporters helped Brown in Maine too, offering him volunteers and mailing lists in the hope that he would drain off some Kennedy votes.) But after he took only 10 percent of the vote in the Maine caucuses, Brown put his under-funded, understaffed effort into neutral. Two months later, he geared up again for a final effort in Wisconsin, another state that seemed to have a made-to-order Brown constituency of old-line liberals and activist students.

Brown's Wisconsin campaign, with the candidate and his staff literally dependent on reporters and supporters to keep them fed, was a flop. But it was a spectacular flop, ending with a bizarre statewide television extravaganza filmed by *Apocalypse Now* producer Francis Ford Coppola that featured blazing strobe lights and helicopter overflights. Even for free-thinking Wisconsin, that was too much. Brown ran a dismal third in the April 1 primary. He withdrew from the race that night with gracious words for his opponents and a promise to try again in 1984.

Wisconsin was a disaster for Kennedy as well. A week before, New York and Connecticut had given his campaign its only injection of that much-desired political commodity known as "momentum." That momentum evaporated on April Fool's day as Kennedy lost by 2 to 1 margins in Wisconsin and Kansas. It seemed final proof, if any more were needed, that the great majority of Democrats were unwilling to nominate Kennedy for president. The campaign went forward, propelled by the candidate's unflagging energy and an ingenious, industrious fund-raising staff. On June 3, Kennedy won five of eight primaries and two of the three biggest states at stake. For the next two months, he conspicuously ignored the delegate count and forged ahead toward the convention. "The jobless . . . the families without adequate health care . . . the farmers who have lost their land do not have floor passes to the convention," he explained in a New York speech in July. "But my campaign does. And we will walk and work the floor of the convention on their behalf."

Kennedy did work the convention, and won some major victories on the party platform. In his memorable speech on the convention's second night, he pumped genuine life into what had been a sullen political gathering and won himself the respect of more than 20,000 people in the hall and 20 million more watching on television. He emerged as the convention's dominant figure, and as a leading prospect for the Democrats in 1984. But when the convention ended, Jimmy Carter was the nominee.

Kennedy's losing campaign in 1980 was an intense, wearying whirlwind of seven-day weeks and seven-speech days that reached 39 states, Puerto Rico, Mexico, and the United Nations. It covered nearly 300,000 air miles and cost some $15 million (with a million-dollar debt left over at the end). An ABC News camera crew that filmed Kennedy every time he arrived somewhere to make a speech counted up at the end of the primaries and found it had shot that scene 2,150 times.

Tight security was standard operating procedure for a Kennedy campaign, and everywhere the candidate went he was surrounded by Secret Service agents and police guards. Even when the treasury was tightest, the campaign paid a doctor and a trauma nurse to accompany Kennedy full-time just in case something happened. Except for three egg-throwing incidents, from which the candidate escaped unsplattered, nothing did.

It was also standard for the Kennedys to turn the campaign into a family effort. At any given time a dozen or more Kennedys, Lawfords, and Shrivers were likely to be out stumping. A fundraiser in Chicago would find Chicago native Ethel Kennedy at the head table next to her brother-in-law; a Greek-American rally in New York would include an appearance by Jacqueline Kennedy Onassis.

The surprise winner of the family's "best campaigner" title was the candidate's wife, Joan, who won respect and admiration with her natural, amiable manner and her frank talk about her successful battle with alcoholism.

Mrs. Kennedy provided the richest personal moment of the whole campaign in the incident that has entered political lore as the "one-question press conference." On the Friday before the Iowa caucuses, Joan Kennedy accompanied her husband to a press conference in Sioux City. To both Kennedys' surprise, the first question was directed at her: in light of new media investigations of the Chappaquiddick incident, did she really believe her husband's explanation? With apparent reluctance Mrs. Kennedy walked to the microphone. She paused for a long while, biting her lip. "'Yes," she finally said. "I believe my husband's story, which he told me right after the incident . . . and so I don't believe that these stories in the last few days are going to come up with anything new . . . we really should be discussing the important issues. It just seems a shame that, you know, it all has to come out again."

Mrs. Kennedy had defended her husband many times before. But her faltering and obviously heartfelt response that day was so moving that nobody present could say a word when she finished. For a long minute, nobody asked another question. Another minute. Finally, everybody just walked away. The press conference was over.

What was not standard for a Kennedy campaign was the long roster of defeats that the last brother suffered during the year. Ted Kennedy became the first member of his family to be rejected by the Democratic party.

It was an experience he had not expected, at the beginning, ever to face. In an interview during the first week of the campaign, when everything looked good, he said, "I think it has been advantageous to be a Kennedy. My father, you know set a very high standard . . . that, you know, coming in first was important."

Nine months later, on the day after the Democratic convention and his campaign had come to an end, the youngest Kennedy looked back at his experience and said that he had learned a somewhat different lesson in 1980. "I learned how to lose," he said. "The series of (primary defeats), it's not, that's not pleasant, but the forces which motivated me became much more significant, much more powerful, than the result on any given primary night.

"And when you have that sense, I suppose you learn to live with your disappointments."

★ Carter ★

by Martin Schram

HAMILTON JORDAN was sitting at his desk, awaiting the word, and when the flashing began on the telephone line that links the Oval Office with his, he jumped to answer.

"Yes sir?"

"I just met with Kennedy," said the President, who was sitting at his own desk, just a few steps down the corridor. "I have the certain feeling that he is going to run."

Jordan paused. "So be it," he recalls saying as he hung up the phone.

For President Carter and most of his advisers this publicly uneventful fall Friday in 1979—September 7—was the day that the battle of the 1980 campaign was officially joined. But for Hamilton Jordan, the conversation between Senator Edward Kennedy and the President was just ratification. For the past nine months, Jordan had already been presiding over the beginnings of a reelection campaign that had always been aimed at defeating Kennedy. When virtually all of the other senior Carter advisers had been doubting that Kennedy would dare to challenge an incumbent Democratic president, Jordan was arguing that Kennedy would—as long as the polls were showing he could win.

In fact, Jordan had built Jimmy Carter's 1980 campaign plan around this assumption, in a lengthy memorandum to the President that filled a black looseleaf notebook and was dated January 17, 1979.

In his memo, Jordan outlined some things that proved right and some that proved wrong, set some goals that were attainable and others that were not. And as he would say later: "An awful lot of what I wrote was just plain obvious."

While he was correct in gauging the nature of Kennedy's eventual decision to run and even the timing of it, he proved unrealistic (and even naive) in setting a goal of raising by the end of 1979 all of the campaign contributions permitted by law in each state. (That goal was not reached until the end of the long 1980 primary campaign.) And Jordan, like virtually every other observer and practitioner of the unscience of politics, did not foresee the overwhelming impact that international crises such as those in Iran and Afghanistan would have upon the 1980 campaign.

The Jordan memo was the Carter campaign blueprint. But its greatest fascination was that it also provided insights into the inner workings of the Carter White House. They were far more revealing than mere blueprints and battle plans.

The Jordan memo disclosed the determination of the Carter White House to play tough, hard power politics in an election year.

It emphasized using the power of incumbency to achieve political goals—showing Jordan carefully attempting to steel the resolve of the President to use these powers by citing Gerald Ford's 1976 campaign as a perfect example of what not to do and how not to do it.

"...President Ford failed to utilize the advantages of incumbency and failed to minimize the disadvantages. He learned a very expensive lesson in the primaries which almost cost him his party's nomination."

It outlined plans for using White House pressure and influence to encourage state officials to shift the dates of various primary elections and caucuses—to create a "preferred version" of the 1980 calendar that would benefit Carter's campaign.

"...The easiest way to establish early momentum...is to win southern delegates by encouraging southern states to hold early caucuses and primaries...It is in our interest to have states that we are likely to win scheduled on the same day with states that we might do poorly in."

And it cited the importance of "playing the expectations game" in 1979 to reduce the impact that any challenge to Carter might have in 1980.

"...I believe that it is to our own benefit to help create the expectation that we will be challenged in our own party..."

This glimpse inside the Carter inner circle, as revealed in

internal memos and lengthy interviews, showed the President and his people seeming far more practical and purposeful and aggressive at politics—some call it hardball—than they had appeared to be at running the government.

They were clearly better prepared for the real contest of 1980 and its real contours than was their principal opponent for the Democratic nomination. And that proved to be a good part of the story of the Democratic presidential campaign. For the party's nomination was both won and lost. When it came to politicking, the Carter crowd began with a better sense of themselves and where they were going and how they were going to get there than did Kennedy's.

The early contrast was pronounced. While the Carter forces were planning and leveraging, Kennedy was giving public exhibition of being somewhat less prepared: Asked in that now famous CBS television interview by Roger Mudd just why he wanted to be president, Kennedy floundered about as though he had been asked to explain the practical application of quantum mechanics.

But perhaps even more revealing of the contrast between the two camps, were the semi-private comments of Kennedy's brother-in-law and campaign chairman, Stephen Smith, just after the Kennedy campaign had mismanaged, misspent, and miscued itself into a stunning defeat in the first political battle of the year, the caucuses in Iowa. He was sitting in his headquarters office with a reporter offering explanations that were at times quick and staccato and at times stream of consciousness:

"Problem was, as soon as we opened our door it was nothing but ragtime . . . We were trying to start up in 50 states all at once . . . Now money's a problem, sure. But the press focused in on what was just horseshit. And out there it was just ragtime . . . When we started, it was three weeks before we even got a wire in . . . So we were going off in 50 directions at once—and going against the best switchboard in the world, and we couldn't even get a phone wire in the beginning . . . It was all happening to us at once . . . It was all moving too quickly . . . It wasn't as orderly as you'd like . . . He got overscheduled . . . We overspent . . . But from the outside, I'll tell you, it's just a lot of ragtime."

While Stephen Smith was caught up in the ragtime—the helter-skelter of politics that can befuddle a campaign—his

Carter counterparts had already implemented most of their master plan.

In its two years, the Carter campaign had three chairmen, but in reality, it always had just one chief: Jordan.

In a rather remarkable interview, the man who ultimately settled in as Carter's permanent campaign chairman, the ever-aggrandizing Robert Strauss, slipped into a moment of uncharacteristic modesty (which is what made it remarkable), when he was asked about the nature of his own role at the committee. "This has never been my operation, as you know," the 61-year-old veteran of important jobs said. ". . . The word 'chairman' is a misnomer. 'Chief spokesman' is really the role I have, and it's a good one for me. . . . That and some fund-raising, the sort that required a senior person—someone with gray hair who could talk with those business council people."

The campaign of 1979–80 saw the President's political fortunes undergo extraordinary change. Having plummeted to the lowest rating accorded a modern president, and facing a challenge from a Kennedy who was already beating him by better than 2 to 1 in the polls, Carter found for himself a new image of leadership—aided immeasurably by the crises in Iran and Afghanistan. And he rode that newfound image and the political skills of those he had kept by his side for four years (preserved in the suspended animation of government jobs) to victories over a challenger who once looked unbeatable.

By the time he captured a majority of the Democratic convention delegates, his presidency was once again coming under unrelenting criticism and attack (and even ridicule) from the Democratic left and right in the Congress, in the editorial columns, and even in the election day interviews of many voters who had just cast their ballots for him.

The pattern was Carter classic. He finished in 1980 as he had in 1976, staggering through a series of late primary defeats even as he was putting a numerical lock on his party's nomination. But in a way, his 1980 showing was more remarkable than the 1976 come-from-nowhere victory that got him into the White House. For in 1980, Jimmy Carter did not have the luxury of coming from nowhere; he came from being thoroughly inspected and seemingly rejected; from being down and apparently out.

It was a comeback that perhaps tells us as much about ourselves as it does about our president. It shows us as being tough in our judgments of our incumbents, but paradoxically, far less willing to release them from their hold on us. Jimmy Carter was viewed by the public as seriously flawed when he began his campaign to win renomination and he was viewed much the same when he finally had the nomination numerically won. His victory came not because he was especially beloved or even greatly respected; it came mostly because he was considered less objectionable than his chief opponent. But even victory on those terms proved a politically difficult task.

Jimmy Carter was always a leader in title more than in public perception. That is why his campaign could leave little to charisma, and even less to chance. The crises in Iran and Afghanistan turned out to be timed to political perfection for Carter, inspiring Americans to rally around their flag and their president just as he was trying to get his campaign off to a fast start. His strategists had nothing to do with summoning those crises, nor timing them. But they did lay the political groundwork for Carter's surefooted start. And the effort began with that memo from Hamilton Jordan.

★

January 17, 1979
EYES ONLY
TO: President Carter
FROM: Hamilton Jordan

INTRODUCTION
The Incumbent President As Candidate
THE MYTH OF THE INCUMBENT PRESIDENT
Over the two hundred year history of our country, the myth developed and was sustained by events that incumbent Presidents are always re-elected.... The history of Presidential incumbents seeking re-election in recent history flies in the face of this historical presumption that all Presidential incumbents are re-elected.

...So, as we think and plan for 1980, we must be prepared to deal with the contradiction that exists. Namely, that while the myth persists that incumbent Presidents are always elected to second terms, the fact is that the fragmentation of political power within the party and the tremendous difficulty the modern President faces in finding practical and attractive solutions to this new generation of complex foreign and domestic problems—make a serious challenge to an incumbent President much more likely.

THE RE-ELECTION CAMPAIGN OF PRESIDENT FORD

...If I had to point to several factors that were the cause of our success (in 1976), one major factor would be that we understood the law, its implications for our political strategy and functioned better under it than any of the other candidates. Because President Ford's people did not understand the law initially and functioned poorly under it, he almost lost the nomination of his party.

Secondly, President Ford failed to utilize the advantages of incumbency and failed to minimize the disadvantages. He learned a very expensive lesson in the primaries which almost cost him his party's nomination. By the general election, President Ford, the White House staff and his campaign staff had learned to maximize the advantages and minimize the disadvantages, and consequently came very close to beating us.

And finally...President Ford and his campaign made classic errors in strategy and judgment in almost every dimension of his campaign to win the Republican nomination. As an indication of what not to do, an analysis of his primary campaign is beneficial.

An Analysis of the Ford Campaign for the Nomination

...There was never an early, conscious effort to develop a coherent strategy for winning the Republican nomination.

...There was never a serious early assessment of President Ford's strengths and weaknesses nor a strategy for the use of the President that was oriented toward his strengths.

...The Ford campaign spent most of 1975 trying to get Ronald Reagan out of the race instead of preparing for a serious challenge.

...The best way to discourage a serious challenge from within your own party is to expect one and prepare for one;

Indications of lack of confidence in our own prospects for re-election will be interpreted as a sign of weakness and will only encourage a serious challenge.

Gerald Ford proved an effective foil for Jordan, as Jordan sought to focus the thinking of his boss upon the perils of incumbency—he put it delicately in terms of the complexity of modern problems, rather than plummeting polls and perceptions of failing leadership. Jordan also used the example of Ford to galvanize the President into endorsing aggressive steps to use the levers of incumbency. At the end of the memo, Jordan would have Carter mark his approval of every proposed step. He did this not because the President's approval was required to effect such action, Jordan would later concede, but because he knew it was important to channel Carter's thinking along the lines of acting firmly and aggressively and early if the nomination was to be won.

Jordan had fashioned himself something of a student of the political appeal of Jimmy Carter, ever since that day in 1966, when he was a 21-year-old college student working at a summer job spraying mosquitos and he happened to hear Carter making a campaign speech during his first, unsuccessful run for governor of Georgia. Like Jody Powell, Jordan had known no other job in his adult life other than the political care of Jimmy Carter. Over the years, Jordan had come to feel that Carter had a political knack for staking out a broad belt of appeal in the political center. But he always felt that Carter never had been truly accepted by the liberal establishment within the Democratic Party, and probably never would be. Thus, in his 1979 memo, Jordan argued that Carter's fight to win his party's nomination would be more difficult than winning the general election once the nomination was won. And winning the nomination, as Jordan saw it, required early demonstrations of party strength.

THE 1980 CAMPAIGN
THE DEMOCRATIC NOMINATION AND THE GENERAL
ELECTION
. . . Due to the fragmentation of political power in our country and in our party and the nature of persons in the Democratic

Party who participate disproportionately in the nomination process, it has always been my feeling that there is a greater chance we will lose the nomination than there is we will lose the general election.

. . . I assume that we will face a strong challenge within our own party. And we should not spend a lot of time worrying about where it comes from or who it may be, but we should be prepared psychologically and politically for a serious challenge.

. . . Another way of discouraging a serious challenge is to demonstrate early political strength and organization in key primary and caucus states.

The thrust of the advice Jordan was giving the President was that the Carter campaign for 1980 had to start early and win early. By the time the first caucus of 1980 was held in Iowa in January, the Carter-Mondale campaign committee had already been operating for almost a year. And in that time, it had already gone through three campaign chairmen.

In that time, the President's campaign had gone through three campaign chairmen.

First was then Democratic Party treasurer Evan Dobelle, who was chosen by Jordan because, although he was then just 33 years old and relatively inexperienced, he was considered capable and mainly supremely loyal to Jordan. By August, Jordan had concluded that Dobelle's skills were in fundraising but not strategic organization.

There is also another explanation for the rise and fall of Evan Dobelle. "Hamilton had wanted Evan to take orders from him," said another of the Carter senior advisors, "but then Hamilton got busy running the White House and he didn't give the orders." (Jordon was also busy at that time in defending himself against allegations that he had used cocaine—allegations from two unreliable plea bargainers that would be dismissed a year and a half later by a special prosecutor.)

In August, Jordan moved his 38-year-old White House political lieutenant, Tim Kraft, over to run the campaign committee, phasing Dobelle into the job of chief fundraiser. Kraft's background was in political organizing but it soon became clear he was not the sort of commanding presence who could command the media's attention and air time nor satiate the appetites of a nation of prominent Democrats who figured they deserved to deal with the President, or perhaps Jordan, but not much less.

And this led to the drafting of the redoubtable Robert Strauss.

At the Carter campaign, Chairman Strauss served as the out front man, handling the network interviews and hitting up the nation's board chairmen and leading Democrats. Kraft remained as campaign manager, tending to the organization and tactical detail. They co-existed and Strauss explained why it worked.

"Hamilton is a close enough friend of mine and of Kraft's that he probably lied enough to each of us about who was really in charge that neither of us resented the other one—and we get along fine."

All the while, Jordan sitting in his office as White House chief of staff (the chamber used to be H.R. Haldeman's) was serving as Carter's campaign chief without portfolio. To the other senior Carter officials, there was no doubt about this. "Hamilton is the chief strategist," said Tim Kraft. "Hamilton is the facilitator . . . and final arbiter," said Patrick Caddell. "Hamilton makes all the big decisions," said campaign counsel Tim Smith.

In an election year, political work and presidential work have a way of blending despite the best of intentions and purest of designs. For a couple of months in 1980, Jordan found himself swept away from the campaign, making secret diplomat forays to Europe and elsewhere as a negotiator ad hoc, hoping to solve the Iranian hostage crisis by dealing with French lawyers who were serving as intermediaries to the government in Tehran.

"It was hard—damn hard—to get anything done on the campaign then," said one senior Carter adviser. "We couldn't get to Hamilton for final decisions."

When the negotiations failed, Jordan returned to his two-hatted routine, overseeing the business of reelecting the President even as he was tending to the business of being the White House chief of staff.

It was a business he had been in, actually, ever since he suggested a reshaping of the primary and caucus calendar in that 1979 memo to Carter.

THE 1980 DELEGATE SELECTION RULES

(Jordan provided Carter with two color-coded charts, one entitled "The 1980 Delegate Selection Calendar—as of Dec. 15, 1978" and the other entitled "Preferred Version." He also offered explanations.)

Preferred Version

It is absolutely essential that we win the early contests and establish momentum. If we win the early contests, it is difficult to see how anyone could defeat us for the nomination. Conversely, if we lose the early contest(s), it is difficult to see how we could recoup and win the nomination... The easiest way to establish early momentum and stress the significant role of the south in the party is to win southern delegates by encouraging southern states to hold early caucuses and primaries.... It is in our interest to have states that we are likely to win scheduled on the same day with states that we might do poorly in.

Jordan wrote Carter that they had what he called limited but significant influence to shape a preferred version of the delegate selection calendar by convincing some states to shift their primary and caucus dates. South Carolina Gov. Dick Riley, Tennessee Speaker of the House Ned McWherter and Florida Gov. Bob Graham would likely be among those who would be helpful, Jordan figured.

As it turned out, Jordan and his assistants had limited but significant success in their efforts to shape the calendar to suit Carter's political aims.

Jordan envisioned dropping the Kennedys' home state Massachusetts primary from its early slot on March 4 (just a week after the New Hampshire primary) to sandwich it among several Southern state elections on March 11. The Carter aides could not move Massachusetts. ("We kind of bungled that one," said one Carter campaign official.) But Connecticut, another state Jordan feared early, was dropped down into April from its original early March 4 pairing with Massachusetts.

Jordan did succeed in making March 11 an early big day

for Carter, however, moving Georgia and eventually Alabama to join Florida on that date, guaranteeing a Carter southern sweep on that Tuesday.

Originally, Jordan had seen Illinois (March 18) as a potentially damaging state for Carter. He had first hoped to move Alabama's primary and then Tennessee's to sandwich Illinois among pro-Carter slices of the South that day. Neither could be done. But then Illinois turned out to be a major landslide victory that came close to demolishing the Kennedy candidacy.

New York was originally scheduled for April 1, as was Kansas, and Jordan, seeing New York as a poor state for Carter, hoped to move the caucuses of Michigan (a state judged as more favorable to Carter) to that date as well. That didn't succeed, but the effort proved irrelevant anyway.

"It should have been obvious all along that New York would have to change," recalls one Carter strategist. "April 1 was the first day of Passover—but Hamilton just didn't see that back then."

Jordan viewed the April 22 Pennsylvania primary as potential bad news for Carter; he proposed trying to shift the caucuses of Missouri, Texas, Louisiana, and Oklahoma to that date as well. Missouri indeed held its caucus on that date and provided a large Carter victory that enabled the Carter officials to eventually proclaim that they had won far more total delegates than Kennedy on April 22 despite Kennedy's razor-thin victory in Pennsylvania.

Jordan believed all along that the nomination had to be won early or it would not be won at all. Fund-raising was a chore that had to be gotten out of the way quickly, to leave time for the business of politics. And when it came to opponents, Jordan's advice came down to: expect the strongest, which means, prepare for the worst—and try to mold public expectations to fit the President's aims.

★

SPENDING LIMITATIONS ON THE 1980 PRESIDENTIAL CAMPAIGN

. . . We should try to raise most—if not all—of our funds in 1979 so that all of our political time and resources can be directed toward the early caucuses and primaries in 1980.

TIMETABLE FOR CANDIDATES TO MAKE DECISIONS
Possible Candidates/Types of Candidates

...*Governor Jerry Brown*. The single candidate who is sure to run and sure to announce early.... And although my strong personal inclination is to discount a Brown candidacy and not treat him seriously, I am reminded of his performance against us in the late primaries and his adept handling of Proposition Thirteen in California...

...*Senator Ted Kennedy.... There is no question in my mind that Senator Kennedy will challenge us for the nomination in 1980 if he believes that there is a very good chance that he can win*. If the odds are 40–60 against him, he will not run. But if the odds are 60–40 in his favor, he will definitely run.... Senator Kennedy will probably have to make a very close and very difficult decision in the late summer or early fall of this year.

...The absolute worst thing that we can do is to behave in a way that suggests we fear a Kennedy candidacy. We should proceed publicly on the same course that we have been on recently, that of praising him, minimizing differences, etc.

PLAYING THE "EXPECTATIONS" GAME

The "expectations" game might be described as the effort by the national media and the political community to establish arbitrary expectations against which to measure the political successes and failures of the various Presidential candidates. And although this game is played on the terrain of the media and the political community, it can be influenced—in varying degrees—by the candidates themselves.

In 1976, we played the "expectations" game well at times, poorly at others and many times it was simply beyond our control. We realized the importance of relating our political strategy to the expectations the media and the political community had of us. To begin with, we had no choice as your candidacy and prospects for winning were not taken seriously by anyone at the national level. Recognizing these "low expectations," we shaped and executed a political strategy that resulted in our exceeding the low expectations in a dramatic way that thrust you into the early role of being the frontrunner for the nomination and the probable nominee of the party.

Based on this early and unexpected success, we lost control of the public expectations of your candidacy...

The 1980 "Expectations" Game

Our situation in 1980 is the converse of 1976. Based on the historical myth of the incumbent President as presented earlier, the expectation is incredibly high that you will be re-nominated by the party and re-elected. This expectation is so high and so great that anything that happens in the next year to eighteen months that challenges that "expectation" will be closely scrutinized and greatly exaggerated by the news media...

...I believe that it is to our own benefit to help create the expectation that we will be challenged in our own party...

★

Of the people within the Carter inner circle, only Hamilton Jordan argued all along that Kennedy would challenge Carter in the fall. (Press Secretary Jody Powell, who gets his political inspiration from glands and visceral sensations, had felt deep down that Kennedy wanted to take on Carter ever since the Massachusetts Democrat went to the party's mid-term conference in Memphis in 1978 and delivered his emotional "sail against the wind" speech. But Powell did not press the point on the basis of politics.)

Most of Carter's other experts within did not share Jordan's view. Not Caddell, who had admired Kennedy and had served as his pollster in his 1976 senate race, and who argued through much of 1979 that it was unlikely Kennedy would run.

Not Strauss, who tried to stay plugged into the Kennedy plans through his friendship with House Speaker Thomas P. (Tip) O'Neill, and who now says: "I was one of the last to say that Kennedy would run." And not Rafshoon, who even wrote the President a memo about it. (Rafshoon would later send a shorter version of his thoughts to then-chairman of the Carter campaign, Evan Dobelle.)

"The only person who can beat Jimmy Carter is Jimmy Carter," Rafshoon wrote to the President early in 1979. "And

this can happen when you fail to follow your own instincts."
This theme (follow-your-own instincts) is the underpinning of
much of the advice that Rafshoon has given Carter during
politically tough times. He went on to discuss the opposition:

"Teddy Kennedy. Kennedy is the only serious potential challenger. The press will promote his candidacy because they like
him and more importantly, because it keeps things interesting . . ."

*"Whatever we do in reaction to or fear of a Kennedy can-
didacy will seriously hurt our chances in both the primaries
and the general.* We should forget about it for two reasons:
he isn't going to run and if he does he'll lose."

To this, Rafshoon added a listing of six points telling Carter
why Kennedy wouldn't run.

Meanwhile, back at the White House, the President was
digesting the advice of aides that was at times in conflict and
at times in concert. He read Jordan's explanations of why
Kennedy would run if the polls showed he could win, and
Rafshoon's explanations of why Kennedy would not. He could
not help but notice that from these divergent views the two
advisers recommended a similar tack: both recommended
against doing anything to suggest "fear" (they both used the
word) of a Kennedy challenge. Both warned against any change
of public course; continue praising Kennedy, Jordan had added.

Apparently, the President felt moved to act. During dinner
at the White House on June 11, Carter told a group of congressmen: "If Kennedy runs, I'll whip his ass." One startled
Democrat, disbelieving, asked the President what he had just
said. The President patiently repeated: "If Kennedy runs, I'll
whip his ass."

Later, White House officials urged the congressmen to have
no qualms about making the comment public, which they dutifully did. Kennedy, who had been insisting in those days that
he would not run, commented: "I'm sure the President must
have been misquoted. I think what he meant to say was that
he was going to whip inflation."

Jordan's study of Gerald Ford's 1976 fight to win the nomination of his party had convinced him that it was important for
the President to remain "in a noncandidate posture" for as long

as possible, even as the campaign organization was getting off to a vital early start. This conviction had led Jordan and the other Carter advisers through a series of political contortions. In informal sessions late in 1978 at the home on Georgetown's R Street shared by Patrick Caddell and Tim Kraft, the Carter advisers had puzzled over how they could possibly put a campaign committee in place without it being taken as an announcement of candidacy. They even discussed the possibility of mounting a grass-roots groundswell of their very own, and then having the committee formed—as if in response to this groundswell—without Carter's blessing. Finally, they just decided to form the exploratory committee, just like every other campaign did, and get on with it.

The President, meanwhile, continued to hint at—but stop short of announcing—his candidacy throughout most of the year. He was maintaining the "noncandidacy posture" Jordan had advocated in his 1979 memo. Jordan had included in that memo what he felt was a key chapter. It was the section in which he outlined the "strategy" for the coming campaign. It contained 11 points. Some of them read like political bromides, emphasizing the importance of a strong record on which to stand and the need to prepare for a strong challenge. Others got down to what is generally considered hard strategy, such as the political reshaping of the delegate selection calendar and an early show of power in the South.

★

STRATEGY FOR 1980

. . . To the extent that we have political decisions to make, they are more tactical than strategic. We will be expected to do well in every primary and caucus against every opponent. Our potential opponents will have the latitude and the luxury of deciding the time and place where they will make their challenge . . .

1. We will be re-elected or not re-elected based largely on your performance as President.

2. The best way to discourage a strong challenge from within the Democratic Party is to prepare for one.

3. I assume a serious challenge will develop from the left. The Brown challenge will be non-ideological and will have to be treated differently.

4. We should not discount any challenge. Remember our campaign and how people laughed at us.

5. The best way to prepare for a strong challenge is to get an early start.

6. At the same time, it is important politically and substantively that the President remain in a non-candidate posture for as long as possible.

7. It is important that we create a positive mood among the party elite toward our candidacy.

8. In accordance with our strategic and tactical decisions, it is important that we use our limited influence to shape the primary and caucus schedule.

9. It is important that we demonstrate early that our Southern base is intact.

10. We should use the next ten months to advantage to get well organized and to raise the bulk of our campaign funds.

11. While displaying basic political confidence in our prospects for re-election, we should not be perceived as taking the Democratic Party or the nomination for granted.

★

INTERLUDE: Hamilton Jordan and campaign counsel Tim Smith are walking into the basement entrance to the West Wing of the White House, dripping with perspiration after a couple of sets on the President's court on a muggy June day in 1979.

Almost casually, Jordan shifts from talking tennis to talking politics.

"Kennedy is going to run and we'll beat him bad," Jordan says, as he enters the elevator that will take him to his office upstairs.

"You know what the one issue will be?" he asks.

Smith, standing outside the elevator, shrugs.

"Kennedy!" Jordan answers, and as the doors close, he shouts a final ebullient observation "—And we're going to be geniuses again!"

★

In the days that followed, however, the President and his strategists did little to impress the outside world that they were about to retire the cup for campaign genius.

Instead, with his standing in the polls at a record low, Carter indulged himself in a unique and rather bizarre experiment in presidential leadership in July, 1979, that came to be known by the misnomer of a "Camp David domestic summit." It was, instead, more of a domestic leadership retreat, in every sense of the word, beginning with the President mysteriously hiding out from the public for a few days. And, reaching for a fitting climax, Carter then opted for a plan that was both wreckless and feckless: he demanded the resignations, en masse, of his entire cabinet and his senior advisers—just so he could fire three of his cabinet secretaries. The two moves had significant impact on the campaign to come.

At the Camp David domestic summit, Carter's pollster Patrick Caddell was very much in control. He had captured Carter's thinking with months of memos and presentations and even pleadings to the President, his wife Rosalynn, and other members of the Carter hierarchy. His warning was that America was mired in a malaise.

One of the results of the summit on malaise was that Caddell—who eventually became perhaps the most highly praised adviser within the inner circle for his polling accuracy and his advice—was for a while very much on the outs within.

Caddell was disputed—and at times derided—by a number of top Carter advisers including Vice President Mondale and domestic policy chief Stuart Eizenstat. They disagreed with the whole thrust of Caddell's malaise thesis and his call for a dramatic and thematic reversal in the President's approach to leading America. To a less vocal degree, Jordan also opposed Caddell's view; in those days at Camp David, the pollster seemed to possess a hold on the President's thinking that not even Jordan could match.

While the summit on malaise—and Carter's speech explaining it—were largely the work of Caddell, the mass resignations were a Gerald Rafshoon production.

Rafshoon had recommended that Carter call for the resignations of his top officials as a fitting dramatic climax to a month of seeming disarray. Instead, it was seen publicly as climaxing a month of disorientation with an image of collapse.

"I'll take full responsibility for the cabinet resignations," Rafshoon later said, confirming that he was the moving force behind the ploy and offering his own candid analysis that indeed it went wrong. "And looking back, I guess the malaise speech would have been a success if we hadn't stepped on it with those cabinet firings. We jumped up 11 points in polls that were taken immediately after that speech. But the reaction to the firings took just about all of that away again."

Jordan had opposed the idea of mass resignations. He did agree that some cabinet changes needed to be made. Another of Carter's senior advisers countered that, if this were the case, then the demand for mass resignations was perhaps the only way to prod the President into making the desired changes— "Jimmy just has a hard time firing people," this adviser later said.

The Camp David summit and the mass resignations occurred at the very time that Kennedy was making his decision on whether or not to run—in fact, Jordan had pinpointed this decision period in his memo months earlier.

Looking back, Jordan said later that the horrendous public response to the call for mass resignations—and the corresponding slippage in the polls—probably helped influence Kennedy's decision to challenge Carter. "That might have been an additional encouragement to Kennedy," Jordan said retrospectively.

In a sense, Carter had made a two-pronged contribution to his challenger. Not only did mass resignations demand and the reaction of the polls help prod Kennedy into the race, but Carter's exposition on the American "malaise" provided Kennedy with considerable campaign stump fodder.

But before the Kennedy forces had even gotten to the serious task of starting up a campaign, the Carter officials had already made most of their initial strategy decisions. A number of them were made at a two-day political gathering on August 19 and 20 at the spacious Easton, Maryland, home of Nathan Landow, a real estate developer and a friend of Jordan's. The decisions taken there proved crucial to Carter's early campaign successes.

★

Easton, Maryland, a setting of blue jeans and bathing suits and tennis shorts has taken on an aura of secrecy worthy of a cell meeting.

As the senior officials of the Carter White House and the Carter campaign committee filed into Landow's home of modern glass and old wood, each of them had been given an agenda book that has been carefully number coded and affixed with the name of the designated adviser. The books were not to leave the meeting and were to be returned at its conclusion, the advisers were told. (This meant that if anything was to be leaked, it must be committed to memory.)

Some of the group had been invited for the full two-day session, Saturday and Sunday; others had been invited only for Sunday and knew nothing of the Saturday session at which the agenda books had been reviewed and a few decisions had been already scripted.

Those meeting on Saturday, August 19, included Hamilton Jordan, the conference master; Tim Kraft, the campaign manager; Richard Moe, Vice President Mondale's chief of staff (a Mondale aide was carefully invited to every major campaign meeting); and two young aides who had prepared the agenda books, Tom Donilon, who would emerge at age 23 as the chief delegate counter for the campaign, and Tim Smith, the campaign counsel.

Sunday's arrivals included Jody Powell, Gerald Rafshoon, Evan Dobelle, Patrick Caddell, White House aides Phil Wise, Sarah Weddington, and Rick Hutcheson, Mondale's administrative assistant Jim Johnson, and a number of the campaign committee's officials.

"It was a watershed meeting for our campaign," one adviser later recalled.

Early in the session on that Sunday, August 20, a number of the Carter advisers voiced doubts that Kennedy would really make the race. Jordan's response was unequivocal: "Kennedy is already running."

Phil Wise, Carter's White House appointments secretary, who ran Carter's Florida campaign in 1976, made a strong pitch for the need to go all out to win the Florida caucus and convention straw vote that would be held in the fall of 1979. They are officially meaningless, but psychologically crucial, he argued; they have nothing to do with electing a single delegate to the convention—but there will be a draft-Kennedy effort in Florida, and Carter cannot afford an early showing of defeat.

They agreed that they would go all out to win the Florida caucus and straw vote. They would invest heavily in money and time—cabinet and White House officials would descend upon the state that fall like boll weevils hitting the cotton belt. As a result, Carter staved off what could have been a disastrous pre-campaign defeat, winning by a margin that was in fact closer than it seemed. And perhaps the best thing for Carter in the victory was that when the caucus results were in, Kennedy would be moved to declare that the contest had been the effort of those draft-Kennedy people and not his own campaign (which was basically true)—and he would add that Iowa would be the true test of strength.

Before the meetings adjourned at the Landow house, there was some tough talk and some tough decision-making about money. It would prove to be perhaps the least titillating, but most important, of the campaign's early decisions.

The Carter advisers were shown three campaign budgets: a high level ($18 million), medium level ($15 million) and a low level ($12 million).

This opened what would be a campaign-long series of disputes between those who advocated increased spending for field operations, chiefly Tim Kraft, and those who advocated increased spending for advertising, chiefly Gerald Rafshoon. In the months that followed, this dispute between Kraft and Rafshoon would be repeated frequently and would escalate in intensity.

The Carter officials were told there was no way they could reach even their mid-level budget goal unless they doubled between Labor Day and Christmas the amount of money raised between March and August. They decided to build a series of fund-raising events around the President's official announcement of candidacy later in the year.

They also decided to cut back sharply on spending—especially on staff travel.

Both decisions were crucial. In the week of Carter's December announcement alone the campaign raised $2.5 million. Because of the fund-raising increases and spending cutbacks, says Tim Smith, "We were in excellent financial shape in January, 1980."

This put the Carter campaign in stark contrast with the Kennedy campaign. The challenger, ill-served by his advisers, wound up spending himself virtually out of existence in the first month of 1980, due to a series of poor management decisions—and often no decisions at all—in the campaign that was presided over by Kennedy's brother-in-law, campaign chairman Stephen Smith.

Kennedy campaigned around the country in those days in a Rolls Royce of jetliners, and it was Smith himself who permitted the plane to sit grounded in Florida at a cost of $5,000 a day while Kennedy enjoyed his Christmas vacation. The Kennedy campaign housed itself in lavish offices in Illinois, and spent at least $50,000 to renovate its own Washington headquarters. From March to December 1979, the Carter campaign spent $2.8 million; in just November and December, 1979, the Kennedy campaign spent almost as much—$2.4 million—a figure that does not include the officially independent spending of the draft-Kennedy forces.

In September, having privately put the word to the President, Kennedy began publicly putting out the word that he would soon be running. The daily press summary and the weekly polls were bringing nothing but bad news. Carter's ratings were low and the spirit of his staff even lower.

"People around here were panicky," Jordan recalls. "That was something I had to fight internally. . . . One of the main jobs I had in the first few days (after Kennedy let it be known that he would run) was calming everybody down. Most of the people here had never been through a campaign before. They just didn't have the confidence I had in our ability to win the nomination."

Another of Carter's senior advisers remembers: "The White House was like the city morgue. It was a very quiet and very depressing place."

In the Oval Office, Patrick Caddell is lecturing to an audience of one, his boss, on the positive value of negative campaigns.

It is September, 1979, and President Carter is at 25 percent in the Gallup Poll, which puts him 38 points behind Edward Kennedy.

"Politics is undergoing a change," Caddell recalls telling President Carter. Caddell, the McGovern wunderkind of '72 who is now growing older and richer as the President's pollster, launches into a discussion of the lessons of the major campaigns of 1978. A Carter victory in 1980 must be a come-from-behind victory; so Caddell focuses upon the comeback victories of governors Hugh Carey of New York, Brendan Byrne of New Jersey and Ella Grasso of Connecticut.

"Negative campaigning worked in these elections, more so than ever before," Caddell explains. He means a "negative" strategy in which a candidate broadcasts his opponent's shortcomings even more than he emphasizes his own virtues.

"All of the winners who had to come back from behind to win did so on the basis of negative campaigns. Given that, we can probably make our opponents the issue in 1980."

Caddell goes on to talk about Kennedy, and Carter listens attentively; Caddell is, after all, the closest thing he has to someone from the other side. In 1976, Caddell worked as pollster for both Carter for President and Kennedy for Senate.

"This has to be a general election type of campaign. Even though it is just a primary election, people have to be made to face all of the complications that go into making an actual choice for the presidency: not just 'Who do you like better?' but 'Who do you *really* want to sit in the Oval Office?'"

At one point, Caddell pointedly warns: "This campaign could get very bloody."

He explains that Kennedy and Carter represent opposite strengths and weaknesses. Kennedy's strength is a public perception of his leadership capabilities; his weakness is the perception of personal characteristics associated with him. Carter's strengths lay in his personal traits (honesty, decency, trustworthiness); his weakness is a widespread public view that he lacks in leadership.

"There is no way that one of you can represent his own strength in a campaign without in effect attacking the other's weakness," Caddell says.

"So it could be very bloody. But at least our weakness is something we can do something about."

As he was saying that, Caddell later recalled, "My mind was spinning—how do we use the White House to do what we wanted to do?"

At the outset, they assume one of their greatest assets will be what they see as the aggressive capabilities of the President as a campaigner, out there among the people, winning them back to the fold. They will prove wrong about that. The unanticipated events in Iran reverse the script. Carter will make his comeback without going anywhere.

But Caddell was right about the "negative" nature of the campaign. Kennedy will emphasize Carter's failures as a leader. The media coverage, plus subtle campaign advertising from Carter, will emphasize the personal questions about Kennedy's character.

Kennedy will deride Carter for the President's famous declaration of American malaise. Carter's TV messages, prepared by media adviser Gerald Rafshoon, will emphasize the President's personal qualities, drawing an unstated-but-clear contrast with Kennedy's.

There is: "President Carter. He's a solid man in a sensitive job."

Which will be escalated to: "Husband, father, President—he's done these three jobs with distinction."

And: "A man brings two things to a presidential ballot. He brings his record and he brings himself. Who he is is frequently more important than what he's done. In the voting booth the voter must weigh both record and character before deciding. Often it's not easy. And this voter winds up asking, 'Is this the person I really want in the White House for the next four years?'"

The personal character question would contribute mightily to Kennedy's early defeats in the caucuses of Iowa and the primaries in New Hampshire, throughout the South, and in Illinois. When Kennedy finally mounted a comeback of his own later in the campaign (too late, in fact), the Carter strategists came up with a new round of ads that would again shift the focus directly back upon Kennedy's character as the issue, and that would be sufficient to see Carter through the primary season.

Throughout the fall, the President kept in touch with his campaign largely through weekly meetings that were never part of his officially disclosed schedule, but which were held at about 5:30 p.m. in the Treaty Room, in the upstairs living quarters of the executive mansion.

The President nominally presided, but in fact Jordan directed the flow of discussion—"Hamilton was the facilitator," one senior adviser explained. Those attending included Rosalynn Carter, the Vice President, Strauss, Powell, Rafshoon, Caddell, Kraft and at times Weddington.

Throughout October, Carter was invariably optimistic about the prospects for defeating Kennedy, even when the moods of most of those at the mid-levels of the White House were ranging from pessimism to panic.

His chief-of-everything, Jordan, was also optimistic. During one meeting in October—this one at Camp David—the campaign advisers were talking about how tight the campaign budget was. "Don't forget, it has to last until June 3," one of them said. Jordan interrupted: "Ridiculous! We've got to go (spend) heavy at the outset. If we do, it'll all be over early."

On October 21, Carter ventured into the heart of Camelot to address the dedication of the John F. Kennedy Memorial Library in Boston. He had accepted the invitation during the summer, based on the advice of Jordan. Jordan's recommendation was based upon a hard calculation of 1980 politics, not 1960 sentiment. If Carter said he would be there, Jordan advised, Kennedy would not dare start up his formal campaign before then.

Carter, usually an unimpressive public speaker, gave a performance at the library dedication so strong that it impressed even the most skeptical of the Kennedy partisans.

★

On November 4, the United States embassy and its personnel in Tehran were seized. The nature of the Carter presidency changed markedly and so did the mood of those meetings in the Treaty Room.

"A change came over the President—you could see it and you could feel it," says one of the regular attendees. "You could tell that he wasn't paying attention at times. Sometimes he would be just distant and sometimes he would interject to ask, 'How long is this meeting going to take?'"

Days were getting shorter as winter approached, and usually they would begin in dusk and finish in nighttime darkness, a gloomy backdrop. "The meetings became somber and even depressing," says one adviser.

But two days after the embassy in Iran was seized, Carter, still trailing badly in the polls, agreed to debate his opponents for the Democratic nomination—unprecedented for an incumbent president.

On December 29, with the Soviets having invaded Afghanistan, with the Iranian crisis continuing, but with Carter having overtaken Kennedy in the polls—the President withdrew from the debate. His decision not to debate would be made into an issue that would last the rest of the campaign—Kennedy would see to that—but it would not seriously hurt Carter.

Carter had declared that he could not debate or campaign because the crises in Iran and Afghanistan required his constant attention. But one of his most senior advisers later conceded that, although indeed, Carter was preoccupied by the crises, he could have continued campaigning through January and into February, which is when the negotiations with Iran reached a truly crucial stage that required frequent presidential consultations and decisions.

Carter's top officials were also saying, at the time the President pulled out of the debate, that all of Carter's political advisers had been urging him to both debate and campaign, because it would be crucial to the success of his campaign.

But in fact, his senior advisers later said, this line was vigorously pressed mainly by his top advisers at the campaign committee—Robert Strauss and Tim Kraft—plus that of White House domestic policy chief Stuart Eizenstat. Others, including Caddell and Rafshoon and Jody Powell, are said to have not been anxious for Carter to go through with the debate or campaign, believing it would be better politics to stay home. And Jordan, they say, may have leaned toward having Carter at least debate, out of concern for damage that the *Des Moines Register* could do to Carter in the upcoming caucuses, but he is portrayed as having not pressed the point vigorously.

"Things were going well for us in the polls," one senior adviser explained, in elaborating on the view of those who counseled that there was a political advantage to pulling out of the debate. "By being president, by leading, he could do more for himself than by campaigning . . . We had nothing to gain by Carter debating."

And another senior adviser, asked what the central reason was for Carter's decision not to debate, offered a somewhat more succinct explanation. He said:

"F——— the fat rich kid."

INTERLUDE: The President's advisers decided to bolster public understanding of Carter's decision to withdraw from the debate with a bit of political gamesmanship. The idea, according to several senior advisers, was Jody Powell's.

Powell wrote a memo to the President that was intended for public consumption. (Powell offers a small variation; he says that he originally wrote the memo as a genuine document and then decided to leak it.) The two-page memo, which was leaked to the *Los Angeles Times*, outlined arguments of Carter's political advisers supposedly urging him to go through with the debate in Iowa. It said that these were the consensus views of Powell, Jordan, Strauss, Kraft and Eizenstat.

For added measure, the leaked memo contained a penned notation in Carter's own handwriting, worded more formally than many of the President's comments that are intended for strictly in-house distribution.

Carter had dutifully written:

"I can't disagree with any of this, but I cannot break away from my duties here, which are extraordinary now and ones which only I can fulfill.

"We will just have to take the adverse political consequences and make the best of it. Right now both Iran and Afghanistan look bad, and will need my constant attention."

Later, asked about the orchestrated memo and the President's notation, Robert Strauss would say: "Well, it was somewhat overwritten."

The dignitaries in the strategy session in the Treaty Room of the White House residence are conducting themselves with all of the decorum of shriners in convention.

The President, the Vice President, the First Lady, and their highest echelon of advisers are celebrating the Illinois primary blowout of the night before—it will be Carter 163 delegates, Kennedy just 16—with backslaps and bellylaughs.

Jimmy Carter is cheerily demanding to know why his crack team allowed Kennedy to win even those few delegates. Robert Strauss is talking about how they are going to get Kennedy out of the race once and for all now. And Patrick Caddell is passing out sheets of paper with the latest poll results for next week's state.

The room falls silent as those assembled read the first sheet, and then the second. They are looking at an unforeseen development that will plague the President for the rest of the campaign: the birth of the anti-Carter protest vote.

All of the public polls have been showing Carter headed for a huge win in the next primary, in New York, that would surely mean the end of the Kennedy candidacy. Caddell's raw data shows that too: Carter 51 percent, Kennedy just 32.

But Caddell's unique technique for adjusting the initial responses—which has produced the most reliable of all political polling figures this year—shows that Kennedy has actually taken the lead: Kennedy 43, Carter 39.

There follows a third statistic that is the most amazing of all.

Kennedy holds this lead despite the fact that he is viewed "unfavorably," as opposed to "favorably," by a majority of people. And Carter is trailing even though he is viewed "favorably" by a substantial majority of the people. (The figure is 60 percent "favorable," 38 percent "unfavorable.")

"Everyone's eyes just popped out," recalls one adviser who was present in that meeting. Caddell explains to the President and his advisers that apparently people are now suddenly willing to vote for Kennedy even though they do not care for him. He says that now that people believe that Carter will be the party's nominee, they are focusing upon Carter almost exclusively, and they are deciding they do not like what they see.

The "protest vote" proves to be at the heart of what is happening throughout the rest of the Democratic primary campaign of 1980.

For a while it will confound the Carter strategists. They will not find a way of coping with it for several weeks, until they are well into the Pennsylvania primary. Finally, they will neutralize it significantly with a new batch of negative ads created by media adviser Gerald Rafshoon that will focus attention—and doubts—upon Kennedy once again. (In the process they will focus controversy upon Rafshoon.)

But it will come back to afflict Carter once more, at the end of the primary campaign. And in fact, it is probably a harbinger of things to come for Carter in a general election contest against Ronald Reagan.

Understanding the "protest vote" means understanding much about what is going on in this country this year; it means understanding ourselves and the way we work our politics.

Just how the President and his campaign came to view this anti-Carter "protest vote" is seen in a study of the internal statistics of Caddell's campaign surveys, some of which have been made available to the *Washington Post*. The statistics basically show numerically what journalists had been gleaning and writing during their own lengthy interviews during the primaries: that many people just did not like Carter's performance as President, and even though they did not like Kennedy, the more they thought about Carter, the more willing they were to vote for his opponent. Kennedy was most successful when he became just Brand X.

The Carter campaign of 1980 could not be like the Carter campaign of 1976. This year, Carter had to make his opponent the issue, which is far different from 1976, when he won the nomination mainly by convincing people to like him. He made them view him as trustworthy and decent and so on; he made them vote *for* him, not *against* Scoop Jackson or Mo Udall.

A glimpse at how the Carter campaign came to cope with this "protest vote" with new negative ads shows how polling and advertising mix in the politics of 1980, and how campaign spending decisions are made. It also offers a marked contrast between the Carter and Kennedy campaign organizations.

For by New York, the Kennedy campaign had mostly run out of money, which greatly limited its polling. And it had been running its advertising at the outset through a consortium of media experts that produced media results about as successful as the storied committee that tried to assemble a horse—and produced a camel instead.

New Yorkers had more than just Jimmy Carter's campaign successes to give them cause to protest his leadership. There was that U.S. vote in the United Nations Security Council for an anti-Israeli resolution—quickly followed by U.S. renunciation of its own vote.

More than one quarter of New York's Democratic primary voters are Jewish, and Caddell's figures showed that in a ten-day period following that United Nations vote, New York's Jewish voters had shifted from favoring Carter by a 9 point margin to favoring Kennedy by a 17 point spread.

This contributed greatly to Carter's problem in New York, Caddell was saying a week before the vote there, but it could not account for all of it. "It wasn't just the Jews," Caddell says. "It was upstate. It was across-the-board. It was something else."

Caddell was more concerned about what he saw as the larger problem for Carter—that Kennedy could have the lead despite the fact that the majority of the people gave him an "unfavorable" rating. Additional speeches by Carter surrogates were scheduled, and new Carter media spots were aired.

Still, publicly, all signs were pointing to a Carter landslide. By the Friday preceding the March 25 primary, the Louis Harris poll in the *New York Daily News* was showing Carter with a huge 27 point lead.

Caddell, using his own technique, was coming up with something else. He and his associate, John Gorman, had devised a two-step procedure this year which had proven very accurate in this tumultuous year.

First a person would be asked whom he would vote for. Next, a short series of questions would be asked designed to get the person being interviewed to think as intensely about the choice as he would on election day, when he walked into the voting booth. Then the person would be asked again, in a "second vote," to choose the candidate he would vote for. Invariably, much of Carter's support dropped away in that second voting.

On Friday, Caddell's own data were showing that Carter had climbed back to a very narrow lead. But that same day, Cyrus Vance was testifying in Congress. The Secretary of State said that the controversial U.N. resolution really had coincided with the Carter administration's policies, after all—an admission that made for stunning front page news in New York on the weekend before the election.

Carter's strategists were apoplectic.

Vance's testimony was politically undiplomatic—in fact, politically disastrous. But also damaging, Caddell felt, was that the Friday Harris poll giving Carter a 27 point lead, which the *New York Daily News* headlined, "Carter's the One—in a Pollslide," could fuel the anti-Carter protest vote.

★

Sunday, 2 p.m., Caddell is in the kitchen of his home on R Street when his associate John Gorman calls with the latest results.

"I have some good news and some bad news," Gorman says. "The good news is that we have now seen the most dramatic shift ever in our regression analysis (of factors that people view as important when they make their voting decisions).

"The bad news is that . . . Ted Kennedy has disappeared as a factor in this election. It's Carter versus Carter. And Carter is going to get murdered."

The anti-Carter protest vote has hit with full force. Publicly, the Harris poll is still showing a 20 point Carter lead, but the bottom has fallen out of the President's prospects for a victory in New York that would have meant the end of Kennedy's challenge. On Friday, Caddell had shown Carter with a 4 point lead. On Saturday it was Kennedy who had a four point lead. Now on Sunday, Kennedy's lead has swelled to 9. It is going that way (even though Monday's Harris poll will still show Carter ahead by 18).

Caddell calls the President, who is at Camp David. He goes over the figures with Carter. He explains how his associates have done this analysis of internal questions to determine what factors are leading people to vote the way they are voting.

Usually trustworthiness of a candidate is the number one factor—that has always been a strong plus for Carter. Now Caddell explains trustworthiness has fallen off the charts, it is not even among the top 12 factors that New Yorkers consider important in the making of their presidential decision.

What is number one is a "protest question" that Caddell has added to his survey—it is a statement that is read to people by his interviewers, "Carter can't handle the presidency; we would be better off trying a new president." Suddenly a majority of the New Yorkers are now agreeing with this statement; two weeks earlier, a majority were disagreeing with it.

The President listens to all of this bad news without commenting. When Caddell finishes his hurried presentation there is still silence.

"We'll try to do everything we can," Caddell says.

"Thank you," says the President.

New York and Connecticut are dual debacles for the President—most pollsters and even the Kennedy camp are stunned by the outcome, which is Kennedy by 18 in New York and by 5 in Connecticut.

No longer are the President's advisers thinking about forcing Kennedy out of the race early. Now they are looking thankfully ahead to a respite in Wisconsin. They call it their "safety net."

For the moment, there is no urgency about figuring out how to solve that protest vote problem—for, after New York and Connecticut, people are no longer looking at Carter as a sure winner. Several weeks down the trail, Pennsylvania looms as a potential New York. But for now, Caddell's polls are showing Carter with a comfortable lead in Wisconsin, where the primary will be held April 1.

This is somewhat of a surprise to Caddell.

Back in the planning stages, he had advocated skipping Wisconsin, contending that the state was simply too liberal, that it would be a Kennedy state, not a Carter state. Vice President Mondale had argued that Caddell was wrong, that the state was solid, Midwestern and a good Carter state.

Caddell took a poll and came back with a report: "Mondale was absolutely right."

With New York behind them and Pennsylvania ahead, the Carter advisers needed a decisive win in Wisconsin, as one adviser noted, "to show that we are not in a complete state of collapse."

Public opinion on Carter's handling of the crisis in Iran had begun to sour and several days before the primary Caddell's surveys showed that Carter's lead was beginning to narrow. "The Iranian thing was clearly a problem," Caddell says. "The President's ratings on his handling of it were declining."

Hamilton Jordan had been deeply involved as a shuttling emissary, meeting overseas with French lawyers representing the Iranian government. Proposals were in the works and a deadline was set for the day before the Wisconsin primary for either the transfer of control of the hostages out of the hands of the Iranian militants or for the imposition of strong American economic sanctions.

Privately, there were signs that an agreement was near. But publicly, things took a turn for the worse when, first, Iran went public with what it said was a message from Carter that was apologetic in tone; next, Jody Powell issued what seemed to be a flat denial that any message had been sent to Iran's leaders; but then Swiss officials said they had indeed delivered some kind of message from Carter. Powell tried to clarify that what he had been saying was that no such apologetic message had been sent, but the effort seemed mostly to be making the worst of a bad thing.

The Carter officials were desperate to turn things around. The President personally met with a group of newspaper representatives, and later talked with television network anchorpersons as well, to let it be known that agreement seemed near.

And on election day, in a rare and even bizarre performance, the President summoned reporters to his office at 7 a.m.—just in time for the network morning news shows—to proclaim that the latest statement out of Iran was a "positive step."

That did the political trick, short-term.

"When it was made clear over the weekend that there was going to be some progress, that bumped the race up for us," Caddell says. "It went from a lead of 15 to 18 points to a win of almost 30 points.

"Wisconsin was the only state where we ever got the undecideds to go for us in the end."

But there are some members of Carter's highest council who feel that there were also long-term setbacks to the last-minute attempt at election day dramatics.

"The President decided that he wanted to do it—and now Jody is kicking himself for going along with it instead of thinking about it and stopping it," one senior adviser said a few weeks later. "We paid a price for that—a real price, especially as far as our relations with reporters are concerned. That 7 a.m. thing crossed the line. Carter no longer seemed decent and honorable, but manipulative. Ironically, it probably had no impact—usually it takes a 24-hour gestation period for big events to have an impact on the public."

The President's strategists are locked in a major strategy dispute.

It is Saturday, and with the overkill of Wisconsin behind

them, the Carter campaign's board of directors has just heard Caddell's latest analysis, which is that the April 22 Pennsylvania primary is looking "very New Yorky."

All of the public polls are showing a huge Carter lead in Pennsylvania, and Caddell's "first response" figures are showing that too: Carter 53 percent, Kennedy 30. But his "second vote" response in those same interviews shows that there has already been a dramatic reversal, with Kennedy leading Carter, 43 to 40.

Once again, "trustworthy" was not listed as a major factor in people's decisions. And people were agreeing in large numbers with that "protest" statement of Caddell's questionnaire that it is time to try a new president.

Tim Kraft argues against pumping new money into the Pennsylvania campaign budget in an attempt to salvage Carter's sinking prospects in the state. His argument—at this meeting attended by Jordan, Rafshoon, Caddell and campaign counsel Tim Smith and campaign finance director Tim Finchem—is that the campaign will be hard pressed for money in the primaries ahead and even harder pressed to stay within the legal spending ceiling for the overall campaign. "Somewhere we've just got to bite the bullet and not spend big just for the chance of one big win," Kraft says. "We've got to exert some of this discipline that we've been talking about."

Rafshoon vehemently disagrees. The advisers had already decided to concentrate most of their field operations money on the caucus states and to spend their media money on primary states. With a new media plan, that protest vote in Pennsylvania can be turned around, Rafshoon argues. The state can be saved. There are too many delegates at stake to surrender them to Kennedy at this late stage, he says, and the psychological impact of another New York-style blowout could be disastrous. It could lead to perilous erosion of Carter's supports. And those upcoming primaries of the big June 3 campaign finale—including California, New Jersey and Ohio—loom as a potentially big day for Kennedy, if only his campaign can make it that far.

Jordan quietly keeps his own counsel. He will spend a couple of days asking if Carter aides think it would be smart to write off Pennsylvania; he seems to be siding with Kraft. But his decision will be to spend for the media plan and trust Rafshoon to deliver.

★

Rafshoon takes a camera crew to Pittsburgh and begins interviewing people on the subject of what they think of Kennedy. The idea, he concedes, is far from original.

"I remembered what Ford was able to do to us at the end of the 1976 campaign with those man-in-the-street ads," Rafshoon says, recalling those devastating ads that featured Georgians saying why they were going to vote against Carter.

It is early morning in Pittsburgh. As Rafshoon is working with his camera crew, he notices a middle-aged woman loitering to the side, studying him suspiciously. Finally she approaches, a sparkle in her eye.

"I know you," she says. "You're . . . you're . . ."

"Dan Rather!" says the short, mop-haired Rafshoon, who is to Dan Rather what Woody Allen is to Sir Laurence Olivier.

"I knew it!" the woman beams, shaking his hand before walking away.

The ads Rafshoon produces are negative—but then again, so is Kennedy's daily stump rhetoric. Among Kennedy's lines:

"The only malaise this country is suffering from is a malaise of its leadership . . . Jimmy Carter keeps wringing his hands, wringing his hands and saying, 'There's nothing anyone can do about our problems.' . . . What is Mr. Carter afraid of? If he won't face the voters in his own party, how does he expect to face Republicans in November? . . . Mr. Carter is going to fight inflation by throwing thousands of people out of work . . ."

Rafshoon's ads show people saying that Kennedy is "too liberal . . . a big spender . . . wrong on welfare . . ." The closest thing to a personal attack is one commercial which deals only subtly with character:

MAN: I don't think Kennedy's qualified to be president.
WOMAN: I don't think he has any credibility.
WOMAN: I don't believe him.
WOMAN: I just don't think he's the man for the job.
MAN: I don't trust him.
WOMAN: You're taking a chance with Kennedy.
WOMAN: I'm going to vote for Carter because I think he's the best qualified.

MAN: Between Kennedy and Carter, I would definitely go with Carter myself. I trust him.

"The ads spoke to the perceptions of Kennedy that people already had in their minds," Rafshoon says, taking care to always refer to them as the man-in-the-street ads, never the negative ads. "We needed to remind people, that's all."

The ads begin running during the last week of the Pennsylvania campaign. Kennedy has been steadily lengthening his lead in the Caddell polls; Friday's "second vote" figures give him a 9 point lead over Carter.

But—significantly—they also show a sharp increase in the number of people who now believe that Kennedy can win the nomination. In the next couple of days, voters begin expressing increased concerns over Kennedy's personal character. The Carter people get the feeling that, like those unpleasant television ads where stomach acid disappears in a beaker, the protest vote is being neutralized right before their eyes. Caddell's polls are showing that people are once again listing "trustworthy" as the main factor in their election day decision-making—just like it used to be in Carter's good old days, when he was winning big. A majority of the people are now agreeing with the statement that Kennedy is a big spender. Caddell's last poll, finished the Sunday before Tuesday's election, shows Carter and Kennedy dead even, at 40 percent.

That is just the way it is on Tuesday night, when Kennedy technically wins by a whisker. The reality of it is that Carter—whose aides almost had him abandoning the state—comes away with half of Pennsylvania's 185 delegates.

And added to the landslide victory in the Missouri caucus the same day, Carter comes away from a day that could have been a disaster with a net delegate gain that is just one less than Kennedy's biggest day of the campaign, back when he rode the newborn protest vote to victory in New York and Connecticut.

"Jerry's (Rafshoon) negative ads made it possible," Caddell will later say. "They made Kennedy the issue again."

Carter will sweep through May with ten victories in eleven primaries—including wins in Maryland, Nebraska and Oregon, which Carter had lost in 1976 and which his advisers had again viewed as likely defeats just a week or so earlier.

May will give Carter a delegate cushion that will provide

crucial comfort as he goes through what has become his traditional, quadrennial June 3 tail-first crash landing. In 1980, as in 1976, he wins in Ohio but loses in New Jersey and California.

"Luckily," Caddell says, "the month of May made June 3 irrelevant."

★

In the Oval Office, back in September of 1979, Patrick Caddell had borrowed a blank sheet of paper from the President and then drawn for his boss an optimistic diagram of the campaign to come.

He had drawn two lines. One started at the bottom left corner of the page and slanted slowly upward as it moved to the right—it was Carter. The other started high on the left but finished low on the right—it was Kennedy. Caddell had them crossing each other in January.

"But Iran changed all that," Caddell later explained. "Iran helped make the lines cross sooner than I expected."

The seizure of the embassy in Iran gave Carter his timely opportunity to gain public opinion points for leadership when he needed it most—only late in the campaign did the hostage crisis prove a liability.

But in fact, Carter had begun his climb from the oblivion of a 2 to 1 deficit in the polls even before the U.S. embassy in Iran was seized. A *Time* poll (conducted by the firm of Yankelovich, Skelly and White Inc.) in late October showed that Carter had cut the margin to just 10 points—49 percent to 39 percent, as compared with a 58 to 25 deficit back in August.

The Carter strategists were able to go on from there and defeat Kennedy in part because of Iran, but also because they followed their own blueprint. They won early—especially in those southern primaries that had been scheduled early in the year, where they were able to pile up huge delegate margins with relatively little expenditure of campaign funds.

But the Carter blueprint did not carry them farther than June 3. And that proved to be a considerable problem for the President and his advisers in June as they faced the unforeseen situation of having won a majority of the delegates but being unable to get Kennedy to abandon his campaign, and unable to rekindle the enthusiasm within the party that Carter titularly headed.

Jimmy Carter never had a strategy for coming out of the Rose Garden. He never had a strategy of reconciliation when he decided to end his self-imposed political isolation. He had only a gambit of public relations. And politically, that got him nowhere. At his press conference of April 29, 1980—with the hostage situation in Iran unresolved, and instead apparently hopelessly out of his control—Carter had planned to say that he felt he could come out and do a little campaigning. But no one asked him about that. So the next day, White House aides planted the question with one of their own kind, Charles Manatt, the Democratic National Committee's finance council chairman, who was attending a party session with Carter at the White House.

With the press looking on, Manatt begged the question: ". . . is there a chance that the people can see you, that you can be with them and you can get out in the countryside—you can get out in the states and be with us?"

The President said sure.

Then he ad libbed that he could campaign because his problems are more "manageable" now—his advisers were grimacing at that choice of words for weeks afterward.

By exiting the Rose Garden without a strategy, Carter had surrendered a crucial initiative. Predictably, Kennedy's first response was that now they should have that debate that Carter had cancelled back in December; predictably, he also set some preconditions that Carter could not accept.

So the Carter people summarily rejected Kennedy's new debate challenge. Both sides hardened their positions. And a bad situation became inexorably bitter.

"Carter does not have to grovel to Kennedy now," said one of the President's most senior advisers.

That was the way they were drawing the battle lines at the White House in June. The Carter advisers never tried to come up with a compromise. They could have, for example, proposed that Carter and Kennedy discuss the issues in a televised, but nonconfrontational setting—perhaps a parlor setting or a town meeting–like affair as part of the process of writing the party platform. Such a session would not have resolved their differences on the issues, but it might well have removed the poison that had come to dominate relations between the two candidates and their camps.

But the President would not yield. "Jimmy Carter just is not about to appear with and debate Teddy Kennedy," said one of his advisers. The bitterness remained.

For Jimmy Carter, who had boasted about whipping Kennedy's ass, his primary campaign victory may have been personally satisfying—but it was not particularly sweet. Carter found himself at the helm of a party that was seriously disaffected. The Kennedy activists remained angry and divided; the liberal and labor establishment chafed under Carter policies that had deepened the recession, boosted unemployment, and seemed alien to decades of cherished Democratic rhetoric. Democrats were expressing little enthusiasm for the man they had chosen to lead them. Jimmy Carter found himself, in victory, the victim of a partywide malaise.

EPILOGUE:They had kept the secret for months, the President and his pollster, ever since those winter days of January, when Edward Kennedy was at his lowest.

Caddell had conducted a special poll in January, and in the Oval Office, he laid the results out for Carter to see. The poll was based on open-ended questions. It showed, Caddell explained, that people can see Kennedy doing very well as their president—despite all of his current personal problems and the re-airing of Chappaquiddick. They can be very comfortable with him sitting in that desk, making decisions, Caddell explained.

"The President was more surprised than I have ever seen him," Caddell said, recalling that winter meeting. The two men agreed that day that the results of the poll would not be shared, not even with the staff, lest they leak. For Kennedy was launching a series of strident attacks on the President at that time, and his pollster did not want him to switch to a more statesmanlike strategy instead. As Carter explained that day:

"I learned this painfully back (in 1976) when I tried attacking Jerry Ford—people don't like you attacking an incumbent president."

★ GOP ★

by Lou Cannon
and William Peterson

IT SNOWED Saturday, two days before the Iowa precinct caucuses, covering the state with a thick, finely textured blanket of white, and making travel hazardous.

Sen. Howard Baker, who had been telling people all week "the real race is for third place," woke up that morning in the old German town of Pella, then headed north for Decorah, Monona and Ames. George Bush had spent half the night curled up on the back seat of a bus. But he was up early, holding a press conference at 8:45 a.m., before heading for the American Legion Hall in the small western Iowa town of Minden.

John B. Connally, acting like a good ole country boy in a pinstriped suit and cowboy boots, was catnapping as his bus rolled into Elberon just after daybreak, completing an 854-mile, 40-hour tour across the state. Reporters traveling with him were still talking about his performance the night before at Bill Deal's livestock auction ring in Waverly.

"Let me tell y'all something," he had told the dairy farmers gathered around the auction ring. "None of you have made the sacrifices for the dairy industry that I have. I got indicted because of it, if you want to know something. You think I don't know about milk producers and milk prices, you're crazy."

Waverly, one cattle trader said, hadn't seen anything like it "in at least 99 years."

It had been that way all January, the most intensively political month in Iowa history. Frenzied, unpredictable, desperate. Campaign '80 was underway, and in those first bone-chilling days of the year, when there were so many candidates with so many hopes, it looked as if it would be the most memorable election year in a generation. The prospects for high drama seemed limitless. An incumbent president was being challenged by a Kennedy. Seven Republicans, representing every conceivable wing of the party, offered the GOP its broadest choice in decades.

The Republican Party entered the campaign with more candidates and less division than at any time in its modern history. The great questions which had divided the party in the recent past had been subsumed by a shared view of the common danger or deep emotions of national pride.

There were, of course, practical reasons for this new-found Republican unity—the prospects of victory and the rewards of success. By 1980 the Republican Party had risen from the ashes of Watergate and the threat of extinction. It remained, as it had for half a century, the minority party, numbering only 20 percent of the nation's registered voters. The Nixon years had left a bitter legacy: the GOP minorities in Congress and the statehouses had shrunk even more, and the party's future appeared bleak when the obscure Jimmy Carter of Georgia recaptured the White House for the Democrats in 1976 and, for the first time in almost a decade, restored one-party rule to Washington. The Democrats held huge majorities in House and Senate, approaching the landslide figures of the FDR-LBJ periods that enabled the legislative packages of the New Deal and Great Society to be enacted. They had also broken the hold of the Republicans in the Deep South, once more giving them back their old springboard to victory in presidential elections. But the Carter presidency brought unexpected Republican opportunities. What Howard Baker called Carter's "failed presidency" and the nation's seeming impotence abroad left the Democrats divided, embittered, and imperiled. Now, in 1980, it wasn't just the hope of winning the White House that so enticed the Republicans; they stood, their pollsters and strategists told them, at the threshold of historic change. The tides appeared running against the Democrats, leaving the GOP with the chance of sweeping back into power in a way they hadn't achieved since Eisenhower's great victory of 1952 gave them control of both ends of Pennsylvania Avenue. And if the survey analysts were correct in detecting a conservative current nationally, the GOP stood poised to gain more than even White

House and Congress; this year, it was said in their private councils, could be the one that brought them back to majority status in public political affections. Out of such dreams were the Republican presidential prospects fueled. And they were, indeed, seemingly united.

The principal Republican candidates—except for John B. Anderson, who decided to run as an independent after his bid for the GOP nomination became hopeless—shared the same values as well as the same views. All of them spoke of restoring American greatness. All blamed Carter for the nation's new problems and sense of national humiliation. All vowed to re-build respect for America. All agreed America must cut the size and scope of government. All called for reduced govern-ment spending and more incentives for American business.

These were the same values Ronald Reagan had articulated and passionately argued for since 1964, and now they had become the shared conventional wisdom of his party. Reagan, with his resurrected 1976 speech and its promise—"There will be no more abandonment of friends of the United States of America"—was himself a symbol of the yearning for the old assured decades of world power. Domestically, all of the Re-publican candidates extolled still older values—the values rep-resented by Reagan's litany of "family, work, neighborhood, freedom, peace." Reagan, more than any other figure, had set the public agenda for the Republicans. The questions that sep-arated him from the pack were not ideological, as they had been for so many years. They were questions of personality, experience, depth, political strategy, and always—age.

Iowa initially looked like Reagan country. He had been a sportscaster on the state's largest radio station, WHO in Des Moines, back in the 1930s, and many Iowans still fondly re-membered "Dutch" Reagan's accounts of Iowa Hawkeye foot-ball games, and the Chicago Cubs games. He also had a large and loyal political organization in place, left over from 1976. But during the Iowa campaign Reagan was the candidate who wasn't there. His opponents were everywhere. But Reagan was a recluse, appearing not to care enough to visit the place where he began his career. Campaign manager John P. Sears rubbed salt in the wound, telling one local newsman, "It wouldn't do any good to have him (Reagan) going to coffees and shaking hands like the others. People will get the idea he's an ordinary man, like the rest of us."

By mid-January, this had hurt Reagan badly. An Iowa poll by the *Des Moines Register* found his popularity had dropped 24 percent in a month. Baker, who had been airing a dramatic commercial in which he shouted down an Iranian student, had regained much of the support he had lost in the fall, and was running second. Connally, who gambled and lost in trying to win a highly publicized straw poll of delegates to the Florida GOP convention in November, was in fourth with 10 percent of the vote, the exact same standing he had in August. But the big surprise was George Bush. Virtually unknown a few months before, he had moved into third in a dead heat with Baker.

Now, on the Saturday before the caucuses, the national media had invaded Iowa in full force. NBC had virtually taken over the Fort Des Moines Hotel, traditionally the state capitol's Republican gathering place. ABC, with well over 100 correspondents and technicians, had taken over the Savery, the Democratic hotel. CBS had rented the entire palatial Des Moines Civic Center, momentarily saving it from financial ruin. That day the network camera crews saw a tired John Connally, a worried Howard Baker, and an exuberant George Bush. Everywhere he went, supporters flocked to his side. "Six months ago a lot of people were for Reagan. But that died down," Roy Pogge, a Council Bluffs attorney said at one rally. "Bush has been going up. I predict he'll beat Reagan or at least be second."

Reagan made one last perfunctory swing through the state. His last—and biggest—event was a rally televised live from Adventureland Amusement Park. The park, isolated from reality in an old cornfield northeast of Des Moines, was covered with an eerie glaze of ice and snow. The park's Palace Theatre was packed with old ladies in straw hats, and bedecked in balloons and colorful banners. But the rally was a staged, plastic event. People cheered, but only on cue. Balloons dropped from the ceiling, but only on cue.

Reagan tried to evoke his old sportscaster days, telling the audience "the long blue shadows are spreading across the field, but this is a more important game than those stadium events I used to broadcast." His voice cracked. His motions were jerky from over-rehearsal. He looked like an old actor on the skids, failing to succeed in a comeback at the Palace Theatre. He left for California with a wave after 30 minutes. He has spent less than 40 hours in the state in three months—far less time than Walter Cronkite or John Chancellor. Bush had spent 27 days.

Looking back, it seemed so easy. After Ronald Wilson Reagan had captured the Republican presidential nomination by winning 29 of the 33 primaries in which he competed and 60 percent of the vote, the outcome appeared to have been pre-ordained and totally predictable. "It was just Reagan's year, wasn't it?" asked a loyal Republican listener of Reagan chief of staff Edwin Meese last May, after hearing a long Meese speech about the primary campaigns. "There's something to that," Meese replied, "but it didn't necessarily have to turn out that way." What follows is an account of why it turned out the way it did.

"In one very important sense, former California Gov. Ronald Reagan has already won the campaign that he enters tonight in New Hampshire," the *Washington Post*'s Mark Shields wrote on the morning of the candidate's declaration of candidacy. "For, in fact, Mr. Reagan, more than any other national figure, has determined the public agenda for the presidential campaign of 1980. Since 1975, he has been arguing—articulately and emphatically—the need to cut the size, scope and spending of government. A perennial critic of government waste and 'social tinkering and experimentation' Mr. Reagan now finds his theme song being sung . . . by every Republican challenger for the nomination with the exception of Rep. John Anderson. As the advocate of a more muscular national defense and a more skeptical approach to the Soviets, Mr. Reagan has now been joined by almost all of his own party and many of the Democrats."

For Reagan, victory began in Iowa in the lessons learned of an unexpected and unnecessary defeat. They were lessons that Reagan would carry with him throughout the primaries. The lessons were that a candidate must be himself, must play to his strengths, must do the things that work for him, must follow his own best instincts even against the advice of those who understand the political process better than the candidate. These are the lessons learned hard in politics, and Reagan believes that his learning of them made the difference between victory and defeat. Others who are close to Reagan believe it, too.

"Iowa brought the whole campaign back to reality," says Nevada Sen. Paul Laxalt, a Reagan intimate. "It enabled the governor and Nancy to campaign on a personal basis. It enabled them to win."

Even before Iowa, many in politics and the press had thought of Reagan as the false favorite of 1980. He led in the polls and attracted more media coverage than any candidate save Sen. Edward M. Kennedy, but the potential for disaster seemed poster-size. He was, after all, 69 years old and six years out of office, an aging ex-actor with no foreign policy experience and a penchant for factual flubs. His aides and his ex-aides told jokes about him. Have you heard about the Ronald Reagan doll? You wind it up and it runs for an hour and then takes a nap. Would President Reagan be a threat to blow up the world? Only between the hours of nine and five.

Reagan inadvertently contributed to the circulation of such stories and of others more grounded in the reality of the campaign. On November 13, 1979, the morning of the night he announced his presidential candidacy, Reagan went on NBC's "Today" show and appeared not to recognize the name of French President Valery Giscard d'Estaing. The explanation given by Reagan's press secretary was not reassuring—he said Reagan hadn't heard the question. For weeks afterward, on the Reagan campaign plane, reporters would repeat Tom Brokaw's words "Valery Giscard d'Estaing of France" and chorus back, in mimicry of Reagan, "Who?" The explanation that Reagan was more hard of hearing than ignorant gained currency as it became apparent that the candidate often had difficulty hearing questions from the audience. Reagan ascribed his problems not to age but, alternately to stuffed-up sinuses caused by flying and to a movie accident of more than 40 years ago when an actor had fired a blank cartridge close to his right ear.

When Reagan did succeed in setting to rest questions about his age and condition, he seemed to raise more serious questions in their place. After his first week of campaigning, the *Washington Post* reported that Reagan had shown a physical vitality equal to any of his younger challengers "while raising new doubts about his capacity to serve as president." The story recounted Reagan's fumbling campaign appearances in New York City, where he seemed unaware that the city was receiving federal loan guarantees with considerable strings attached, and in Grand Rapids, Michigan, where Reagan proved misinformed about pending legislation aimed at rescuing Chrysler Corporation. Reagan, in fact, performed so badly on this opening tour that his strategists resolved to expose him as little as possible in the weeks ahead. By December, front-runner Reagan was engaged in little more than a front-walking campaign. The pace was so leisurely that on one South Carolina trip baggage call was listed as an "event."

In these early weeks, Reagan was essentially an airborne candidate who flew everywhere without establishing a real presence anywhere. While Bush was concentrating on Iowa and New Hampshire and John B. Connally was focusing on Florida and South Carolina, Reagan was hopscotching around the country in expensive charter flights which usually ended with a late-night weekend flight home to Los Angeles. Because of the three-hour time difference on the coast, Reagan often failed to meet the deadlines of evening newscasts or Eastern newspapers. "Reagan was very much aloof at this time," recalls strategist and pollster Richard B. Wirthlin. "He was giving cameo appearances, he wasn't staying in any state long enough to make an impact. His advantage was frittered away by the refusal to debate (in Iowa), which was viewed unkindly by Iowa Republicans."

In part, Reagan's early strategy was dictated by the belief of campaign manager John P. Sears that his candidate was so far ahead that he had everything to lose and little to gain from public exposure. In part, it reflected the new political realities of 1980 which required candidates to campaign in far more primaries than ever before with far less financial resources than they had enjoyed in the past. Under the new federal campaign laws, candidates who accepted federal matching funds (everyone of importance except Connally) were limited to total expenditures of $17.6 million in the primaries. Reagan said frequently on the campaign trail that the spending limits had been conceived without reference to the explosive growth of primaries, and he was right. When Barry Goldwater won the Republican presidential nomination in 1964, he had participated in seven primaries, winning five of them. When Richard Nixon won the Republican nomination four years later, he entered nine of the 12 Republican primaries, winning eight of them. Nixon spent $10 million on that effort and $20 million more in winning renomination in 1972. Reagan entered 33 of the 35 primaries in 1980, skipping only Puerto Rico and the District of Columbia. But his campaign spent money as if the sky's-the-limit approach of 1972 were still allowed. By the time of the first primary in New Hampshire on February 26, Reagan had spent two-thirds of his allowable limit for the entire 33 primaries.

In politics, no less than war, the lessons of the last campaign are prized beyond their application to the present one. Each political campaign, like every battle, is dependent upon the experience of past campaigns but is itself unique. In different ways, Reagan and Sears were misled in their early campaigning because of what had happened to them in 1976. Reagan's obsession was what had happened to him in New Hampshire, where in 1976 he had sought to score a quick knockout victory over President Gerald Ford. Instead, he lost narrowly, winning 49 percent of the two-candidate vote and finishing only 1,587 votes behind the President. This narrow Ford victory became the basis of a bigger Ford win in the subsequent Florida primary and may well, as Reagan still believes, have meant the difference in the nomination. Reagan had brooded about this loss in the intervening years, at times criticizing the press for reporting Ford's victory as a victory and sometimes darkly hinting that votes had somehow been taken from him in a mysterious manner. Narrow losses do that to politicians. Few people sit around second-guessing, say, Barry Goldwater's landslide loss of 1964 or George McGovern's big defeat of 1972, but there are still plenty of politicians who will tell anyone willing to listen how Nixon could have pulled it off in 1960 or how Hubert H. Humphrey could have won in 1968. The Reagan people, going into 1980, talked that way about the New Hampshire primary of 1976.

Though Sears was not above second-guessing New Hampshire, he had his own separate and interlocking obsession. It was called the Northeast. After Reagan bounced back in North Carolina and subsequent primaries in 1976, Sears tried to win the nomination for his candidate by prying loose pro-Ford delegates in New York, Pennsylvania and other Northeast states. He failed, not from lack of effort but because Nelson Rockefeller was alive and politically powerful and because Reagan remained a suspect candidate in the region. With Rockefeller gone and no incumbent of his own party to contend with, Sears was convinced that the Northeast was ripe for Reagan in 1980. This viewpoint was Sears's central contribution to the Reagan campaign, and it was an important one. Reagan announced his candidacy in New York and he was campaigning in New York and Connecticut the fateful week before the Iowa precinct caucuses. To some reporters, both Sears and Reagan seemed almost uninterested in questions about the Iowa caucuses. New Hampshire was the first primary, after all, and Reagan would do well there. Then he would start scooping up the Eastern delegates. It was almost as if Iowa did not exist.

But New Hampshire was no longer really first in 1980. Sen. Howard H. Baker Jr. of Tennessee, better at political analysis than he proved at running a presidential campaign, said it best when he told reporters early in January that the Iowa caucuses had become "the functional equivalent of a primary." In the aftermath of Iowa, there would be a lot of finger-pointing within the Reagan organization about who was responsible for not recognizing the obvious, with Reagan's Californians blaming Sears and his loyalists, and Sears pointing the finger back at them and Reagan. The truth is that everyone in the Reagan campaign, from the candidate on down, missed the importance of Iowa. "In organizing their front-running campaign and concentrating on the Northeast and New Hampshire and lining up all the party people, they failed to recognize that Iowa was the linchpin of their strategy and that they needed to win there to accomplish it," said Bush political director David Keene after it was all over. Reagan agreed.

Iowa was an unlikely—some argued unrepresentative—place for the campaign to begin. With its endless rolling terrain and quiet small towns, the state reminds the casual visitor of an America that used to be. It is largely rural (the population of Des Moines, its largest city, is only 200,000); almost all white (98.4 percent) and heavily dependent on agriculture and agribusiness. Its skies are clean, its land rich, and its people decidedly middle American. Despite their cornhusker image, Iowans are better educated (the state has the lowest literacy rate in the nation), better paid, healthier and better governed on the local and state level than residents of all but a handful of states. They take their politics and institutions seriously. "In God we trust, and state troopers too," the *Des Moines Register* reported on one statewide poll. "But not in labor unions, government agencies or real estate agents."

Historically, Iowa is a Republican state, but its size, location and preoccupation with agriculture have worked against it being a real power in national affairs. Not surprisingly, the only president the state has produced was a Republican, Herbert Hoover, who grew up in the tiny hamlet of West Branch. It was also a caucus, not a primary state, with only 37 delegates to send to the 1980 GOP national convention. So cumbersome and complex was the machinery for selecting those delegates that only one party member in 14 took part in the process in 1976.

This changed radically in 1980 for two simple reasons: the Iowa precinct caucuses were the first formal test in a presidential race that had already been underway for more than a year, and Iowa was the place that an obscure former governor of Georgia, Jimmy Carter, got his first big boost on the way to the White House.

No one recognized the importance of Iowa more than George Bush, or capitalized on it better. In part, Bush, out of office and unknown, had to, for his survival depended on a strong showing in the early tests of the season. That he survived longer than any other Reagan challenger was the great surprise of the presidential season.

When he began his long distance run in the fall of 1977, three full years before the election, Bush had never won an election outside his Houston congressional district. His first confidant and later campaign manager was James Baker, a calm, precise tactician who managed Gerald Ford's 1976 race. Their most crucial early decision was to take advantage of Bush's two biggest assets—his time, which Bush out of office had plenty of, and his energy. They formed a political action committee, the Fund for Limited Government, to finance Bush's travel, and in 1978, he hit the rubber chicken circuit, traveling more than 96,000 miles, visiting 42 states. Every party functionary he met along the way received a handwritten note from Bush.

By mid-1978, a strategy to wrestle the nomination from Reagan evolved. It was a carbon copy of the game plan that put Jimmy Carter in the White House. The emphasis was on grassroots organizing in a small group of early primary and caucus states, primarily in the Midwest and Northeast. All but the most general issues—leadership, experience and Carter's failings—would be soft pedaled. More precise positions and national exposure would come later. "You have to win early—the same way Jimmy Carter did—and you can't win those early ones by standing in the Waldorf-Astoria in New York," Baker said.

It is hard to imagine two individuals from more varied backgrounds than Reagan and Bush. Reagan is the son of a small-town shoe salesman; his roots are in the Midwest. Though a Texan by residence for three decades, George Herbert Walker Bush is the product of a far different class: the moneyed and established Eastern elite. His father, Prescott, was managing director of the investment banking house of Brown Brothers, Harriman, and then a senator from Connecticut. He grew up in Fairfield County, Connecticut, in a world of stone mansions, wood paneling and vast lawns. Young George was sent to Andover, where he excelled, and Yale, where he excelled even more, graduating with a Phi Beta Kappa key and a membership in the senior society called Skull and Bones, a redoubt for the Wasp elite. "He always seemed a little like Scott Fitzgerald made him up, intent and earnest and ambitious with the easy grace of a man charmed," a friend once wrote.

Bush's resume indeed could have been crafted by Fitzgerald. By his 55th birthday, he had been a star athlete (captain of his Yale baseball team), war hero (he was gunned down over the Pacific as a young Navy pilot), successful businessman (oil), congressman, ambassador to the United Nations, envoy to China, Republican National Committee chairman, and director of the CIA. The posts gave him a nationwide network of contacts to structure a campaign around: An "old blue" Yale network, an intelligence community network, a business network, a Capital Hill network, a foreign policy network, and a Republican organization network.

Bush's many jobs also gave his media advisor, Robert Goodman, a skeleton to build a candidate around. Bush, Goodman felt, had the makings of a new American hero about him, and he promptly nicknamed him "the American Eagle." The fact that few voters had ever heard of the candidate didn't bother Goodman. "George Bush was that new face people were hungering for," he told one interviewer. "We had a great advantage of lack of perception of him really, which meant we could present a fresh perception that would be considered new and current and different." The trick was convincing voters that Bush was different from the fresh face—Jimmy Carter—

they had bought four years before. So Goodman crafted a catchy campaign slogan, and an elaborate, richly textured set of TV commercials which stressed the candidate's experience. "This time there will be no repeating past mistakes," a voice said. "This time there can be George Bush: A president we won't have to train."

But there were liabilities in Bush's background, a lingering hard-to-define uneasiness about the man, a sense that he lacked toughness and grit. It led his opponents and the press to dismiss him as a fragile, rich Ivy Leaguer, a Texan who didn't own a single cow. Why, in all his jobs, had Bush never made a single wave? Why had no one ever heard of him. Was he afraid of conflict?

A Carter campaign aide captured the feeling with a tongue-in-cheek slogan for a Carter-Bush campaign: "Why change wimps in the middle of the stream?"

His quip captured the problems that would plague the Bush campaign.

The strategy for Bush's Iowa campaign was born in the Dallas Center, Iowa, living room of Ralph Brown, a soft-spoken young attorney, on the last day of February, 1979. Bush, then still an asterisk in national polls, didn't attend. But two of the state's top Republicans who would play crucial roles in the campaign did: Mary Louise Smith, Bush's co-chairman back in his days at the Republican National Committee, and John McDonald, GOP national committeeman. They provided Bush's link to the state's party structure, recruiting 68 prominent GOP leaders to his national steering committee at a time when the candidate was still "George Who?" The committee was big news in Iowa. "Bush Builds Impressive Iowa support," the influential *Des Moines Register* declared in a front-page headline.

By April, Bush dispatched a full-time campaign director, Rich Bond, an intense, young political operative from Long Island, to Iowa and the candidate and his family began making regular trips to the state. Only Rep. Philip Crane, the longshot conservative, was there so early, and his candidacy faltered after encountering financial problems in late spring. Bond built up list after list of names of supporters, slowly putting the bricks of a campaign organization together. Once he obtained a name, a phone call went out, then a packet asking the recipient to sign on with Bush and supply names of neighbors likely to be similarly inclined. It was tedious, boring work. But by fall, when Bush won a series of five consecutive straw polls, results had begun to pay off. "It's a two-man race now in Iowa," declared Bond.

There was more truth than fiction to that remark. But Bush still had two far better known Reagan challengers to deal with.

Of all the Republicans, none was feared more by the Carter White House—or Reagan strategist John Sears—than Howard H. Baker Jr. of Tennessee, the Senate Minority Leader. After 13 years in Congress, he was a respected and well-liked figure on Capitol Hill, a proven Republican vote getter in a Democratic state. He could, the White House feared, damage the President where it would hurt worst—in his political base in the South, and in the vast middle ground of moderate American voters.

Baker, at 53 the youngest of the major GOP contenders, grew up in the tiny mountain town of Huntsville, Tennessee, the member of a political family, and he has the bearing of a man comfortable with himself and his place in life. His father, mother and father-in-law, the late Sen. Everett Dirksen of Illinois, all served in Congress. A compromiser by nature, he relished the "big issues" of the day, and tended to gravitate toward the political middle. His service on the Senate Watergate Committee had given Baker invaluable national exposure, and proven a showcase for his two greatest strengths as a candidate: his ability to project on television, and to cloak even the most partisan political rhetoric in Olympian prose. On paper, he was clearly the most formidable moderate in the race. The Reagan camp viewed him, correctly, as the most articulate of the former California governor's opponents.

The lessons of Carter's 1976 victory made a deep impression on Baker. Almost immediately after the election he began talking about making a run for the 1980 nomination. He briefly considered not seeking reelection to the Senate in 1978, then thought about running for governor of Tennessee. But Baker eventually decided to return to the Senate, winning handily, despite an unpopular vote cast in favor of the Panama Canal Treaty. But the race showed a certain disregard for the grubby organizational work of politics that would haunt him in 1980.

After conferring with his family over the Christmas recess, Baker made a final decision to run. He would campaign from the Senate, a place he felt guaranteed national exposure because of his minority leader status. He would demonstrate his leadership claims by being leader. His vehicle would be President Carter's Strategic Arms Limitations Treaty which he opposed. By mid-February, he had visited Russia, and made his first pilgrimage to New Hampshire. Baker's friends said he was off and running. But the senator kept delaying his formal announcement, first until July 4, then week by week, later and later, due to delays in the SALT debate, a debate that never made it to the Senate floor. It wasn't until November 1 that he formally announced. By that time his rivals had a long head-start.

Few people who had watched John Bowdein Connally over the years ever doubted that someday he, like his old mentor and fellow Texan Lyndon B. Johnson, would be a candidate for president. A major player on the national stage for two decades, Connally had proven himself a man of genuine ability with an ego to match. But always before obstacles stood in the path of his candidacy. First, his thirst for money, then his old boss Johnson, who brought him to Washington fresh out of the University of Texas in 1940, then his switch from the Democratic to Republican Party and his indictment on charges of taking a $10,000 bribe from milk producers during the Nixon administration, stood in his way.

Now, at age 61, the former Texas governor and adviser to three presidents, made his move, offering himself to the nation as the man who would be, for "the fourth major period of crisis in our history," what Washington, Lincoln, and Franklin D. Roosevelt were for theirs:

"Someone in charge who knows what he is doing and why."

This reflected both Connally's natural swashbuckling style and his analysis of the race. As he saw it, Jimmy Carter had proven himself inept. He was an embarrassment to the nation, a man with neither the vision nor ability to play on the world stage, someone the Democrats surely wouldn't nominate for reelection. Teddy Kennedy would be the nominee. Connally would run against him as the Texan on the white horse, the fastest gun in the West, the only Republican charismatic enough to take on the Kennedy legend. Thus, Connally would convert his biggest liability—a wheeler-dealer image—into an asset.

But first there was Reagan. Connally, his advisers felt, had to take on the former governor head on in each of the 50 states and show strength in the national polls. Grassroots organizing was ruled out. "We could generate major coverage and major crowds," said Eddie Mahe, Connally's chief strategist. "To use John Connally in someone's kitchen didn't make any sense when he could be speaking to 2,000 people in a convention center."

Connally started fast. He scored his earliest and most significant victories in the corporate boardrooms of America. He courted them shamelessly, and they adopted him as their own. By early fall, his list of financial backers read like a who's who of American business. Among them were one of every four of the very top executive officers of the nation's 500 largest firms. Connally talked their language; he acted like many of them wish they dared act. To Reagan adviser Ed Meese it appeared Connally felt "if you get people by the boardrooms their hearts and minds will follow."

★

By January, 1980, when the candidates moved into Iowa for a final push, the campaign had been underway for more than a year. For months, the candidates had been crisscrossing the nation, courting, courting hard. But little of it had to do directly with voters. Basically, the candidates were courting the press and the people the press talks to—the established politicians and political activists. And they were building organizations and financial support.

Since Reagan had begun the race far ahead of the other candidates, the race already was cast as Reagan vs. Stop Reagan. Each candidate wanted to be Stop Reagan, the Republican who could demonstrate by some success or gimmick that he was the person most deserving of becoming the rallying point for anti-Reagan forces. Gerald Ford was playing a waiting game in California, with no one certain where he would come out in the end. The other candidates tried to demonstrate their specialness by winning straw votes in states where they thought they were strong. Connally and Crane chose straw polls in Florida. Baker picked Maine. Bush, Bob Dole, and to a lesser extent, Baker, tried to make an impression in Iowa, where Dole tried to influence the result of a poll taken at a GOP fundraising dinner by buying up $75,000 worth of tickets and distributing them to his supposed supporters, many of whom actually voted for Bush or other candidates. Baker and Connally came out the big losers in this stage by failing to produce up to the expectations their campaigns had created. In many ways, their campaigns never really recovered.

★

The formal opening act of the 1980 season, like so many other major events of the campaign year, was a television event, a debate sponsored by the *Des Moines Register*. The crowd in the new, 2,600 seat Des Moines Civic Center was an opening night crowd, slightly apprehensive about the show and its cast of characters. Almost everyone was pleasantly surprised. The most striking impression from the evening was that the Republican Party, after all its years of travail, had fielded six articulate spokesmen, representing a broad range of experience. Not a one embarrassed himself.

By the luck of the draw, Rep. Philip M. Crane, the longshot conservative, was on the far right of the gray carpeted podium. Somber and handsome, he sounded professorial—more reasonable than his image would indicate. Bush, wearing a mortician-like black suit, sat on the far left. With his campaign gaining momentum ("Big Mo," he called it), Bush had more to lose than any of the debaters. The prospect weighed heavily on him. He looked tired, taut, nervous. Media adviser Goodman was disappointed. "The Eagle performing alone in his own (TV) ads is terrific," he later said. "That debate format is a terrible format for George . . . It's a letdown. You see six guys instead of the Eagle and five others."

Sen. Robert Dole of Kansas, the weakest candidate in the field, had the best lines. "If you want a younger Ronald Reagan with experience, I'm here," he said.

John Connally, asked how he differed with Reagan on issues, struck the first blow on the absent ex-movie actor. "I wish Governor Reagan were here. Oh, I wish he were here. I don't know where the governor stands."

One by one the other candidates picked up the same theme. In retrospect, Reagan's hopes for Iowa, where he began his career as a radio sportscaster, died that hour as candidate after candidate deftly jabbed at him. Reagan made two more quick hops across the state, spending a total of less than eight hours, but he never reversed the impression that he didn't care enough about Iowa to talk to its people.

In a strange way, the nationally televised debate had the opposite effect on the candidacy of John Anderson of Illinois, making him, for the first time, a national figure. Anderson struck a responsive cord by questioning the conventional wisdom at the table. "How do you balance the budget, cut taxes, and increase defense spending at the same time?" he asked indignantly. "It's very simple. You do it with mirrors." How responsive wouldn't be seen until later.

At 8 o'clock on the night of January 21, 150,000 Iowans gathered in living rooms, schools, city halls and firehouses to vote in the Republican precinct caucuses. Bush strategists, anticipating a strong showing, had met two nights earlier in a suite at the Fort Des Moines Hotel to talk about the future. Up to this point, Bush had avoided all but the most general issues, trying to be all things to all people, a conservative for conservatives, a moderate for moderates. Now, it was argued, was the time to move into a second phase strategy in which the candidate would identify with issues, a time to give people a reason to vote for the new fresh face of the Republican Party. In a decision that plagued his campaign for months, Bush rejected the advice. "It was determined that we should not change something that was working," said campaign manager James Baker.

The Iowa results were better than even Bush had dared hope. He had collected 33 percent of the vote, six points better than Reagan. Baker had 14 percent, Connally 10 percent, Crane 7 percent, Anderson, who hadn't contested the state, 4 percent, and Dole 3 percent.

Bush was suddenly the hottest property in American politics. "What's wrong with good organization and working harder than the next guy?" he told a cheering crowd. "Because of what's happened in Iowa we are going to go all the way to the White House."

Reagan heard the news about Iowa at the home of movie producer Hal Wallis in posh Bel Air, where Reagan had gone the night of January 21 to watch a private screening of *Kramer vs. Kramer*. But Reagan's mind was not on the movie but on his own contest against himself—the contest of the vigorous candidate Reagan believed himself to be versus the absentee, aging ex-actor he had portrayed in Iowa. "There are going to be some changes made," Meese recalls Reagan saying to him grimly the same night. And Reagan was emotionally ready to make them. "I sensed for weeks before that, psychologically, Ron felt trapped," recalls Nevada Sen. Paul Laxalt. "He concurred in avoiding the Iowa debate but subconsciously he didn't feel right about it. When he changed, he was liberated and it enabled him to perform in New Hampshire."

Laxalt is one of the few politicians who is a close friend of Reagan's, and he was less philosophical and lots more blunt when Reagan called him the day after the Iowa caucuses. Then, the Nevada senator urged Reagan not to rationalize his loss but accept his own campaign in Iowa as the reason for what happened. Both Reagan and Laxalt are sports fans, and both had watched the week before when the Pittsburgh Steelers beat Reagan's beloved Los Angeles Rams in the Super Bowl. "The Steelers wouldn't have won if (quarterback) Terry Bradshaw had been sitting on his ass for three quarters, and you were sitting on your ass in Iowa," Laxalt told Reagan.

Reagan understandably remembers Iowa as "the lowest point" of the campaign for him. Everyone, including Sears, agreed that he needed to change his style and his tactics.

On one stretch, Reagan spent 21 days in a row on the road, most of it in New Hampshire with side trips to the early primary states of South Carolina and Florida. Reporters no longer found the pace leisurely, and a sign appeared in the Reagan press room. "Free the Reagan 44." On February 6, when Reagan turned 69, he barnstormed New Hampshire, visited a George Bush headquarters at the request of a Bush worker and knocked a plaster moosehead off a wall in a Kingston coffee shop. On this same day he announced for the first time that he would debate Bush, thus formally abandoning the questionable strategy which President Carter would use to the end against Senator Kennedy. But it was different in Reagan's case. As longtime aide Lyn Nofziger put it, "If you're going to use a Rose Garden strategy, you better have a Rose Garden."

Reagan did something other than campaign hard in New Hampshire. He also, for the first time, directly tackled the nettlesome issue of his age, which was raised early and often by reporters and also by his audiences, particularly at New Hampshire high schools. Reagan's usual answer at the high schools was the slightly defensive line, "It's better than the alternative." But in the first week of February—in an idea attributed to a shrewd California supporter, Lorelei Kinder, and picked up and pushed by Sears and Gerald P. Carmen, the Republican state chairman in New Hampshire—the Reagan campaign decided to defuse the issue by calling attention to the supposed problem. "You might as well," said Sears. "You can't deny it." It was a classic demonstration of how to take the edge off an issue by celebrating a liability. For days there were cakes and balloons and "Happy Birthday, Ron" signs. The height of this excess was reached in Greenville, South Carolina, on February 6, where Reagan stumbled into a huge cake and emerged with icing all over his coat. The verdict of the two-day celebration on the press bus was "Reagan 6, Cakes 1," but the campaign had succeeded in its purpose. Through the rest of the primaries, the issue was rarely raised by anyone.

The most important consequences of Reagan's new strategy flowed from his decision to debate. Before Iowa, everyone in the Reagan entourage opposed debates, fearing that some Reagan blooper would puncture his front-running balloon. Afterward, when Wirthlin's surveys showed Bush ahead in New Hampshire, there were no dissenters to Reagan's new view that he must now meet his opponents face-to-face. The two New Hampshire debates became the most important events of the Republican primary campaign. One of these debates, a dramatic encounter between Reagan and Bush in Nashua on February 23, will be remembered as one of the most exciting evenings in American politics. But the other debate, an undramatic meeting of seven candidates in Manchester on February 20, may have been even more important.

Reagan was visibly nervous the night of the Manchester debate. He fumbled questions and at one point appeared to suggest that it would be all right for U.S. corporations to bribe foreign governments. Bush was no ball of fire, either. The prevailing view among the press was that the debate was a dull affair, with no winner, and that Reagan may have done a little worse than his rivals. This press judgment was summed up in a headline in the *Washington Post*: "GOP debaters restate basic positions in N.H. Debate." But Wirthlin's polls showed Reagan

moving from a point behind to 20 points ahead on the strength
of this debate. And Bush aides now believe that the Manchester
debate may have been the turning point against their candidate.

What happened? The survey findings taken for Reagan and
Bush afterward show that the debate was watched by a huge
audience which was making a different assessment than the
reporters. Reagan had started out the campaign far ahead. His
conservatism—unorthodox, perhaps, in 1964—now represented the mainstream thinking of the Republican Party. The
questions about him were not ideological—they were personal
questions about whether he was up to the job or too old to be
president, questions which had been raised as much by Reagan's non-presence in Iowa as by anything else. "Bush did
better in this debate than he had done in Iowa," said Keene
afterward. "We didn't think Reagan had done that well and
neither did the traveling press. But the voters watching it on
television were making a different kind of comparison—they
were comparing Bush with this super-candidate they had heard
about who had knocked off Reagan in Iowa. On camera, Bush
looked pretty much like a guy who puts his pants on one leg
at a time like everyone else. And Reagan had started with the
strongest base in the Republican Party, with the only question
being, 'Was he up to it?' If he looked as good as anyone else,
and he did, why not vote for him?"

Wirthlin thought that Reagan looked "more uptight than he
had ever been in a public forum" but that his forcefulness came
through in contrast to Bush. Reagan also gained in the last
moment of the debate when a supporter for another candidate
in the audience crossed up the sponsoring League of Women
Voters by asking a question about a relatively inoffensive ethnic
joke Reagan had told during the campaign. The questioner
implied that Reagan was prejudiced against Italians. Reagan
replied, with some heat, that he had been "stiffed" by a reporter
who had overheard him telling a story he was using as an
example of a joke that should not be told. "I don't tell them,"
Reagan said of ethnic jokes. "I don't like them. I'm going to
look over both shoulders from now on and I'm only going to
tell stories about Irishmen because I'm Irish." The reply, while
not strictly true, drew applause. Wirthlin's polls showed that
Reagan's answer also provoked sympathy from the television
audience, many of whom thought the question unfair. The

result was that the ethnic joke wound up helping Reagan instead of hurting him.

The climax of the New Hampshire campaign came Saturday night in Nashua three days before the primary. Its impact is summarized by a *Boston Globe* headline: "A Golden Night for Reagan. At a high school gym in Nashua the Gipper grabbed the brass ring." What Reagan really grabbed was a microphone. Angered by *Nashua Telegraph* editor Jon Breen, who had threatened to have Reagan's microphone turned off, Reagan, said, "I paid for this microphone, Mr. Green (sic)." The gym erupted in applause. A combination of skillful maneuvering and the personal characteristics of the leading candidates had come together in a way that proved elevating for Reagan and devastating for Bush. Reagan is a competitor, a former high school and college athlete who revels in the metaphors and mindsets of sports. As a governor and as candidate for governor, he was sometimes lazy but invariably impressive when aroused. He has a temper, and he knows how to use it to his advantage. Bush, articulate and informed in conversation, does not like confrontation, as he was to show throughout the series of debates. The Nashua debate made him simultaneously appear weak and arrogant, an impression from which he never recovered.

What happened is this. Understanding that Reagan was effective in face-to-face encounter and that Bush was leading in New Hampshire, Carmen had proposed the two-candidate debate. Hugh Gregg, the Bush campaign manager in New Hampshire who had played a similar role for Reagan in 1976, accepted the proposal but only on the grounds that the debate be held in Nashua, where he had strong personal ties to the newspaper and community. The week of the debate the Federal Elections Committee ruled that the paper could not sponsor the debate because it would be an illegal contribution to Reagan and Bush. When Gregg balked at paying any of the expenses, Carmen paid the entire $3,500 in debate costs from Reagan campaign funds, a ploy which enabled Reagan to truthfully say that he was paying for the microphone. At the same time, Sears had opened negotiations with other candidates, inviting them to the debate without telling Bush. But on the evening of the debate, when Bush realized what had happened, he refused to meet with the other candidates or with Sen. Gordon Humphrey of New Hampshire, a Reagan supporter who wanted Bush to invite the other candidates. Without any apparent recognition of how his actions would look to an audience or the press, Bush took refuge in the fact that he had been invited by the newspaper and that it was up to the *Telegraph* to decide who should participate in the debate. Bush strode on stage, as pro-Reagan *Manchester Union Leader* publisher William Loeb wrote afterward, looking "like a small boy who had been dropped off at the wrong birthday party." When Breen announced that the other four candidates at the gym—Baker, Bob Dole, John B. Anderson and Philip M. Crane—would not be allowed to speak, Reagan protested that they were being silenced unfairly. The other four strode onto the stage, waving to the crowd. "Get them some chairs," cried voices from the audience. Bush did nothing, refusing even to acknowledge the presence of his unseated rivals. The four candidates then walked off, to hold press conferences in adjoining rooms denouncing Bush. Reagan, aroused by the confrontation, proceeded to best Bush in the debate. Two days later, irreverent Bush press secretary Pete Teeley told his candidate: "The bad news is that the media is playing up the confrontation. The good news is that they're ignoring the debate and you lost that, too."

Bush also lost the primary, in a big way, and quite possibly the nomination. The Nashua debate added to a trend that was already running deep toward Reagan, who defeated Bush by nearly a 2 to 1 margin. The margin approached 8 to 1 in Manchester where the *Union Leader* had run a virulent campaign against Bush, depicting him as a weak, ineffective man who was the candidate of "liberal leftists" and "clean fingernails Republicans." Though Bush was to narrowly win the Massachusetts primary the next week, he never really recovered from his New Hampshire defeat.

Reagan took advantage of his recovered front-running position to follow a course which conservatives and Californians in his campaign had been urging ever since Iowa—the firing of Sears. Dumped with Sears were political director Charles Black, whose loss would be the most severely felt of the three, and hard-driving press secretary James Lake. It was turnabout time for Sears and his allies, who had been steadily divesting the campaign of old Reagan aides for several months. Nofziger had been forced out in August and Michael K. Deaver, a close

Reagan associate, had resigned after a confrontation with Sears and Black in November. The same month domestic issues adviser Martin Anderson was pressured into a sidelines role by Sears. But when Sears also urged the demotion or firing of Meese, who had been Reagan's executive secretary in Sacramento, Reagan decided to get rid of Sears instead. Reagan chose the afternoon of the New Hampshire primary, when it became clear that he was winning by a landslide. Doing it that way, Reagan said later, showed that he wasn't simply retaliating against aides because of a defeat. The timing of the firings also subordinated the shake-up to Reagan's big win in New Hampshire.

That night at a well-known watering hole in Bedford, White House Press Secretary Jody Powell and White House pollster Pat Caddell were celebrating the results with reporters. They were very happy. Carter had just demolished Kennedy and Reagan, the man they wanted Carter to face in the general election, had taken care of Bush. Furthermore, Sears—the most respected of the Republican strategists—was out. "Maybe Reagan doesn't need a staff," Caddell joked to a reporter who had covered the Reagan campaign. "You tell Reagan that he's giving staff people a bad name." But for Reagan, who had complained that Sears looked him in the tie rather than the eye, it was a liberating experience. He was his own man once again, he thought, and the conservatives and Californians he felt most comfortable with were back in the saddle with him. For better or worse, Reagan was doing it now his own way, and he was winning.

One candidate who wasn't winning but was beginning to attract significant coverage was Anderson, celebrated as the thinking man's candidate by the popular "Doonesbury" cartoon strip of Gary Trudeau. Despite a well-publicized performance in which he defied a meeting of the New Hampshire Gun Owners by coming out for gun control, Anderson failed really to catch on in New Hampshire, drawing only 9.8 percent of the vote and failing to win a delegate. But he won 30.1 percent of the vote the next week in Massachusetts, where he finished second to Bush, and 29 percent of the vote in Vermont, where he was second to Reagan. The networks, however, treated Anderson as the real winner of these March 4 primaries, diminishing the impact of Bush's victory and his chances to stay competitive with Reagan. The impact of this treatment was helpful in the long run to Reagan, as Sears realized, because it kept Stop Reagan a multiple candidacy.

For the same reason, the success of Anderson was damaging to Bush. "We got a bad break from Anderson emerging," believes Bush campaign manager Jim Baker. "Just at the point we had gotten to be the alternative to Reagan, along came Anderson. The media hype was perfect for him—right before the primary in his home state."

But Bush received one benefit from the March 4 round of primaries. In typical low-key style, Baker bowed out of the race the following day at a press conference in his Senate office where he acknowledged without bitterness that his campaign "isn't going anywhere . . . I'm doing everything I know how to do, doing it well . . . and it's still producing third- and fourth-place finishes," Baker said.

Bush, of course, was glad to see Baker go, and so was Reagan campaign manager Sears. "Had Howard been in Bush's shoes, he might have made more of his position than George did," said Sears. He had no such worries about Anderson.

★

It was in South Carolina that John Connally choose to make his stand.

Big John was always the best show in town. In his cowboy boots and perfectly tailored three-piece suits, he was a bigger than life figure, a superb orator, quick on his feet, tough, decisive, blustery. He looked like a president, tall, jut-jawed and silver-haired. He acted like a president. He was, his friends insisted, the most qualified and electable candidate for the job in history.

Trouble was, hardly anyone wanted to vote for him in the early primaries.

What happened?

Connally's credentials were certainly impressive enough: three-time governor of Texas, Secretary of Navy, Secretary of Treasury, lawyer able to command $500,000 in fees, rancher, businessman, family man, son of a tenant farmer, a man who could honestly say, "I've been poor and I've been rich and rich is better."

But Connally was plagued by what political professionals call "a high negative," which many felt doomed his candidacy from the start. About one-third of the voters polled in every national survey said they simply wouldn't vote for Connally under any circumstance. They felt he was a reckless—perhaps even crooked—wheeler dealer, a political turncoat, and a handmaiden of big business.

No matter what Connally did, the negatives followed him. One of the most embarrassing times came during the middle of a crudely staged, TV call-in show on a cold, January evening in Cedar Rapids, Iowa. Connally and a local television personality were on the air taking direct telephone calls from listeners when a hearty sounding man said he intended to vote for Connally, who he described as a great American. But, he added, he needed Connally's help in dealing with his wife.

"What's the problem," asked the grinning candidate.

"She thinks you're a crook."

This gave Connally a chance to launch into a lengthy explanation of his acquittal on charges of taking a $10,000 bribe from milk producers in exchange for lobbying for higher milk support prices in the Nixon administration.

"I'm the only certified non-guilty political figure in the country," Connally declared.

"I've told my wife all of that," the man responded.

"What did she say?"

"She still thinks you're a crook."

By the time his campaign moved South, Connally was desperate. Money had run so short that staff salaries were suspended, and plans for an elaborate media blitz drastically reduced.

From Connally's point of view, South Carolina seemed to be the ideal spot for a comeback. What he didn't realize was that he was choosing the state where Reagan's polls showed him running strongest outside of California, the one state among the earliest primaries where Reagan experienced no serious slump after his loss in Iowa. Nevertheless, Connally's pragmatic conservatism, saber-rattling bravado about national defense and faint Southern drawl seemed tailored to South Carolina. Even more important, he had the backing of the state's two most powerful Republicans, former Governor James

B. Edwards and Sen. Strom Thurmond. Reagan, he theorized, would come out of the New England primaries bruised and battered, ripe for kill. A Connally win in South Carolina, followed by strong showings in Florida, Alabama and Georgia three days later, would send the GOP race back to square one. And Connally would be sitting there.

Thurmond was the key. In Washington, he is regarded as an eccentric anachronism. But back home in South Carolina, Thurmond is routinely introduced as a "living legend," a title he has aptly earned by being elected, over the last five decades, as a Democrat, an independent, a Dixiecrat and a Republican. At 77, he still has that rare peculiar magic that few politicians ever achieve. Teenagers flock to his side for autographs. College girls fawn over him. Old men shake their heads in wonder at his four children, all 8 and under, and his beautiful young wife. "This morning in Aiken at 3 o'clock Strom's third wife was born," goes a standard line.

Thurmond pulled out all stops for Connally. He made television commercials. He placed countless phone calls to political cronies. And he climbed aboard a bus with Connally and criss-crossed the state with him for the better part of three weeks, introducing the Texan as "a fellow Southerner, a patriot and a great American."

"I don't know any man of the political scene today who is more dynamic, more aggressive and more forceful, who is as tough as this man, and we need a tough man," Strom told audiences as they moved from the red hills of the Piedmont, across the piney wood foothills and into the South Carolina low country.

On the stump, Connally was one of the last of the old-fashioned political orators, a real hell-fire-and-brimstone figure. He would give the same speech a dozen times, always talking without notes, and make it sound different each time. But the lines that drew the most applause were always the same:

"We've got to quit taking scientific advice from the Jane Fondas and Ralph Naders of this world and start taking it from the Edward Tellers" . . . "If appeasement were an art form, the Carter Administration would be the Rembrandt of the age" . . . "Unless the Japanese ease trade barriers for U.S. products they should be made to sit on the docks of Yokohama in their own Toyotas watching their own Sony television sets."

The Strom and John show was a sure crowd pleaser. People came out everywhere. They listened. They cheered. The funny thing was that when Connally finished it was hard to find anyone who said they intended to vote for him. His message simply didn't sell. On election night, he finished an embarrassing 24 percentage points behind Reagan.

The next afternoon in the Grand Ballroom of the Marriott West Loop Hotel in Houston, John Connally pulled out of the race, saying it "would not contribute to the good of the party or the good of the country" to continue.

He had campaigned for 14 months and spent $11 million. All he had to show for it was one delegate, Ada Mills of Arkansas.

New Hampshire had been the watershed for Reagan, but his narrow victory in Vermont and third-place finish in Massachusetts a week later suggested that there was still a contest in the Republican primaries. South Carolina demonstrated that this contest did not exist in the South. It also rid Reagan of the nagging presence of Connally, whom Reagan regarded as his potentially most difficult opponent after Gerald Ford. "If Connally had developed credibility, his vote would have come out of ours," says Wirthlin, "and in a multi-candidate race this would have posed a danger." That danger now was gone.

Reagan was a happy, confident candidate after South Carolina. On the night of the South Carolina primary, with early results showing him leading Connally 2–1, a smiling Reagan and his wife left a black-tie dinner to meet with reporters. "I have been telling some of you that I'm cautiously optimistic," Reagan said in a line he was to use over and over again in the months ahead. "Now I'm cautiously ecstatic."

This was on March 8, a Saturday. Reagan expected to sweep the three Southern primaries in Florida, Georgia and Alabama the following Tuesday, and he exceeded even his own expectations. He polled more than two-thirds of the vote in Georgia and Alabama and 56 percent in Florida, where Bush had waged a determined campaign in selected districts. Overall, Reagan picked up 105 of the 114 delegates in the three states, building up a lead that even at this early date rapidly was becoming insurmountable. He was now pointed squarely toward the

March 18 primary in Illinois, a state viewed by both the candidate and his strategists as potentially decisive, and a state where Reagan had been wiped out by Ford in 1976.

Now, in 1980, Ford remained the last troublesome problem for Reagan. The surefire way to dispel some of the euphoria which now prevailed on the Reagan campaign plane was to mention the name of the former president. Ford and a group of his closest friends and advisers met in Washington on March 12, the day after the Southern primaries, at a time when the deadlines for entering enough primaries to head off Reagan had already passed. But Reagan didn't want head-to-head combat with his former foe, even if he could beat him, because he knew this presaged a long and difficult struggle that probably would last until the Republican convention. On March 10, in Mobile, Alabama, Reagan said Ford could "hang up his golf clubs" if he wanted to and enter the race but under prodding from reporters finally declared: "I will tell you right now that I will probably be just as happy if he doesn't (run)."

Ford didn't. On March 15, he accepted the analysis of his advisers that it was too late to take on Reagan. Beset by conflicting advice from within his own family and the resentment of other candidates, principally Bush, who thought that his entry into the race would only further divide the anti-Reagan vote, Ford declared that he would not be a candidate. All that remained now was for Reagan to win in Illinois.

From the beginning of the primaries, Illinois had been seen as the shake-out state by the Republican candidates. Reagan hoped to clinch the nomination there, and most of the others knew that they needed a strong Illinois showing if they were to remain in the race. The importance of Illinois derived from many factors—its size, its historic importance to Republican candidates, its crossover voting law and, above all, its strategic placement in the primaries as the first major industrial state in which the candidates competed.

After Iowa, Bush had seemed the most likely alternative to Reagan but his once-promising candidacy had been shattered by his defeats in New Hampshire and the South. Anderson, boosted by a wave of national press coverage, had replaced Bush as the real alternative to Reagan even though Anderson had fared poorly in New Hampshire and had not even competed in the South. But he had exceeded the low initial expectations for him with those two second-place finishes in Vermont and

Massachusetts, and he had used these as the springboard to campaign directly in Illinois where the newspapers were favorable and the "Anderson difference" ads on television had caught the imagination of voters.

Debates had been key in the earlier Republican encounters, and a debate now played a major role in Illinois. On March 13 in Chicago, Anderson rivals Philip M. Crane and Bush used the opportunity of another multi-candidate debate to depict Anderson as a liberal-in-Republican-clothing who did not deserve the support of GOP voters. Crane, never known for using a stiletto when a broad ax is available, put it bluntly to Anderson during one exchange: "You are in the wrong party."

This attack gave Reagan an opportunity to try out a new role—"Ronald Reagan, Statesman"—and he made the most of it. *Newsweek*'s Jerry Lubenow observed that at times in this debate Reagan looked to be more the moderator than Howard K. Smith, who followed a new format of letting the candidates fight. Reagan had anticipated this, and he was carefully, and effectively, low-key and witty in his approach. At one point, repeating a standard campaign line that wage-and-price controls had never worked, even when capital punishment had been used to enforce them under the emperor Diocletian, Reagan added the comment, "And I'm one of the few persons old enough to remember that." Another time, in an exchange with Anderson, Reagan asked in apparent astonishment, "John, would you *really* find Teddy Kennedy preferable to me?" Anderson, who had been the star of the Iowa debate and effective in Manchester, found the going more difficult in Chicago. Once he snapped at Bush, saying that Bush's comments reflected the kind of "narrow partisanship" that might be expected of the "former chairman of the Republican Party under Richard Nixon."

Wirthlin's polls in Illinois found that, as in New Hampshire, the debate was widely watched by persons who intended to vote in the primary and that they thought Reagan, by a wide margin, was the winner. He also was the winner on election day, with 48.4 percent of the vote compared to 36.7 percent for Anderson and only 11 percent for Bush. It was the first time in a major industrial state that Reagan demonstrated the ability to attract working-class crossover voters, an appeal which became an important thrust of his fall campaign. Already, Reagan was campaigning almost entirely against Jimmy

Carter. And from now through the last round of primaries June 3, it would be Carter rather than his Republican opponents whom Reagan mostly had in mind.

Reagan's appeal to working-class voters was rooted both in his own background and in the findings of pollster Wirthlin on who the best targets for a Reagan campaign would be. Reagan has been a millionaire for years, but he grew up as a New Deal Democrat with vivid memories of his father being fired during the Depression. He has always believed that he can speak the language of the working class and he demonstrated this to a high degree in his successful California campaigns for governor.

From the beginning of the campaign, Wirthlin surveyed Reagan potential with a series of highly sophisticated questions measuring the value systems of voters who were pro-Reagan. Wirthlin found a strong correlation between Reagan support and a "self-assertive" ethic which holds that individuals are responsible for their own actions. This value is widely shared among working-class voters, particularly identifiable ethnic voters who are Catholic or orthodox in religion. Such voters are a necessary target of a Republican presidential campaign because they tend to live in strategically located cities in key states and because their historic voting pattern is Democratic.

These voters, Wirthlin found, tended to agree with Reagan's stands against gun control and abortion. And the values of "family" and "neighborhood" which Reagan extols are also to a large degree working-class values.

There were other confirmations of Wirthlin's findings. A *Boston Globe* poll in New Hampshire, taken at a time when Reagan and Bush were tied, showed the former California governor winning decisively among voters who made less than $20,000 a year and even more decisively among voters who make less than $10,000. Reagan lost Connecticut to Bush, but he carried industrial Bridgeport by a wide margin. *Washington Post* reporter Nicholas Lemann, interviewing Reagan voters in working-class Altoona, Pennsylvania, found that Reagan's appeal had much to do with the old ethic of hard work and upward mobility which is the basis of the American Dream. "George Bush is, to me, the rich kid down the block," Lemann quoted one voter as saying. "How many kids from Altoona are gonna go to Yale? How many have the opportunities he was automatically given? Ronnie Reagan is the grandfather next door. He started with nothing. He's built that American Dream. He's gonna be the guy who really understands Joe Lunchbucket's problems."

The biggest struggle within the Reagan campaign was now with the bank account. Because of the profligacy of the early months, the campaign was bumping up against federal spending ceilings with little money for travel and less for advertising. Reagan's last media spending of any significance came in the crossover primary of Wisconsin. He won big there, with 40.3 percent of the vote to 30.6 for Bush and 27.6 for Anderson, in effect knocking the Illinois congressman out of the race and into his independent candidacy. However, it was only April 1, with two months of primaries to go. From now on, Reagan was a sitting duck vulnerable to a big-spending media campaign, as Bush showed in defeating Reagan in Pennsylvania April 22 and coming close to him in Texas May 3. But back at headquarters in Los Angeles, Bill Casey, Reagan's campaign chairman, and his allies were beginning to win the battle of the books.

For campaign treasurer Bay Buchanan, the campaign had been a frustrating experience. She had warned as early as January 5 that the spending level of the Reagan campaign was dangerously high, but no one seemed to be paying attention. Sears said that everything would come out all right. The Californians, who later would blame Sears for most of the trouble, seemed unable to get a grip on things either. Had Reagan lost in New Hampshire, no matter what the reason, he seemed likely to lose the nomination because he lacked the resources for a long fight.

The handful of reporters regularly covering the Reagan campaign at this point found out how bad things were on March 6, when Casey abruptly cancelled three airplane charters in the South, leaving reporters stranded in Columbia, South Carolina, while the candidate took off on a small jet to Atlanta. Various loyal staffers in Washington and Los Angeles received an even less pleasant message the same week, often from Casey himself. The staffers, some of whom were barely thanked for their services, were told they had been fired. Most persons in the campaign with strong ties to Sears already had been purged or had left of their own accord. One Reagan aide, recalling the days of the Nixon shake-up of the Interior Department after the firing of Secretary Walter Hickel, echoed an old joke: "If my boss calls while I'm at lunch, get his name." But Casey, with the assistance of Buchanan and Verne Orr, a former Reagan state finance director in California, succeeded in doing what needed to be done. The campaign's last half million dollars, the only contingency fund available, was saved for the Republican convention. The eventual withdrawal of Bush on May 26 meant that the Republican National Committee could begin to spend some of its funds on the fall campaign. However, the survivors on the Reagan staff would never forget what "the money situation," as they called it, had meant. "We would have become totally dependent on California," said one of them in the week after Reagan's narrow victory in Texas. "If we hadn't stopped the hemorrhaging when we did, we would have had the candidate at home, literally unable to campaign."

Reagan was still winning. He won on the basis of natural strength in such states as Kansas, Louisiana, North Carolina, Tennessee, Nebraska, Idaho, Nevada and Kentucky. He won on the basis of superior organization in New York, Indiana and Maryland. He lost in Connecticut, the most convincing of Bush's several home states. He lost in Pennsylvania, where he was heavily outspent. He lost in Michigan by nearly 2 to 1 after Gov. William G. Milliken gave Bush the most effective support of any politician during the entire campaign. It no longer mattered, however, because the story the next day was how Reagan's victory in Oregon, also on May 20, had clinched the nomination for him.

The amazing thing about Bush's candidacy was not that it failed, but that it kept going as long as it did. No one took more beatings. No one was written off more. No one bounced back with more tenacity. Bush came out of Iowa as the first hot media candidate of 1980, the Texas Yankee with the energy and resume that wouldn't quit. His picture, jogging ahead of the pack, suddenly appeared on the cover of *Newsweek*. His name was on television every night. His quick rise and fall provides some of the most telling commentary on the state of politics in 1980. "Geez, the ups and downs of this business, the triumphs, and tragedies—it's a bitch isn't it," media adviser Goodman said later.

His advisers attribute the fall to a failure to adapt to cir-

cumstances after Iowa. When asked what went wrong, they
invariably went back to the meeting in Des Moines on January
18 when the decision was made not to stick with the same
strategy that had served them so well up to that point. Bush's
failure, one adviser said, "wasn't a failure of precinct organization or advertising." Rather, it was a failure in character and
strategy on the part of the candidate, an over-reliance on momentum. Bush called the momentum Iowa gave him "Big Mo."
He embraced it. He boasted about it. The pamphlets and advertisements his campaign produced talked of little else. But
when the momentum disappeared, Bush was left naked. "When
you looked behind Bush's campaign, there was nothing there.
He was a hollow shell . . . People thought he was a lightweight,"
said Dick Bennett, one of Anderson's pollsters. "We didn't
put the issues base under the momentum like we should have,"
conceded campaign manager Baker.

After Illinois and Wisconsin, Bush sharpened his positions
on issues, and attacks on Reagan. He won a few impressive
victories, helped along by his campaign's skillful managing
of funds which allowed him to mount major media efforts at
a time when Reagan was broke. His advisers kept hoping the
victories would change the tide, and build up to a grand finale
on June 3. But the perception of the Bush candidacy had
changed. He was regarded as a hopeless loser, no matter how
hard he tried to come back. Every time a reporter rejoined
Bush's traveling entourage, they were asked, "You writing
another Bush obituary?"

Every campaign has its own cadence and rhythm, an atmosphere that sets it apart. Bush's marched to a country music
beat. This was partially due to Bush's professed fondness for
country music and the open comfortableness of his staff. But
it also reflected the genuine country blues quality about his
campaign, a combination of frustration, down and out despair
and eternal hope. Two songs played constantly on a tape recorder at the back of Bush's campaign bus captured this mood.
The first was a Jimmy Buffett tune, adopted as the unofficial
campaign theme song. It reflected the weariness of the endless
days of campaigning and late night drinking habits of the press
and his traveling entourage. It went like this:

> My head hurts. My feet stink
> And I don't love Jesus.

It's that kind of morning.
Cause it was that kind of night.
I'm telling myself my condition is improving
If I don't die by Thursday,
I'll be roaring Friday night.

The second, such a favorite that Bush used several lines from it in a press conference, was a Kenny Rogers song, called "The Gambler." The key lines went like this:

You've got to
know when to
hold 'em
Know when to
fold 'em
Know when to
walk away.
And know
when to run.

In the end, Bush didn't want to quit, and those last final days were wrenchingly painful for the happy warrior of the 1980 presidential race. He was a man torn between his head and his heart. His advisers told him it was time to drop out. The numbers told him he was finished. But he had invested too much of his time and soul. He had run too long, been underestimated too long, come back too often. So, he kept campaigning, cut off from his closest friends and advisers, wrestling with what he called "the toughest decision of my life" in one of the worst Holiday Inns in America, located in a smelly swamp off the New Jersey Turnpike. When he finally returned to his home in Houston, he anguished two full days before deciding the inevitable.

He announced he was finished in the same hotel Connally had three months before, saying it went against "my every gut instinct, my every bit of training."

But this time Republican voters had lost interest in a race they regarded as over. The GOP primary turnout had increased 32 percent in Massachusetts over 1976, 46 percent in Illinois and 52 percent in Wisconsin. By the time of Michigan the turnout was down 49 percent from 1976. And it was down, also, in most of the nine states which voted in the final round of GOP primaries on June 3, after Bush had dropped out of the race and only the coronation of Reagan at the Republican convention remained.

Reagan had begun the campaign as the front-runner whose ancient agenda had prevailed within his own party and had in many respects determined the dialogue for the presidential campaign of 1980. The doubts about him, at least among most participants in the Republican primaries, were personal rather than philosophical. He would never have won if this were not the case, would not have won if the time had not been right for him. But it is difficult, also, to dispute the accuracy of Reagan's own assessment that he would not have won either, if he had not changed his strategy and climbed aboard that bus in New Hampshire or if he had not debated Bush and the other candidates in New Hampshire and Illinois. "We had more respect for their candidate than they did," said David Keene after Reagan had ducked the first debate in Iowa. As it turned out, Reagan also had more respect for himself than his strategists had. "There was no magic," says Wirthlin. "The candidate won the primaries." And Meese, agreeing, adds this thought: "I think we did better than we had any right to expect."

★ III ★

The Parties

William Greider
David S. Broder

★ Republicans ★

By William Greider

BY MAY, when the carpenters began to construct the three-story television anchor booths inside Detroit's new Joe Louis Arena, the suspense was already gone from the event. Even the densest television producers knew by then that when the Republicans assembled in convention in July the nominee, without question, would be Ronald Reagan. It was likewise obvious to them that the three great national networks had put forth more than $7 million in order to broadcast a turkey.

Reagan's competition for the nomination was not merely weak and outnumbered; it was gone. One by one, the rivals had studied the primary returns, counted their delegates and their dwindling campaign funds and, in the gracious manner of loyal Republicans, dropped out. Dole and Baker, Crane and Connally, and finally the last, lone eagle of resistance to the Reagan movement, George Bush—all stepped aside and said the requisite number of words about party unity and their new fealty to the former movie actor.

The news media, reporters and editors, producers and correspondents, were feeling a bit sheepish about their own reflexive behavior, as they prepared to send casts of thousands—6,000 of them, in fact—to cover an event which they all agreed would be devoid of essential news. How dumb, how boring, they said to one another. Never again, they vowed.

In the meantime, with their troops already committed to expensive hotel accommodations, they tried to imagine plausible reasons why they were still going to Detroit and what they could possibly write about, in the absence of real news. Some imagined, with the kind of perverse nostalgia only reporters would indulge, a city in riot, like Chicago in 1968, a week of diverting turmoil in which the poor blacks and unemployed industrial workers of the Motor City poured forth to vent their anger on innocent Republicans. Some remembered the conservative hour of 1964, the vengeful spirit of the Republican convention which nominated Barry Goldwater, and they foresaw a replay of that self-defeating orgy of purist extremism. Others dwelt upon the vice presidency, the morsel of suspense which remained in whom Reagan would select as a running mate, a question which would bore them if there had been anything else available. Still others settled on a modest, intangible question that events in Detroit might help to answer: What sort of leader was Ronald Reagan, now that he was in triumph and control of the Republican party? And what was the nature of this conservative movement that he led on its stubborn, 20-year crusade to win the soul of the Grand Old Party? These were valuable questions, but not exactly the stuff of screaming headlines.

The cynical expectations were misplaced. Notwithstanding the fluff and fakery and boilerplate oratory which are always associated with these undertakings, the 32nd convention of the Republican Party became, in its own tone and flavor, a pivotal event of 1980, one of those rare, clarifying moments in politics, when ideas and feelings merge successfully into a broadly worded message. In the sum of its party, the Republican convention broadcast a rather joyful message to the uncommitted voters who were watching and listening: the meaning of Republican has changed. In place of the party's old scolding, exclusionary style, there was a new open-armed and confident movement, one that has suppressed the nativist resentments of its past. Through its candidate, the convention broadcast a rather clear warning to the Democratic opposition: the majority party would not in 1980 be able to paint Ronald Reagan into the old nay-saying corner, the way it had so easily characterized Republican candidates since the baleful days of Herbert Hoover—against the working man, against the security systems erected by the New Deal, against growth and prosperity for average Americans. Ronald Reagan, whatever else one would say about his qualifications, was leading the Republican party to new ground—not with the rancor of purists but with the good-natured optimism of people who believed that they had seized the future and events would deliver them into power.

"Four years ago, they wouldn't listen to us," William Evans, a San Diego businessman was saying on the convention floor, wearing the white cowboy hat that was the trademark of Reagan's homestate delegation. At the airport, Evans encountered the New York delegation which, at the Republican convention in 1976, had helped to defeat his candidate. "Now they were all wearing Reagan buttons and all gung ho. It kind of restores your faith," he said.

Like so many of the Reagan delegates who came to Detroit, who controlled more than three quarters of the convention votes, Evans has been among the conservative faithful for nearly a generation. He heard Ronald Reagan's speech at the ill-fated 1964 convention which nominated Goldwater and he became a convert. That man should be president someday. Someday he will be. If people will only listen. Finally, after two unsuccessful campaigns, the country was listening to Reagan and Evans was fulfilled, not doubting what the results in November would be, feeling charitable toward the vanquished, even toward that old nemesis, the liberal press.

"I think the national press has been very good to Ronald Reagan," Evans observed pleasantly. "In the last six weeks," he added shyly.

On the convention floor, while a drum-and-bugle corps blared patriotic anthems or preliminary speakers droned through inconsequential speeches, the Reagan delegates shared their own sense of history, of the significance of what they had accomplished and the great watershed which they felt sure was ahead for America. "The country," as Bill Tribe, a furniture dealer from Ogden, Utah, put it, "is just exploding with conservatism."

Tribe, like so many delegates, carried his own Instamatic camera to capture the moment. He had a sunny, sunburnt face and gee-whiz manner, as he patiently explained to an Eastern reporter how the nation was on the brink of a great decision—either to pull back from the morass of the liberal welfare state and save itself or to sink forever beneath the tyranny of all-powerful government.

"This is our last chance to turn around the liberal philosophy," Tribe said. "By 1984, about 60 percent of all the employables will be working directly or indirectly for the federal government. That coalition can't be turned around. This is the last gasp for free enterprise."

Larry Pepper, a 35-year-old lawyer from Vineland, New Jersey, attending his first national convention, drew the portrait which held these Reagan delegates in thrall:

"Ronald Reagan's America would be back to grassroots principles and old-fashioned American ideals. I think we'd see an America that began to look again at the work ethic, at production, entrepreneurship, an America where the family unit became once again important, back to the traditional values that made America great."

The Reagan conservatism, as these delegates suggested, was, first of all, a coalition built upon sentiment, the terrible feeling that something was lost from the American experience and that we must go back and find it, restore it to the pantheon of shared values. Family. Freedom. Love of country—the simple verities which seemed tarnished and corrupted by an age of complexity, in which the United States lost foreign conflicts or was humiliated by unwashed terrorists, in which Washington wrote rules for the most obscure corners of commerce and industry, in which groups once closeted as deviants or shunned as the racial underclass were now "liberated" by the new fashion of tolerance and even assisted by the government programs of affirmative action.

Joe Walker, a schoolteacher from Tallahassee, Florida, saw Reagan as a unifying force: "We're adrift now and we're going to get that patriotism back. America is longing for this unity, to get back to the basis of what this country's all about."

But, beneath this glow of confidence and sectarian conviction, there was another feeling widely shared among most Reagan delegates—a sense of political practicality which had been missing in all the previous chapters of this conservative movement's long struggle for dominance. In 1964, having captured the nomination for Goldwater, they took splenetic delight in driving away the moderates of their own party and offending virtually every voter group identified as Democratic. That uncompromising spirit, expressed by the candidate and his followers, produced in the autumn of 1964 one of the great landslide defeats of American history; it elected a Democratic majority to Congress powerful enough to enact most of the liberal agenda, programs which had waited a full generation for political triumph. Medicare for the aged and the poor, more federal aid to schools, a network of social programs, from job training to pre-kindergarten classes for poor children, which reached breathlessly for an awesome liberal goal, nothing less than eliminating poverty in America.

The Reaganites had learned something from defeat. It was as though they had studied the election disaster of 1964 and puzzled over why Americans did not eagerly embrace their candidate when Reagan ran for the nomination in 1968 and 1976. If Reagan's message was self-evidently what Americans wanted, why was it so difficult to sell? The answer, as it permeated the conservative perspective, explains why the Detroit convention was a pivotal political event. For, when they gathered in triumph, the Reaganites were tempered by their own sense of tolerance; they recognized that, first, they could not dismantle the New Deal in one clean stroke without terrifying the majority, the citizens who depended, either directly or at least psychically, on the security networks constructed by liberalism, and, second, they could not reach across to those great vote pools of traditional Democrats without extending a friendly hand to them. In short, they knew they were different from the Democratic majority and, in order to win a national election, they would have to build bridges. To those who work with their hands, to families who will never see the inside of a country club, even to black Americans who had watched only a few years before as the Republican Party attempted to exploit racial antagonism.

They were different, these Republicans assembled in Detroit: richer, more conservative, older, whiter, more Protestant than the profile of America itself. According to survey data collected by the *Washington Post* and CBS News, only 3 percent of the delegates were black (compared with 15 percent of the Democratic delegates who went to New York in August). Only 4 percent were members of labor unions (compared with 27 percent of the Democratic delegates). Only 29 percent were women (compared with half of the Democrats). The Republican delegates, as one might expect, were overrepresentative of business, particularly small business, and underrepresentative of government employees (while the Democratic Convention was distorted in opposite directions—15 percent of the Democratic delegates were schoolteachers).

In any case, what really set these Republicans apart from the voting center was their beliefs. They were, issue by issue, well to the right of the majority and they knew it. The Equal

Rights Amendment, despite its failures in the ratification process, was supported by two thirds of the citizenry; 70 percent
of the Republican delegates opposed it. A majority of Americans favor comprehensive national health insurance; 88 percent of the Detroit delegates were against it. On down the list
of policy viewpoints, the Republicans opposed those positions
which a majority of the public has consistently embraced: a
government guarantee of jobs for everyone willing to work,
wage and price controls to halt inflation, gas rationing instead
of higher gas prices. These conservatives believed, on the other
hand, that the federal budget should be balanced, even if it
means cutting those liberal social programs.

And yet, recognizing the differences, knowing the difficulty
of selling their beliefs to others, the delegates in the main
expressed a pragmatism which they had lacked in their past
battles. The *Washington Post* survey asked the Republican
delegates what advice they would give to their nominee for the
fall campaign. While some answered with the old sectarian
spitefulness ("Do not compromise in order to get votes" and
"Continue to shoot from the hip"), the overwhelming theme
of the responses was: be reasonable.

"Listen to the broad spectrum of the public and do not mold
ideas but accommodate those views in policymaking," a very
conservative delegate from Georgia advised.

A Reaganite from Washington state suggested: "Make certain you select a running mate with a light conservative background or you'll turn too many people off."

"Temper your ideology with pragmatism—up to a point,"
said a Republican office holder from Virginia, a woman who
regards herself as very conservative. "Don't depend totally on
the right wing groups. Be sensibly conservative."

A Utah lawyer advised: "Talk to the working man, the man
who carries the lunch bucket. That's where we'll win or lose."

This was all good advice. It was, after all, the common
sense of electoral politics. What made this advice remarkable—
and potentially historic—was that the Republican nominee of
1980 was actually following it.

★

On Monday, the opening day, 4,500 distraught Republicans
marched through downtown Detroit, demonstrating their contempt for the party's platform, specifically its refusal for the

first time in 40 years to endorse the Equal Rights Amendment. The protest was moderate, like the people themselves, but the distress was real enough. They had lost, totally, in the pre-convention skirmishing over platform-drafting and the right-wingers had won. The protesters included the wife of the governor of Michigan, Rep. Margaret Heckler of Massachusetts, Sen. Charles Mathias of Maryland, Senate GOP Whip Ted Stevens of Alaska, a who's who of middle-of-the-road Republicanism. "Dwight Eisenhower endorsed ERA, Richard Nixon endorsed ERA, Gerald Ford endorsed ERA," bellowed Jill Ruckelshaus, party activist and wife of a Nixon Administration executive. "But something happened in Detroit last week. Give me back my party!"

Along the parade route, one heckler held up this sign: "ERA Libbers. Read the Bible. Repent while there is still time." Everyone knew that the platform would be ratified as drafted and it was. The minority of delegates who wished to fight over restoring the ERA endorsement did not even have enough support on Tuesday evening to bring the issue to the floor for a full-scale, prime-time debate. The Republican Party had changed and it was the Bible-reading hecklers whose views prevailed. They called themselves the Moral Majority.

A video evangelist from Lynchburg, Virginia, the Reverend Jerry Falwell, one of the Baptist preachers who organized evangelicals for political action in 1980, found himself widely quoted at the Republican Convention. He obliged interviewers with fulsome descriptions of his own political power, the millions of Christians whom he was mobilizing in behalf of Reagan. He made occasional threats and warnings; if the party strayed from the moral agenda, if Reagan selected a tainted running mate, the Rev. Falwell might take his Christians back to church and tell them to sit on their hands. This fundamentalist crusade, delegate Don White of Alaska explained, "does not represent any religion. We represent morals. We're pro-life, pro-family, pro-morals and pro-America." In translation, that meant the complex of social issues which the Reagan platform expressed in concrete policy positions. For the traditional American family and against the ERA which was seen as threatening to it. For restoring prayer in public schools, against equal rights for homosexuals. For a constitutional amendment to prohibit abortions, against the busing of school children for racial integration.

These platform planks, some of which went a bit further

than Reagan's political managers had wished, represented an essential glue in the building of Reagan's coalition. In spirit, they expressed the troubled orthodoxy of American life, the fears of people confronted by vast social changes and deviations from tradition. They spoke to the longing for restoration, the return to the simple verities that delegate Larry Pepper foresaw. Whether that was a practical political objective, whether in fact government had the power to reverse deep social changes like the modern feminist movement, there was no question that millions of Americans shared in the discontent. Would the Republican Party be able to deliver what it was promising? Probably not, but that is not a consideration which deters people who are mobilized for political action by their own moral concerns. The conservatives who wanted government to restore a regular order to American social values—no abortions, no equal rights for homosexuals, no pornography, no more social engineering by government—believed they would triumph because they believed they were right, just as an earlier generation of liberal Americans devoted their energies to the civil rights movement, in the face of extraordinary political obstacles, because they believed racial equality was right.

In any case, the Rev. Falwell and like-minded delegates represented only one element at the convention, a special-interest group of sorts like all the schoolteachers who turned up as delegates under the National Education Association banner at the Democratic Convention. The Reagan platform and his candidacy would play to their political goals, would recite the code words which excited their loyalty, but the crusaders would not be allowed to run things. The evangelicals were welcomed as followers in the movement and their needs were addressed but, when hard political choices were made, they were not the leaders in Detroit or in the campaign that followed. Indeed, some of them went home from the convention feeling disappointed, even betrayed by their candidate's pragmatism.

Some commentators, dreaming of the discord of 1964, listened to the ramblings from Rev. Falwell and others and concluded that a mean-spirited authoritarianism dominated the convention. They saw a frightening reactionary movement being born and offered cheap comparisons with the rise of Fascism. They missed the evident joy of the event and the rather important ideological realignment which was underway in the Republican Party, accompanying the social theme but dwarfing them in importance.

Roughly speaking, the Republican Party had played the national scold for 40 years, the permanent nay-sayer who objected to every new idea, who smugly dismissed the claims of the underprivileged and insisted that counting pennies at the national treasury came before social security for all citizens. This is caricature, of course, but it seemed accurate enough to voters that Democratic candidates could regularly win congressional seats and the White House by describing the choice in those terms. Are you a Democrat who works for a living and believes in progress, who is compassionate and practical, who wants growth and prosperity? Or are you a Republican who dines at the country club and clips coupons and worries most about a balanced budget? Most Americans, not surprisingly, called themselves Democrats, when the choice was put that way, and the Republican Party was a shrinking organization, representing only one fifth of the adult populace.

Now, in the summer of 1980, the Republicans made a bold grab for the high ground. They were the ones now preaching growth and prosperity. They were the party of progress and hope and it was the Democrats, in the person of President Carter, who had become the scolds. Forget the caricature, elect Ronald Reagan and let the good times roll.

Rep. Jack Kemp of New York, the quarterback who retired from Buffalo's pro football team to become the city's glamorous congressman, was the leading apostle of this new Republicanism. Reagan did not invent it and seemed considerably less enthusiastic about some of the new economic theory than did its younger advocates like Kemp, but the nominee's general belief system was completely compatible with the tone and direction of the new rhetoric. Indeed, Reagan had been running on a generalized version of the same theme for years. The theme was optimism. It used to belong to the Democrats. But when Kemp, a potential choice for Reagan's running mate, addressed the convention in midweek, he niftily reversed the images of the two political parties. Somehow, he began, the country has lost its vitality, America's robust faith in its own strength.

"Even President Carter senses this," Kemp told the delegates. "But somehow he has persuaded himself that *people* are to blame. One year ago tonight in a televised address, he told us that the country is in the grip of a malaise, an economic and social crisis of confidence. 'Too many of us now tend to worship self-indulgence and consumption,' Mr. Carter lectured us in that speech. He told us we are demanding too much, expecting too much, and are too unwilling to give. His solution is to impose limits on us, to shrink our opportunities for personal and national growth.

"Again and again, in word and deed, Jimmy Carter has clearly stated his belief that people are the problem and austerity is the answer.

"Ladies and gentlemen, austerity is not the answer. Austerity is the problem. And the American people are not the problem. They are the answer.

"This Malthusian idea that 'less is more' is nonsense. Less is less. You can't help America's poor by making America poor. But the policies of this administration are making the whole country poorer."

Kemp and the hardy band of young Republican thinkers had something more to offer than artful rhetoric. They had ideas which were new—at least new to Republicans. They jettisoned the old anti-union bromides that were once the boilerplate of Republican oratory and replaced them with broad appeals to working people. Organized labor is not the problem. Business is not the problem. The problem is the federal government and how it mismanages, wastes and depreciates the wages and assets of ordinary working people.

The message had a resonance with many Americans who were Democrats, at least in their inherited status. Political loyalties had been weakened for both parties, but the appeal of the GOP's new theology really sprang from two separate economic facts. First, in the postwar prosperity, millions of laboring families had struggled upward, found secured lives which allowed them to see themselves and their children's futures—not as oppressed workers, struggling against heartless capitalists—but as solidly middle-class. They owned homes in the suburbs, they hoped for a new car every few years and college for the kids, perhaps a boat or even a cabin at the lake. For these people, the Democratic Party which had been their voice and protector, the faith of their fathers, now represented something else as well: the party of government spending and high taxes and, worst of all, outrageous inflation.

The second economic fact was the outrageous inflation. It had persisted through the 1970s, regardless of the shifting government policies to combat it. If the Keynesian rules of economics by which liberal Democrats had produced prosperity were not quite dead, they were certainly badly tattered. If a labor family, newly arrived at middle-class status, saw government gradually pulling them off that comfortable plateau, eroding their paychecks and savings with inflation, that family began to see things differently—more like Republicans.

These anxieties leaped over the usual boundaries of class interests, the economic divisions which had worked so effectively to sustain Democratic hegemony. A steel worker, among the best-paid industrial workers in America, might be as upset by inflation and stagnated economic growth as that country-club Republican who worried about the stock market. Kemp, knowing his party already had the stock market investors, was talking directly to the steel workers.

What the Republicans of 1980 promised as remedy was something called "supply-side economics," which meant a series of huge federal tax cuts, meant to restimulate the private sector, launch a new era of economic expansion and halt, permanently, the growth of government. The rhetoric was different, but the fundamental theory was an exaggerated version of the old Democratic philosophy: cut taxes to stimulate growth and the expanding economy will return more tax dollars soon enough to the federal treasury. Indeed, when challenged, Kemp would say that he was merely proposing what John F. Kennedy had done so successfully in the early 1960s—a tax cut which stimulated investment and also redistributed spending money to consumers, launching the long period of high growth of the middle sixties.

There was one flaw in the comparison—a potential danger which President Carter would exploit fully as an issue in the fall campaign. When John Kennedy proposed his tax cut legislation in 1962, the annual inflation rate fluctuated around 2 percent. If the government applied the same fiscal dynamics to the economy of the 1980s, when the inflation rate zoomed in and out of double figures, it could produce monstrous federal deficits which would touch off even scarier inflation. Carter called Kemp's plan irresponsible and many mainstream economists, including Republican economists, agreed.

In a sense, that debate completed the role reversal of the two parties. In 1980, either as an act of political courage or simply by mismanagement, President Carter had followed the old Republican formula for curbing inflation—raise interest rates, hold down the budget deficit, induce a recession with higher unemployment—in order to bring down inflation. Roughly speaking, it worked. But the Republicans, instead of applauding, were fundamentally changing the argument. They attacked Carter for his heartless policy which put so many Democratic voters out of work; they promised a new tomorrow of growth and prosperity, not unlike the old Democratic promises of the liberal past. Would voters believe them? That question, as much as any other, would decide the election.

But one other bridge had to be crossed in order to make this new Republican Party convincing to once-hostile constituencies. The Republicans must reassure the vast majority that, notwithstanding the purist conservative speeches of other seasons, the New Deal was here to stay. Ronald Reagan would not try to dismantle the main engines of economic security constructed by modern liberalism—Medicare, Social Security, unemployment compensation and the others. He would not continue the longstanding right wing crusade to break labor unions. He would not attempt to repeal the fundamental victories of the civil rights movement or even to disturb greatly the huge troughs of federal aid which nourished schools and colleges, housing and highway industries and agriculture. This message was embedded in the Republican platform, explicit and contradictory to the other theme of opposition to the federal government. It was intended to pacify the many sectors which might feel threatened by a huge cut in federal spending. Fear not, the platform said, without ever quite explaining how America could cut the size of the federal pie and yet no one would lose their slice.

To consumers, to small businessmen, to farmers and senior citizens, the Republican platform promised that the old guarantees would not be disrupted, but made better—less costly, less encumbered by bureaucracy—if power and dollars were shifted away from Washington and to other control points, state and local governments, private institutions like church schools, families themselves. To suspicious groups, the party made direct promises.

To organized labor: "Wage demands today often represent the attempt of working men and women to catch up with government-caused inflation and high taxes. With the blessing of the Democrats' majority in Congress, the Council on Wage and Price Stability has put a de facto ceiling of 7 to 8½ percent on workers' wages, while the Administration devalues their paychecks at a rate of 13 to 15 percent. The government, not the worker, is the principal cause of inflation."

To blacks: "We remain fully committed to the fair enforcement of all federal civil rights statutes and to continue minority business enterprise and similar programs begun by Republican administrations but bungled by overregulation and duplication during the Carter Administration."

To the urban poor: "Republican programs will revitalize the inner cities. New jobs will be created. The federal government's role will be substantially reduced. The individual citizen will reclaim his or her independence."

Like most political programs, which are derived from the process of coalition-building among diverse interests, the Republican program straddled important contradictions. How could the federal government, for instance, desist from "social engineering" and at the same time fulfill the moral agenda of the Rev. Falwell? Would it not require an increase of governmental power over individuals to prescribe the prayer for school children to recite each day? Or to prohibit, once again, the choice of abortion? Or to exclude homosexuals from certain kinds of jobs? One citizen's decadence is another's liberation. To require orthodox social behavior or to punish deviations implies a new order of government intervention in private lives, repealing the libertarian trends of the last generation.

The economic contradictions were perhaps more serious and threatening to the Reagan movement. If a party ran on a platform which promised that no one would lose his or her share of the pie, if a candidate was elected to the White House by reassuring all the diverse interest groups that he was their ally, the new president would discover soon enough that he had traded away the political power to do much in office. Even in abundant America, you cannot have your cake and eat it too, any more than you can cut federal spending without hurting someone, somewhere. Jimmy Carter, who made similar promises in his own 1976 campaign, learned the hard way that he could not easily assemble the necessary majority against the particular interests. If the Republicans won in 1980, with their version of the "free lunch," they would have to learn that lesson all over again.

But nobody at Detroit talked much about that. Their eyes

were on victory and on their candidate who, in his hour of triumph, revealed some contradictions about himself as well.

Ronald Reagan's week in Detroit was, if the players were faithful to the script, going to have the quality of ritual, like the convention itself. He arrived on Monday in the afternoon, performed briefly at a greeting rally at the Renaissance Center, the gleaming towers by the river, then retired to his penthouse suite on the 69th floor of the Plaza Hotel. While the convention proceeded through its dozens of speakers and pro forma approval of rules and platform, Reagan would remain out of the public eye, letting suspense build. He spent Tuesday laying on hands, in the Biblical manner, meeting with delegations of women and blacks, congressional leaders and mayors, listening and reassuring. This was all necessary to the chemistry of successful party politics, but unexceptional. On Wednesday, after the convention had ratified his own nomination, Reagan would make known—presumably late at night after the TV cameras had gone to bed—his selection as a running mate. On Thursday night, in brilliant climax, the vice presidential choice would be ratified and then Ronald Reagan, candidate for president, would address the nation, via television, in his acceptance speech.

But all of the players did not follow the script and Reagan found himself confronted with a sticky dilemma which tested his capacities in a way that no one had anticipated, a test that revealed weakness as well as strength. Svetlana, the astrologer who writes for the *Washington Post*'s "Style" section on Sundays had predicted as much, but neither the political reporters nor the Reagan high command got the message. She blamed Mercury in retrograde. Her prophecy: "I can say that people selected may not necessarily remain on the ticket and that the results will be not as hoped for. Some changes will occur for Retrograde Mercury implies changes and redeliberations."

As the week began, the hopeful politicians who wanted to be chosen had been winnowed to a short list of those who were real possibilities. Kemp was among them, buoyed by a rather crude campaign among convention delegates to generate an irresistible bandwagon effect. The hall was plastered with Reagan-Kemp placards and hats and balloons, but the presidential nominee had other imperatives besides pleasing the very conservative movement he was leading. Kemp, Sen. Richard Lugar of Indiana, Rep. Guy Vander Jagt of Michigan—all these and a few others would have delighted the hard-core conservatives, including the evangelicals, but this was an opportunity for Reagan to broaden his appeal. If he selected a running mate from the moderate wing of the party, the conservatives led by former President Gerald Ford, Reagan could mobilize them for a vigorous campaign in the fall and, simultaneously, reassure the nation that he was, as so many delegates had counseled him to be, a reasonable man.

How would he choose? Would he be hard-headed and ideological? Or practical in political terms? Would he keep his own counsel, listen to the many voices offering advice but then make his own very private selection? Or would he let events drift along and shape the decision for him? The answers, to the extent that they predict how Reagan would behave with presidential power, were both reassuring and disturbing. John Sears, the masterly political strategist who had been dumped from command of the Reagan campaign following the New Hampshire primary, was now serving as an incisive political commentator for the editorial pages of the *Washington Post*. On the eve of Reagan's selection of a running mate, Sears wrote a prescient description of how Ronald Reagan goes about making decisions:

"By the time a man reaches the age of 69, a large portion of his predictability can be discovered by studying those experiences that were important to him.

"If you're an actor, you get up in the middle of the night to go to work. Your place of business is a set designed to look real. You get into a costume, people bring you coffee, you're made up. A crew in charge of cameras, lighting, scripts and other details moves about. You don't question what they're doing. Someone explains today's scene. You perform. Then you do the same thing over and over again until the director is satisfied. Critics ultimately review the picture. You become used to receiving the credit or taking the blame for a product that was not wholly yours...

"I have been asked many times how Reagan goes about making a decision. The answer is that his decisions rarely originate with him. He is an endorser. It is fair to say that on some occasions he is presented with options and selects one, but it is also true in other instances he simply looks to someone to tell him what to do.

"It is this endorsing process that accounts for the difference between Reagan the campaigner and Reagan's more moderate record as governor of California. The white-carded stump speeches are Reagan the performer playing to a known audience and sending the crowd away with its money's worth. As governor, there was no crowd, merely decisions to be made, only a few of which were very exciting. Reagan sat with his California cabinet more as an equal than as its leader. Once consensus was derived or conflict resolved, he emerged as the spokesman, as the performer."

Sears proved to be uncannily accurate. The selection process, involving scores of consultations, the weighing of options for political benefit, was going on in private. The inner network of Reagan advisers, very conservative men themselves but committed to political practicality, were gently steering toward their own consensus which, in turn, would be presented to the candidate for his endorsement. Lou Cannon of the *Post*, who was probably more closely tuned to the private vibrations of the Reagan command than any other national correspondent, reported on Monday morning that the consensus was settling on one name—George Bush. The choice of Bush, the last challenger to Reagan's nomination, would outrage some of the folks from the Moral Majority, who saw the former CIA director in conspiratorial terms. Bush was a member of the dreaded Trilateral Commission created by David Rockefeller, which many conservatives saw as the vehicle of a one-worlder, neo-communist, Eastern-establishment plot to rule the world. No matter. While these delegates of the fringe would be furious, Bush would cement Reagan's ties to the Ford wing of the party. Bush was a dutiful No. 2 man who would lend the credentials of his Washington experience to the ticket with absolutely no risk that he would outshine the presidential candidate.

In the process of consultation, however, Ronald Reagan and his circle of advisers lost control over events. Late on Tuesday afternoon, the candidate had a ritual meeting with Gerald Ford, the man who defeated him for the nomination in 1976. Reagan asked the expected question: Might Ford himself be interested in joining the ticket? Reagan and his advisers were startled by the answer. Ford did not say no. He gave the kind of hedged

disclaimer—"I think I can help you more on the outside"—
which in political negotiation translates as: maybe, let's talk.
Reagan urged him: "Think it over and don't answer right now."

If George Bush would be good for the ticket, Gerald Ford
would be super. Ford was familiar and trustworthy, if less than
brilliant. He would protect Reagan from the expected Democratic effort to caricature; he would unite the Republican Party's
various elements as no other ticket had since Eisenhower-Nixon
in 1952. A dream ticket, they concluded in the Reagan suite,
and his advisers began immediately to negotiate with the circle
of advisers around Ford, men like former Secretary of State
Henry Kissinger and economic counselor Alan Greenspan, former White House aides Jack Marsh and Bryce Harlow. These
men and others could hardly separate their own interests from
Ford's. Privately, many of them were dubious about Reagan's
abilities and of the quality of advisers in the Reagan camp.
They wanted a Republican victory certainly, but they also
wanted a new administration that would not tear apart their
own moderate policies in domestic management and foreign
affairs. Some of them, just possibly, may also have envisioned
themselves returning to power in Washington after four dull
years as the outsiders.

In any case, a 24-hour private dialogue developed between
Ford's circle and Reagan's and the decisive question became
whether Gerald Ford, ex-president, could return to a lesser job
as Reagan's deputy with some positive assurances that he
would have real influence in government. Reagan responded
generously to the question and directed his staff to explore the
subject in greater detail with Ford's advisers. The Reagan people met with the Ford people Wednesday and, the more they
talked, the more both sides believed that this "dream ticket"
was possible. The Reagan advisers worked up a "talking paper"
which sketched the outlines of an understanding between the
two principals, not a contract for signature, but a summary of
good intentions. Ford, as vice president, would be "super director of the executive office of the president," as one top
Reagan aide put it. He would be given a vital role in the
National Security Council, in shaping the federal budget and
in congressional relations.

But, as the general principles underwent further discussion,
they began evolving into hard bargaining points. What did a
vital role mean exactly? Could Ford veto staff proposals from

elsewhere in the government or from Reagan's own staff? Could he be given power to approve or veto certain key appointments—director of the budget or national security, perhaps cabinet posts like Defense or State?

Reagan and Ford met again on late Wednesday afternoon, amicably and in the same spirit of fruitfully searching for accord. But the tantalizing "dream ticket" was already dying. From the Reagan camp: "They were playing hardball with us. You could say we made a very thorough investigation of creating a dream ticket but the closer we got, the further apart we seemed to get." From the Ford camp: "He (Ford) knew exactly what he was going to need if he went into the government and he knew it was something he probably wasn't going to get."

Other questions ought to have occurred sooner to a politician who regards himself as a true conservative. How could a president truly divide up his executive authority without distorting—perhaps even violating—the Constitutional design of the office? Others more familiar with the realities of power in the federal government were instantly staggered by the naivete of the idea. It took Reagan and his staff an unusually long look in order to grasp that, even among friends, the concept of sharing presidential powers was not negotiable.

But, first, the former president threw a trick curve into the private discussions. After chatting amiably with Reagan, Ford and his wife Betty went around to the anchor booth of CBS News for a promised interview with the avuncular anchorman, Walter Cronkite. To a bland question about the vice presidency, Ford responded with a startling confession: he and Betty were, yes indeed, thinking about it. "Neither Betty nor myself would have any sense that our pride would be hurt if we went there as number two instead of number one," Ford said.

It was a little like a political black-jacking, televised to the nation. Ford proceeded to ABC's booth where he gave even sharper hints to correspondent Barbara Walters.

Reagan and his advisers were stunned. The candidate was talking with aides in his suite when he noticed Ford on television, discussing with Cronkite something about a "co-presidency." "Is that Ford?" Reagan asked, incredulous. "It was a power squeeze," one Reagan aide complained. "They were putting us in a box."

Indeed, the squeeze nearly worked, for, after Ford's TV appearances, the convention delegates, by now assembled for their evening session, were delirious with speculation and congratulation. The TV correspondents, roaming the floor and interviewing random sources, picked up the unconfirmed gossip and amplified it to the nation. The authoritative voices of the floor correspondents repeated through the evening the latest bulletins on Gerald Ford's selection as Ronald Reagan's running mate. It was certain now to happen, they reported confidently.

Only it wasn't certain and it didn't happen. In the Reagan suite, they watched the Reagan-Ford euphoria of the TV coverage sweeping the convention—and maybe the nation—along on a deal they now realized was not as ideal as they first believed. Ford's people were now suggesting specific control over specific jobs and it did not take great imagination for the Reagan advisers to see that they might be bargaining away the prize they had worked so hard to win. If Ford chose the secretary of state, for instance, who would he choose but Henry Kissinger, still despised in the Reagan camp and one of the brokers who were arguing for the shared presidency. This would mean, not a Reagan administration with new directions, but "a return of the Ford White House," as one Reaganite complained.

As the evening drew on and the convention's enthusiasm continued to swell, both men realized that the deal would not work. Sometime after 10 p.m. the mutual discussions were terminated. Now, anxious to stop the political damage of false hopes, Reagan turned swiftly to his advisers for the second reasonable choice after Ford. They proposed George Bush, the candidate who they told Lou Cannon earlier in the week was the logical choice. Reagan had little time for further thought. He quickly endorsed their suggestion and, approaching midnight, the word went forth at last. It was not Ford, after all. It would be Bush. Reagan himself drove to the convention hall, disrupting the ritual taboo against having a nominee appear before his acceptance speech, and announced his selection from the podium.

The political damage was negligible. Many of the evangelicals grumbled, complaining that the Trilateralists had triumphed after all, but their anger would subside in time and they would support the Reagan-Bush ticket. What may have hurt more was what the episode said about the Republican nominee. Lou Cannon wrote this analysis afterwards:

"His political instincts are sure and pragmatic. He tries for the best outcome, even if it means a long reach toward the improbable. His decision-making, however, can be hesitant and reactive. He lets himself be pulled along by events, listening to this group and that group. Sometimes those events can pull him off the track he wanted to follow."

Cannon ended with an unanswered question: "The lingering doubts that always have been there were heightened by the episode. This time Reagan came to the rescue of his own confusion. What would happen, as president, if he did not get there in time?"

★ Democrats ★

by David S. Broder

THE FIRST phase in the struggle for the presidency ended on June 3 with the last of the primaries. Nearly 100 weeks had gone by since the first candidate announced in the summer of 1978; tens of millions of dollars had been spent and 32 million people—about a fifth of the electorate—had taken part in the nominating process. When it was over, little had changed in the public's perception of Jimmy Carter. His character ratings in the Gallup Poll remained high. But doubts about his competence and his ability to lead the country were as deep-seated as ever.

He had another problem. He had won 1,764 delegates in the primaries, 100 more than he needed for the nomination. But he presided over a Democratic Party that was badly divided. These divisions boiled over in the weeks leading up to the party convention in New York and were reflected dramatically in Barry Sussman's preconvention poll of the delegates. In effect, Sussman found two Democratic parties—a moderate to conservative party led by Carter and a liberal-leftist party led, symbolically at least, by Edward Kennedy. They were badly split on a host of issues ranging from national defense to abortion to nuclear power.

Kennedy exploited these tensions and divisions. He refused to acknowledge the reality that he had lost the nomination. He refused to close down his campaign, to make his peace with the victor or to allow the president to begin preparations for the fall campaign.

Ten weeks remained after the primaries until the convention in New York. There was time to put things in order. Accordingly, Carter on June 5 invited Kennedy to the White House for an hour's conversation. Just the two men were present. No advisers were brought in.

It was their first face-to-face meeting since the dedication of the John F. Kennedy Library the previous October, and the alteration in the circumstances could not have been more dramatic—or obvious to either man. Then, on the eve of Kennedy's candidacy, Carter had been the beleaguered incumbent, lagging in the polls, and Kennedy the heir apparent to the nomination. Now, Carter had, as he had promised, "whipped his ass," and done it almost without stirring from the White House.

The meeting was tense—as almost all their encounters had been from the time they had first met in Atlanta on the Law Day celebration in 1974.

Carter had remarked to his own associates that Kennedy, more than any other of the Senate liberals, had held himself aloof during the first 30 months of the Carter presidency; even when they talked, Carter complained, Kennedy never seemed to say what he was really thinking. Carter attributed the coldness to Kennedy's jealousy and to the influence of Kennedy's staff, a group that Carter believed manipulated the senator for their own ideological and political ends.

Kennedy, for his part, was at least as suspicious of Carter. As far back as the 1976 primaries, he observed Carter's rise with distaste, telling one newspaper friend, "Why don't you guys take care of him (Carter), so I don't have to?" Personally, he resented the social snubs from the Carter White House—the belated invitation to the state dinner for Chinese Vice Premier Deng Xiaoping, the pointed exclusion from the Camp David policy talks in the summer of 1979. Substantively, he complained that Carter's personal stubbornness had blocked prospects for an almost-negotiated agreement on a national health insurance proposal that both men could have worked to push through Congress. Politically, Kennedy was seething at Carter's use of television ads attacking his character and credibility while the President stayed out of reach in his White House sanctuary.

"I finally got to see the Rose Garden," Kennedy told the mob of reporters waiting outside the White House, "through a window."

He laughed at his own line, but made no effort to disguise

the failure of the meeting or his own resistance to rapprochement. Judging from what both men said to the press that day, and what each of them subsequently told associates, there was no real communication between them.

Kennedy told reporters that he was still a candidate and had pressed Carter, once again, to meet him in a debate. That, he added drily, "appears unlikely." When Kennedy had finished his sidewalk interview, Carter called the reporters into the Oval Office, confirmed that the discussion had snagged on the debate question and said once again that "the platform process" was the best way to settle the policy differences between the two men.

Carter promised to "bend over backwards" to assure Kennedy and his supporters a voice in the platform, and, as a signal of his sincerity, the Democratic National Committee announced that Rep. Morris K. Udall of Arizona, Carter's most persistent challenger in the 1976 nomination fight and a declared Kennedy supporter, had been asked to make the keynote speech at the convention.

Privately, however, Carter complained that he had asked Kennedy three times during their meeting whether the challenger would support him in the fall campaign. Each time, Carter said, Kennedy refused a direct answer, sliding off into a discussion about the need for a debate.

While Kennedy later said that he knew as early as the night of the Iowa caucuses that his chances for defeating Carter were evaporating, to many of his close associates, the senator seemed in June and July gripped by the belief that Carter's failings as a president and vulnerabilities as a candidate were so obvious that the delegates to the convention would surely, as he put it, "not jump off that cliff." There was a ten-week gap between the last primary and the nominating convention roll call. And that, Kennedy believed, would be a period of soul-searching and sober second thoughts for the Democratic Party.

In fact, nothing like that happened. Carter's shortcomings and vulnerabilities were dramatized. A door was opened that would have let the delegates bolt—to Kennedy or a third candidate—if they had chosen. And nobody moved. Carter's majority on the eventual roll call was almost exactly what would have been expected once the results of the final caucuses were added to the June 3 delegate totals.

What the period between the primaries and the convention revealed—in bold relief—was how fundamentally the nature of the nominating system and therefore of the convention itself had been altered by the "reforms" the Democrats began after their disastrous 1968 convention in Chicago. The arguments of the ten weeks could well prove to be the opening barrage in a counter-revolution against those "reforms." But as Carter understood perfectly well, they could not be undone retroactively in 1980. As he told reporters in the Oval Office after Kennedy's visit, he was confident of renomination "regardless of any conceivable circumstances."

A man in Carter's position might not have been so confident in an earlier era. Old-pro politicians were in control of the nominating process and they liked to prolong the suspense by staying uncommitted as long as possible, in part to enhance their own bargaining position and in part to watch how the contenders stood up to high-pressure situations.

When John F. Kennedy ran in 1960, many in the public believed he cinched his nomination when he defeated Hubert H. Humphrey in the West Virginia primary on May 10. But Kennedy knew better. After that, he had to negotiate for support from leaders of key state and interest-group delegations: Carmine DeSapio, "Soapy" Williams, Walter Reuther, David McDonald. The key endorsements that put him over the top came only on the Sunday before the convention opened, when Richard J. Daley delivered Illinois and David Lawrence and William J. Green, Pennsylvania.

Some of those men and their successors were instrumental in delivering the 1968 nomination to Humphrey, who missed most of the primary filing deadlines because of Lyndon Johnson's late withdrawal from the race. But their power was resented by the backers of Eugene McCarthy and the late Robert F. Kennedy. Systematically, the losers in 1968 set about to change the nominating system, in the party "reform" commissions headed by George S. McGovern, Donald M. Fraser, Barbara Mikulski and Morley Winograd (all of them, except Minnesota's Fraser, allies and supporters of the Kennedy brothers).

It was the "reforms" put through by these Kennedy allies and the like-minded members of the "reform" commissions that operated from 1969 through 1979 which ultimately frustrated the effort of the last of the Kennedys to break Carter's grip on the nomination.

At the level of rhetoric—and, in some cases, belief—the thrust of the commissions was to shift power from "the bosses" to "the people" by making the delegate-selection process far more "open" and "accessible" than it had been. The theory was that a more "open" convention would also be more "representative" than the 1968 convention had been—at least in the eyes of those who had seen their candidates beaten there.

Some of the "reforms" were long overdue: simple procedural safeguards, requiring, for example, that state parties publish their delegate-selection rules in advance and publicize the dates and times of the meeting place. The idea was to stop the county chairman or governor who simply pulled his delegate list from his pocket and showed it to anyone who happened to be in the room at that moment.

But once past that stage of curing obvious outrages, the "reformers" ran into hard questions—the same kind of questions that confronted the makers of the American Constitution and anyone else who ever tried to establish a representative governing body. The most fundamental were: Who are you representing and how will you represent them?

Almost from the beginning of the discussions, the "reform" commissions began wobbling toward a fateful intellectual confusion between the concepts of representation and participation. The original indictment of the 1968 convention was its alleged lack of representative character: McCarthy and Kennedy had gotten the votes (in the primaries) but Humphrey had been given the nomination.

But, in keeping with the spirit of the times, a period of assertiveness by blacks, women, youths, poor people and other self-conscious groups, the complaint about the "unrepresentative" character of the convention was soon engulfed in the clamor to "open" the convention to greater participation by those enumerated categories of citizens—and any others who might want to come in as well.

The first of the "reform" commissions made clear the underlying ideology when it said, in its report:

> The guidelines that we have adopted are designed to open the door to all Democrats who seek a voice in their

party's most important decision: The choice of its presidential nominee. . . . If we are not an open party; if we do not represent the demands of change, then the danger is not that people will go to the Republican Party; it is that there will no longer be a way for people committed to orderly change to fulfill their needs and desires within our traditional political system. It is that they will turn to third- and fourth-party politics or the anti-politics of the street.

In seeking to channel the social and political movements of the discontented into the Democratic Party, the traditional pragmatism of the victory-oriented professional politician was deliberately downplayed. McGovern, the first man nominated in the new system, rejoiced that "my nomination is all the more precious in that it is the gift of the most open political process in our national history." But he carried only Massachusetts and the District of Columbia. As he later joked, "We opened the doors and windows to the Democratic Party—and everybody walked out."

But that was not the most important of the unforeseen and unintended by-products of "reform." The most significant effect was the explosion in the number of primaries—and that was something no one intended.

As Austin Ranney, a professor of political science and member of the original "reform" commission, has written:

> I well remember that the first thing we members . . . agreed on—and about the only matter on which we approached unanimity—was that we did not want a national presidential primary or any great increase in the number of state primaries. Indeed, we hoped to prevent any such development by reforming the delegate-selection rules so that the party's non-primary processes would be open and fair, participation in them would greatly increase, and consequently the demand for more primaries would fade away.

Exactly the opposite happened. John Kennedy ran in four contested primaries on his way to the 1960 nomination. Eugene McCarthy competed in 11 in 1968. McGovern ran in 16 in 1972; Carter in 26 in 1976; and Kennedy in 34 in 1980. In the most recent year, 70.1 percent of the delegates were chosen through the primary process.

That growth was unexpected—but it was not accidental. In some states, the old-guard politicians, when confronted with the rigorous procedural requirements the new rules set for caucuses and conventions, decided that the simplest way to avoid credentials challenges and all the other hassles was to let the voters pick the delegates directly in a primary.

In other states, the prospect of hordes of "outsiders" and "amateurs" invading the caucuses to support their favorite presidential candidates frightened the "regulars." Far better, they decided, to let the "outsiders" have their fun in a primary, and keep control of important things—like state central committee jobs—in the hands of the few who regularly attend the caucuses.

But the main reason for the upsurge in primaries was the populist, democraticizing, participatory impulse that lay behind the rules "reforms" themselves—the belief that "the people" should prevail over the old powerbrokers. No caucus, however "open," will attract as many participants as a primary; if participation is the goal, why settle for a half-measure?

Besides, it was noted that the television networks were paying ever-increasing attention to the presidential primaries, turning the Tuesday contests into a weekly winter-and-spring entertainment series every fourth year. The way to cash in on the publicity was to run a primary in your state. So the cameras, which had begun remaking general-election campaigns and candidates 20 years earlier, now contributed to the remaking of the nominating system as well.

If the proliferation of primaries was a device for "democratizing" the delegate-selection system, it did not achieve other aims the "reformers" cherished. They wanted to be sure the convention was representative of the Democratic constituency in substantive and not just mechanical terms. But representative in what respect? That has always been the conundrum for theoreticians of democracy, since each individual has so many aspects of personality, character, and viewpoint that no one can truly "represent" another in every regard.

The "reformers" decreed that there were two aspects of the Democratic constituents that were critical to be represented, or, as the jargon of the commissions had it, be given "fair reflection" in convention hall.

One was their dominant demographic characteristics, and the other was their candidate preference. Political experience, past party service, election to public office or organizational leadership of any kind were ruled irrelevant, as were such subjective standards as judgment, reliability or loyalty. Sex and race were critically important. (Age enjoyed a similar cachet at first, but youth lost its political chic when the anti-Vietnam-war protests stopped with the ending of the draft, and many young people turned out not even to be interested in voting.) Over the years, the mandate was written that 50 percent of the delegates be women and that appropriate portions in each state be blacks, Hispanics, Asian-Americans, Native Americans and what-have-you.

A similar but cross-cutting standard was applied to reflect candidate preference. An early and obvious target of "reform" was the unit rule, a relic of bossism that deprived the minority within a delegation from expressing its sincere views. From the abolition of the unit rule, it was a short step to a form of proportional representation, giving each candidate, winner or loser, his share of the votes in the primary or caucus or convention. (A 15 percent cutoff became the accepted minimal standard.)

But then the question arose as to how to assure each candidate that his delegates were sincere supporters. Since these were no longer a handful of political insiders who had dealt with each other over the years, but an assembly of strangers, gathered for the moment, it became necessary to check the credentials of someone who purported to be a supporter of Candidate A—to assure that he was not a "ringer" for Candidate B. It clearly would be as improper to have a B "ringer" sitting in an A delegate's seat as it would to have a male delegate in a female's seat, or a Filipino where there should be an American Indian.

The solution that evolved from successive commissions' struggle with this question was the doctrine of "candidate right of approval"—in effect, a veto power by the candidate or his political staff over the identity of his delegates.

As embodied in Rule 11-H of the 1980 delegate-selection procedures, it said:

"All delegates to the national convention shall be bound to vote for the presidential candidate whom they were elected to support for at least the first convention ballot, unless released in writing by the presidential candidate. Delegates who seek to violate this rule may be replaced with an alternate of the same presidential preference by the presidential candidate or that candidate's authorized representative at any time up to and including the presidential balloting at the national convention."

The same principle was extended to the convention itself in Rule F-3 (c) of the convention call. Both these provisions whisked through the Democratic National Committee with a minimum of debate and no serious controversy. But when the Kennedy forces began searching for a way to prevent Carter's seemingly inevitable nomination, they focused on this loyalty rule.

Talk of challenging the candidate commitments began coming from the Kennedy camp as early as March 19 with the senator himself sometimes hinting in this direction and at other times denying any such intention. But when the last of the primaries and caucuses left Kennedy 700 votes in arrears in committed delegates, it was the only card left to play.

In what some Kennedy aides later conceded was an unexpectedly successful public relations ploy, they adopted the slogan of the "open convention" and began trumpeting the claim that hundreds of Carter delegates—and the Democratic Party itself—were being forced to walk the plank unwillingly by a despotic president.

Even by the standards of presidential politics, there was an extraordinary amount of hypocrisy on both sides of the formal "open convention" debate. Kennedy staff members like Richard Stearns, who had been in the middle of the ten year effort to "reform" the delegate-selection rules, now discovered that they objected to a new form of "bossism"—by the presidential candidates. Carter supporters like South Carolina's veteran Democratic chairman, Donald Fowler, who had fought a dogged rearguard action against the "reforms" of the past decade, now discovered that they contained essential, timeless principles which could not be compromised. George McGovern told a group of reporters over lunch in late spring that "I couldn't go along with Ted" on a challenge to F-3 (c) but ended up in August as Kennedy's main speaker in the convention debate on the issue.

Meantime, behind-the-scenes operators like Carter campaign chairman Robert S. Strauss solemnly invoked the concept of a sacred contract between the 19 million voters in the Democratic primaries and the delegates—implying that only a desperate knave like Kennedy would trespass on such sanctified ground. (Strauss, it must be said, had trouble keeping a straight face about the whole solemn argument. Appearing before New York delegates, he quoted that old Lyndon Johnson line about the novice school teacher in Texas who was asked by the board of education, which was weighing his job application, if he believed the earth was round: "I can teach it round, or I can teach it flat.")

But behind all the made-up arguments and moral posturing was a political reality: Carter was into another of the sudden, sharp descents in public esteem that had marked his presidency and measured the thinness of his personal support.

He had begun 1980 with a 56 percent approval rating in the Gallup Poll, had stayed in the 50s until March, then fluctuated between 38 and 43 percent through May. But about the time of the last primaries, he took a 10 point drop, and when the convention rules committee met in Washington in early July, the last published rating was only 32 percent favorable.

The rhetoric at that meeting was fiery. Veteran liberal Joseph L. Rauh Jr., arguing that for 150 years the Democratic conventions had protected the right of individual delegates to change their minds, said Carter was trying "to turn a deliberative body into a bunch of robots . . . serving in handcuffs." But Don Fowler noted that, in 1972, when Rauh was protesting an effort to change the rules retroactively to the disadvantage of front-runner McGovern, Rauh had argued that "if the rules can be changed at the end of the game, then all that remains is naked political power." The rules committee vote—87 to 65 in favor of locking the delegates to their pledges—exactly mirrored the candidate preference of its members. Which was no surprise to anyone past the third grade.

The next month, however, was unsettling for the Carter forces. Every economic indicator continued to suggest that the "free-fall" recession was continuing. One hostage was sent home from Iran, suffering from multiple sclerosis, and his accounts of his captivity only deepened the frustration about the 52 men and women he left behind. The Republicans staged a successful convention, climaxing with the picture of Jerry Ford holding aloft the arms of Ronald Reagan and George Bush.

And on the second day of the Detroit GOP convention,

Tuesday, July 15, a portion of every front page was occupied by the news that Billy Carter had slipped into the Justice Department the previous afternoon, registered as a foreign agent for the Libyan government, and thereby, apparently, avoided criminal prosecution for having received $220,000 of a promised $500,000 payment (or, as he insisted, loan) from the regime of Muammar Qaddafi.

Brother Billy had been a loose cannon on the deck of the Carter Administration for years. Twelve years the president's junior, Billy ran a gas station in Plains and shared in the management of the peanut-processing business, disguising a shrewd intelligence and voracious reading habit behind the pose of the beer-swilling, profane, redneck good-ole-boy who loved to mock his brother's ambition and sanctimony. When the family business was placed in trust, Billy earned a living through personal appearances at conventions and carnivals— a kind of freak show that he despised as much as it demeaned him. Driven out of Plains by the horde of tourists, he was living in a kind of limbo, when the Libyans made their pitch for him. The outcast brother was an obvious target for an outcast regime, which was vital to the United States as the source of 9.7 percent of its oil imports but was despised for its sponsorship of terrorist activities around the world and its bitter opposition to the U.S. efforts to negotiate a settlement of the Arab-Israeli conflict.

The Libyans invited Billy and some of his Georgia pals to visit in 1978, and in 1979, he played host to a return delegation, using the occasion for some gratuitous anti-Semitic remarks for which his brother, the president, publicly chastised him. Questions were raised then about whether Billy was working for the Libyans, but for months, he stiff-armed the routine inquiries from the Justice Department's foreign agent registration section.

When the horde of reporters returned to Washington from the Detroit convention, they pounced on the Billy Carter story as the best vehicle to get through the summer doldrums. In short order, it was revealed that: a criminal prosecution of Billy had been imminent and he was somehow advised that a registration statement might be prudent; he had discussed the problem with the president's White House National Security Adviser and Legal Counsel and had been referred by the latter to a private attorney; the president himself and his national security adviser, Zbigniew Brzezinski, had enhanced Billy's standing in the eyes of the Libyans by using Billy as a back-channel to persuade Qaddafi to intervene with the Ayatollah Khomeini on behalf of the U.S. hostages, and both had later met with Billy and a Libyan official at the White House; the president had shared with his brother official State Department communications on his trip to Libya and had discussed the foreign agent registration issue with Billy; and, finally, after his repeated denials, the Attorney General, Benjamin Civiletti, had at least casually advised the president that it might be prudent for Billy to file the registration form.

These disclosures, coming serially over two weeks, and often belatedly confirmed by the White House, were enough to generate a special Senate investigating committee and send fresh tremors of nervousness through the Democrats in Congress. The post-GOP convention Gallup Poll showed Reagan leading Carter, 52 to 38 percent, and the President's job rating dropped to an all-time low, 21 percent.

The impact of all this hit hardest among junior Democratic members of the House of Representatives, a conspicuously nervous bunch. Many of them had won in previously Republican districts in 1974, 1976 or 1978; they lived with the fear that in any election, the voters back home would discover that they were Democrats and retire them. Some 40 or 50 of these junior Democrats met on Capitol Hill on July 24 and 25 and threw their support behind the "open convention" drive. Many were Kennedy backers, some Carter supporters, but their spokesmen were not identified with either side. One of them, freshman Rep. Michael Barnes of Maryland, a onetime aide to Ed Muskie, was invited on "Meet the Press" on July 27 and predicted that the "open convention" movement would gain recruits among Democratic governors and then sweep the delegate ranks as well.

As if on cue, independent movements sprang up to "draft" Muskie from the Secretary of State's job, Mondale from the vice presidency or Sen. Henry M. Jackson from his vacation home in Washington state, to lead the Democrats, in unity, to political salvation.

Gov. Hugh Carey of New York added his voice to the chorus and a group of Democratic fund-raisers, who had backed Muskie or Jackson in their past campaigns, enlisted Washington lawyer Edward Bennett Williams as a spokesman for the "open convention" forces.

For about 96 hours, a full-scale revolt appeared to be gathering and the White House was concerned enough that Strauss was ordered back to duty from his annual vacation at the Del Mar, California, race track—a sacrifice of no small importance to him.

And then the "open convention" movement died in its tracks. It died for several reasons. On August 4, a week before the convention was to open, the White House finally assembled a full statement of the administration's involvement with Billy Carter, with supporting documentation, and that night, in an hour-long, prime-time press conference, the president dealt effectively with every question that had been on the case.

Meantime, the "open convention" forces were running into problems. While people like Barnes and Williams and their allies had other candidates they hoped to see nominated, they were never able to separate their efforts from the Kennedy campaign's original try to break the delegate pledges. And as long as Carter and uncommitted delegates thought Kennedy would be the beneficiary of the rules fight, they were not buying.

Nine months earlier—when Kennedy was on top of the polls—there was an element of political prudence. The same polls that showed Carter losing to Reagan showed Kennedy losing worse. And the alternative candidates, Jackson, Muskie, Mondale, were all men who had faltered in their own past bids for the presidential nomination.

But the main reason the "open convention" movement failed was that it ran up against the character of the delegates this kind of selection system produced. These were not veteran Democrats, anxious for a chance to wheel and deal with each other. They were political newcomers—70 percent, in the *Washington Post* survey, attending their first national convention—whose main mission was to support the candidate to whom they had pledged themselves months before. Had they been cast free of their candidate commitment, as the open-convention people were advocating, most of them would have suffered the kind of political anomie that results when a person is stripped of identity.

Moreover, most of them saw no reason to change. The

Washington Post poll, taken from July 22 to July 30, when "Billygate" hysteria was at its height and the polls were most alarming, showed that 98 percent of the Carter-pledged delegates said he remained their personal choice for the nomination. Contrary to the polls, they believed he had an excellent chance of winning the election and they thought his record in office merited reelection.

The original commitment had not been made lightly, because these were not casual people. Whatever the theory of the "reformers" who opened the door to participation in the Democratic delegate-selection process, it was not a random cross-section of the party's constituency that chose to involve itself in the new game. Being chosen as a delegate required attending a great many meetings, understanding the rules, and enlisting others with similar leisure time and intelligence. It was not a game for ignoramuses or those with a marginal interest in politics: two-thirds of the Democratic national convention delegates were college graduates, 40 percent with graduate school training; 61 percent held some other elective or appointive post in the party; and 40 percent were government employees.

As some were quick to note, it was also a game where organized groups with the right kind of membership could become extraordinarily successful. And no group was quicker or more effective in seizing that opportunity than the National Education Association, (NEA) the 1.8 million-member teachers union.

During the 1970s, NEA had transformed itself from a nonpartisan professional lobby at the state and local levels into a highly politicized union. The reason was simple: the younger people moving into its leadership, like executive director Terry Herndon, 41, recognized that teacher salaries, teacher benefits, classroom facilities, and school budgets all depended on decisions made by politicians. As the source of funds shifted from the local to the state to the national level, NEA's political focus shifted with it. And in 1976 the organization made its first-ever presidential endorsement: Jimmy Carter.

But that move came after the primaries and in 1980, Herndon and Co. were determined to play a more conspicuous role. The endorsement of Carter by the NEA board came in September, 1979, when Carter was trailing Kennedy badly in the polls (and when NEA's smaller rival, the American Federation of Teachers, endorsed Kennedy). It was very old-fashioned politics. Carter had delivered on his main promises to NEA: education funding went up 73 percent in the first three years of the Carter Administration and the first Cabinet-level Department of Education was created.

By endorsing Carter early and at a lowpoint in the polls, Ken Melley, the NEA's chief political operative said, "We felt we could demonstrate to other politicians, as well as to Carter, that our endorsement meant something."

Indeed it did. With an average of 6,000 members per congressional district, and a big field staff of organizers in national and state headquarters, NEA was perfectly positioned to move its people into the "open" Democratic delegate-selection system. Teachers were accustomed to going to workshops, taking notes, and learning procedures. Their evenings and weekends were free for political activity. Many could find a personal motivation for helping a pro-education president.

In Iowa, teachers were at work four months before the first caucuses in January, and they elected 12 of the state's 50 delegates. When the Oklahoma Democrats had their state convention in May, they learned that 43 percent of the 932 delegates were teachers. Teachers claimed 14 of the 42 national convention delegate posts, and could have had more.

Overall, more than one out of seven of the Carter delegates—279 in all—were NEA members. With 23 Kennedy supporters, they constituted the second largest bloc in the convention—outranked only by California's 306 delegates.

Teachers also understand discipline—in politics as in the classroom—and the NEA tied its teacher-delegates close to the organization. The Iowa teacher-delegates were given $400 apiece toward their expenses from their fellow teachers' contributions to IPACE, the state association's political action fund, and another $250 from NEA's national political treasury. Those who needed more help could get no-cost loans from a teachers' credit union in Pennsylvania, with NEA picking up the interest fees.

With the help went a claim of loyalty. There were NEA caucuses on every major issue in New York, NEA whips working the convention floor. As George Brown, executive director of the Iowa State Education Association, told its teacher-delegates before they left for New York, "Let me give you a small piece of advice. Your first caucus in New York will be at 3 p.m. Sunday at the Statler, a pleasant 24-block walk from your

hotel. Be there. Because if you don't show, you don't get your
dough."

NEA President Willard McGuire reminded them of their
obligations at the Sunday caucus and said in blunt terms that
they had not been sent to New York to act independently or
in contravention of their policy instructions.

★

A notion has taken hold in recent years that national political
conventions no longer have a function or utility. Since the
nominees are chosen in the primary elections, the argument
goes, the delegates have nothing to do; they are irrelevant or,
in Joseph Rauh's words, have been reduced to the status of
robots. David Brinkley of NBC News observed in New York
that the television networks were covering "rampant inactivity
on the floor."

In fact, however, not everything was preordained when the
Democrats gathered in Madison Square Garden in August.
Three events occurred that might have had different outcomes
and might have affected profoundly the course of that convention and the course of the campaign that followed.

The first was the vote on the celebrated rule F-3 (c) which
required every delegate to vote on the first ballot for the candidate to whom the delegate was pledged.

On the eve of that vote, Kennedy claimed that he was within
50 votes of "breaking the convention open." He was wrong.
With disciplined cadres such as the NEA, Carter's forces won
that test by 540 votes. Carter's nomination was thus assured.
But two other problems remained—the platform controversy
and the necessity, in Carter's view, of winning the support
(if not the affection) of Kennedy and his followers.

On these issues, Kennedy had many cards to play.

Defeated soundly on the rules issue, Kennedy promptly
announced that his candidacy was over and that his name would
not be placed in nomination. But he conspicuously withheld
any endorsement of Carter and made it very plain that he had
not abandoned his plans to make a fight of it on the platform.

From the time of his Georgetown University speech in January, Kennedy had been running an issue-oriented campaign,
insisting that the Democrats must not recant their support of
social and economic programs aimed at the needy, just because

fiscal pressures were pushing the country in a conservative direction.

On that crucial policy question, he spoke for a majority of the delegates. The diversity represented in Madison Square Garden was greater than that of any previous Democratic convention—and far greater than the Republican convention.

By party rule, 50 percent of the delegates were women— up from 13 percent in 1972 and 33 percent in 1976. About 14 percent of the delegates were blacks and 6 percent came from other minority groups.

As Stuart Eizenstat, Carter's chief domestic policy assistant and main spokesman on platform issues said, that kind of convention was "to the left of the country—and of the president" on many issues. "As long as you have to draw your delegates from these groups (activist women and minorities), you are going to have people from the liberal side of the spectrum," he pointed out.

And he was right. In The *Washington Post*'s survey, delegates to both conventions and a cross section of the general public were asked to rank themselves on a scale where 1 was very liberal and 7 was very conservative. The median point for the public was 4.2, significantly to the right of center. The GOP rank-and-file was at 4.6, the typical Democratic voter at 3.9. But the greatest gap was between the two sets of delegates—the Republican being at 5.5 and the Democrat at 2.9.

On specific issues, the liberalism of the Democratic convention delegates was obvious. Some 85 percent favored the Equal Rights Amendment. Some 72 percent opposed balancing the budget if that meant cutting social programs. By a 2 to 1 majority, they favored immediate enactment of a comprehensive national health insurance program, an issue Kennedy had made his own. And most significant for the convention battles ahead, by a ratio of 56 to 39 percent, they agreed with the proposition that the government should see to it that anyone who wants to work has a job.

During the platform hearings preceding the convention, Carter's forces were in control. They put together a platform tailored to Carter's needs but a platform unacceptable in various ways to Kennedy and his allies. His major economic planks were rejected in favor of Carter's "fiscal conservatism." To Kennedy, this meant that the Democrats were preparing to "turn their backs on the millions of Americans who are unemployed or... who are being victimized by higher interest rates or high rates of inflation."

While Carter prevailed on all the essential questions, there was less celebration among his strategists than one would have supposed. Defeating Kennedy was one thing, but sending his 40 percent of the party home empty-handed from the convention was something else.

A confrontation in New York was inevitable.

Richard Moe, an aide to Vice President Mondale, and Paul Kirk, Kennedy's assistant (old friends from their days as heads of Mondale's and Kennedy's Senate staffs), had been meeting for weekly breakfasts at the Mayflower Hotel coffee shop ever since Carter and Kennedy agreed at their June 5 White House get-together that some direct channel of communication was needed. But the meetings had been unproductive until late July, after the Republicans adjourned and the Carter side began to see the need for concessions.

From discussions of convention scheduling, they moved on to more substantive questions. On August 5, an agreement was reached and announced, in which Kennedy was promised a prime-time debate on the economic planks and, in turn, withdrew a number of his secondary platform amendments. A joint statement said, "Whoever is on our ticket, we are determined to conclude our convention united behind our nominees."

But still Kennedy held back a direct pledge of support, saying he wanted to see what the convention did with his plank calling for a $12 billion jobs program, a plank Eizenstat continued to insist Carter would reject.

Even in the Monday statement ending his candidacy, Kennedy said, "I continue to care deeply about where this party stands and I hope the delegates will stand with me for a truly Democratic platform.

"Tomorrow," he said, "I will speak to the convention about the economic concerns that have been the heart of my campaign and about the commitments in the future of the Democratic party. I will speak again for the people I have seen and for the cause I have carried across this country."

The next 24 hours were a building drumroll of anticipation for that speech. The delegates came at midday Tuesday to

Madison Square Garden and it soon became clear that the tight discipline of the rules fight would not prevail on the ideological platform issues.

When Kennedy arrived on the podium, the Garden floor and galleries were a sea of Navy-blue Kennedy posters. Even some Carter delegates joined in waving them. But the senator cut the demonstration short and got into his speech—his expression conveying that this was a moment he had long awaited. Later, some of his aides would say that one reason Kennedy had pressed Carter so often to reschedule the canceled debate was that he wanted the voters to know he was not the mumbling, uncertain man he had appeared to be on the Roger Mudd/ CBS interview, but a political leader who knew his mind and could express himself with power and authority.

He did that and more on that Tuesday night. The speech, written by Robert Shrum and Carey Parker, was a distillation of 1,000 campaign talks. Like William Jennings Bryan's "Cross of Gold" speech to the 1896 Democratic convention, it had gained in repetition.

He had a prime-time audience and he did not miss the chance. His voice was deep and his timing certain, as he hit the rhythm of the text in its opening, cadenced phrases: "I have come here tonight not to argue for a candidacy but to affirm a cause. I am asking you to renew the commitment of the Democratic Party to economic justice. I am asking you to renew our commitment to a fair and lasting prosperity that can put America back to work."

The cheers began with the first sentence, and they continued as Kennedy outlined, in broad strokes, the heart of his platform dispute with the president:

"Let us pledge that we will never misuse unemployment, high interest rates and human misery as false weapons against inflation.

"Let us pledge that employment will be the first priority of our economic policy.

"Let us pledge that there will be security for all who are now at work. And let us pledge that there will be jobs for all who are out of work.

"These are not simplistic pledges. Simply put, they are the heart of our tradition; they have been the soul of our party across the generations. . . . We dare not forsake that tradition."

The cheers were coming from around the hall, but many

of the Carter delegates—recognizing this for what it was, the basic campaign speech of the candidate they had rejected and defeated—were listening in silence.

And then, before they realized what was happening, he had glided on a smooth transition into an assault on Ronald Reagan—the most effective counterattack any Democrat had yet mounted on the Republican nominee.

In five striking paragraphs, he recaptured Franklin Delano Roosevelt from the smothering embrace of Reagan's acceptance speech, transformed the spirit of the convention, and reminded the party's factions that they could cheer and laugh together at the Republicans' expense.

By quoting Reagan against Reagan in such "preposterous" statements as "Unemployment insurance is a prepaid vacation plan for freeloaders," and "I have included in my . . . prayers . . . that the Federal government not bail out New York," and "Eighty percent of air pollution comes from plants and trees," Kennedy showed the Democrats how to isolate Reagan from the Democratic constituencies the Republican nominee had been trying to capture. A man who said such things, he roared, is "no friend of labor . . . of great urban centers . . . of the senior citizen . . . of the environment."

And he brought the delegates to their feet shouting when he indignantly recalled that in 1976 the new Republican nominee had said, "Fascism was really the basis of the New Deal."

"That nominee," Kennedy roared, "whose name is Ronald Reagan, has no right to quote Franklin Delano Roosevelt."

For a full half-hour, the convention let Kennedy's oratory lift it and bring it back down, as he moved through a recital of his views on tax reform, health insurance, and the rest of the liberal litany from opposition to nuclear power to support of the E.R.A.

And in the end, when he spoke of his own failed campaign, he recalled not his own defeats but his meetings with "young workers out of work, students without the tuition for college, and families without the chance to own a home."

It was a bleak and intentionally somber setting for the ritualistic words that followed: "I can congratulate President Carter on his victory here. I am confident that the Democratic Party will reunite on the basis of Democratic principles—and that together we will march toward a Democratic victory in 1980."

As for himself, Kennedy said, "A few hours ago, this campaign came to an end. For all those whose cares have been our concern, the work goes on, the cause endures, the hope still lives, and the dream shall never die."

It was the same peroration he had used at the dedication of the John F. Kennedy Library the previous October, when his own hopes were in the ascendancy, but to the hypnotized, weeping followers in Madison Square Garden, it seemed a promise of another campaign to come. And when he stopped and turned, they let their emotions go in a tumultuous sobbing shout that turned into the first real demonstration of the convention.

On the convention floor, Geraldine Wales of Ardsley, Pennsylvania, a Kennedy delegate, had been sobbing almost uncontrollably during the final moments of his speech. Fifteen minutes later, she was boogeying on her chair, waving her sign, shouting "We Want Ted." A *Washington Post* reporter clambered over the rows of seats to ask her what was happening.

"I worked my ass off for that son-of-a-bitch Carter in 1976," she said, never stopping her motion. "And I feel rotten now, rotten. I'm just trying to get my enthusiasm up so I can work for Carter this fall." Is it working? she was asked. "It's not quite working yet," she said, and she went back to her chanting and swaying.

The convention managers were smart enough to see the demonstration as psychotherapy for bruised egos like Wales's. But they had another reason for letting the demonstration go. A deal was being cut, below the podium, to dispose of the remaining platform issues.

All day, the Carter forces had been trying to find a compromise acceptable to Kennedy on the main remaining economic plank—the $12 billion jobs program. And, insistently, Kennedy had said, "Let's let the convention vote." With the results of the previous roll calls indicating how tenuous was their control, with the impact of Kennedy's speech still palpable in the hall, the last thing the Carter side wanted was a roll call. At best, it would be 45 minutes of prime-time demonstration of the down-the-middle division in the Democratic Party. At worst, it could be another defeat.

The decision was made: give Kennedy his jobs program victory and everything else on the table—except the imposition of wage-and-price controls, which Carter had said he could never accept.

Tip O'Neill was given his instructions and executed them with dispatch. Almost before most delegates knew what had happened (and before CBS could halt a Walter Cronkite monologue and switch back to the podium), O'Neill had intoned his catechism:

"The question is on Minority Report 3. All in favor say 'Aye.' All opposed 'Nay.' In the opinion of the chair, the 'ayes' have it." Twice more, he ruled for the affirmative. Once, in equally indecipherable confusion, he ruled for the nays.

Somehow, in the "reformed" convention, with all its participatory openness, some old-fashioned, backroom politics had prevailed.

Once the platform deal was made, there was little real work left. The final two days of the convention became a sweeping-up exercise and a therapy session aimed at sending the delegates home in the mood to wage battle on Reagan and the Republicans.

The convention roll call Wednesday night confirmed Carter's renomination (and also the tenacity of the Kennedy supporters, 1,146 of whom voted for the withdrawn challenger), and Kennedy promptly issued a statement vowing to "support and work for" Carter's election.

The spotlights from high inside Madison Square Garden shone down on the podium and the band played "Hail to the Chief." The president looked out on the crowd, looked but did not wave or raise his arms as politicians usually did at such moments of triumph. Carter simply looked, enjoying a sight many said he would never see again.

This was not the end of Carter's race against Edward Kennedy but the beginning of his campaign against Ronald Reagan. And as he was on that October Saturday when he flew to Boston to confront Kennedy, he was far behind, some thought in an almost hopeless position.

But by then everyone had learned not to count him out until the ballots were tallied.

The president and his aides were confident that three months later they would be vindicated in the polling places of America.

They were prepared to argue that, despite all the mistakes and reversals, the country was better off because Carter had been its president.

The country was at peace and had been throughout the Carter presidency. The president had proved to be a realistically cautious chief executive in the use of military power.

Carter's record was also not the unmitigated disaster his critics said it was. There were some important achievements: a treaty with Panama, the Egyptian-Israeli peace treaty, diplomatic recognition of China, at long last an energy program, movement toward the deregulation of industry, an overhaul of the Civil Service System.

He had been honest and people believed him. The "scandals" of his administration had been minor league. His judicial appointments, for the most part, had been excellent. His environmental record was strong.

But balancing this were other factors, many of them, the president's aides argued, out of his control, but not out of the minds of voters. He boasted that the work force had expanded at a record rate under his leadership, but by the summer of 1980 the unemployment rate had reversed itself and was higher than when he took office. He assured the country that inflation was abating, but it had been at an almost 20 percent annual rate just a few months before his renomination and was still more than twice the rate he inherited in 1977.

Some of the promises of 1976 lay in ruins. The tax system had not been reformed, nor had the welfare system. There was no national health insurance program, not even hospital-cost-containment legislation. The budget wasn't balanced. He had campaigned for the presidency promising to cut defense spending and was campaigning for reelection by boasting that he had increased military expenditures.

There were American hostages in Iran and Russian troops in Afghanistan but there was not a strategic arms limitation treaty with the Soviets. He had identified and tried to face up to the great issues of the time—energy, arms control, the need to increase the productivity of American workers and streamline the functions of American government. But he had met with only mixed success and the voters were restless.

Carter's political advisers knew this. They planned to defeat Reagan not by dwelling on the past but by focusing attention on the future—the "two futures," the president said in his acceptance speech, that the country would choose between when it selected him or Reagan.

Carter's own view of the future was tempered by the experience of the last four years. His deepest commitments—to human rights or the control of nuclear weapons, for example—remained unchanged, but he had grown philosophical over the prospects for rapid and dramatic progress on the major problems facing the country.

Carter's basic political instincts were conservative. "I am a very conservative Southern businessman by heritage," he told the Illinois legislature in 1978. The president had signalled the coming clash with Kennedy over economic policy a year before it officially began in a speech to a Democratic National Committee fund-raising dinner in Washington.

"We have proved that the Democratic Party is the party of fiscal responsibility . . . I would like to caution all of you Democrats—those in my administration, those in the Congress—that we here in Washington must set an example. We cannot pass legislation that is identifiably wasteful . . . This is the future of our Democratic Party."

The president's ridicule of "simple solutions" to complex problems was a campaign tactic aimed at Reagan, whom he accused of living in a "fantasy world." But it was also what he believed. Carter summoned the nation to no lifting, driving dream, and his promises for a second term, if there were to be one, were far less extravagant than they had been four years earlier. Part of this may have reflected the realism gained in four years in the White House. Part of it may have reflected the fatalistic aspects of his religious beliefs. Part of it may have had to do with where his roots were.

In 1960, a distinguished historian, C. Vann Woodward, published a collection of essays under the title *The Burden of Southern History*. It was one of Woodward's main theses that what set Southerners apart from Americans of other regions was the experience of their history, which allowed them no illusions about the "legends" of endless American abundance and inevitable American success.

"For Southern history, unlike American, includes large components of frustration, failure and defeat," Woodward wrote. "It includes not only an overwhelming military defeat but long decades of defeat in the provinces of economic, social and political life. Such a heritage affords the Southern people no basis for the delusion that there is nothing whatever that is beyond their power to accomplish. They have had it forcibly and repeatedly borne in upon them that this is not the case. Since their experience in this respect is more common among the general run of mankind than that of their fellow Americans, it would seem to be a part of their heritage worth cherishing."

Woodward wrote before the Vietnam War, before the Watergate scandal, when gasoline was cheap and plentiful. Jimmy Carter, the first president from the Deep South in more than 100 years, was trying to govern in a far different time. Judging by his public comments, he had concluded that it was his fate to steer the country through a painful transition in which the old American legends would be further battered. Carter did not pretend to know what perils that transition would hold, but he was convinced that he was far better equipped to handle them than Reagan.

In 1976, Carter told the Democratic National Convention, "I say to you that our nation's best is still ahead." Now, returning to the same sports arena where he first accepted his party's nomination, the president asked mostly for a reaffirmation of faith, not just in his own goodness, but in his ability to bring the country safely through whatever dangers awaited it.

"I am wiser tonight than I was four years ago," he said.

★ IV ★

Ordinary Men

Dan Balz
Edward Walsh
Lou Cannon

★ Anderson ★

by Dan Balz

SOME CAMPAIGNS are born of bright ideals. John Anderson's began in bitterness and despair.

It was the summer of 1978 and the congressman from Illinois was already looking past his expected reelection that fall to the end of his political career. He was a bruised man. Earlier in the year, the New Right had picked him as a target for political extinction; he barely survived a bitter primary fight.

The experience left scars—and new fears. Anderson realized the conservatives would be back to try again. After almost 18 years of what he considered to be distinguished (and conservative) service in Congress, he only wanted them to go away.

During that period he sought out an old friend, Rep. Morris Udall, the liberal Democrat from Arizona. Udall remembers a discouraged Anderson who felt he'd reached dead end in the House, who wanted out, whose wife wanted out.

Anderson and Udall had come to Washington together in 1961, and though they were of different parties and opposing political views, they found a common bond in their rural and religious upbringings. Over the years they became close friends, as did their outspoken and independent-minded wives. In 1976, Udall had run unsuccessfully for the Democratic presidential nomination, and Ella Udall often talked to Keke Anderson about the excitement and exhilaration of a presidential campaign.

In that summer of 1978, some of Anderson's friends in Illinois had approached him about running for president and offered him seed money. The idea appealed to Anderson. It would be a way to take the fight back to those in his party who opposed him, who said he should find another home. He felt he was a better Republican than they were and wanted to prove it—and anyway, it was better than staying in the House of Representatives. Keke Anderson felt even more strongly about the idea than he did.

It was both a preposterous and slightly mischievous notion. Anderson was a highly respected member of Congress, but he knew almost nothing about campaign politics. He had no money, no political base, was hardly known outside of northern Illinois and was perceived as a liberal in an increasingly conservative party. To run for president was an exercise in political fantasy.

That a man like John Anderson would even consider running is testimony to the revolution that has occurred in presidential politics in the past 20 years.

The revolution has come in two forms: changes in the way parties choose their candidates and changes in the way voters pick their presidents. The new nominating system has made it possible for almost any serious politician to offer himself for the presidency and have a hope of winning. New delegate selection rules, campaign financing laws, the proliferation of primaries and the diminished influence of party leaders have opened up the process to more and more candidates. Over the years, men with no logical chance of winning their party's nomination exploited these changes to beat heavily favored opponents.

In 1972 George McGovern took advantage of the delegate selection rules he and others had fathered to win the Democratic nomination though he was representative of only the party's left wing. In 1976, Jimmy Carter, the ex-governor of an unimportant southern state, built his nomination out of a series of marginal primary victories, shrewdly using the long primary schedule to create the illusion of unstoppable momentum early in 1976.

Candidates in 1980 also played to a different electorate than the candidates of only a decade ago. Voters were more independent, more likely to split their tickets, more sophisticated about many issues and more cynical about their representatives. They refused to be swayed by party bosses, in contrast to their parents and grandparents. Many devoted themselves to causes— abortion, environment, the Vietnam war, equal rights, gay rights—rather than to the major parties.

THE PURSUIT OF THE PRESIDENCY 1980
A Campaign Portfolio

PHOTO BY MERRETT IN CENTURY CITY

by Frank Johnston,
award-winning Washington Post photographer
with captions from the text

THE REPUBLICANS

They shared the same values as well as the same views.
(Left to right) Crane, Connally, Anderson, Baker,
Dole, Reagan, Bush.

Reagan: He spoke to the future in the accents of the past.

Anderson: An exercise in political fantasy.

Bush: Like Scott Fitzgerald
had made him up.

Connally: "You think
I don't know about
milk prices, you're crazy."

Baker: Better at analysis
than presidential campaigns.

THE DEMOCRATS

Kennedy was, in a sense, the leading
political figure in the nation.

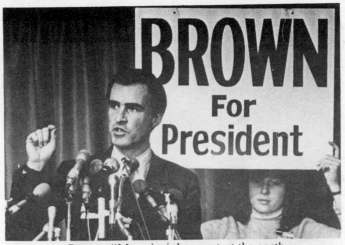

Brown: "My principles: protect the earth, serve the people, and explore the universe."

Carter's strongest point was that he wasn't Kennedy, and Kennedy's strongest point was that he wasn't Carter.

THE PRIMARIES

New Hampshire Primary voters go to the polls.

The political industry was operating at full strength in 1980, essential to the fortunes of every major candidate.

The amazing thing about Bush's candidacy was not that it failed, but that it kept going as long as it did.

THE REPUBLICAN CONVENTION

...a widespread perception that the nation was in danger.

A "masterful and intuitive" politician meets with his
Policy Advisory: (left to right) Ed Meese, Charles Walker,
George Schultz...William Simon, Alan Greenspan,
Caspar Weinberger, Jim Lynn.

It is hard to imagine two individuals from more varied
backgrounds than Reagan and Bush.

"We are being called upon again..."
The candidates with former President Ford.

THE DEMOCRATIC CONVENTION

The Democrats at Madison Square Garden.

He had been the Democrats' idea of a dream candidate
for the better part of ten years.

One of the longest-lived bubbles
in American politics had burst. Kennedy concedes.

A study in contrasts as the Democrats choose.

THE GREAT DEBATES

The "brief encounter" in Baltimore was tame and inconclusive:
The Reagan-Anderson debate.

Reagan's aides: "We did better than we had any right
to expect."

"If all of the unemployed today were in a single line...
that line would reach from New York City to
Los Angeles, California."

"We have demanded that the American
people sacrifice, and they have done very
well..."

NOVEMBER 4th

Carter knew the shape of the whole as he flew through the night to the home place in Plains...With Jody Powell on Air Force One.

Before the polls had closed, the President knew. Addressing well-wishers in Plains after voting.

The voting was over and now the waiting would begin...
Mr. and Mrs. Reagan at the polls in California.

Reagan had not merely won an election. He was the
beneficiary of an electoral landslide. At a victory rally at
Los Angeles' Century City.

THE WINNING TEAM

President-elect Ronald Reagan
Vice President-elect George Bush

The electorate grew accustomed to direct contact with candidates, and their link was television. Smart politicians used television to manipulate images of themselves to appeal to the changing American mood, but increasingly it was television news, not paid ads, that shaped the consciousness of the voters. Television provided the visual world of presidential politics and the networks spent millions catering to the appetites of a mobile, fast-changing society. In 1980, this would be the foundation of Anderson's campaign.

It no longer mattered much what experts said about a candidate's chances of winning the White House; they had been wrong so many times. What mattered was creating an audience of voters large enough to affect a few early contests. The system encouraged more and more politicians to run; all it took was ego, money, stamina and a strong, clear voice.

What motivated John Anderson to think about running for president in that summer of 1978 is not altogether clear, but it is doubtful that winning the presidency was the overriding influence. Anderson recognized that with television the presidential campaign offered him a pulpit. That was enough.

"After spending an adult life of unfulfilled dreams and promises, a man has to prove something to himself," he told a *Washington Post* reporter in late 1979. "Maybe I'm trying to convince myself that everything I've been doing makes sense. I guess I just want to get it all off my chest before I close up the books."

By the time he had gotten it off his chest, he had reshaped the 1980 presidential election—shucking off 30 years of loyalty to the Republican Party to form the first serious independent candidacy since George Wallace—and become perhaps the first pure television candidate in the history of American politics.

How it happened is a marvelous human story, the continual metamorphosis of a small-town man and a peek into the future of American politics.

By January, 1979, Anderson was ready to take the first formal step toward a presidential candidacy, the creation of an exploratory committee. But even then, he had reservations.

For many candidates, the exploratory committee is a misnomer, for it is generally formed after the final decision has been made to run for president. For Anderson it was literally a committee to explore the receptiveness to his candidacy.

Anderson had asked Jim Nowlan, who had managed Senator Charles Percy's 1978 reelection campaign, to head the committee and one day that month the two met in Anderson's congressional office, along with Anderson's administrative assistant Michael MacLeod, to lay out a preliminary road map.

Anderson expressed confidence that he could handle himself in a presidential campaign, that he could discuss the issues, confront his opponents, and present himself to the public effectively. What he worried about was looking like a fool. Anderson is a proud man, as are most politicians, and he wanted to be taken seriously. If everyone greeted his candidacy with hoots of disbelief, he wasn't sure he wanted to run.

The three men agreed that the main objectives of the exploratory period would be to raise enough money to keep Anderson moving around the country that year and from that, try to determine if there were sufficient interest in Anderson to justify a formal candidacy.

The next few months were discouraging to everyone. Anderson was uncomfortable with the details of politicking. He distrusted public opinion surveys and refused to think about using them to shape his candidacy. He disliked the fundamental courtesies of any campaign. Once he was asked to call a number of state chairmen around the country to let them know he and his staff would be doing some work in their states. Anderson looked at the list and replied, "I don't want to call those guys. They're all politicians." Like most politicians he disliked asking people for money. Finally Nowlan and others convinced him he had to do it.

On March 3, 1979, Nowlan drafted a memo to Anderson. It was a gloomy report. "Adequate financing is uncertain, staffing is less than skeletal," he wrote. "At this point there is no finance committee nor any nationally known heavy hitters identified as JBA (John B. Anderson) fund-raisers." He said the campaign needed to spend $1 million by the end of the year if Anderson wanted to come close to being a serious candidate. Nowlan suggested four potential constituencies to tap, and in retrospect it is an ironic list: Anderson's "friends" in Congress, the Jewish community because of his strong defense of Israel, evangelical Christians because of his own religious background, and energy companies, especially the nuclear industry, because of his record of support.

Nowlan's memo also contained the outlines of a strategy for Anderson's longshot campaign. Quoting Republican pollster Robert Teeter, Nowlan said the public was looking for (1) something different, (2) a return to traditional values, and (3) proven capability.

Anderson still was not convinced he should formally declare as a candidate. Nowlan and his deputy Dean Brown found themselves giving Anderson pep talks, trying to make him believe that he could run without being embarrassed, but the congressman seemed unmoved.

One weekend in March he came back to Illinois almost despondent. He had sought the support of his friends in the Illinois congressional delegation, and almost all of them, responded by telling him not to run. Anderson asked Nowlan to explore possible support for an Anderson Senate campaign for the seat being vacated by Adlai Stevenson. Nowlan made some checks around the state and determined that Anderson could raise the necessary money and a week later reported this to Anderson. But by then Anderson had given up the idea. Either he would run for president or quit politics.

At the end of April it was clear to Nowlan that by any objective standard the exploratory effort was a failure. The campaign still wasn't raising money and without money Anderson couldn't get enough attention to stay afloat. Over breakfast one Sunday at the Andersons' home in Rockford, Nowlan said he saw no way for Anderson to win the Republican nomination and didn't want to spend a year of his life on a hopeless cause. He told Anderson and Keke that if the campaign went ahead, he would bow out, that Anderson deserved a campaign manager with real enthusiasm.

But by then Nowlan's pep talks had had an effect. Anderson said he had decided to run after all. He told Nowlan he wanted to announce his candidacy in early June, and the lame-duck campaign manager went to work on a strategy, which culminated in a May 17 memo to Anderson.

"JBA will have to develop a campaign approach which (1) gives him high visibility in New Hampshire and (2) sets him apart as different, better, far and away the most serious, thoughtful candidate," he wrote. "I believe the way to do this is by taking on, challenging, the absurd conventions of presidential campaigning which magnify the inane and are destructive of political leadership because of the incessant, never-ending public demands upon the candidates. I recommend that JBA become a kind of anti-candidate."

Nowlan argued that this would produce "substantial unpaid media coverage and the appreciation of editorial writers and commentators." Given the campaign's empty treasury, Nowlan's blueprint for survival was the only sensible course to take. Given the media's own plans for covering the 1980 campaign, it was brilliant.

On June 8, 1979, having raised less than $200,000 since January and standing at less than 1 percent in the national polls, Anderson formally announced his candidacy in the U.S. Capitol. A suggestion by Keke that he stage the event at the Lincoln Memorial was rejected as a gimmick.

In the fall Keke rented a house in New Hampshire and moved there to build up a campaign organization for the first primary state. Anderson became a political circuit rider, preaching his gospel around America wherever he could find an audience. He relied on a few loyal friends in a few states to find them. He often traveled alone, using volunteer drivers to shuttle him around a city. He talked issues until he was hoarse, but no one listened. And he was running one of the most unorthodox Republican campaigns in modern history.

He courted the black vote. "I don't know of any other candidate who's talked to as many black groups as I have," he said that fall. He courted women. "I'm trying to convince women I'm the best candidate on women's rights. Who else has gone to New Hampshire to participate in a candlelight vigil in front of the *Manchester Union Leader* for freedom of choice?"

He had a string of positions that set him apart from other Republicans. He advocated a 50-cents-a-gallon tax on gasoline to cut consumption and reduce U.S. dependence on foreign oil. With the proceeds from the tax he proposed to cut social security taxes in half. The Anderson 50-50 plan he called it.

He was the only Republican actively calling for Senate ratification of the SALT II treaty. He criticized proposed increases in the defense budget, opposed the MX missile, decried a "missile madness" in the world that he said could set off another dangerous arms race, spoke out against the "idolatrous worship of the Kissinger era" of foreign policy, warned against listening to President Carter's advisers who talked of playing the "China card" in dealing with the Soviet Union.

He mocked the issue of leadership, which at the time was the rallying cry of everyone else in the race. "Leadership is suddenly a banner to be held aloft," he told one audience. "When are you and I going to look in the mirror and take some of the blame?" To a reporter he said, "If I hear about leadership once more I think I'll throw up."

Along the way Anderson developed one of the most impressive clip files in the history of presidential politics. No one writing for a major newspaper could find anything wrong with him. The *Des Moines Register* called him "a silver-haired orator with a golden tongue, a 17-jewel mind and a brass backbone." The *Wall Street Journal* said he was "a loner, a thinker and probably the best orator in Congress." Hugh Sidey of *Time* magazine wrote: "Common sense and compassion have consistently overwhelmed him during these legislative years. Intelligence and independence have probably kept him from more prominence within the party."

These nice stories, however, always ended with the same conclusions that he didn't have a chance to win the GOP nomination because he was too liberal for the party. This seemed to be Anderson's catch 22. Many of these same journalists had helped make Anderson's national reputation as a politician by writing glowingly of his work in the House, but when Anderson began to take their words seriously enough to offer himself as a candidate, they ridiculed his chances.

Most of the national press corps knew and liked John Anderson and probably believed he was as well qualified to be president as some of the better known Republican candidates. Since they were convinced he had no chance to win and would have to say it in their articles, they eased their own guilt feelings about dismissing him by writing superlative-laden stories stressing his best personal qualities: his intelligence, his articulateness, his independence. Unconsciously they created the illusion that he was almost without fault, and when the public began to notice his candidacy, there was nothing on the public record that approached a balanced portrait of his career. At the time, none of the press corps understood the consequences of this.

Still, Anderson knew all those newspaper stories weren't enough. Late one night in November, 1979, he found himself in the Gaslight Club at the O'Hare Hilton Hotel in the company of a reporter from the *Washington Post*. He had spent a dismal and invisible day campaigning around Chicago and now at the end of the trip he sat in a garish lounge and talked about his own frustrations.

"I can make these piddly speeches and it's not going to get me anywhere," he said. "I'm not stupid. This is a country of 230 million people. You've got to have what you say resonate. If you can have your ideas reported, that's the way to get votes. I just don't have enough days left to make speeches."

The opportunity to reach that larger audience came January 5, in Des Moines, Iowa, in the first televised debate among the Republican candidates—an opportunity Anderson almost missed. The congressman was not competing in the Iowa caucuses, the first major event of the 1980 campaign, and when the initial invitation came in from the *Des Moines Register* to participate in the Iowa debate, his staff politely sent regrets.

Anderson was stunned when he heard what his staff had done. He didn't care about the politics of the event, he wanted a forum and a chance to stand up beside his better-known opponents and talk about issues.

All the candidates except Reagan came to the debate that night, mostly hoping to gain ground against Reagan in Iowa. But Anderson wanted to prove he was different, and in the opening minutes, he quickly made his point by supporting President Carter's newly imposed grain embargo against the Soviet Union as retaliation for the Soviet invasion of Afghanistan. He was the only man on the platform to side with the President.

His answers to the questions that night were crisp and often at odds with the other candidates. How do you balance the budget, cut taxes and raise defense spending? "It's simple," he said. "You do it with mirrors." Is there anything in your public life you regret? "If I had one (vote) that I could change, it would have been the vote that I cast in favor of the Gulf of Tonkin Resolution in 1965," he replied.

Anderson's staff had prepared a closing statement for the candidate but he threw it away and spoke extemporaneously at the end. "When my father, my Swedish father, journeyed as an immigrant to this country almost 80 years ago, he didn't come because he thought life would be easy. He came because he knew this country stood for hard work, it stood for opportunity, it stood for individual freedom, it stood for basic moral courage. A lot of Americans today are wondering—my generation and younger generations in this audience everywhere across America—are wondering about the future of this country, because they see inflation. They see mounting deficits. They see the weakened dollar. They see the economic subservience to the oil cartel. They worry about the decline in our international position.

"And yet they see the politicians by and large playing the game the same old way. It is the same old politics. We'll come out here to Iowa and we won't talk to the Iowa farmer and tell him we're going to expect some sacrifice. . . . I'm afraid that there's too much old politics being practiced, even among Republicans. . . . And yet I think the country is looking for something different.

"We've got to pull up our socks in this country. We've got to be willing to sacrifice something today in order to secure a better future and a better tomorrow. It's not going to be easy. It wasn't easy for my father. It won't be easy for us. But we can do it."

The audience erupted in applause, and the next day, as he walked through the airport, strangers came up to Anderson to cheer his performance.

If anything, Anderson's showing in the debate reinforced the experts' belief that the Illinois congressman could not win the Republican presidential nomination and so their analyses focused on whether Reagan had been hurt by failing to participate. But Anderson's message that night was in fact beginning to resonate across the country, as television encapsulated his words into video images that seared into living rooms of Republicans, Democrats and Independents, most of whom were only beginning to think about a new president. The subliminal message that night was that John Anderson was a courageous politician willing to stand alone, a plainspoken man surrounded by double-talking candidates. Television had created—for the moment—a new political star and launched his independent candidacy.

And yet the public had learned little about Anderson from that performance in Iowa, and did not seem to care. Some were in love with the images.

★

It was a measure of the Anderson phenomenon of 1980 that admirers ascribed to him virtues that would have made an ordinary man blush. Because what's good about any presidential candidate naturally gets exaggerated, the heroism of John Anderson was overstated. He did not change from cornbelt congressman to hero overnight when he declared for the presidency; nor was he born a hero; nor, really, was he one during those early months of 1980.

John Anderson was born in 1922 in the northern Illinois city of Rockford. His father was a Swedish immigrant, his mother the daughter of immigrants. His father, who is 95 today, ran a grocery store in the predominantly Swedish section of town. Anderson's parents had six children but three died during childhood of scarlet fever and pneumonia.

He grew up in a deeply religious family. "They believed that outside of the home and school, time should be devoted to church," Anderson wrote in a 1970 book called *Between Two Worlds*. "That not only meant Sunday evening evangelistic service. It meant Sunday morning church service when a 45-minute sermon was not considered unduly long, young people's service at five o'clock and then a Sunday evening evangelistic service. It meant attendance at Wednesday night prayer meeting services as well as the frequent 'special' meeting which would bring well-known evangelists and Bible teachers to our city."

The Andersons went to tent meetings on hot August nights, and it was at one of these gatherings that 9-year-old John accepted Jesus Christ as his personal savior.

"Seated there beside my parents on the rough planking of a makeshift church pew, I was suddenly gripped as never before in my young life by the message of . . . God. There under the canvas of what had once been the 'Big Top' of one of those innumerable little circuses that toured the country but have now become as sanctified as any great cathedral, I fell on my knees and beseeched God's mercy," he later wrote.

"For me personally, the recollection of the night of my rebirth does far more than provoke a nostalgia for the carefree days of childhood. It serves as a constant reminder of the miracle of regeneration. It provides the assurance that the same Christ who could touch the heart of a child is also sufficient unto all of my needs today."

As a young man, Anderson settled into law and politics in his home town. A graduate of the University of Illinois at Champaign-Urbana, and of the law school there, he went to Harvard for an advanced law degree and while in Boston taught at Northeastern University School of Law in Boston. His law school education was interrupted by two and a half years in the Army in the field artillery.

In 1952 a "wave of restlessness" got him and he decided to get a State Department job. He took the Foreign Service test in Chicago and that year was sent to Berlin as an adviser on the staff of the United States high commissioner. On his way to Berlin, he met his wife, Keke. She worked in the State Department, taking passport photos for the foreign service officers. "Alas, the first photograph proved entirely unsuitable," Anderson wrote in his book. "I had closed my eyes as she clicked the shutter." He returned for another photo and the romance blossomed. They were married in Germany and their first child was born there.

Two years later they returned to Rockford, where he again picked up on his law practice and politics. In the spring of 1956 he won a five-man race for the Republican nomination for state attorney. "I prayed over this initial decision to seek public office, just as I have prayed over every major decision in my life," he wrote later.

He was three years into his term when the longtime congressman from that part of the state decided to retire. Anderson beat four other Republicans in the primary and went on to win the conservative 16th district seat that fall. He arrived in Washington at the beginning of John F. Kennedy's New Frontier.

Anderson's first six years in Congress were distinguished by solid, Midwestern conservatism, an almost perfect party-line voting record and an appointment to the House Rules Committee. Anderson, in those early years voted against raising the national debt, buying U.N. bonds, foreign aid, public service jobs, food stamps, mass transit, Medicare, the war on poverty, the new Department of Housing and Urban Development.

He also introduced in 1961, and again in 1963 and 1965, an amendment to the Constitution saying the nation "devoutly recognizes the authority and law of Jesus Christ, Saviour and Ruler of nations, through whom are bestowed the blessing of Almighty God." He would later regret the action, call it a naive and foolish act, and a political embarrassment, but it reflected the real John Anderson in those early years in Congress.

He almost never broke with his own party in those days. On 68 key votes during his first six years, he sided with the Republican majority 66 times. Once he abandoned the GOP majority to side with the conservatives in his party against a college funding bill. Another time he broke with his party to vote for a pay raise for members of Congress, judges and other federal officials.

"You are plunged into a frightening environment," he later recalled. "I followed a man who had the reputation (of being a party voter) in the district. But there is a process of maturation that occurs. We in the House have a somewhat provincial outlook, which is the way it should be because we are supposed to be closer to the people. But the longer you serve, the more you realize that what you try to do is to reconcile the views of your district with the larger goals of trying to be aware of issues on a national scale."

A change in Anderson's political career came in 1968 over civil rights. "The whole atmosphere (of the 1960s) began to register itself on my conscience," he said. "It began to convince me that times had changed, and that some of us—grudgingly— were going to have to change. Old habit patterns die hard. Some people have a fetish about consistency. I think it ignores the kind of accelerated change taking place in society."

As Anderson sought to harmonize the world he had known as a boy in Rockford with the world he saw as an adult from Washington, he was forced to resolve the growing tension between his religious and intellectual convictions. It was a period of extraordinary stress as he sought to embrace the new world without rejecting the old, but it was also a period of enormous personal change and he gradually developed his own version of a social gospel.

"The Great Commandments simply mean that, given an interdependent society, we are all accountable for what's around us," he said. "There are some people who say that's dangerous radicalism, approaching socialism. But Christ himself was concerned enough that when the people were hungry, they were fed."

The 1968 open housing bill gave Anderson the opportunity to make public his personal conversion and he did it with a passion that was to thrust him almost overnight into the national limelight.

It happened on the April day Martin Luther King Jr. was buried in Atlanta. In Washington, the House Rules Committee gathered for a showdown on the open housing bill, with the choice of sending the bill to the House floor or to a House-Senate conference committee that meant almost certain death. In 1966 Anderson had opposed the bill. But on that Tuesday in April, with the fumes from the city's riots fresh in his nostrils, with the rhetoric of the Kerner Commission report on the violence in the cities ringing in his ears, he broke with his party and cast the deciding vote that sent the bill to the floor.

The next day, his eloquent defense of the bill helped change enough votes to secure its passage: "I do not see this particular piece of legislation as any memorial to the dead. I see it rather as that cloud and that pillar that will guide the way of the living. . . . Let all men, black or white, understand that the religion of liberty is based on a reverence and respect for the law. But let us not be blind to the necessity of also rendering justice to the patient and the long suffering who do not riot but who will be brought to the brink of despair if, like the priest and the Levite, we simply turn aside."

He was for a moment a hero of the civil rights movement in America, and the next January his colleagues elected him chairman of the Republican Conference Committee, a remarkable accomplishment given his now increasingly moderate voting record. It was a measure of the admiration other Republicans had for him, despite occasional maverick votes.

But the next few years were not so glorious for Anderson, as he found it more difficult to harmonize his changing personal convictions with the responsibilities of party leadership. He satisfied neither during much of the period.

Once converted on civil rights, he confronted America's involvement in Vietnam. Those who were close to him in the early 70s believe he was undergoing another important change, from hawk to dove. It began to show up in his growing fears of an unbridled arms race between the two superpowers, and in his sympathy for many of the students on college campuses who were protesting the war. But he would not break with the new Nixon administration over its war policies. Time and again he voted to support Nixon's policy of Vietnamization, in part because he was strongly influenced by the generals in the Pentagon who briefed him at GOP leadership meetings in the White House. As late as August, 1972, when the House took up a bill that would have terminated U.S. involvement in Indochina by October 1 of that year, Anderson was voting with the White House.

He was not so reluctant to break with the White House over Watergate, however, an episode in his life that changed him as much as the open housing bill had. Legend now has it that he was the first Republican to call for Nixon's resignation, though documenting that fact is difficult. Nonetheless he was a critic of the White House's performance during that period and remembers vividly the reaction from his House colleagues to a speech in 1973 in which he said he was disturbed that Nixon seemed intent on a grudging, step-by-step admission of wrongdoing rather than a true confession.

"I was rebuked," he said, "for not being totally loyal."

The repudiation of Anderson by many of his colleagues and constituents back in Illinois was more complicated than that, however, and Anderson has had difficulty understanding why. During the Watergate years, Anderson became for many reporters—and especially the television networks—the one Republican leader willing to criticize the President. He was regularly quoted and showed up frequently on the nightly news shows. It was wonderful publicity, though it was not clear that Anderson sought it for any personal political gain. Nor was he deceitful about his feelings.

But with his denunciations came a moral righteousness that was impossible to disguise. While his civil rights conversion had been carried out with a feeling of humility, his performance on Watergate was rich with high-toned moralism. Back home it played terribly. Anderson appeared to be going out of his way to kick Dick Nixon, and his friends in Illinois took it out on him. There were times when he and Keke would go back to Rockford and go to the country club for dinner and old friends wouldn't speak. They resented him and in time he grew to resent them. Though his motives on Watergate may have been pure, it was a poisonous period in his life and he and Keke never again looked at Rockford in the same way. It wasn't that they couldn't go home again; they didn't want to.

When his friend Gerald Ford became president, Anderson settled into a more conventional Republican role. He played partisan politics in the House, laying the lash on the Democrats in floor debates, voting with his party in many of the economic and energy issues that had come to dominate the Congress. He voted against such liberal Democratic articles of faith as the repeal of the oil depletion allowance, public service jobs and common situs picketing. He supported deregulation of natural gas, an end to price controls on oil and even voted against a 20-cents-a-gallon tax on gasoline. He backed the Kemp-Roth tax cut bill that became the centerpiece of Ronald Reagan's campaign economic program.

But party loyalty went only so far with him and he walked away on enough important bills to add to his reputation as a Republican who belonged in another party. He often voted with Democrats on civil rights and social programs and he backed a tough strip mine bill that Ford vetoed. Nor did he make his dissents quietly. Once he joined his friend Udall to co-sponsor an Alaska lands bill that became the Democratic alternative to a Republican version that had been approved by Udall's own Interior Committee. One young House Republican vowed at the time never again to support Anderson for a leadership post.

By the time Jimmy Carter came into office, Anderson was neither a liberal nor a conservative, and though he still called himself a Republican he was more a political maverick. It was, therefore, a surprise mostly to Anderson that the vigorous New Right, then beginning to feel its way into power, would challenge him in the 1978 Republican primary by offering up a right wing preacher who built a campaign around abortion, equal rights, and the Panama Canal. It was a mean campaign that disoriented Anderson, who by then enjoyed being a respected member of the Washington establishment. He felt it was an affront to him to have to fight off the challenge, and it brought back to him the memories of the Watergate period. He won the primary, but never found his way back into the party.

★

Anderson left Iowa the day after the debate and did not return, campaigning as planned that month in New England and elsewhere. The political industry, its eyes focused only on the upcoming Iowa caucuses, largely ignored his guerilla war for the hearts and minds of the Republican party. He made almost no news, and yet his campaign took on new life, thanks mostly to the video images of that Saturday night encounter in Des

Moines. Among the monied and insulated Left in America, Anderson suddenly became the darling of the 1980 campaign and for several weeks the chic thing was to "discover" John Anderson.

Anderson's staff sensed something had changed in the campaign but didn't understand its meaning. The changes were manifested in odd ways for an obscure Republican congressman from the Midwest. On Manhattan's Upper East Side, more than 200 elegantly dressed men and women crowded into an apartment on the night of January 10 to get a look at this man and to contribute to his campaign. Stewart Mott, the gadfly philanthropist and barometer of social politics, gave Anderson $1,000, the legal limit. Similar scenes were repeated that month in Cambridge, Massachusetts, and Beverly Hills, where liberal Democrat Stanley Scheinbaum organized an Anderson fundraiser that drew more than 300 persons, including television producers Norman Lear and Grant Tinker and authors Gore Vidal and Irving Wallace. That month Anderson appeared on NBC's "Saturday Night Live" in perhaps the most curious juxtaposition of candidate and audience of the campaign.

In the course of a few weeks, the liberals remade John Anderson into one of their own, discarding 20 years of recorded votes in Congress and his long membership in the Republican party in favor of superficial impressions from the debate. Anderson suddenly came to embody what the liberals had hoped for in the candidacy of Sen. Edward M. Kennedy. They saw Anderson as an eloquent apostle for the politics of "sacrifice and compassion," and contrasted that to Kennedy's failures on the stump. As Kennedy had stumbled and stammered his way through the early months of the campaign, each "uh" and "er" amplified by the horde of journalists traveling with him, Anderson had benefitted from what one aide called "the stunning indifference of obscurity." His new liberal admirers seemed to believe he had been born politically in Iowa on the night of January 5.

The embrace of the liberals made some of Anderson's Republican advisers uneasy, but they were willing to ignore it because all the new attention meant money that Anderson needed desperately. In all of 1979, his campaign had raised $453,000 from just 4,000 contributors. At the end of the year Anderson had been forced to take out a personal loan for $50,000 to pay staff salaries. But after the debate, money began to roll in and by the end of January, $150,000 had been collected—peanuts compared to his competitors, but big money to Anderson's bargain-basement operation.

Still, it wasn't enough to continue a serious campaign, and that is where Tom Mathews stepped in.

Anderson, whose political instincts are as finely tuned as a sputtering old car, continued to set his sights on the February 26 New Hampshire primary, while his staff, many of them liberal Republicans dreaming still of taking away the party from the crazy conservatives from the West, kept their heads buried in the minutiae of devising a strategy to help Anderson finish "better than expected" in one of the early primaries.

None of them had stopped to analyze the impact of the Iowa debate in any but the most conventional of terms. But Mathews had a different sense as he analyzed Anderson's performance in Des Moines and the reaction to it. He thought Anderson had the potential for appealing to a new and unique audience in American politics.

Tom Mathews had made his living trying to define audiences and get money from them for clients. He was part of the direct mail firm of Craver, Mathews & Smith, which had made its reputation raising money for a variety of Democratic and liberal politicians and organizations. Their client list included Ted Kennedy, the Democratic National Committee, Common Cause, the National Organization for Women, the Sierra Club, the American Civil Liberties Union.

When Jim Nowlan was still running Anderson's campaign in 1979, he had contacted the firm to see if they would help Anderson raise money. The firm knew Anderson only by reputation, but felt he was one of the few Republicans they would willingly work for. They sent out one test letter for Anderson in August, 1979, but it was a failure and the whole matter was dropped.

After watching the Iowa debate, however, Mathews was encouraged to try again. "I realized that Anderson's appeal was not to the Republicans but to the alienated middle, which is turned off to both parties, which is suspicious and distrustful of the two parties."

The firm contacted Anderson's campaign staff and recommended they go back into the market with a new letter, which Mathews drafted with the new audience in mind. It read:

> Dear Friend,
>   When it comes to electing Presidents . . .

. . . The politicians and press don't think you count.

. . . You may exist, but you don't count.

. . . You may have strong beliefs, but you don't count.

You may be a well-informed, intelligent, courageous, fair-minded citizen, but you don't count.

The reason they think you don't count is simple. They believe that presidential candidates are selected by fools, by citizens who believe lies, evasions, half-truths and soft soap.

I simply refuse to believe that. I've based my last act of political faith on your existence. I do believe you count. That you and I can make a difference in this country.

I'm assuming you want an honest man with sound experience to be president of the United States. I also assume you'd be willing to help such a man run for office. That's why I'm writing: to ask you to judge me and if you then think I'm worthy, to send my campaign a contribution for whatever you can afford.

If you and enough other concerned, issue-oriented citizens do, we'll make some history together. We'll refute a lot of political nonsense that passes for truth in this country.

The letter went on for an additional four pages, detailing Anderson's positions on energy, the economy, defense, abortion and gun control—never once mentioning Anderson's Republican credentials or his goal of winning the GOP nomination. It ended this way:

Other candidates may boast of superior organization or financial resources. Still others speak in glittering generalities of their talents for leadership. But, I want to arouse the conscience and reason of America. To speak of the America yet to be. To return to the spirit that made America great.

Yes, I am a dark horse. I do not pretend that the task will be easy, or the burden light.

But I know I can do it if I can count on help from people like you. Whether you are a Democrat, Republican or Independent, your help is crucial if we are to raise the issues which must be raised in this campaign.

According to the conventional and miserable commentary on the ability of Americans to make political decisions, I have committed public suicide because of my willingness to speak clearly and independently on the issues. But I feel the issues must be addressed specifically. The times are simply too difficult, too dangerous, for candidates not to make clear where they stand or how they intend to approach our problems.

Craver, Mathews & Smith prepared two versions of the letter, one signed by Anderson and the other by Gloria Steinem (because another letter signed by her was doing well and the firm needed a way to assess Anderson's own appeal) and on February 3 sent out a test mailing of 48,000 pieces.

The response was impressive: a rate of return better than 5 percent (the August test letter was less than 1 percent) and an average contribution of $32. The firm had tested 16 different mailing lists and each one had performed magnificently.

While the test letter was still in circulation, two other events occurred to reinforce Mathews' feelings about Anderson's appeal.

The first began on February 11 and continued for two weeks in hundreds of newspapers across the country. The cartoonist, G. B. Trudeau, through the comic strip, "Doonesbury," fell in love with John Anderson. It started with Michael Doonesbury as an audience of one listening to an Anderson speech and telling the candidate, "You are . . . uncommonly well-spoken. You have quite a gift, sir. What do you expect to do with it?" "Run for president," comes the reply. "Oh, right, sorry," Doonesbury says. Another day's panel had Anderson warning against "missile madness" while extolling the virtues of SALT II. "Excuse me, Congressman Anderson, but are you sure you're a Republican? You sure don't sound like a Republican," Doonesbury says. "Great," says John Anderson.

Anderson didn't seem much like a Republican when the second event occurred. It was February 18 in Concord, New Hampshire, and the gun owners of New Hampshire had constructed their own charming political gantlet for the candidates to run. All the Republican hopefuls were there, and all except one groveled before the group, invoking their histories as hunters, patriots, and war veterans to ingratiate themselves with one of the most powerful special interests in America. Anderson, who almost missed the event because his staff, as with the Iowa debate, thought it wasn't a good forum for him and rejected an initial invitation, stood up before the gun owners and asked, "What is so wrong about telling the law-abiding public of this country we will license gun owners? We will tell them . . ." Anderson never got to finish the sentence, the chorus of boos was so loud and so instantaneous. It looked like another of these campaign manager's nightmares, but with the network camera crews rolling, it was for Anderson the most memorable moment of his campaign.

The next night, on the "CBS Evening News," Walter Cronkite led into the piece this way: "John Anderson often has found himself standing apart from the crowd in this Campaign '80."

By that time, Mathews knew he had a political phenomenon on his hands. It was still clear the Illinois congressman had little chance to win the GOP nomination, but a sizable number of voters seemed to be convinced that he was superior to any of the candidates who could. And they were saying so with money that continued to pour into headquarters. Mathews decided he needed to sit down personally with Anderson to try to explain what was happening.

The meeting occurred on February 27, the night after Anderson had finished a somewhat surprising third in the New Hampshire primary behind Ronald Reagan and George Bush. Mathews had asked for just 20 minutes of Anderson's time, and it had been agreed that Mathews would fly to Boston to meet with the candidate in the home of a supporter in the suburbs who was hosting a fund-raiser that night.

"I wanted to tell him about the constituency he had," Mathews said later. "I felt he did not know much about it or what its size was. I wanted to describe it to him."

"I realized his appeal was not to the Republicans but to the alienated middle which is turned off to both parties, which is suspicious and distrustful of the parties. It is the group that has turned to single issue activities."

Others, less kindly, called it the "chablis and brie" set of suburban America.

Anderson arrived in a somewhat sour mood, having learned on his way down to Boston that, after appearing to have won two delegates in New Hampshire, he had fallen just short of the qualifying 10 percent cutoff. The fundraiser was scheduled for later in the evening, and about 8 p.m., Mathews joined Anderson, Keke and Mike MacLeod, the campaign manager, in an upstairs bedroom for their meeting.

Mathews began by comparing Anderson to a man speaking to a roomful of people who sat politely, their hands folded in their laps, listening to his message, but not responding. But, Mathews said, the man's voice is being piped into another room filled with more people and they were going crazy, yelling, cheering, jumping up and down. Those people, Mathews told Anderson, were not Republicans, and they were the audience he believed Anderson should begin to appeal to more directly in his campaign.

"I told him it was possible to build a constituency in this campaign that would last for many years—whether he won or lost," Mathews said.

Keke Anderson began to talk excitedly about creating a third party, but Mathews said he thought it was too early to know what the best strategy would be, though he did suggest that Anderson could build enough support in the coming primaries to make a run at both the major parties. Mathews was pointing toward an independent candidacy but believed the political climate was too cloudy then for final decisions.

Anderson called Mathews's analogy "a shattering concept," but there is little evidence that he gave it more thought than that. His campaign in Massachusetts was moving too quickly that week to think about an independent candidacy.

Six days later, in a hotel ballroom in Boston, an astonished John Anderson came down to greet a sweaty, cheering, beer-drinking throng of young supporters. At the time he was leading the pack in both Massachusetts and Vermont, and though he would later lose both by an eyelash, the night was his. The networks devoted their late-night wrapups to exuberant coverage of the Anderson breakthrough and showed him before his supporters quoting Lincoln, Cicero and Ralph Waldo Emerson. ("There is nothing that astonishes man so much as common sense and plain dealing.") He raved about his "campaign of ideas" and went off to Illinois believing, as did his staff, that he could still win the Republican nomination.

But it was his home state that destroyed the dream, first in a debate with Reagan, Bush and Phil Crane, in which his three opponents took turns attacking him, and later in the primary itself, which Reagan won easily despite Democratic crossovers for Anderson.

After the Illinois primary, it was clear that Reagan and Carter were the likely nominees of the two parties—and equally clear that many Americans regarded that as a dismal choice. The pressure on Anderson to consider running as an independent began to grow. Yet within Anderson's campaign there was no appetite for such a contest. The bonds of party held even the Ripon Society members of his staff tightly, and Anderson's closest aides spurned any talk of his bolting the party.

Anderson too seemed mystified by events, unable to understand why it was impossible for him to win the GOP nomination at a time when there seemed to be enthusiasm for him as a candidate. Money continued to come into the campaign (although it had fallen off immediately after the Illinois debate in which Anderson had gotten trapped into a discussion of party loyalty) and the media still praised his candor and intelligence. The lecture from Tom Mathews back in Massachusetts had not taken hold and the campaign began to drift.

Though his campaign then had come to symbolize a new sort of unconventional politics, Anderson remained the most conventional of politicians. His mind operated in old thought patterns, his celebrated campaign of ideas was at best a reflection of the thoughts being offered up at such East Coast think tanks as the Brookings Institution, MIT and the Council on Foreign Relations. He clung to the two party system and put his faith in its ability to deliver the country from a Carter-Reagan election. He was not daring, as his new admirers seemed to believe, but cautious and conservative.

Thus the independent candidacy came in stages, as Anderson was shoved a few steps at a time away from his lifelong party into the political netherworld of new politics.

The first step came on March 25 at a meeting in the Hotel Pfister in Milwaukee. The participants, in addition to Anderson and his wife, were MacLeod, Mathews and his partner Roger Craver, issues director Cliff Brown, Norman Lear, Stanley Scheinbaum and New York political consultant David Garth, who had first encountered Anderson the previous fall and found him interesting but too poor to afford the services of Garth's prestigious firm.

By the time of the meeting, there was agreement that Anderson had no real hope of winning the Republican nomination, leaving as options (1) to continue on in the primaries for the sake of the cause of broadening the party's base, (2) dropping out, or (3) going independent. Mathews argued in the strongest possible terms for Anderson to drop his Republican identification and declare as an independent, and he was joined by Lear and Scheinbaum. Garth told Anderson he would not urge any particular course but said the best shot at winning the White House was as an independent. Others advised staying in the Republican race despite the expected outcome, citing the cost of an independent candidacy, the uncertainty and the potential for Anderson to run again in 1984 as a Republican and win. The meeting lasted several hours and there were some heated exchanges. The candidate mostly listened. At the end Anderson agreed to think seriously about running as an independent and asked Garth to investigate what it would entail.

The next week he lost badly in Wisconsin to Reagan and flew back to Washington for some rest. Tom Mathews went to work again. On April 2, Mathews went to New York for an afternoon meeting with Garth. If Anderson asks you to take on this campaign, will you do it and how much will you charge? Garth, who had helped elect unknown Edward Koch as mayor of New York, who had helped New York Governor Hugh Carey and New Jersey Governor Brendan Byrne win reelection against overwhelming odds, was intrigued at the prospect of electing the first non-party president in American history. He told Mathews he would accept an Anderson offer for something less than $35,000 a month.

Next Mathews contacted Arnold Siner at the Washington law firm of Arnold & Porter, and asked him if the firm would be willing to undertake the legal fight to get Anderson on ballots around the country. Siner said he would have to take the question to the firm's managing partners, but he was interested.

On the day Mathews met with Garth, Anderson flew to California, where he said he would sit under a eucalyptus tree and think about an independent candidacy. No better at knowing the flora of California than he had been in estimating his appeal to Republican voters, Anderson found no trees on the beach at Malibu where he and Keke were to spend the Easter weekend, but he did find Tom Mathews.

Mathews met with the Andersons on April 6 to urge again

that Anderson go independent. This time, on the flight out, he carefully prepared his presentation in the form of a speech. After his Massachusetts experience, he didn't want to leave anything to chance.

"I did not come here to urge you to undertake an independent campaign," he told Anderson. "I'm setting aside my own feelings because I know the decision to run as an independent requires heroism, and nobody can urge heroism on anyone else. No normal person would do it. It is not reasonable. You're excused by the risk, the sacrifice, the magnitude of the task and its incredible complexity."

Mathews said he was there to describe the shape of a plausible campaign that would let Anderson "present a powerful message to the American people and to affect national politics for years to come."

Mathews likened the campaign to an airplane. "You and your vision of politics and government are the wings and fuselage, the unifying structure that provides lift and simplicity.

"Carter and Reagan have their simple messages. Carter's is 'Trust me, I'm doing the best I can and nobody can do it better.' Reagan's is 'We can return to a happy, secure, simpler, stronger time.' I'll not presume to define your message (something he later regretted) but it's there. Your people feel it. To articulate it in the most powerful and effective way, I suggest you conduct some conversations with ordinary people who support you. I think it would be invaluable to hear what it is in their hearts and minds that connects them to you."

Mathews then described "the engines of the plane," and told of his meetings with Garth and Arnold & Porter, making clear to Anderson that he had said he was acting without authorization from the candidate. He told Anderson he expected Arnold & Porter to agree to help get him on the ballots and said Garth would do it and ended by telling Anderson that he and Garth believed an announcement should come around the time of the April 22 Pennsylvania primary.

Anderson paused, and then looked up. "When do we button it up?" he asked.

"Next Thursday in New York," Mathews replied.

On April 24, standing in the ballroom at the National Press Club in Washington, Anderson made history by announcing for the second time in less than a year that he was a candidate for President of the United States. He had neither party nor money, neither a tested organization nor a clear sense of his own campaign. He had only an abiding belief that the Carter-Reagan choice was a disaster for the country and enough ego to offer himself as the savior. His old friends couldn't quite believe it, and deep down, John Anderson probably couldn't either.

★ Carter ★

by Edward J. Walsh

AIR FORCE ONE, the shiny blue and white supreme symbol of the presidency, hurried down a taxiway at Andrews Air Force Base outside of Washington. At the end of the taxiway, the plane turned right, and then right again, never pausing as it swung onto the runway and began picking up speed.

It was a brilliant autumn day along the East Coast, an October Saturday in 1979. Inside the plane, an unimposing man looked over the speech he was to deliver in a few hours. Two weeks earlier, he had celebrated his 55th birthday, in the third year of his presidency. Now Jimmy Carter was on his way to confront face-to-face the man who wanted to end that presidency the next year.

A little more than an hour later, Carter landed at Boston's Logan International Airport where, as on dozens of other occasions, he was greeted by a lineup of state and local politicians. He was driven through the city's streets, to a slice of land that jutted out into its harbor and stopped in front of a graceful modern building that had been designed by the architect I. M. Pei.

The building was the John F. Kennedy Presidential Library and Carter had come to Boston to dedicate it. But he knew, and those around him knew, that the day's events would be more political than ceremonial, that there would be a silent sizing up and measuring of him and the man who met him at the library door—Senator Edward M. Kennedy.

It didn't seem fair; Kennedy, as usual, seemed to have all of the advantages, just as his yet unannounced campaign against Carter then looked invincible.

The crowd outside the library was dotted with familiar faces from 20 years earlier. This was Kennedy turf and it was a Kennedy crowd, watched over by an unusually large press contingent attracted by the inherent political drama of the event. The master of ceremonies was Stephen Smith, a suave New Yorker who would shortly be heading his brother-in-law's campaign for the presidency.

Carter toured the library and, with Kennedy nearby, moved out into the bright midday sun for the dedication ceremonies. Mounting the stage that had been erected for the occasion, he began greeting the other dignitaries. When he reached Jacqueline Kennedy Onassis, he leaned forward and kissed her.

Mrs. Onassis recoiled in horror and the instant was fixed in time by dozens of photographers peering through their powerful lenses. It was just the sort of awkward, embarrassing moment—a Polish translator who spoke about "lust," the collapse of the President as marathon runner—that seemed to haunt the Carter presidency.

Carter is a modestly built man, fragile-looking and soft. He looks vulnerable, and never more so than on that day in Boston.

"If Kennedy runs, I'll whip his ass."

The President made that boast the previous spring at a White House dinner for members of Congress. Few believed him. But now, when it was finally his turn to speak, Carter began to make good on that bold prediction.

He spoke for 18 minutes, and in that time gave probably the best speech of his presidency. He broke the ice early, reminding Kennedy that years earlier the senator had publicly said he might never be interested in the burdens of being president. He spoke as a Southerner, paying tribute to what the Kennedy administration had meant to his region of the country and the struggle for racial equality. He spoke personally, recalling in moving terms what the death of John Kennedy had meant to him, how he cried openly "for the first time since the day my own father died."

And Carter spoke as president, about his time and his vision.

"President Kennedy was right: change is the law of life," he said. "The world of 1980 is as different from the world of 1960 as the world of 1960 was from that of 1940. Our means of improving the world must also be different.

"After a decade of high inflation and growing oil imports our economic cup no longer overflows. Because of inflation, fiscal restraint has become a matter of simple public duty . . . We have a keener appreciation of limits now, the limits of government, limits on the use of military power abroad, the limits of manipulation without harm to ourselves (and) a delicate and balanced natural environment.

"We are struggling with a profound transition from a time of abundance to a time of growing scarcity in energy . . . And we face these times when centrifugal forces in our society and in our political system—forces of regionalism, forces of ethnicity, of narrow economic interest, of single issue politics— are testing the resiliency of American pluralism and of our ability to govern."

It was a carefully crafted message designed to make a political point—that Edward Kennedy was not his brother, and that nostalgia for the 1960s would not solve the problems of the 1980s. But it was also what Carter devoutly believed. For much of his presidency, his public comments were filled with words meant to convey this message. Change. Limits. Sacrifice. The common good versus "the narrow special interests."

It was a harsh message preached by a dour little man the Secret Service had mischievously dubbed "Deacon." But no one seemed to be listening. The more Carter spoke, as he did in his first State of the Union message, about the need for a "reconciliation of private needs and interests into a higher purpose," the more the national unity he sought behind his programs eluded him.

He had campaigned for the presidency promising to restore trust and integrity to the White House, saying it was time that Americans once again could believe their president. In this he succeeded. Even after almost three years in the Oval Office, Carter was invariably described as "decent," "sincere," "well-meaning." He was believed. But judging by the polls and other barometers of public opinion, most Americans did not believe *in* him—in his ability to master the complex government he was elected to head, or to inspire the country to meet the noble goals he set for it.

By an uncommonly strong performance that day in Boston, Carter "won" the first preliminary skirmish with his Democratic adversary. But he still looked like a loser.

"He knew what sort of a president he wanted to be. He wanted to get things done, and he wanted them done the day before yesterday."

Jody Powell, the President's press secretary and one of his two closest advisers, was reflecting on three and one-half years in the White House. Like Carter's other aides, he was defensive and protective of the man he worked for, and a bit melancholy about the experience.

Carter's record was much better than generally perceived, Powell said. He hoped there would soon be a "revisionist history" on that topic, in time for the general election test against Ronald Reagan.

They had not done a good enough job in communicating the President's accomplishments, he said. But maybe that was inevitable, he went on, given how in modern America the media "devours news at an alarming rate," shying away from complexity to spotlight one problem, and then another, never pausing to examine what could or should or had been done to solve them. Too much attention was paid to the process of government, to the human failings that invariably are a part of it, and not enough to the end product, to the legislation that was finally enacted, to the appropriations that were increased, to the bureaucracies that were shaken up and made to work better.

Powell's views were widely shared by the President's other senior aides and what was most striking was the change in tone from the early days of the administration. Carter took office amid extraordinarily high expectations which he had carefully nurtured. He was the first Democratic president in eight years; before him, a Republican vice president and then a president had been forced from office in disgrace. If he was still something of an unknown quality, the subject of much guessing about what he would really be like, he was going to be given more than the usual benefit of the doubt afforded to new presidents.

But three and one-half years later, the expectations for Carter were exceedingly low. He nurtured that feeling, too. The country is in a difficult transition period, with no easy or painless solutions to its problems, he said. The film used to introduce him at the 1980 Democratic National Convention reminded viewers that many of the presidents revered in the history books—Lincoln, Wilson, the two Roosevelts—were criticized, even vilified, in their own time. It's a tough job and he's a good man doing his best, the message said.

There was no single, traumatic event or experience that the analysts could point to as the root cause of the loss of faith in the President, no Vietnam War or Watergate scandal. In three and one-half years as commander-in-chief, Carter had mounted one military operation—the attempt to rescue 53 American embassy employees being held by Iranian terrorists in Tehran.

It was a thoroughly botched affair, mislabeled a "humanitarian" mission by the president, that left eight American servicemen burned to death in the Iranian desert. But the public, at least at first, seemed not to blame Carter personally for the tragedy. The crowds still applauded when he boasted—even after the eight deaths—that no American had died "in combat" while he was president.

Similarly, there had been instances of questionable behavior in the Carter Administration, but nothing that touched the President personally or remotely suggested a pattern of abuse of power. The first, and worst, of these cases involved Carter's first Cabinet appointee and one of his closest confidants, Bert Lance, Director of the Office of Management and Budget. Before the Carter presidency was a year old, Lance had been driven from public office by the revelations of his questionable wheeling and dealing as a Georgia banker.

Carter was not held personally accountable for the sins of Lance's past. But in its own way, the Lance affair was as badly botched as the Iranian rescue mission. Carter's stubborn defense of his old friend, his foolish declaration on national television ("Bert, I'm proud of you"), undermined confidence not in his personal integrity but in his judgment and his understanding of the presidency. When, two and one-half years later, American helicopters were left burning in the Iranian desert, it was just the sort of tragically flawed comedy of errors the public had come to expect from its president—a nice try, too bad the little guy couldn't pull it off.

So it went over the months and years, a gradual squandering of the "fresh faith" Carter had asked of the public in his Inaugural Address. There was a tax rebate plan proposed and then abruptly dropped because of "changed circumstances"; an energy proposal was declared "the moral equivalent of war" and was then torn to shreds by a Congress controlled by the President's own party; other legislation, embodying many of the promises of 1976, was stalled on Capitol Hill and eventually abandoned; American power was said to be "second to none," but it was helpless in the face of raging mobs in Third World countries that burned American embassies and held American diplomats for ransom.

And Carter seemed helpless, too, as these and other events ground down public faith in him. His was a "passionless presidency" wrote James Fallows, a speechwriter who left the White House after two years still expressing his belief in Carter the man but thorough disillusionment with Carter the President. Passionless, and similar terms, were applied regularly to the Carter presidency to describe the curious phenomenon of a man who held the most visible and powerful public office in the world and yet seemed incapable of touching any kind of emotional cord in the public or of providing his followers with anything more than the vaguest outline of his vision and direction.

"It soon became clear," Fallows wrote of the early months of the Carter Amdinistration, "that Carter and those closest to him took office in profound ignorance of their jobs. They were ignorant of the possibilities and the most likely pitfalls. They fell prey to predictable dangers and squandered precious time."

Fallows's testimony, and the experience of three and one-half years, made at least arguable Powell's contention that Carter knew from the first the sort of president he wanted to be. Jimmy Carter spent four years planning, plotting and running to be president, which left very little time to think about how he would use the office once he attained it.

In a political system that now threatens to make running for president a permanent and full-time occupation, this is perhaps inevitable; certainly none of the other candidates who scrambled through the 1976 primaries alongside Carter gave evidence of deep reflection on the presidency. But Carter, who made being a Washington "outsider" into the great political virtue of 1976, was particularly ill-equipped by experience for the job he had won. He may have wanted to "get things done"—what president didn't—but aside from a laundry list of legislative and diplomatic objectives, Carter took office without giving the public a clear sense of where he was headed or how he would get there. Perhaps he didn't know himself.

Over the years, however, Carter had demonstrated that he is a master of one art—the art of elective politics. Elective politics is largely a matter of positioning, of getting the public to focus on your opponent's shortcomings, making the other guy the issue. Carter has always understood that elections finally come down to a question of choice and that even if you are viewed as the proverbial lesser of two evils you still win.

Thus, when Carter took office in January, 1977, he turned his presidency into an extension of his campaign. He no longer had an opponent as such, but he could still position himself. If he was not sure of what kind of a president he wanted to be, he knew what kind of president he did not want to be: he would not be Richard M. Nixon.

Beginning with the first act of his presidency—his walk down Pennsylvania Avenue on Inauguration Day—Carter set out with a vengeance to set himself apart from Nixon, who had turned the term "Imperial Presidency" into a political cliche. It was a no lose proposition, at least for a while, for a new president. However history might ultimately judge him, Nixon, the only American president forced to resign from office, represented the lowest common denominator in national politics. So long as he was the standard against which a successor was measured, it was no contest.

In 1976, Carter had run against the ghost of the Nixon presidency, but he had not defeated or succeeded Nixon himself. He had defeated, and succeeded, Gerald R. Ford, an outgoing, affable creature of Capitol Hill who was as different from Nixon in his own way as was the new straightlaced, moralistic Democratic president. In two and one-half years in the Oval Office, Ford did little to change the external trappings or internal structure of the White House. But he was a comfortable figure, perceived as a decent, honest and hard-working man, and that made all the difference. Carter had recognized this and publicly acknowledged it in the stunning opening line of his Inaugural Address:

"For myself and for our nation, I want to thank my predecessor for all he has done to heal our land."

Ford's appealing human qualities were undoubtedly a major reason his uphill campaign against his relatively unknown and strangely distant Democratic challenger turned out to be so close. In the end, he lost not because of doubts about his personal integrity or his good intentions, but because of questions over whether he was really up to the job. Americans, it turned out, wanted more than an honest man in the Oval Office and were even willing to take a chance on an enigmatic, inexperienced one-term governor of a Deep South state to find the right combination of honesty *and* competence.

But the new president, whether out of calculation of the short-term benefits or uncertainty over how else to approach the presidency, misread or chose to ignore the meaning of his own election. Style, "the Carter style," meant in all its aspects to contrast with the lingering memory of the Nixon style, became his hallmark.

"Hail to the Chief" no longer was played at presidential appearances. The long black presidential limousine, with the national and presidential flags fluttering in the wind, was retired in favor of a relatively modest tan Mercury. Carter had denounced the size of the Nixon-Ford White House staffs, so his own White House complement would be slashed to the arbitrary number of 350 without much if any thought of how this might affect the functioning of government.

The President walked to work his first day on the job. He spent one afternoon taking telephone calls from around the country, earnestly replying to questions while a national radio audience listened. He appeared on television dressed in a cardigan sweater and told the country, "I've spent a lot of time deciding how I can be a good president."

Many of these steps were proposed to Carter in a pre-inaugural memo from his political pollster, Patrick Caddell. "He can do much to both restore confidence, build credibility and gain support for his programs by the style with which he undertakes the presidency," Caddell argued.

There was nothing wrong with Caddell's analysis as far as it went and for a time the strategy he proposed worked brilliantly. A narrow winner over Ford, Carter quickly rose in public esteem. Sophisticated and jaded Washington might sneer at the cardigan sweater and other homey props the new president used, but in the White House they were convinced the rest of the country liked it, liked Jimmy Carter, and that the President was building a strong political base he could then use "to get things done."

Style, however, has its limits, and an obsession with style can be crippling. There was no better example of this than

Carter's devotion to a concept he called "cabinet government."

Nixon had abused his cabinet, dominated the departments, and sought to run the whole government through a powerful palace guard inside the White House. Carter would have none of that. Each of his cabinet appointees was introduced to the country as "superb," the best in his or her field, and the White House would not attempt to tell them how to run their business, the president-elect promised.

No one stopped to ask: if the President, and those authorized to speak for him from the White House, were not to dictate the direction and policies of the cabinet departments, who, then, would?

"They gave away the government," a disillusioned official said later of this experiment with "cabinet government."

Fifteen months after taking office, with the bright hopes of the early days dissipated, Jimmy Carter tried to regain control of his own government. He summoned the cabinet and his senior White House advisers to Camp David, the presidential retreat in Maryland's Catoctin Mountains, for two days of soul-searching over what had gone wrong.

"The shakedown cruise is over," Carter told the high and mighty of the government as they reviewed the reversals and missed opportunities of the then not-so-new administration.

Precious time, in Fallows's words, had been squandered. And after all the sound and fury of this first crisis meeting at Camp David, little changed. Anné Wexler, a veteran political activist, was brought into the White House to improve the President's liaison with constituent groups. Gerald Rafshoon, the director of Carter's campaign advertising in 1976, joined the staff to improve his public relations and image.

But the Carter Cabinet, which the President had "read the riot act to" at Camp David, remained intact, and so did his tight circle of senior aides from Georgia.

"The Georgians" were an odd lot, not at all the tightly knit cadre of Southern good-ole-boys they came to be thought of. They ranged from Stuart Eizenstat, the President's bookish and cautious domestic policy adviser, to Frank Moore, his beer-bellied congressional relations chief who, accurately or not, gave the impression of not having peered inside a book in years. But their public image was forever set in cement by the manners and mores of the two closest, the two most important of the Georgians.

One was Jody Powell, 33 years old when he became press secretary to the President. He had started as Carter's driver on the dusty back roads of Georgia during a gubernatorial campaign and went on to be his constant companion on the long march to the White House.

The other was Hamilton Jordan, 32 in 1977, an intense and nervous man who was the grand strategist of Carter's campaign for the presidency. Jordan would not be the President's chief of staff—Nixon had had one of those, so Carter would not—but he was to be Carter's closest, most trusted adviser.

Hamilton and Jody, "Butch Cassidy and the Sundance Kid" as they were portrayed in a photograph in *Rolling Stone*, set the public tone for the new White House. They were not close personally and, like others of "the Georgians," they were held together by their loyalty to Jimmy Carter and little else.

But they shared certain values. One was a fierce pride and defensiveness about their Southern heritage. The other was a deep distrust and distaste for what Carter called "the power elites" that dominated politics in Washington and which all of them—Carter, Jordan and Powell—believed were remote from and uncaring for what the President called "The People."

Carter returned the loyalty of "the Georgians" with a blanket of protective defensiveness. The more someone like Moore was criticized for ineptitude in dealing with Congress, the more secure became his position in the White House hierarchy.

But the President was ill-served by many of the Georgians and others he cared for and protected.

He was ill-served by Lance, who brought enormous talent and energy to his job but was burdened by a fatal background that would wipe out much of the public faith in the new administration that Carter had so assiduously built up.

He was ill-served by Jordan, who in his zeal not to be thought of as a part of the hated Washington establishment turned himself into the Dennis the Menace of the national capital. Powell smoldered with many of the same emotions, but Powell, the most public of the administration's public men, usually allowed them to show only in private. Jordan found other outlets, prancing around the White House in blue jeans, flaunting his contempt for the way things had been done pre-Carter. Finally, he made himself an easy target for a disgruntled woman and a gossip columnist who turned a murky barroom incident into a national spectacle, and for two indicted New

York nightclub owners who sought to trade on Jordan's bad boy image, delivering him on unsubstantiated cocaine possession charges in return for better treatment themselves.

Carter was ill-served by Dr. Peter Bourne, his health adviser and an early supporter, who in the summer after Lance resigned was forced to follow him after writing a phony drug prescription for a woman employee in his White House office.

He was ill-served by his brother, Billy, who sought to capitalize on his relationship with the President by turning himself into a professional buffoon. Billy started as an embarrassment to the President, but he ended up a threat, the subject of a Senate inquiry into his ties to a government that stood for everything the administration said was repugnant.

And some of those who served Carter best were seldom publicly rewarded. One of these was Jack H. Watson Jr., another of "the Georgians" but as different from Powell and Jordan as was Cyrus R. Vance, the President's Wall Street-bred Secretary of State. An ex-Marine with the air of an earnest altar boy about him, Watson had headed the Carter "transition team" before the inauguration and flirted with the idea of becoming the de facto White House chief of staff. But he was quickly cut to pieces in a brief power struggle with Jordan and relegated to the obscurity of handling intergovernmental relations for the White House.

While Jordan became a regular gossip column item, Watson kept his name out of the newspapers and he did his job thoroughly. Three years later, when Carter was in his desperate struggle to turn back the Kennedy challenge, his strongest allies in the Democratic Party were the mayors and governors who had come to like and respect Jack Watson for what he had helped to do for their cities and states.

But most of all, the President was ill-served by himself. For in case after case, he tolerated what was going on around him, even at enormous cost to his presidency. For all the talk by his senior aides about how "tough" Jimmy Carter was, how his "steely blue eyes" could burn right through you, the President shrank from personal confrontation. He tinkered with, and enlarged, the circle of those deemed his senior advisers, but the core never changed. Of the eight original members of the Carter senior staff, five would still be with him at the end of the term and a sixth, Jordan, would be in charge of the far more immediate and important business of running his reelection campaign.

Carter never asked Lance—or chose to ignore it if he knew—about his background as a hustling country banker and financial corner cutter.

He tolerated Jordan's juvenile antics, defended his aide on national television and shared the bitterness of others in the White House who felt Jordan had been unfairly singled out by a vicious Washington press corps.

He tolerated his brother's public buffoonery, perhaps because he had been so willing to exploit Billy's "redneck" image when it was politically useful, and then thoughtlessly compounded the matter by recruiting his brother as a quasi-diplomat, asking him to use his ties to Libya in an effort to free the American hostages in Iran.

Carter tolerated Moore's mistakes on Capitol Hill, which were frequent and serious enough that years later the congressional relations chief confessed to the *Wall Street Journal* that he probably should have been fired. When the President looked at his original White House counsel, Robert Lipshutz, he saw a kind and gentle lawyer from Atlanta, a friend and loyal aide who was ill-suited for the high-pressure task given him in the White House. But the President never asked, "Why not the best?"

Carter tolerated, even encouraged, a kind of schizophrenia in his foreign policy as personified by Vance, the careful and cautious negotiator from Wall Street, and National Security Adviser Zbigniew Brzezinski, a glib and vain academician who was given to long theoretical discourses on his "global view" of virtually any issue in international life.

In the oversimplified world of Washington journalism, Vance came to stand for reasoned incrementalism and accommodation, and Brzezinski for the bold historic gamble and, especially when it came to the Soviet Union, for confrontation. Carter let both flourish, picking and choosing between them as the times and circumstances dictated, and later complaining when the critics said his foreign policy lacked coherence.

Fifteen more months of precious time passed before Carter again retreated to Camp David to consider his plight. This time desperation and despair overcame uncertainty. Heads rolled in the cabinet, but the theatrics surrounding the shakeup—the President's mysterious disappearance into the Maryland mountains and his later demand for the temporary resignation of the entire cabinet—proved to be unsettling.

And even with the change of a handful of cabinet secretaries, it was a debatable proposition to say that Jimmy Carter's presidency had changed in any fundamental way. Lipshutz had been gently eased out with a maximum of dignity. He was replaced by Lloyd Cutler, a lawyer skilled in the ways of Washington, a paragon of the "power elites" Carter so despised. But otherwise the inner circle, the people with whom Carter was most comfortable, remained unchanged.

When the administration was being formed, one of those named a senior adviser to the new president was a woman named Midge Costanza. A former deputy mayor of Rochester, N.Y., she was a short, slender bundle of energy given to talking rapidly and too much. Although she had been helpful to Carter in his campaign, she brought no readily discernible expertise to the White House. But Costanza, other than Brzezinski the only non-Georgian on the original Carter senior staff, had one great virtue to the President and the men closest to him—she was a woman, and a woman who need not be taken too seriously by them.

She left the White House shortly after the first Camp David conference and "shakeup," perhaps realizing that she had never been much more than a prop, to be slipped on or discarded as easily as a cardigan sweater.

Now, in the summer of 1979, having gone through a far more traumatic "shakeup," the President once again reached out beyond his inner circle for help. He tapped Hedley Donovan, 65, who had had a distinguished career as editor of *Time* magazine, a courtly and worldly gentleman with a full head of gray hair.

Donovan was named a senior counselor to the President, with free reign to range over all the domestic and foreign policy questions confronting the administration. He was given an office in the coveted West Wing of the White House, and occasionally his appointments with Carter were included in the President's daily public schedule.

Donovan put together a presidential commission on the issues facing the country in the 1980s. But otherwise no one, inside or outside the White House, knew exactly what he did. Carter had reached out for him at a time when the criticism of the White House for ineptitude and amateurism had reached withering proportions, when there was a discernible need for a symbol of maturity close to the President. A latter day Costanza, Donovan served for a year and then left quietly.

Once again an uncertain president had settled for style and symbolism. As in the beginning, it proved inadequate. And the President could not say he had not been warned.

Back in the days when guessing what kind of a president Jimmy Carter would turn out to be was a favorite game in the nation's capital, James David Barber concluded the second edition of his book *The Presidential Character* with these words:

"We have become a nation of uneasy skeptics, suspicious of all the powers that be, listening in the political cacophony for some reliable theme. Carter has an enormous advantage in following Nixon, who was thought to be unprincipled, and Ford, who was thought to be incompetent. But uneasy eyes are on him. The politics of gestures will not sustain hope long, and political faith is fragile. It will take achievement—real progress—to convince a nervous nation that this president named Jimmy is "The People's man."

Three weeks after taking office, the new president left Washington and flew south to a place he said he would return to often to renew his spirit from the pressures that inevitably closed in around him. His airplane—the shiny symbol of the presidency was his now—took him to Warner Robins Air Force Base outside of Macon, Georgia. There was no airport large enough for the big, four-engine Air Force jet close to his ultimate destination, which was still almost 100 miles away. From Warner Robins, of course, the new president could make the rest of the trip by helicopter; he had one of those, too, a shiny, olive-colored machine with the number one painted on its side. It belonged to the Marine Corps.

But Jimmy Carter had promised to be a different kind of president and no aspect of his way of doing things was too small or unimportant not to be included in his determined show of differentness. He had calculated, not because he had an engineer's mind and an eye for detail, because any fool could figure this out, that it cost more fuel and more money to travel by helicopter than by automobile. Therefore, he would go by car.

It was not until later that Carter realized that he had miscalculated. For now when he traveled by car it was not alone, but as part of a caravan of police, Secret Service, staff and press vehicles. He had forgotten that the Secret Service would insist that every intersection he passed, every bridge he went under, be closed off temporarily by state troopers. When you included the extra cost to the state, not to mention the inconvenience to the motorists along his route, it turned out to be better to go by helicopter after all.

But on this first trip, the President arrived in the back seat of an automobile. His motorcade glided into the little town on the main highway, passed the old school house and the softball field, within sight of the town's single block of modest business establishments that had become as familiar as, and in a way resembled, the artificial set for a television series. The President had come home to Plains.

Not everyone was thrilled by the arrival, least of all many of those who accompanied Carter. Even those who had not been assigned to his campaign the previous year had become depressingly familiar with the little town during the long transition between administrations, which the president-elect had decided to spend at home rather than in Washington.

The reporters and Secret Service agents assigned to Carter remembered too well the drab routine, the dreary motel in nearby Americus where they stayed, the ramshackle steak house where they almost always ate dinner. Most of them loathed the place and so when the President decided to return to it so soon after his inauguration, it sent a shutter through their ranks.

My God, they thought, this guy really meant it when he said he would be coming home often.

But Carter didn't mean it or, more likely, he changed his mind about it, as he was to change his mind about the helicopter and the tax rebate he had already proposed to Congress and dozens of other matters. He spent a few days during the Christmas seasons at Plains, but otherwise his ancestral home, which had been the perfect backdrop for an outsider politician waging an anti-Washington campaign, seldom saw him in the next four years.

He never said why but soon enough it became apparent. All one had to do was to see Carter on one of those infrequent visits, like a bright spring afternoon in 1979 when he stopped in Plains briefly on his way back to Washington from a vacation of fishing and solitude on Sapelo Island off the Georgia coast.

Shortly after he arrived, with his wife at his side, he strode out of his house, walking along the main highway, cutting across the road and along a residential street where he could remember the houses in which his childhood friends had lived until he reached the tiny business district. Then the ritual began. The President would pop into the stores along Main Street, not missing a one, shaking hands with old friends, recalling times past and assuring them all was going well with him. As always, a mob swirled about him. Pushing and shoving was the order of the day as reporters, cameramen, tourists and Secret Service agents jockeyed for position near him. As he moved from one store to the next along the street, the mob, like an oversized huddle of demented football players, moved with him.

Why do you do this? he was asked and a look of pained resignation crossed his face. "Because they expect it," he said, nodding toward the stores where the townspeople awaited their president.

He hated the ritual as much as the reporters hated the place. Years later Jody Powell tried to explain why Carter so seldom returned to Plains.

"He was either trapped in his house or he was a totally public figure," Powell said.

But if not Plains, where was the President to go if he wished to escape the White House, as all presidents sooner or later did? Over the years, presidents tended to become identified with the places where they sought refuge. For Roosevelt, such a place was the "Little White House" in Warm Springs, Georgia. For Eisenhower, it was his farm near Gettysburg, for Kennedy the "family compound" on Cape Cod. Johnson had his ranch in Texas and Nixon his grandiose "Western White House" in California.

For Jimmy Carter, that place would be Camp David.

Roosevelt had first used it and Eisenhower renamed it for his grandson but it was made to order for Carter. Two hundred acres of woods and trails tucked away in the gentle Catoctin Mountains, it offered both space and privacy.

Carter used it at moments of crisis—it was to Camp David that he retreated in 1978 and again in 1979 to consider the state of his presidency and the country.

He used it when the stakes were highest—a peace treaty, tenuous to be sure but thought of as his supreme achievement in foreign affairs, bore its name after the 13 agonizing days he spent there with the leaders of Israel and Egypt.

He used it constantly, on weekends and holidays, usually sharing it with only his wife and family, grimly pursuing there his recreational pastimes, one ancient and the other modern, but both singularly solitary endeavors—fishing and jogging.

His election had changed Plains, but it had not changed him. If he had spent much of his adulthood in public life, or the pursuit of public responsibilities, he despised being a public figure.

Carter is a true loner—not a lonely neurotic afraid of the outside world but a man at ease with himself and what is inside his head. He is the kind of man—they are common enough in ordinary life but rare in the upper echelons of national politics—who needs and wants little more than the company of his wife and family to sustain him.

Carter's relationship with his wife, Rosalynn, was extraordinary simply because it was so close—the kind of closeness not always evident in the marriages of ambitious politicians. Through the long campaign for the presidency and the official duties of the White House years, they were forced to spend days and weeks apart. But they gave the impression of never being far apart, of thinking and acting as one.

This may have been because Rosalynn Carter apparently had only one ambition in life: the success of her husband. She was called "the Steel Magnolia" not because her sweet Southern smile was necessarily disingenuous, but because it obviously masked so much more about her and her fierce devotion to her common endeavor with the man she always called "Jimmy."

She came to the White House determined to make her mark. Carter said often in pre-Inaugural interviews that he intended to be an "activist" president, and she intended to be an activist First Lady.

She had her First Lady-type projects, like a mental health commission, and the President often sent her on foreign missions. But over the years, it gradually became apparent that Rosalynn was no ordinary First Lady and that it would not do to pigeonhole her with some typical First Lady-type label, as Jacqueline Kennedy was with redecorating the White House or Lady Bird Johnson was with highway beautification.

It was impossible to measure her influence, except that it was clearly important and pervasive. The President spent more time with his wife than with anyone else and it was clear they did not pass the hours in mundane husband and wife conversation. If they disagreed—fought even over the direction of Jimmy's presidency—no one would know because she wore her sweet smile in public and was defensive about references to her as "the deputy president."

But it was to Rosalynn Carter that Pat Caddell first went with his disturbing poll findings on the mood of the country in 1979, which in turn led to that summer's "domestic summit conference" at Camp David, taking notes on the legal pad while a stream of visitors told Carter what he must do to salvage his presidency. It was she whom the President talked to at night, at the end of each of those ten days in the mountains that ended with the Cabinet shakeup and the attempt to redefine and restructure the Carter presidency.

Rosalynn Carter was the President's friend; so was Charles Kirbo, the Atlanta lawyer and trustee of his financial holdings who years earlier had come to his rescue when one of the courthouse gangs in southwest Georgia tried to cheat him out of his first elective victory.

But there were few others, none in the White House after Lance left. Carter had come to Washington as the "outsider," a title he bore proudly and which remained with him through three and one-half years in the White House. It was said often of the President that he had no real friends in the nation's capital and even those closest and most loyal to him, such as Powell, did not dispute that.

This was particularly evident in the President's relations with the Congress, a Congress controlled by his own party. Carter arrived in Washington with a reputation as a stiff-necked, uncompromising autocrat. He quickly dispelled the fear that he would never bend—some thought he compromised too soon and too often—but the mutual wariness that separated him and the gregarious creatures of Capitol Hill was never completely bridged.

Frank Moore might not have been a wizard at congressional relations, but the President's loner instincts did not make Moore's job any easier. Carter was simply not given to small talk or quick surface friendships. The cool detachment of his personality, his political background, which was entirely outside of Washington, and the circumstances of his election, after a campaign in which he seemed to be waging holy war against the ways of the capital, made that gulf all the wider.

As a state senator in Atlanta, his only legislative experience, Carter had read every bill thrown into the Senate hopper. It made him a walking encyclopedia of facts, sought after for advice on various bills, but it left little time for the after hours good times by which state legislators cement their relationships. He didn't have many friends in the Georgia Senate either.

Carter is an "executive type," at home with the lonely business of decision making, a distinctly different political creature from the "legislative type" to be found on Capitol Hill, Powell believed. And the President recognized this, his press secretary said. Sometimes, after the day's business at the White House was concluded, Carter would wonder aloud what might have happened had he won his first race for the Georgia governorship in 1966 and then, after the single term the state constitution then allowed its governors, had run for the U.S. Senate.

"He would say how miserable he would have been in the Senate," Powell recalled.

But Carter, while different from the Tip O'Neills and Bob Byrds of the world, compromised and reached out. The White House could prove it, show with cold, hard numbers that Jimmy Carter was an extraordinarily accessible chief executive constantly conferring with members of Congress.

And the President's public pronouncements were filled with flowery tributes to the great men of the Congress, how they had shown extraordinary courage or been exceptionally cooperative in overcoming this problem or that.

Only it never quite took; the chemistry wasn't quite right. The reports of Carter's meetings with the members of Congress became depressingly similar—they would talk, he would listen, always politely, assuring them, "I understand," but giving them little feel for the state of his mind or his heart.

In public, the President could not seem to make up his mind about the Congress and its 535 members. At times he would rage against their faint-hearted ways, warn them of "the people's" wrath and denounce their subservience to "the special interests." He threatened to go over their heads directly to "the people," but he never really did. How could he? Most of them were Democrats, and so was he.

At other times, he reverted to the effusive language of compromise and accommodation, understanding the pressures they worked under and praising their excruciatingly slow steps toward goals he wanted met the day before yesterday. The members, accustomed to the daily ritual of posturing and overblown language that passed for debate on the floors of their chambers, never seemed to take either the warnings or the praise very seriously.

The President was a man apart from the members of Congress, but he was a man apart from more than them. There were no simple answers to the riddle of why Carter still seemed a distant figure, but part of it may have had to do with instincts and values that were rooted in a much different America than the one he was trying to lead.

In a country that continued to grow more urban and suburban, Carter was the quintessential small-town president. His outlook was shaped by small-town life and when he spoke about the basic decency and goodness of the American people it was the small towns that he had visited that he had in mind. He owed his election to the small towns of states like Ohio and when he held his celebrated "town meetings" to hear directly from the people they were in places like Clinton, Massachusetts, Yazoo City, Mississippi, Bardstown, Kentucky, and Elk City, Oklahoma.

In a country where the institution of the family is increasingly battered and seemed at times about to come apart, he was an intense family man. Carter was a realist about the inability of anyone to turn back the clock, but sometimes a wistful longing for a simpler time filtered through his public remarks. "Our life was confined to a tiny community," he recalled for the Future Farmers of America at the end of 1978. "And the center of my own existence was my family—close knit, mutually dependent on one another. Americans were not mobile then. It was a very rare occasion for a family to move. How different it is today."

In a country where the state of organized religion had been in decline for years, Carter was an intensely religious man. His religion was not the ordinary, go to church on Sunday type that many Americans adhered to. It permeated his life, comforted him and made him somewhat fatalistic about life's trials, which he knew to be unfair. He was not embarrassed to make his deep religious convictions public or to lecture government employees about the evils of "living in sin." At first there was some skepticism about all this, but it did not last long. In a business, politics, that is replete with hypocrisy, and never more so than when it touches matters of religion, the President's faith passed the acid test of genuineness: Billy Graham never preached in Jimmy Carter's White House.

After three and one-half years, he was still an enigmatic, contradictory figure. Carter seemed to have an almost mystical relationship with something he called "The People," which presumably did not include "the power brokers" and the members of the "political and economic elite" he denounced in his 1976 acceptance speech. The people were good, the President said, and he would try to reflect their virtue.

But in matters of daily life, when it came to dealing with individual people, he could be mean and appear small-minded. He started out by personally controlling access to the White House tennis court, wasting time on that and hundreds of other insignificant details that bogged down his presidency from the beginning. Sometimes his mean streak, which was undeniable, surfaced publicly—as when, after Vance had resigned because of differences over the hostage rescue raid, he needlessly and ungraciously compared the departed secretary to his successor, Edmund S. Muskie.

And complicating all the judgments about Carter's character was one other undeniable trait—he was a seeker after power and single-minded in his determination to retain it. No one who knew him could doubt the sincerity of his effort to free the hostages or the personal anguish he suffered over their plight. But when the rescue raid failed, after Kennedy's campaign had been smashed against the patriotic fervor he had called for earlier, he stopped talking about the captive Americans and glided easily back into the everyday business of politics.

Sometimes he seemed like Charlie Brown, the hapless hero of the "Peanuts" comic strip, who was forever being victimized by people and forces less virtuous than himself. At other times, he seemed more like Lucy Van Pelt, the crabby little girl of the same comic strip, who angrily and defiantly shouted her philosophy of life: "I love Mankind; it's people I can't stand."

★ Reagan ★

by Lou Cannon

HE SEEMED to many, from beginning to end, a most unlikely leader of the nation. As the United States of America entered the complex, computer age of the 1980s, Ronald Wilson Reagan reached backward and spoke to the future in the accents of the past. His suits were as out of date as his metaphors, most of which derived from the Great Depression or World War II. He quoted freely from the Founding Fathers and from his early hero, Franklin Delano Roosevelt. He viewed Soviet expansionism much as Roosevelt had viewed Nazi aggression. When others protested that he saw the world in stark and simple terms, Reagan would say: "For many years, you and I have been shushed like children and told there are no simple answers to complex problems that are beyond our comprehension. Well, the truth is there *are* simple answers—just not easy ones."

By the historical standards of the American presidency, Reagan seemed an even more unlikely leader. Though he was vigorous and athletic, he was 69 years old and would be 70 within a month of taking the presidential oath of office. The age showed in the dewlapped wrinkles of his neck. It showed in the Reagan campaign schedules, which were generously endowed with "staff time" that was the euphemistic reference to Reagan's afternoon nap. And Reagan in other ways seemed singularly unprepared for the office which he and others have ritualistically referred to as "the most important in the free world."

He had not held public office in six years. He had no foreign policy experience. He had never worked in Washington. He was a divorced man espousing the values of the family, a wartime stateside noncombatant advocating military preparedness, a fiscal conservative who as governor of California had sponsored the largest tax increases in the state's history.

But despite all this and the majority party and the White House incumbency against him, Reagan was a formidable candidate with an appeal that reached beyond his natural, conservative constituency. He was larger than the sum of his parts. Some said this was because he was a superb television performer whose skills were honed by years of professional experience. Others said he was a lucky politician (as some had said of Jimmy Carter), with the good fortune to face overrated opponents at the time they were most vulnerable. But there was another reason, and it was more important than the others. It was that whatever Reagan lacked in complexity or youth or consistency, he made up for in an unremitting vision of America. The vision was the thing. It was a vision frozen in time, which made it more powerful than transitory visions. Reagan believed in it, which made it even more powerful. A close personal aide, Michael K. Deaver, said this about Reagan's belief: "He's resolved something, his being or what he is, a long time ago. He seems to know what is right."

And whether Reagan did, in fact, know what was right, his vision of America was what made this aging, out-of-date ex-actor credible to other Americans. Reporters and Reagan aides would smile at one another and head for the press buses when Reagan approached his standard tear-jerker ending of the basic speech he used in early 1980. They would laugh outright when Reagan, for the thousandth time, quoted John Winthrop aboard "the tiny Arabella" in 1630 as telling his followers that they should be "as a city on a hill."

"The eyes of all mankind are still upon us," Reagan would conclude. "Our party came into being more than 100 years ago, born of a great crisis at that time. We led this nation through that crisis. We are being called upon again. Let us keep our rendezvous with destiny, let us build a shining city upon a hill."

This was part of Reagan's vision, and the audience did not laugh at it. Most of the people who heard the speech applauded. A few of them cried. And they came back for the equally simplistic and more materialistic versions of the vision: "At the heart of our message should be five simple familiar words. No big economic theories. No sermons on political philosophy.

Just five short words: Family, work, neighborhood, freedom, peace."

Historically, Reagan's vision was rooted in small-town Midwestern America of the early 20th century—then the real and symbolic heartland of the nation. His values were shaped in a day when most Americans lived not in the great, cluttered urban landscapes of our time but in towns and small cities surrounding a more pastoral land. When he was trying out self-characterizations early in the 1980 campaign, Reagan briefly referred to himself as a "Main Street Republican," a phrase intended to show that he was not a boardroom candidate like John Connally or an Ivy Leaguer like George Bush. The phrase, quietly discarded after the primaries because Reagan's advisers thought it made the candidate seem partisan and out of date, was an appropriate description of Reagan. Like all persons, he is a product of his time and region, his experience and his culture. For Reagan it was small-town Illinois, the quintessential Main Street celebrated in Middle America and satirized by Sinclair Lewis's famous novel of the same name. "Main Street is the climax of civilization," Lewis wrote in the preface to his novel, which appeared in 1920 when Reagan was nine years old. Lewis meant these words sardonically but Reagan would accept them as literal truth. In his autobiography, *Where's The Rest of Me?*, Reagan describes his childhood as "a rare Huck Finn–Tom Sawyer idyll."

"Reagan was shaped by the small towns of the Midwest, and that explains in large part the simple moral and conservative approach he brought to public life," wrote early biographer Bill Boyarsky in *The Rise of Ronald Reagan*. "Where Lewis satirized the Midwest communities, Reagan glorifies them. He enthusiastically accepts the values that Lewis criticized. As a result, he is deeply respectful of business; determinedly conservative; mistrusting of change; unintellectual and slightly suspicious of higher education . . . convinced that, as his father said, 'All men were created equal and man's own ambition determines what happens to him the rest of his life.'"

Reagan's father, John Reagan, known as Jack, was a gregarious, nomadic, hard-drinking Irish-American whose own life seems to have fallen far short of his ambition. He was a Catholic in a Protestant land and in Reagan's childhood a fierce opponent of the Ku Klux Klan, which was at the time a national force in American politics. In his autobiography, Reagan related how his father, then a traveling salesman, was told by a small-town hotel clerk that he would appreciate the accommodations because Jews weren't permitted there. "I'm a Catholic," Reagan quotes his father as saying, "and if it's come to the point where you won't take Jews, you won't take me, either." Jack Reagan then stalked out, spent a cold winter night in his car and became seriously ill.

At the time his second son Ronald was born, Jack was working as a clerk in the Pitney General Store in Tampico. Jack's ambition was to own his own store, a goal briefly realized but quickly crushed by the Depression. Ronald Reagan still seems troubled by what happened to his father. When he announced his presidential candidacy on November 13, 1979, Reagan repeated an oft-told story of Christmas Eve in 1931 when Reagan and his older brother Neil were home from college.

Their father received a special delivery letter he hoped would be a bonus. It was instead a "blue slip" telling him that he had been fired.

Ronald Reagan was born in a five-room flat above the Pitney General Store on February 6, 1911. For the first nine years of his life he lived in a procession of Illinois cities and towns: Chicago, Galesburg, Monmouth, Tampico again and finally Dixon, the place Reagan still calls his hometown and where he lived until he was 21. His mother, and the anchor of the Reagan family, was Nelle Wilson Reagan. She was a do-gooder, a lifelong member of the Christian Church who practiced what she preached. Reagan and his older brother remember many instances of her finding food or jobs for needy persons. Sometimes the Reagan home became—in a day when the phrase was unknown—a halfway house for released convicts.

Reagan was a prodigy. Born with a remarkable memory, he learned to read at an early age and dazzled his mother, who encouraged him to read newspapers aloud to her friends. Reagan recalls reading an account of the Preparedness Day bombing in San Francisco on July 22, 1916, when he was five years old.

There were other ways in which the Reagan home was avant-garde for Dixon. The Reagan boys called their parents by their first names and they called the boys by their nicknames—"Dutch" for Ronald and "Moon" for Neil. The Reagans were the town Democrats in a place and time devotedly

Republican. Both Jack and Nelle participated in amateur theatricals which stimulated the imagination of their children and which made both of them talk about an acting career.

But there also was the dark side of Jack Reagan's alcoholism. Even the relentlessly cheerful Reagan autobiography, written in 1965 with one eye to his coming political career, cannot disguise Reagan's feelings about his father's drinking. "I was 11 years old the first time I came home to find my father flat on his back on the front porch and no one there to lend a hand but me," Reagan writes. "He was drunk, dead to the world. I bent over him, smelling the sharp odor of whiskey from the speakeasy. I got a fistful of his overcoat. Opening the door, I managed to drag him inside and get him to bed. In a few days, he was the bluff, hearty man I knew and loved and will always remember."

Children are stronger than we expect them to be, and there is no evidence that Jack Reagan's alcoholism cast any permanent blight on the lives of his sons. Ronald Reagan would not drink at all for many years, and he was repelled by the Hollywood cocktail circuit. But by all accounts, including his own, he grew up to be a resolute, cheerful young man, hardworking and unintellectual, interested in football and girls and theatricals. Athletic and well-built, Reagan enjoyed the role of local lifeguard, and the varying numbers of persons he saved from drowning became an obligatory part of his political biography. Most of all, he enjoyed talking. He had a nonstop gift of gab that had been encouraged by his mother's showing off of his precocious reading ability. As a freshman at tiny Eureka College, Reagan's fiery speechmaking made him the leader of a student strike (over Depression-cancelled classes that would have prevented some students from graduating) which cost the college president his job. He developed a consuming interest, which has never left him, in the medium of radio, which Franklin Roosevelt was then using to carry the gospel of the New Deal to the countryside. At Eureka, Reagan would listen for hours to sports broadcasts, sometimes interspersed with Roosevelt's "fireside chats." Thirty-five years later, as governor of California, Reagan would use the fireside chats as his model for broadcast and televised reports to the people on the public issues of the day.

The Depression and Hollywood stand with Main Street as the shaping symbols in the life of Ronald Reagan. Reagan still considers the Depression as the single most important influence upon him. The Depression cost his father a partnership in a Dixon shoe store. It sent his mother to work in a dress shop for $14 a week. Reagan, then working his way through Eureka, sent $50 a week home so that his parents could continue to get credit at the local grocery store. But there were many others in as difficult a predicament, or worse. Often, in his days as governor, when Reagan was asked whether he had been poor as a child, he replied with the bromide that "we were poor but we didn't think of ourselves as poor." Sometimes he used the line when he was talking about limiting welfare, the way out for the modern poor. As a historical reference, however, Reagan's statement is an accurate one. What had happened to the Reagans had happened to America.

In his senior year at Eureka, Reagan won an acting award for his role in *Aria de Campo*, an anti-war play by Edna St. Vincent Millay, and he had thoughts of an acting career. But he had no job and he returned to Dixon, uncertain of his future and thinking of radio as an entry into show business. Reagan applied for work at several Chicago radio stations and was turned down. Then, in the fall of 1932, came a chance to broadcast University of Iowa football games for WHO, the NBC affiliate in Des Moines. Reagan had been a starting guard at Eureka, and he loved football. From his first broadcast, he gave a tense and evocative account of what was going on on the field of play below. When baseball season began, Reagan's proclivity for nonstop talking plunged him into the since-lost art of recreating baseball games from the laconic summaries of the action furnished by Western Union telegraph. At a time when everyone listened to radio, Dutch Reagan became a sportscasting star.

He used radio as his springboard to Hollywood. In 1937 he accompanied the Chicago Cubs to Catalina Island off the Southern California coast for spring training, and a friend arranged a screen test for him at Warner Brothers. Reagan passed easily and Hollywood proved even more suitable for Reagan's talents than had radio. Starting out on low-budget pictures, where his ability to quickly memorize scripts proved an enormous asset, Reagan advanced to become "the Errol Flynn of the B's." He made 31 movies in five years, progressing from his $200-a-week starting salary to the princely figure of $1,650 a week in 1941. Popular and invariably cast as a good guy, Reagan had mastered his craft and seemed to be rising to the pinnacle of stardom. Though burdened with "B" pictures, he won critical acclaim for performances in *Brother Rat* (where Eddie Albert made his debut and where Reagan met his first wife, Jane Wyman), in *Knute Rockne* (where Reagan plays the doomed Notre Dame football player George Gipp and Pat O'Brien plays Rockne), in *Dark Victory* (with Humphrey Bogart) and, especially, in *King's Row*, where the cast included Claude Rains, Robert Cummings and Charles Coburn.

King's Row, the story of a small Southern town more malevolent than Dixon, was Reagan's best picture. He portrayed Drake McHugh, a playboy whose legs are amputated by sadistic surgeon Coburn as revenge for the seduction of his daughter. "Where's the rest of me?" yells McHugh, coming to without his legs and uttering the future title of Reagan's autobiography. *Commonweal* praised Reagan for a "splendid performance," and other reviews were uniformly good. Reagan liked the film too, and in the tradition of ego-laden Hollywood would often show it to house guests after dinner. After Jane Wyman divorced him, she was quoted as saying, "I just couldn't stand to watch that damn *King's Row* one more time."

Reagan never quite fulfilled the acting promise of this period. His career, like so many others, was interrupted by World War II, most of which Reagan spent in Hollywood making training films with the First Motion Picture Unit of the Army Air Corps. Reagan's career couldn't hit its stride after the war, when newer, younger stars were coming along and Hollywood was fighting its own multifront war with television, labor unrest, foreign films, and domestic investigating committees. At the beginning of the war, Reagan had lost out to Humphrey Bogart for a role in a picture that was retitled *Casablanca*. When the war was over he lost his chance to play in another film classic which also starred Bogart, *The Treasure of the Sierra Madre*. Reagan's choice of films, when he had a choice, had never been exceptional and by now his luck was running bad. Given a role in the movie version of the John Van Druten play, *The Voice of the Turtle*, Reagan objected to playing with a new leading lady and asked for June Allyson instead. The actress he objected to was the richly talented Eleanor Parker, subsequently to be nominated for four Oscars. "It took me only one scene with Eleanor to realize that I'd be lucky if I could stay even," Reagan acknowledges in his autobiography.

Reagan's marriage was on the skids along with his movie career. The low point of the career came in 1951, when Reagan played opposite a chimpanzee in *Bedtime for Bonzo*. His marriage had come to an end three years earlier, during Wyman's filming of *Johnny Belinda*, for which she won an Academy Award. Reagan quipped to a gossip columnist that *Johnny Belinda* should be named as correspondent in the divorce action. If Miss Wyman's testimony in the divorce action is to be believed, a better choice would be the Screen Actors Guild which increasingly was taking more and more of her husband's time. The picture she painted, both in court and outside of it, was of a bored wife who no longer shared her husband's interests.

Exit Ronald Reagan actor. Enter Reagan, labor negotiator, public spokesman and future politician. By the early 1950s, although he was still appearing in occasional films, Reagan had in effect established a new career. As leader of the Screen Actors Guild and six times its president, Reagan had become fully embroiled in the economic and cultural issues which shook Hollywood after the war.

If Main Street represented the climax of American civilization in the 1920s, Hollywood was in this post-war era the undisputed capital of American mass culture. Everything that affected Hollywood was a page one story in Peoria—or in Dixon, where the preferred reading matter was the *Chicago Tribune*. These stories included sensational accusations that the movie industry was honeycombed with Communists, disclosures that a key union was operated by gangsters, the emergence of both television and foreign films as a major competitor and taxation-induced "runaway" of U.S. films to foreign countries. Reagan was in the midst of these battles. During the Red-hunting days which Hollywood now remembers with embarrassment and some shame, Reagan opposed Communists but also disputed the basis thesis of the House Committee on Un-American Activities in these words: "I do not believe the Communists have ever at any time been able to use the motion picture screen as a sounding board for their philosophy or ideology." At the time of the Congressional investigations, his stand fully pleased neither side. But he emerged from that period as an effective and adroit political leader who had kept his union intact.

Reagan's personal life and political views were now changing. He had described himself as a "near hopeless hemophiliac liberal." But in 1952, four years after his divorce from Wyman, Ronald Reagan married Nancy Davis, adopted daughter of a conservative and wealthy Chicago surgeon Loyal Davis. In 1954, he became the host for "General Electric Theater," a new half-hour television series, with a salary of $125,000 a year and generous expenses. The G.E. contract, which might be said to have launched Reagan's political career, gave him an opportunity to be seen each week on television and to talk to G.E. employees all over the country.

While some old Hollywood friends ascribe Reagan's increasing conservatism of this time to Nancy or her father, it is probable that General Electric, and Reagan's growing prosperity, had much to do with Reagan's changing political views.

At the outset, Reagan's message in his speeches to G.E. employees was patriotic, anti-Communist, pro-Hollywood. Reacting to the general nature of his talk, G.E. Board Chairman Ralph Cordiner suggested to Reagan that "you work out a philosophy for yourself." Increasingly, that philosophy became pro-business, anti-government conservatism. It was a philosophy more congenial to the Republican Party than to the Democrats, at least in California. But Reagan, like many Americans, found it easier to embrace Republican principles than to abandon the political faith of his family. As a Democrat, Reagan had supported Helen Gahagan Douglas in her U.S. Senate race against Richard Nixon in 1950. By 1952, he was a Democrat for Eisenhower. When Nixon ran for president in 1960, Reagan was still a Democrat but this time supporting Nixon. Two years later, when Reagan was speaking for Nixon during his unsuccessful campaign for governor of California, a woman in the audience asked him if he were a registered Republican. Reagan said he wasn't, but indicated his willingness to join the GOP. The woman, a volunteer registrar, marched down the aisle and signed him up as a Republican on the spot.

By this time, Reagan had become a partisan politician almost without recognizing it. He was becoming an embarrassment to General Electric, which did much business with the government Reagan was consistently denouncing. When Reagan used the Tennessee Valley Authority, a major customer of G.E., as an example of government waste, the company asked him to delete the reference. Reagan complied, but there were those at General Electric who now wanted to be rid of

Reagan altogether. In 1962, G.E. suggested that Reagan limit his speeches to touting the company's products. By then, "General Electric Theater" also was in trouble, facing competition from "Bonanza," a show which became one of Reagan's favorites. When Reagan balked at the limitations G.E. wanted to place on him, the company abruptly cancelled "G.E. Theater." Reagan never knew whether it was his speeches or "Bonanza" which hurt him most.

However, Reagan was now prepared for a political career. He had shaken hands with 250,000 G.E. employees during his eight years as company spokesman and made speeches from one end of the country to the other. He had a philosophy, name recognition and a winning smile. He also had money, and owned valuable ranch land in the Malibu hills. Increasingly active in Republican politics, Reagan in 1964 was named California chairman of the Barry Goldwater presidential campaign. The leaders of that floundering effort, short on money and party unity, decided to put Reagan on national television. The result, wrote David S. Broder after that campaign, was "the most successful national political debut since William Jennings Bryan electrified the 1896 Democratic convention with his 'Cross of Gold' speech."

Reagan's emotional speech on the night of October 27, 1964, stirred millions of Americans, but it was familiar to those who had heard him on the G.E. circuit. Basically, it was the same speech he had given for eight years and would give for another 16 until it grudgingly gave way to new material in the 1980 campaign. There was the celebration of economic individualism: "We need true tax reform that will at least make a start toward restoring for our children the American dream that wealth is denied to no one." And, there were statistics: "The Defense Department runs 269 supermarkets. They do a gross business of $730 million a year and lose $150 million." And, there was democratic idealism: "This idea that government was beholden to the people, that it had no other source of power except the sovereign people, is still the newest, most unique idea in the long history of man's relation to man." And, finally, inevitably, there was the influence of Franklin Roosevelt, who first discovered an American "rendezvous with destiny" while accepting the Democratic renomination for president in 1936. Americans have been holding clandestine meetings with destiny ever since, this one from the peroration of the Reagan speech for Goldwater: "You and I have a rendezvous with destiny. We can preserve for our children this the last best hope of man on earth or we can sentence them to take the first step into a thousand years of darkness. If we fail, at least let our children, and our children's children, say of us we justified our brief moment here. We did all that could be done."

Although Reagan didn't know it then—and though he resisted the idea for nearly a year and a half—this speech stands as his opening address in the campaign for the California governorship in 1966. It raised nearly $1 million for the Republican Party and its candidates. And it caused wealthy Republican contributors in California, such as auto dealer Holmes Tuttle, industrialist Henry Salvatori and the late A.C. (Cy) Rubel, chairman of the board of Union Oil Company, to consider Reagan the best hope to wrest the governorship of the nation's most populous state from the Democrats. When an exploratory committee run by his millionaire GOP backers, "The Friends of Ronald Reagan," raised both money and enthusiasm, Reagan agreed to make the race. The rest, as they say, is history.

Reagan's eight years as governor of California also are history—and there is general agreement among the historians that he was at least an adequate governor and perhaps a good one. State Treasurer Jesse Unruh, a Democratic legislative powerhouse at the time Reagan arrived in Sacramento and the man Reagan defeated to win his second term as governor, offered this balanced viewpoint to the *Los Angeles Times* in 1974: "As a governor, I think he has been better than most Democrats would concede and not nearly as good as most Republicans and conservatives might like to think." Bob Moretti, the Democratic speaker with whom Reagan negotiated his historic welfare bill in 1971, wound up liking and respecting his adversary. In the legislative hyperbole of the time Moretti (and Unruh, and most other Democrats) frequently described Reagan as a heartless, know-nothing foe of the poor, higher education, and racial minorities. But in retrospect, Moretti finds Reagan both a reasonable politician and a man of his word, saying of him: "His bark was worse than his bite."

Any serious evaluation of the Reagan governorship collides squarely with Reagan's own exalted view of his accomplishments. As Reagan told the story on the campaign trail in 1980, it was a golden age during the eight years he served as great

helmsman of California's ship of state. "Every time we had
a surplus, because I don't think government has a right to take
one dollar more than government needs, we gave the surpluses
back to the people in the form of tax rebates," Reagan would
tell his approving audiences. "We gave back over eight years
$5.7 billion to the people of California. We stopped the bu-
reaucracy dead in its tracks, the same way I would like to stop
it at the national level."

This account omits as much as it relates. What Reagan does
not say is that these surpluses, in part, were a result of his own
policies. He does not say that he sponsored what was then the
largest tax increase in California state history and that state
spending and taxes more than doubled during his tenure. Corporation, bank, sales, and personal income taxes all rose
sharply during the Reagan years. The annual state budget increased from $4.6 billion to $10.2 billion and the operations
portion of the budget, over which the governor has more control, increased from $2.2 billion to $3.5 billion. State taxes per
$100 of personal income, a better measurement because it
adjusts for population and price changes, went from $6.64 to
$7.62.

But a case can be made that, despite these figures, Reagan
succeeded in his basic goal of controlling the cost of government. "Reagan was not so much an under-achiever as he was
an over-committer," says one-time legislative aide Judson
Clark of the Sacramento consulting firm, California Research.
"He did some important things, but not as much as he said he
would do and not as much as he said he did." Among the things
Reagan did do was slow the growth of the state work force,
which had increased nearly 50 percent during the eight years
of his Democratic predecessor, Edmund G. (Pat) Brown. There
are different measurements of work force growth, but the generally accepted one shows a 7 percent increase during the Reagan years at a time when state workforces elsewhere were
growing far more rapidly. Reagan cut by 40 percent a capital
outlay budget which had increased 200 percent during the
Brown years. And if the $4 billion which the state gave back
in property tax relief is subtracted from Reagan's budgets, they
roughly kept pace with inflation during his two administrations.

Had Reagan accomplished this result with the tax structure
he inherited, the result would have been that low-income taxpayers would have shouldered most of the financial burden.

The supreme irony of his governorship is that the burden was instead thrust in great part on the corporations and middle-class taxpayers which Reagan had been ritually defending in his speeches to conservative audiences. Under Reagan, in that first tax bill, the levy on banks was boosted from 9.5 to 13 percent. The tax on corporations increased 61 percent—from a 5.5 to a 9 percent rate. This happened, in part, because of Reagan's ignorance of the way government actually worked. And it happened, also, because even in his ignorance he proved a masterful and intuitive politician.

This combination of ignorance and intuition worked reasonably well for Reagan as he struggled to understand the intricacies of government. At least it did on most issues. Where it failed him was on the emotional issue of abortion. In 1967, sponsors of liberal abortion legislation had chosen California as the testing ground on which to promote the nation's first liberal abortion law. California at the time, like a majority of other states, permitted abortions only to save the life of the mother. The liberalizing U.S. Supreme Court decision opening the abortion floodgates was yet to come, as was the counter-revolution of the Pro-Life Movement. In those days the leading body of opposition was the Roman Catholic Church, which launched a letter-writing campaign that produced more mail than most legislators have ever seen. Reagan, as he puts it, had never thought much about the issue one way or the other. At one critical press conference, after the bill had advanced through key committees, Reagan showed almost total confusion about the measure's provisions, freely contradicting himself and describing as "loopholes" provisions which sponsors said were the major purpose of the bill. On one side, Reagan was lobbied for the bill by physicians including his father-in-law, Chicago surgeon Loyal Davis. On the other, the church brought its big guns to bear, and Francis Cardinal McIntyre called the governor and urged him to veto the legislation. Reagan finally signed the bill after the author had made some amendments which supposedly made abortions more difficult to obtain. The statistics of what happened after enactment tell another story. In 1967, there were 518 legal abortions in California hospitals. In 1978, the last year for which complete figures are available, there were 171,982 abortions. From 1967 through 1978 there were 1,230,359 abortions performed under the bill signed by Reagan, now the ardent champion of a U.S.

Constitutional amendment that would impose the restrictions on abortion that were on the books in California when he became governor.

Reagan did better on other issues. He conducted his office with integrity and his governmental appointments, many of them drawn from the business community, were of high quality. So were his judicial appointments, which usually followed the recommendations of the bar. Sometimes this produced a judiciary more independent than Reagan would have liked—as it did when Reagan-appointed Supreme Court Justice Donald Wright tipped the balance in striking down a Reagan-backed capital punishment law.

Occasionally, Reagan approved truly innovative programs, as in authorizing conjugal visits for prisoners with good behavior records. Reagan supported legislation increasing the length of sentences for criminals and more funding for state prisons. Originally, he slashed the funds for state mental hospitals. Then, he restored the funds and gave additional money to community health programs being pioneered in California. State expenditures for mental health doubled during the Reagan administration.

He entered office waging what some called a vendetta against the University of California, scene of a controversial and prophetic "free speech" demonstration. "Obey the rules or get out," thundered Reagan, as he called upon campus authorities to expel "undesirables." Under threat of budget cuts, Reagan tried to force the university to abandon its historic policy of "free tuition" and make students pay more of the costs of higher education. Reagan helped force out University of California Administrator Clark Kerr, who had unwisely provoked a vote of confidence, and he did persuade the regents to accept tuition under another name. But the budget-cutting never materialized. Once Reagan had made his point, he was generous to the university. State spending for higher education rose 136 percent during the Reagan years compared to an overall state spending increase of 100 percent and an enrollment growth of 40 percent. Even educators who resented the anti-intellectualism of Reagan's approach—he had once accused universities of "subsidizing intellectual curiosity"—praised the governor for the increased funding. There is disagreement to this day, however, on whether the verbal attacks on the university caused intangible damage which cost the university top-flight faculty.

It was the performance of the Reagan administration on environmental issues which proved the greatest surprise. "A tree's a tree—how many do you need to look at," Reagan had said during his campaign for governor. Environmentalists viewed Reagan's election as the coming of the dark ages in a state which always has been in the forefront of the conservationist movement. Reagan fought this impression by choosing William Penn Mott, a nationally known park director, as director of state parks. He picked Norman (Ike) Livermore, a lumberman who also was a Sierra Club member, as director of resources. Together, Livermore and Mott compiled a generally enviable record for the Reagan administration—although it was notably pro-industry on smog control issues. A total of 145,000 acres, including 41 miles of ocean frontage, were added to an already impressive state park system. Two underwater park preserves were set aside off the Pacific coast. A major bond issue for park development was proposed and the endangered middle fork of the Feather River was preserved.

What some think was Reagan's finest hour as governor came on the issue of the Dos Rios Dam, a proposed 730-foot structure on the middle fork of the Eel River, a steelhead-spawning stream that is one of California's few remaining wild rivers. The California water bureaucracy, then considered more powerful than the highway lobby, was enthusiastic about the Dos Rios high dam. When the Army Corps of Engineers joined forces to formally propose Dos Rios under the battlecry of water for populous Southern California, its approval was considered a foregone conclusion. Against an array of big battalions, which included wealthy Reagan contributors, were a few Reagan aides (including Livermore, State Finance Director Caspar W. Weinberger, and Reagan's present chief of staff Edwin Meese) and a few conservationists from Round Valley, which would have been flooded by the impounded waters of Dos Rios. Among these residents were descendants of Indian tribes which had been herded into the valley by Army troops late in the 19th century. The Indians argued that Round Valley contained gravesites and valley land that was secured by treaty. It was their plea which proved decisive. "We've broken too damn many treaties," Reagan said in turning down the Dos Rios Dam. "We're not going to flood them (the Indians) out."

The major legislative achievement of Reagan's eight years in office was the 1971 Welfare Reform Act. It is one of many bills which looks good on its own and insufficient when matched against the Reagan rhetoric. "When I took office, California was the welfare capital of the nation," Reagan says on the stump. "Sixteen percent of all those receiving welfare in the country were in California. The caseload was increasing 40,000 a month. We turned that 40,000 a month increase into an 8,000 a month decrease. We returned to the taxpayers $2 billion and we increased grants to the truly needy by 43 percent." Most of these figures are exaggerations, or otherwise misleading. The average caseload increase for the two years prior to enactment of the welfare reform measure was 26,000 not 40,000. Reagan's bill did increase the grants for the poorest recipients—which had not been raised a penny during the supposedly liberal regime of Pat Brown—but half of this increase was mandated by federal litigation. The $2 billion which Reagan talks about is a legislative projection which made no allowance for the dropping birth rate or increasing employment in California at this time.

Still, the Welfare Reform Act was good legislation which could be defended as easily in New Deal terms as the ones Reagan used for his conservative audiences. The Urban Institute, a non-profit Washington research group, called the legislation "a major policy success" in a report issued in 1980. Even taking into account the birth rate, and increasing employment, the institute said that the Reagan program had reduced the welfare rolls by 6 percent under what they otherwise would have been while increasing maximum grants. Frank Levy, the senior research associate who wrote the report, said there were "big symbolic differences in the rhetoric" between what Reagan and various liberals had proposed to improve the welfare system but that the substantive differences were far less than either side was likely to admit. The Reagan program, said Levy, was "reoriented toward fiscal control" but "on balance, more recipients appear to have been helped than hurt." By the time the legislation was passed, there were 1,608,000 persons on the welfare rolls—about one in every eleven Californians. In the next three years the total declined to 1,330,000—significantly lower but still among the highest in the nation. The Urban Institute study found that the major feature of the control was a simple device requiring each recipient of a welfare check to mail a signed postcard each month certifying income and eligibility. In the face of this rudimentary requirement, welfare fraud seemed to melt away. On the other hand, Reagan's ballyhooed required-work program had little direct effect on the rolls, with only 9,600 persons assigned to jobs during a three-year period.

At ground level, Ronald Reagan is decent, likable and homespun, used to being the center of attention but reserved to the point of occasional shyness. Unless aroused by some challenge, he is basically a passive person—reacting to Nancy, reacting to staff, reacting to autograph seekers and to questions that are put to him. He seems to like who he is, and the names other men have called him—"Dutch" and "the Gipper" and "the cowboy"—are names of affection and respect. He is considerate of other people. Many who have seen Reagan up close think he is literally considerate to a fault with aides, neither demanding enough of them nor reprimanding them when they do poor work. But he is sensible about some things that other men are not sensible about.

When Nancy Reagan was incensed by an anti-Reagan editorial campaign in the *Sacramento Bee*, Governor Reagan acceded to her request and cancelled the subscription at home. Then he took the paper at the office, confiding that it was a way to have the *Bee* (which he regularly read) and keep Nancy happy at the same time.

Reagan has a genuine sense of humor. When students pressed around his limousine during a college demonstration and yelled, "We are the future," Reagan scrawled a reply on a piece of paper and held it up to the window. "I'll sell my bonds," it said. And when a wire-service reporter of long acquaintance brought him a reissued promotion picture from *Bedtime for Bonzo* showing Reagan and the chimpanzee in bed together, Reagan autographed it with the words, "I'm the one with the watch."

Reagan comes from a milieu where reaction is required. An actor must be prepared, but he awaits the call of others before he can come onto the stage. And the working hours are different, or at least they were in Reagan's day. The phrase "9 to 5 governor" is accurate in a sort of rough-hewn way, but it is not a complete description of Reagan's working habits. As an actor, Reagan might work with great concentration on a film for six weeks or two months and then have a long period of inactivity. He is capable of bursts of very intensive campaigning, as anyone who saw him in New Hampshire in 1980 can attest. But he does not function well working long and hard over an extended period, and he does not want to work that way. "Show me an executive that works long overtime hours and I'll show you a bad executive," Reagan once said. What's more, he really believes this.

Reagan's nature and working habits combine to make him a delegator of authority. Edwin Meese, who served Reagan as chief of staff in Sacramento and then again in the 1980 presidential campaign, once remarked that Reagan was a near-perfect delegator because he gave a grant of authority that was clearly defined. "If you operated within the limits of what he wanted to accomplish, he wouldn't second-guess you," Meese said. "And he was decisive when you brought something to him."

Even those who concede that Reagan delegates well and decides quickly have questions about his basic intelligence. Reagan is, as they say, no rocket scientist. Many find him lacking in imagination. But Reagan consistently has confounded those who have underestimated him. There is a kind of small-town common sense about him that serves him well and shows in moments when it is least expected. And more than most people would suspect, Reagan has an appreciation of his own limitations. "I think any adult man knows his shortcomings and knows his strengths," Reagan has said. "I've never claimed to be the originator of every idea we had in Sacramento, but I do think I have the ability to recognize good ideas. I do think, also, that I set the tone and direction in which we wanted to go. We were fortunate enough in surrounding ourselves with people who shared our beliefs and whose talent was turned in the direction of implementing them." These are not the words of a stupid man. But Reagan's intelligence is functional rather than reflective. He is best under pressure— as at the Nashua debate and again on August 9 in the South Bronx where Reagan turned a disastrously advanced event into a triumph by telling a woman who was screaming at him: "I can't do a damn thing for you if I'm not elected."

Reagan's most unnerving quality is his proclivity for giving verbatim memorized responses he has used repeatedly as if he were saying them for the first time. It is like punching the button of a tape recorder and hearing the coded message, complete with sincere gestures and that "aw shucks" smile. Partly, this may be a learned defense mechanism which permits Reagan to talk safely to reporters and supporters on the campaign trail. But he has done this with friends in private conversations, too, and it leaves some of them wondering whether he has an original thought in his head. Others, more charitably, regard the mind-taped messages as a natural consequence of Reagan's combined acting and speaking career and say he gives memorized answers without realizing that he is doing it.

Perhaps Reagan has simply made too many speeches. There is much to recommend the observation of old foe Hale Champion (Pat Brown's last finance director) that Reagan is "the Reader's Digest of politics." At least well into the 1980 campaign, *Reader's Digest* was certainly Reagan's favorite reading material. "In both cases," wrote Champion in the *Washington Post*, "their statistics and illustrations have a folklore character. They are, if I may use a non-word, factitious. The figures aren't very good, they often don't prove anything and sometimes they are barely tangential to the issue at hand. But they sound great, and they seem to strengthen the message by making it seem more real, even more concrete." These dubious statistics also enable Reagan, in public or private, to tell his audiences what they want to hear. And this desire to please, more than anything else, has been the source of Reagan's trouble in presidential campaigns. Reagan is almost never embarrassed in direct confrontation, where both the physical and the mental juices are flowing. But before a friendly audience he is likely to say almost anything—once calling for a "bloodbath" if necessary to quell student demonstrations, and, in this year's election campaign blandly referring to the Vietnam War as "a noble cause" before a veterans convention and then four days later questioning the theory of evolution before an audience of fundamentalist ministers.

Reagan's nature and way of doing business make him a natural target for anyone on his staff or in his constituency who wants to foist off a pet proposal on him. Reagan is considerate of others and he wants people to bring ideas to him. While he is pragmatic enough to know that he can't accomplish everything contained in his rhetoric, he nonetheless has real goals and fundamental beliefs.

Watching Reagan struggling to find himself after Noble Cause and Evolution and Taiwan, it occurred to me that he may be more complicated than we have made him out to be. Most of us are. I have been covering Reagan, on and off, since his first campaign for office 14 years ago, have covered him in office and have written a book about him. I have seen him on bad days and good, in triumph and defeat. He seemes to me a good, if limited, man who has demonstrated that it is possible to govern constructively from a conservative ideological base. And yet there is something about Reagan which remains hidden, never glimpsed in those predictable airplane interviews or in the dreary accounts of how Reagan would use the experience he gained in Sacramento to remake Washington. The something shows occasionally in those "vision of America" endings which drive reporters to the press buses. But it shows even more on those rare occasions when Reagan admits visitors to Rancho del Cielo, the remote fog-shrouded ranch north of Santa Barbara which he has chosen as a haven for himself and his wife Nancy. Watching him tell proudly of how he laid the floors and rebuilt the roof of his understated ranch house and put in the fence around it, watching him saddling horses for the obligatory media ride down the old Western trail, watching him look at Nancy to see if she approved of what he was doing and saying, I thought of the passage in *Death of a Salesman* where the son tells about the porch his father built and says that there is more of Willy Loman in that porch than in all the sales he ever made. I wondered if this were also true of Reagan. He had grown up in Main Street America in the first third of this century believing as his father had told him that the only limits on what he could accomplish were those imposed by his ambition. It is a conceit of our system that anyone can be president and Reagan had taken this idea—this fundamental democratic notion which is close to the wellsprings of our national existence—quite literally. He had become a popular sportscaster, a well-known actor, the leader of his labor union and twice the governor of the nation's most populous state. Now he was the Republican nominee for president. Because of what he had done, Reagan was Everyman. And because this is America, and it is what America expects of its Everymans, Reagan had not been ruined by this, at least not that I could see. He still liked working with his hands, and he liked to ride. He still hammed it up for his friends, as he must have done in Dixon, and he still needed and desired the public and private approval of those closest to him. But he was not riding off into the sunset, at least not this day. The sun was behind him as he rode down into the television cameras. Ronald Reagan was about to put the democratic ideal to one of its sternest tests. And he had every confidence that he could do it.

★ V ★

The Race

Richard Harwood

★ Labor Day 1980 ★

by Richard Harwood

THE SUMMER was extraordinarily hot and dry. The grasslands of the Great Plains and the Southwest withered and died. Pictures of dead cattle were seen on the evening news, evoking memories of the Great Depression. The great cities of the East sweltered. There was water rationing in New Jersey. Lawns in suburban Washington turned dusty and brown.

It was not an auspicious time for politics or politicians. The enervation of the cruel summer was compounded by a weariness with public affairs. Barry Sussman's first post-convention poll found that only three Americans in ten thought it made a great deal of difference which party elected the next president. Curtis Gans of the Committee for the Study of the American Electorate predicted that fewer than 55% of the 160 million potential voters would go to the polls in November. Throughout the country—and in Europe, too—journalists, intellectuals, statesmen and other elements of the educated class lamented the Hobson's choice of Jimmy Carter and Ronald Reagan. Ordinary Americans shared these misgivings.

The *Post*'s national correspondent, William Prochnau, took soundings on a meandering, 6,000 mile drive from the West Coast to Washington, D.C. He began with an Oregon raft trip with his nephew, Steve:

> *In the forests along the river strong, sinewy young men like Steve are gathering ferns for florists instead of felling trees no one wants. This is because no one is building houses because no one can afford the mortgage*

275

rates because someone in far-off Washington decided to put the clamps on.

Steve can beat the Umpqua River and the tide, applying the sinew to the oars. He can beat a rain-forest downpour, digging pitch out of a rotting tree to light a fire in the sheets of water, the way his father taught him, the way his father, my brother, taught me and all of us. He is not sure he can beat the far-off Washington that has his friends picking ferns.

At the mouth of the Umpqua, in Reedsport and down the Oregon Coast in Coos Bay, the mills are chewing up finished lumber, which no one wants to buy, and converting it to chips for pulp, which people don't need mortgages to afford. It's as if Chrysler were transforming its unwanted Imperials into beer cans because financing isn't needed for a sixpack.

"Shit," says Steve and it is a word I will hear over and over, as a description of presidential candidates, and Washington's whimsies, in a hundred sentences that defy parsing and occasionally defy logic but are loaded with quiet passion.

Not far north of Reedsport, Carter Lake lies almost hidden in the mists that billow each day over the Oregon dunes. It lies next to Lost Lake.

On the day President Carter was renominated in far-off New York, 13-year-old Ching Mei, a Chinese-American from San Francisco, stood alone in the reeds along the shore of Carter Lake, staring at a single loon mournfully wailing.

The country, young Ching Mei said, was "going down." He wrote off Jimmy Carter with a graceful sweep of the hand, a Tai Chi exercise sweep taught him by his father, a Tai Chi master in San Francisco.

And Ronald Reagan? Reagan was too old for Ching Mei, a "wrinkled old actor" who offered no hope either. Ching Mei's father fled Inner Mongolia in his 60s, started a new family here in his 70s, sired the boy when he was 74 and still practices as a Tai Chi master at 87. So goes it.

In far-off Washington, D.C., it was the same. A September poll of the Federal bureaucrats, government contractors and

scientists who inhabit the rich suburban satellite of Montgomery County, Maryland, were as baffled as Ching Mei: two
thirds of the Democrats and a fifth of the Republicans were
undecided on a presidential choice. "There's a general feeling
of malaise among the voters that includes all of the candidates,"
said Dr. Allen Levey, the chairman of the state Republican
Party. "It's very troublesome—I think we're going to have a
very low turnout in Maryland."

MALAISE.

We began this book with Barry Sussman's exploration of
"malaise," a word Jimmy Carter discovered in the summer of
1979 to describe the failings of the American people. This
"malaise," we concluded, had little to do with the personal
lives or capacities or the personal hopes and fears of Americans.
It was rather an expression of a widespread loss of faith in the
competence of the great institutions in our society, most notably
in the competence of the institution of government and the men
who directed it. That had not changed by Labor Day, 1980.
One of Bill Prochnau's subjects, a man in Las Vegas, expressed
a common view: "The people I talk to think their own future
is bright, the world's future is grim. I guess that's the way I
look at it, too."

There was a fascinating lesson in this for those who manage
and manipulate our public and political affairs. This campaign
had been underway for more than two years, since a day in
1978 when the soon-forgotten Philip Crane announced that he
would seek the presidency. In the endless months that followed,
the sophisticated operatives of the American political industry
had been mobilized and thrown into a battle for the minds of
the people. They had spent tens of millions of dollars to create
images and shape attitudes through clever television and radio
advertising, through carefully crafted speeches and position
papers, through scientifically selected "media market" events.
The mass media had deluged the citizens with facts, analyses,
criticisms, praise and ridicule. Tens of millions of people had
been persuaded to take part in primary elections and caucuses
and precinct cajoleries.

In the end, in the most fundamental sense, nothing had
changed. Neither the political industry nor the mass media left

any significant traces on the outcome. A parade of articulate, photogenic candidates had been offered up as alternatives to Ronald Reagan, who had been the choice of ordinary Republicans since 1976, and to Jimmy Carter, who had been the choice of ordinary Democrats since the start of the year. The challengers, despite the lavish efforts of advertising experts, demographers and imagery consultants, fell like carnival dolls—Crane, Connally, Baker, Brown, Kennedy, Bush, Dole.

The political industry, moreover, had failed to change or redirect in any way the bedrock concerns of the American people or the qualities they sought in their president. As the final match began on Labor Day, the simple agenda of most Americans was the agenda Barry Sussman defined at the beginning of 1980:

"We wanted peace and prosperity and good health. We were afraid of being unloved and alone. We were ambitious for our children. We sought in our presidential candidates two prime virtues: competence and character."

Those issues would decide the 1980 election in the nine weeks and two days that remained until November 4, a date that would mark the first anniversary of the hostage-taking in Iran.

★

"Character" is a concept over which philosophers and semanticists may endlessly debate. We have used the word repeatedly in this book and we mean by it what the dictionary says: "the complex of mental and ethical traits marking and often individualizing a person . . ."

"Competence," as we have used the word, means nothing more than the ability of a man to get things done and to do them well.

Jimmy Carter was renominated by his party because of his character. He was perceived, as the polls of Barry Sussman and George Gallup and all the rest have shown, as a decent, honorable, well-intentioned man, who embodied virtues that are widely admired.

He worked hard. He was a dedicated family man. He was not a privileged "elitist." He had come out of a small Southern town from a family of modest means. He had served in the Navy and was a patriot. He had made a success of a small business. He was a Christian whose Christianity was verbalized in terms of love and tolerance for all mankind. He was intelligent and self-confident. His goal, he said in 1976, was an American government "as good as the American people." He was, in short, an uncommon, common man. When Sussman and other pollsters asked if he "understands the problems of people like you" or asked if he "could be trusted to do the right thing," the results were always favorable to Carter. There was empathy between Jimmy Carter and the American majority.

The "competence" question was another matter. After only two years in the White House, Carter's competence had become something of an international joke and by Labor Day, 1980, that perception had not changed. As a candidate in 1976 he had promised an inflation rate of 4 percent, an unemployment rate of 4 percent, a balanced budget, less dependence on oil imports, 2.5 million housing starts each year, a smaller federal government, national health insurance, a reduction of $5 billion to $7 billion annually in defense expenditures. None of those things had been achieved. The annual inflation rate, on Labor Day, was estimated at 13 percent; the unemployment rate was 8 percent; the budget was $61 billion in deficit; oil imports were 24 percent higher than when he had taken office; no health insurance bill had been enacted; the defense budget was rising faster than the rate of inflation.

"Competence" is getting things done. Carter had failed on that test. Indeed, "things" seemed out of control as Ching Mei and countless other Americans saw it.

Ronald Reagan became the candidate of the Republican Party because of his "character." Like Carter, he was a small-town boy who had made his way in a competitive society without the advantages of wealth or the credentials of the Eastern Establishment—a Harvard degree, for example. He was an achiever who, in his personal life, could claim most of the virtues that enhanced Jimmy Carter's image of character. He symbolized in his appearance, his choice of clothing, his age, his rhetoric and, even in the movies he had made in Hollywood, an idealized remembrance of an idealized past. He was a strong patriot. He believed in an America existing in this troubled world as Number One. He evoked in many minds a vision of the United States during World War II, a proud, victorious nation that stood for the noble and true things in life, a nation that would stand up to the bullies in international affairs and set things right.

As for "competence," he could boast of his two terms as governor of California and if the claims—like Carter's in 1976—were inflated now and then, it was not important. He had been a successful governor, had been reelected overwhelmingly and had left no legacies of disaster.

It was both interesting and fitting that on Labor Day, 1980, these two small-town boys should stand precisely equal in the national political polls. They had survived the longest, most difficult and most open political process in our nation's history. If they were regarded by many as pygmies, as a Hobson's choice, then the American people could take responsibility for that. They had not been forced on an unsuspecting and unwilling electorate by fat men in fedoras, smoking long cigars. They were the people's choice.

And whichever of them made it to the White House would make it essentially on his own because the time had long since passed when either party could automatically assemble a winning majority. The grand coalition built by Franklin Roosevelt in the 1930s had been shattered in the years after World War II by ideological realignments that affected virtually every segment of society. The once Solid South was now a competitive, two-party region. The powerful political machines of the great northern cities had been broken up by reformers, population migrations, ethnic antagonisms and by the inexorable intrusion of the federal government into local affairs. The labor movement was divided on ideological and programmatic lines. The suburbs, now more populous than the central cities, were politically volatile.

In the euphoria of Richard Nixon's landslide reelection in 1972, there was hope among Republican intellectuals that a new Republican majority could be formed out of the uncommitted electoral fragments that had been deciding elections for two decades. Those hopes foundered as Nixon was driven from office in disgrace. They were revived by Reagan who symbolized, as did Nixon, the counter-revolution to the counter-culture of the 1960s and 1970s. Professor James Wilson of Harvard defined the essence of this counter-revolution:

> "Reaganism stands in opposition to those who believe in the unrestrained right of personal self-expression and the need for government to rationalize all other aspects of human affairs by rule and procedure. Reaganism opposes those who would legalize marijuana, abortions and pornography and tolerate or encourage draft resistance, all in the name of personal freedom, and who would support court-ordered school busing, bans on gun ownership, affirmative action, and racial quotas, all in the name of rationalizing and perfecting society. Indeed, Reaganism is based on a profound conviction that the opposite policies are more nearly correct: if communal constraints on individual self-expression are sustained, then people will grow up to do the right thing with respect to blacks and the use of guns. Reagan's acceptance speech at the Republican National Convention described his cause as one based on a 'community of values embodied in these words: family, work, neighborhood, peace and freedom!' Family, work and neighborhood came first." (From *Commentary*, October, 1980.)

There was no doubt that these social issues evoked powerful emotions in the American people. Busing was intensely unpopular. There was widespread uneasiness over the epidemic of drug abuse that had created by 1979 nearly 9 million addicts or heavy users, over the epidemic of lawlessness that involved more than 12 million serious crimes each year and over the growing number of abortions—more than 1.5 million annually. Some of these concerns found expression in the Republican Party platform, in the call, for example, for a Constitutional amendment prohibiting abortions.

But for all the public concern and despite the rise of Right-to-Life groups, anti-ERA organizations and the political efforts of evangelical ministers, nothing approaching a majority based on "Reaganism" had emerged in the last weeks before the election. Reagan, himself, largely ignored these "social issues" in his speeches and advertising campaign. Furthermore, it was not easy to identify Carter with the "counter-culture." If anything, he was Reagan's superior as a puritan moralist, as strongly opposed to abortion and drugs, as strongly devoted to family and neighborhood. A Gallup poll in early September found that among the millions of "born-again" Christians in America, Carter led Reagan 52 percent to 31 percent.

So neither man brought a majority coalition to the last weeks of the campaign. It was to be a choice of personalities, a judgment on character and competence.

The League of Women Voters symbolizes a longing in the United States for an orderly and highminded political process. We have a kind of Jungian memory of dramatic and principled debates in our past that dealt, in a rational way, with the grand issues of slavery and free soil, federalism and states rights, free land and the coinage of silver, expansionism, the League of Nations, war and peace.

The memory is tainted with romanticism. Yet it is possible that the series of debates the League wished to sponsor in the campaign of 1980 might have come to something, because the underlying and sometimes unstated issues between Ronald Reagan and Jimmy Carter were not trivial. The electorate might have been offered, in the words of an earlier politician, a "choice, not an echo."

The impulses of the Reagan campaign and of the forces behind it involved two fundamental changes of tone and policy that were in direct collision with the impulses of the Carter campaign and of the forces behind it.

The intellectual essence of the Reagan program was that in domestic affairs a laissez-faire economic program with minimal government interference would achieve greater prosperity. In foreign affairs, the ability and willingness to use military power in the "national interest" was essential to the survival of Western civilization and would ensure peace.

These concepts were profoundly at odds with the intellectual foundations of the Carter Administration. In domestic affairs, Carter and Carterites were interventionist, committed to federal social and economic management. In foreign affairs, Carter was a non-interventionist, a moralist and conciliator who cringed from the use of military force except in extraordinary circumstances. He was proud, he often said, to be "the first American President in 50 years who has never sent troops to combat."

The American people were as divided on these issues as the politicians. They wanted, in theory at least, to "get government off our backs." At the same time, they welcomed government interventions that enhanced economic security and employment. They wanted peace but, as Barry Sussman's polls showed us, they were almost evenly divided on the use of force to secure the release of the hostages in Iran.

The debates the League wished to sponsor on these matters failed to materialize in September because they failed to satisfy the tactical needs of the candidates. There was a brief encounter in Baltimore between Ronald Reagan and John Anderson, the independent candidate with the hopeless cause. But it was tame and inconclusive. As for Reagan and Carter, their perceived self-interest drew them together in centrist postures. Their differences were muted and compromised and by the first of October, there had been hung on them the label of "Tweedledum and Tweedledum."

Lacking substantive intellectual conflict, there was an inevitable preoccupation with "character and competence," not with programs or visions of America in the 1980s and beyond. Personality and self-revelation became a near obsession of the media, of the campaign organizations and, to some extent, of the electorate.

In early September, Reagan seemed to be stumbling badly. His image of "competence" was tarred by what came to be called the "gaffe game." There was a storm in the newspapers and on the television networks over his statement that he would seek "official" ties to Taiwan, which had lost all "official" but not "unofficial" status with the United States after the normalization of diplomatic relations with China. In an appearance before a Christian fundamentalist rally he had expressed doubts about the validity of the Darwinian theory of evolution and had endorsed the teaching of "creationist" theory in the public schools. In a speech in Ohio he used the word "depression" rather than "recession" to describe the state of the economy. He criticized President Carter for opening his campaign in Tuscumbia, Alabama, which he erroneously referred to as the "birthplace of the Ku Klux Klan." Speaking to a group of veterans he revived a painful issue out of the past by referring to the Vietnam war as a "noble cause."

A respectable intellectual case might have been made for most of these statements. But as they were rendered by the media and transmitted to the electorate, they took on a life of their own. They lent credence to the charge that Reagan was too old and old-fashioned, too simple-minded or shallow to occupy the White House. They terrified his advisers and after only a week of campaigning, Lou Cannon of our staff reported: "Ronald Reagan campaigned today in gloomy weather, which matched some of the omens for his own campaign."

Historians of a later time will review the periodicals and videotapes of the first days of the fall campaign of 1980 and look in vain for the grand debate that might have been. The distinct themes laid out by Reagan in a speech accepting his party's nomination will not be found, nor Carter's for that matter. (See Appendix   for the acceptance speeches.) The "gaffe game" dominated the news.

We have called ourselves a "throw-away" society that discards plastic cups, values, ideas, fashions and personal relationships with equal facility, a society in which all things have an instant half-life.

That cynical and depressing view of our political processes seemed validated in September, 1980, as future historians will also discover. By mid-month the "gaffe game" that appeared to be "destroying" Ronald Reagan and his claim to "competence" had been replaced by the "mean" issue that, overnight, seemed to be "destroying" Jimmy Carter and his claim to "character."

In one of his first post-Labor Day speeches, Carter declared that "Reagan is different from me in almost every basic element of commitment and experience and promise to the American people. . . . I believe in peace. I believe in arms control, I believe in controlling nuclear weapons. I believe in the rights of working people of this country, I believe in looking forward and not backward. I don't believe the nation ought to be divided one region from another. In all these respects Governor Reagan is different from me. . . ."

Before a black audience in the South, Carter accused Reagan of injecting "racism" and "hatred" into the campaign. On the West Coast the President asserted that the election, in effect, was a choice between "war and peace." In Chicago he said a Reagan victory would mean that "America might be separated, blacks from whites, Jews from Christians, North from South, rural from urban." A national television advertising campaign drove home the point night after night that Reagan "shot from the hip" and was a threat to peace.

Thus was born the issue of Jimmy Carter as a "mean" mudslinger, as a "ruthless and reckless" political opportunist. Editorials and cartoons denouncing "low road" politics poured off the printing presses. The network news programs responded in kind. A presidential news conference was dominated by the issue, with Carter asked repeatedly if he *really* believed Reagan to be a "racist" and a warmonger. The reply was "No" and finally, as the criticisms continued, Carter granted a television interview in which he disavowed his earlier tactics and promised to raise the campaign to a higher level.

These were the surface issues of September, "gaffes" and "mudslinging." What, if any, impact they had on the electorate was not to be found in the opinion polls. September ended as it had begun with the candidates tied in voter preference and with millions of Americans wracked by indecision.

Political campaigns are complex undertakings, conducted at many levels on many fronts. Journalists tend to focus on rhetorical events, "gaffes" and "mudslinging," for example. These are intellectual transactions between candidates and electors. Other and sometimes more substantive transactions occur—economic transactions, emotional transactions.

The issue of "racism," raised by President Carter, was one of those emotional transactions. It was essential to his strategy that there should be a large turnout of black voters in 1980. Their loyalties were overwhelmingly Democratic. They held the theoretical balance of power in a score of states, both North and South, especially in an election in which the white vote seemed evenly divided. A black academician, Eddie Williams of the Joint Center for Political Studies in Washington, D.C., observed: "Jimmy Carter will undoubtedly again get 90 percent of the black vote, as he did in 1976. The question is: 90 percent of what?" Inflation, unemployment and the recession had hit American blacks especially hard during Carter's years in the White House. They needed a reason to vote in 1980 and that reason, as Democratic Representative Parren Mitchell put it, was that "Reagan represents a distinct danger to black Americans. . . ."

There was nothing in Reagan's record to support a charge that he was "racist." But soon after the Republican convention,

a group of Ku Klux Klansmen endorsed him. He repudiated
the endorsement but the potential for embarrassment remained
and the Democrats exploited it. In a speech to black Southern
political activists Carter called up the issue: "You've seen in
this campaign the stirrings of hate and the rebirth of code words
like 'states' rights' in a speech in Mississippi; in a campaign
reference to the Ku Klux Klan relating to the South. That is
a message that creates a cloud on the political horizon. Hatred
has no place in this country."

Parren Mitchell told the same audience: "I'm going to talk
about a man (Reagan) who has embraced a platform that some
men known as the Ku Klux Klan said couldn't be better if
they'd written it themselves... who seeks the presidency of
the United States with the endorsement of the Ku Klux Klan."
Coretta King, widow of the Rev. Martin Luther King Jr., and
Patricia Harris, Carter's Secretary for Health and Human Services, carried the same message to other audiences. Reagan's
endorsement of "states' rights," said the black leader Andrew
Young, means "it's going to be all right to kill niggers when
he's president." Advertisements were placed in black-oriented
publications. They carried pictures of the president with Supreme Court Justice Thurgood Marshall and with Mrs. Harris.
The caption said: "Jimmy Carter named 37 black judges.
Cracked down on job bias. And created 1 million jobs. That's
why the Republicans are out to beat him." These advertisements—and Young's statement—were later disavowed by the
White House, but the point was made. An emotional transaction had taken place. Its purpose was quite clear: to provide
black voters with a motivation to go to the polls.

Transactions of this kind are commonplace in the American
political process. The Republican platform's call for a Constitutional amendment against abortion was an emotional transaction which Reagan exploited with a promise to appoint to
the Supreme Court judges who have "respect for innocent life.
Now, I don't think that's a bad idea. I think all of us should
have a respect for innocent life. With regard to the freedom
of the individual for choice (of) abortion, there's one individual
who is not being considered at all. That's the one who's being
aborted. And I've noticed that everybody that is for abortion
has already been born."

That position had emotional resonance. Barry Sussman's
polls revealed that only one out of five Americans supported

abortion on demand. Four out of five had reservations or ambivalent reactions. The Democratic Congress reflected those numbers in adopting, on October 1, strict restrictions on the use of federal monies to pay for abortions. But the fact remained that, for Reagan, it was more of an emotional than an intellectual transaction. As governor of California he had signed one of the most liberal abortion laws in the United States under which 1.3 million abortions have been carried out since 1967.

Both Reagan and Carter made extravagant commitments to American Jews over the emotional issue of Israel and its future. They made emotional commitments to beleaguered industries—steel, autos, textiles. They scheduled major speeches before ethnic groups—Poles, Italians, Hispanics—in which emotional rhetoric overtook or blurred the ability of an American president to deliver. Reagan's comments on Darwinism and the "creationist" theory of the origin of man were calculated to strike emotional chords with Fundamentalist Christians.

The economic transactions consummated in the first weeks of the campaign represented another level of political reality. Carter, using to the hilt the possibilities of incumbency, announced for the dairy industry a new and costlier program of milk-price supports, new work for the Philadelphia Navy Yard, the award of $150 million in urban development grants, federal funds to deal with the chemical problems at Love Canal in upstate New York, $200 million from the Department of Transportation for buses, $300 million for farmers suffering from the drought. Cabinet officers, from the Secretary of State to the Secretary of Labor, traversed the country reassuring various constituencies, challenging Reagan's policies and announcing various kinds of federal aid.

Reagan, long identified as the candidate of corporate America, made open bargains with American labor unions and, in the process, reversed long-held positions. He would preserve—not abolish—the Occupational Safety and Health Administration; he would no longer seek a national right-to-work law; he would no longer propose extension of the anti-trust laws to labor unions and would no longer seek repeal of the Davis-Bacon Act, requiring that federal contractors pay union wages.

He promised, contrary to some earlier comments, not to tamper with the Social Security system.

Carter had likewise changed many positions. He had promised in 1976 to cut the defense budget. In 1980, he boasted of

defense budget increases. He had opposed in 1976 the deregulation of oil prices. In 1980 he boasted that he had achieved
that result. He had promised never to use unemployment to
combat inflation, but that had been his policy.

We tried at the end of September to assess the impact of
personality, of emotional and economic transactions on the
fortunes of the candidates. Barry Sussman's polltakers interviewed more than 5,500 people in eight large and diverse
states—New York, Michigan, Ohio, Illinois, Texas, New Jersey, Pennsylvania and Florida. The "horse race" numbers were
virtually unchanged from the beginning of the month—35 percent for Carter, 33 percent for Reagan, 12 percent for Anderson. The rest were undecided or voting for "others" or not
intending to vote.

On the questions of character and competence, two trends
had set in. Reagan's attacks on Carter's economic policies and
the state of the economy itself were clearly enhancing Reagan's
position. He was regarded as more competent than Carter in
his ability to "get things done" and in his ability to "preserve
the value of the dollar."

Carter, on the other hand, had a distinct advantage on the
character issue. By substantial margins, Sussman's voters had
more trust in Carter to "do the right thing" as president, to
better handle negotiations with Iran, to work effectively with
Congress, to deal with difficult foreign problems.

These findings suggested very strongly that Carter and his
political advisers knew precisely what they were doing in their
September attacks on Reagan as a "risky" president who might
lead the country into war. And there was no evidence that these
attacks had damaged perceptions of Carter's own "character."
Rather, they had instilled serious doubts about Reagan, doubts
that surfaced in the finding that voters in these eight crucial
states were divided equally on the issue of whether Reagan
was "well qualified" to be a good president—44 percent said
"yes," 44 percent said "no" and the rest were unsure.

There was further evidence of the success of the Carter
strategy in the attitudes of women toward the candidates. They
were "dovish," our polls showed, on the issue of war and peace
and they favored Carter over Reagan by a significant margin—
38 to 31 percent.

It was remarkable, given the enormous media attention to
the issue of Carter's "mean" character and his "mudslinger"

tactics, to find at the end of this spasm that his image as "a nice man" was virtually unimpaired. And he evoked widespread sympathy for the burdens he carried.

Sharon, a 39-year-old Texan who runs a day care center, spoke of the "problems he has had to contend with. Anyone— Republican or Democrat—would find it hard." Otis, an 80-year-old retired telegraph operator, saw Carter as a "good, honest man, doing the best he can." Tony, a 28-year-old student in Pennsylvania, said, "He's had a lot of bad luck. A lot of things have gone wrong which haven't totally been his fault."

For Reagan, the month's events had been hurtful in some ways. We encountered frequently comments such as these: "He's just auditioning for another part. He's just an actor. He's just too old."

"He was a good actor but I don't think Reagan would be a good president."

"He is a good actor and will not make a good president."

On the positive side, many voters—responding to the Reagan advertising campaign—were impressed by his record as governor. Even those comments, however, defined one of his major problems; he was a figure out of the past—out of Hollywood and Sacramento—a figure whose present views and capacities were dimly perceived. He had thus failed to draw sharp distinctions between his own policies and Carter's and had, in the meantime, suffered from Democratic accusations of impulsiveness and inexperience.

As September ended, the crucial question for both parties was simple enough:

Who is Ronald Reagan?

How the question was defined for the electorate would determine the outcome.

★ October ★

by Richard Harwood

RONALD REAGAN suffered a small indignity on a California campus early in October. A banner was strung across an old and lovely tree. It carried this message: "Chop me down before I kill again." It was a prank, inspired by a clumsy Reagan statement to the effect that trees pollute the air. Beyond its literal message, the banner symbolized a serious problem for Reagan. Put bluntly it was this: Was he too ignorant or too dumb for the presidency?

At a symposium of public opinion analysts in Washington at about that time, Peter Hart, a consultant to Democrats, spoke at length about the negativism that was coming to dominate the campaign. Feelings of hostility and dislike outweighed any positive feelings toward the major candidates. The result, said Lance Tarrance, who had conducted polls for John Connally, was that "we are going to elect the next president based upon some dimple or wart, rather than an issue or positive personality traits."

Jimmy Carter's warts and wens had been under public scrutiny for more than four years, as a candidate and as a president. He had created among millions of Americans an image of indecisiveness and weakness; more than 40 percent of the people in Barry Sussman's October polls thought he "just can't cut it as president." But he was, in any case, a known quantity, a real person in the American consciousness.

Reagan was vulnerable because he was not "real" in the American mind. There was a fictional dimension to him derived from the fact that Americans knew him best as a whole series of fictional characters they had encountered on countless film and television screens. Even through this long campaign of 1980 the only encounters he had with the masses were through the television medium. His commercials had the quality of old film and newsreels. They left unanswered the question of the "real" Reagan. Who was he? Were his warts and dimples real? Was he slow-witted and dangerous, as the Democrats claimed? Peter Hart referred to this Reagan mystery in describing a conversation with a 45-year-old school teacher in Independence, Missouri. She wanted to vote for Reagan even though she had many unanswered questions in her mind. One of them was this: "I want to know if he dyes his hair. If he does, I will not vote for him." That trivial concern suggested the dimensions of his problem. Even his children professed not to know him well. T. R. Reid of our national staff went searching for the "real" Reagan in the autumn of 1980 and discovered quicksilver. There was no "real" Reagan in ideological terms, he reported. On the contrary, Reagan had performed many ideological roles—college radical, New Deal liberal, moderate Republican, conservative Republican and, as 1980 wore on, neo-conservative who had made a grudging peace with the ideology of the New Frontier and Great Society. "The ability to charm and, as he sometimes puts it, to 'sell' an audience," Reid wrote, "has been the rock on which Reagan has built his three media careers—in radio, in Hollywood and in politics. Politics has always involved the 'need for showmanship,' Reagan told the *Hollywood Reporter* at the start of his first campaign, and performance (the acting out of a role) has always been the central element of his political style."

Lou Cannon, who has followed Reagan's career for more than 15 years and who traveled with him throughout the campaign of 1980, had a complementary view of Reagan's apparent ideological flexibility. In a memorandum written late in September Cannon told his editors at the *Post*:

> In my view, it is useful to look at Reagan's September emergence as a born-again New Dealer not as a sudden shift in strategy but as the third act in a long drama in which Reagan is the central player. There has never been any doubt that Reagan would campaign as a centrist in the general election campaign. He has done that in the past in his campaigns for governor of California. He planned to do it this time through three campaign man-

agements—John Sears, an interim committee management and the present system in which Stu Spencer is the
de facto campaign manager while William Casey retains
the title. He would probably do it by instinct, if he hadn't
planned to do it, for Reagan is a natural politician who
senses moods and issues.

Reagan is a "man of parts," as (David) Broder and
(Stephen) Hess once described him and there has always
been a distinction between Candidate Reagan in the primaries and Candidate Reagan in the general election. In
the primaries the candidate is the figure familiar on the
conservative banquet circuit—confrontational rhetoric,
militant anti-communism and gibes at government, all
of which play well with business audiences. This is the
Reagan who tried to outflank Nixon on the right in his
short Southern campaign of 1968 and it is the Reagan
who battered Ford on the Panama Canal Treaty issues
in the nearly successful campaign of 1976. . . . It is the
Reagan who emphasized his opposition to gun control
and abortion in New Hampshire this year.

Then there is the general election Reagan. In 1966
Reagan relegated the John Birchers, then a big number
in California, to the task of canvassing each other and
said that any Bircher who supported him was "buying
my philosophy; I'm not buying theirs." His issues were
student disorders . . . plus inflation and the tax increases
under the Brown administration.

(In 1980) you would probabably have seen a different,
though still centrist, Reagan if Ted Kennedy had been
the nominee, a Reagan who stressed "family values"
rather than economic ones.

James David Barber is an historian and political scientist
at Duke University who applies the craft of psycho-history to
the study of public figures. He attempts to discover, through
their personal careers and life experiences, what kind of people
they are and how they are likely to behave in office. In an
interview with *U.S. News and World Report* shortly before the
election, Barber attempted an analysis of Reagan's character:

His would be a rhetorical presidency. Reagan's style
is centered on speechmaking. He has been a speechmaker

ever since, as a young college freshman, he made a dramatic speech that won great support on the campus . . .

Reagan also is likely to try to please people. His political life centers on collecting affection from his environment. He wants to be at the center of a friendly crew of colleagues who are appreciative of him and like him. The man, after all, is an actor who wants to please his audiences. He has spent his lifetime trying to do that. (He) uses rhetoric to get along with his audiences without being very serious about what he says. He is not at all the rigid right wing ideologue that Carter and company suggest. Once he got to be governor of California, he didn't act in an extreme fashion. He said many foolish and extreme things, but those are poor indicators of what he would do as president, because they were poor predictors of what he did in California.

I don't think you would have in Reagan the danger of a mean, tough person pushing the government around or getting the United States into tragic difficulties because of his personal lust for power.

He is what I call a "passive positive" type. He has always been a kind of booster, an optimist, a conveyor of hopefulness. He is passive in the sense that he has a long record of saving his energies, of not working too hard. He was a 9-to-5 governor and as a campaigner he takes it pretty easy. The danger is that people with this kind of personality give in to pressure too quickly.

The role playing that had marked Reagan's life and had brought him substantial success seemed to be the very source of his difficulties as the October campaign proceeded. Carter and Reagan, at that stage, resembled the salmon of the Columbia River trying to climb the fish ladders at Grand Coulee. They lunged upward, fell back, lunged upward again and again fell back. Neither could break clearly in front. It was now obvious that John Anderson was out of it. He might deny votes to one or the other of the major candidates and thus, in at least a few states, affect the outcome in the electoral college. But he had no hope of victory for himself; his followers were drifting away and his standing in the polls had dropped below 10 percent.

By the reckoning of his advisers, Reagan at this point should have enjoyed a comfortable lead over a president whose liabilities were known to virtually all Americans. The economy remained in distress. The world outside our shores was troubled and volatile. A war raged between Iran and Iraq in the Persian Gulf, posing real dangers to the petroleum supplies on which Western civilization depends. American, French, British and Australian warships were on station nearby. U.S. military aircraft were on station in Saudi Arabia. New fears arose over the safety of the American hostages, still held in Iran after nearly a year. The Soviet occupation of Afghanistan continued and there was apprehension over a Soviet invasion of Poland where workers were engaged in a bloodless revolt against their government.

But these events had no perceptible impact on Reagan's fortunes. If anything, he seemed to be slipping as Carter continued to assault him on the "war and peace" issue and as the media, focusing on new verbal gaffes, raised doubts about his intellectual qualifications for high office. His vulnerability on these points was related to that nagging question: Who is Ronald Reagan, what about him is real, what about him is playacting?

If, as James David Barber believed, Reagan needed "affection from his environment," October was becoming a month of deprivation. The mass media, as Robert Kaiser of our staff reported on Saturday, October 18, were giving him no comfort:

> Two weeks ago, Ronald Reagan was enjoying his best moment in the fall campaign on two counts. First, the media coverage, particularly on television, was friendly and upbeat, while President Carter was getting the treatment for his "mean" campaigning. Second, a large part of the media seemed to be forming a consensus over the weekend of October 4–5 that Reagan was moving into a real lead in the horse race.
>
> It was a time for good feeling and the Reagan camp felt good. "Optimism" was the one-word headline on a report about the Reagan campaign that appeared in the *Post* on October 4.
>
> Now the moment has passed. First, the horse race no longer appears to favor Reagan. Second, the media coverage of Reagan has turned negative. The 1980 yo-yo has reversed directions again. Both changes deserve scru-

tiny. Both are instructive examples of the dynamics of a presidential campaign in the mass media era.

If there is a first law governing media behavior in an election campaign, this may be it: never fall behind a trend, never miss a new situation. Following this law, reporters, producers and editors trip repeatedly into the snapshot trap. They take new snapshots constantly, then periodically misinterpret one of them as a genuine portrait.

The snapshot ten days ago showed Reagan leading in enough states to win the election, at least according to the surveys done by NBC News, *Newsweek*, the *Washington Star* and the *New York Times*. . . . The snapshot showed Carter struggling with a spreading perception that he was campaigning nastily, meanly, unpresidentially.

But this was just a snapshot, not an accurate portrait of the complex American organism at the height of a presidential campaign. And virtually the moment it was developed and pasted into the media album, it started to turn brown. Within a couple of days it was thoroughly out of date; now, ten days later, it has been replaced with a new snapshot.

During exactly this same period, the tone of the media coverage of Reagan—particularly on television—has changed from passive and friendly to much more skeptical. Arguably, the change in perception of Reagan's chances affected the perception of Reagan the candidate, but in fact, there were three separate developments beyond the perception of the horse race that came into play:

First, the mass media was coming to the end of a cycle in its campaign reporting. After more than a week of friendly, upbeat Reagan coverage, reporters, producers and editors were due for one of the periodic moments of reevaluation that is typical of their trade. Shouldn't we be taking a closer look at Reagan now? That question was asked at the *Washington Post*, and at other media offices, too, particularly CBS News, about which more in a moment.

Second, the White House—in the persons of press secretary Jody Powell, pollster Pat Caddell and others—had begun a concerted effort to put pressure on the media, pressure to end what they called Reagan's "free ride" on television and in the papers. These Carter aides approached reporters and editors personally, complaining that Reagan's record deserved much closer scrutiny than it was getting.

Third, and crucially important, Reagan himself made an enormous contribution. On October 9, he caught himself in a rhetorical thicket over the sources of air pollution, declaring that Mount St. Helens and the nation's stands of timber were important sources of pollutants. Reagan looked silly on the network news shows that night, and he revived doubts about his intellectual capacities at a thoroughly (for his campaign) inopportune moment.

The first sign that the media yo-yo was beginning a new ride down for Reagan came on Tuesday evening, October 7, by coincidence a disastrous day for the Carter campaign. That was the day after Carter asserted that electing Reagan would divide North from South, Christian from Jew and "rural from urban," the piece of excessive rhetoric that finally enabled Carter's handlers to convince the President he was going too far.

On the network news that night, viewers saw Carter let fly with this zinger, then saw Reagan at his Hollywood best responding more in sadness than in anger. "He's reaching a point of hysteria that's hard to understand," Reagan said in a gentle, philosophic voice.

On NBC, correspondent Chris Wallace said it was the sort of episode the Reagan camp loved, because it showed "Mr. Carter as mean and unpresidential, Reagan as caring and mature." On ABC, Sam Donaldson reported: "Carter campaign officials are deeply worried tonight that the president's reelection is slipping away . . ."

CBS gave its 25 million viewers a negative account of Carter's day, too, then added one of the strongest pieces of television journalism that has appeared on the networks all fall.

It was a report by Bill Plante, one of television's best reporters, who has covered Reagan all year. Since this campaign began, Plante reported, "Ronald Reagan has been shifting from the right to the center of the political spectrum."

Plante cited five examples, using film clips with most of them showing Reagan saying something during last winter's primaries or earlier that he is no longer saying today. For example, Reagan used to talk about getting "the federal government out of the classroom," and of abolishing the Departments of Education and Energy.

"No more is heard about that," Plante said, while on the screen a big white X was drawn electronically through the face of the Reagan who had just spoken.

Plante went on, citing Reagan's shifting positions on abolishing the inheritance tax, subjecting big unions to antitrust laws, aiding Chrysler and New York City. The big white X's kept on obliterating pictures of the old Reagan. Then Plante closed the report like this:

"Which is the real Ronald Reagan? Does he plan to deliver on his conservative promise? Or is he really a closet moderate? His aides say that it's simply that he understands the politics of getting elected. In any case it presents President Carter with the problem of convincing voters that he's talking about the same Ronald Reagan who looks and sounds so much more moderate today."

This is tough stuff for television. CBS switchboards lit up with complaints from viewers who thought the X's obliterating Reagan's face were unfair. (The next night, Walter Cronkite apologized to viewers for this "graphic," but not for the report itself.)

Forty-eight hours later all three networks were showing "negative" Reagan material, most of it based on the self-induced confusion over air pollution. In quick snippets of videotape, viewers saw Reagan contradict himself twice, first saying he hadn't said that air pollution was substantially under control (after viewers saw him say it), then saying he thought air pollution was indeed substantially under control.

Carter, meanwhile, had launched a new phase in his campaign after promising (to Barbara Walters in an exclusive interview on ABC, shown on October 15) not to be nasty any more. The networks began showing more of Carter's specific attacks on Reagan's positions and past statements, in effect helping the Carter campaign pursue its principal tactic—raising doubts about Reagan.

By October 18 the whole tone of campaign coverage on the networks had changed. The "CBS Evening News" on October 14, for example, reported extensively on Carter's accusations against the Reagan economic program. Anchorman Dan Rather then noted that a Republican "truth squad" held a press conference to respond to Carter, "but the participants . . . offered little to rebut what Mr. Carter said and not much more about specific costs of Reagan's programs."

It was a moot point whether anything of substance had occurred in the campaign to account for this journalistic trendiness. It may have been nothing more than a reflection of how the national media functioned, as Kaiser suggested. But the candidates and their recruits from the political industry thought there had been a sea change of sorts. The Carter strategists, for example, had concluded by the third week in October that their assaults on Reagan's "warlike" tendencies were not only politically profitable but politically essential to Carter's success; whatever harm might be done to the President's "nice guy" image was easily offset by the harm being inflicted on Reagan. Thus, the architect of his television commercials, Gerald Rafshoon, continued to exploit that theme. Carter, too, followed that script. Reagan's proposal to scrap the SALT II nuclear arms limitation scheme in favor of a new agreement to not only limit but reduce nuclear arsenals was ridiculed by the president as "extraordinarily naive," although the truth was that Carter had made an almost identical proposal soon after taking office. "I'm concerned," said the president, "that he does not understand the serious consequences of what he is proposing . . . (it would be) a devasting and perhaps fatal blow to the long term process of nuclear arms control." This notion that Reagan did not understand what he was about, that he was trigger-happy and impulsive was broadcast by the Carter campaign organizations in countless forums by countless surrogates. There were signs in mid-October, as we have noted, that the message was getting through to women and was affecting their voting intentions. There were signs, too, that it was having an impact in some of the Central and Northeastern industrial states. In the South, however, the reverse seemed to be true. Carter's strength in his native region appeared to be fading as October went on, another indication that the sciences professed by the political industry had their limitations.

Nevertheless, the Reagan people were not unimpressed. For

weeks they had planned to hold fast to a passive campaign strategy based on the belief that Carter, in effect, was preordained to lose on the basis of his record and the state of the economy. Accordingly, they avoided Carter's challenge that the two men meet in debate; since, by their calculations, they were well ahead, they had nothing to gain from such an encounter. It was an unnecessary risk.

On October 18, in the midst of his week of media troubles, Reagan changed course. He agreed to a debate with Carter on October 28 in Cleveland. Why he changed course is a matter of considerable speculation. The obvious answer was that his campaign was going badly—as the newspapers insisted. But the polling data from that period was inconclusive at best. The contest was as close, in terms of popular sentiment, as it had been since Labor Day. Among probable voters, the *New York Times* reported on October 23, Carter had 39 percent, Reagan 38 percent and Anderson 9 percent in the period from October 16 to 20. That was an infinitesimal change from the previous 30 days, hardly cause for a drastic change in strategy. And it was drastic because, in the view of Reagan's people, the election would be decided by the debate, by a single roll of the dice.

There was another possible explanation—the October "surprise," which the Reagan strategists had feared for weeks. History had taught them that while American presidents are frequently at the mercy of events, they may also be the beneficiary of events they sometimes set in motion. And on more than one occasion October has been an eventful month. In October 1956, the invasion of Hungary by the Soviet Union destroyed Adlai Stevenson's modest hopes of election as the country rallied to President Eisenhower's side. In October 1968, President Johnson announced a halt to the bombing in North Vietnam, giving Hubert Humphrey a boost that nearly defeated Richard Nixon. In 1972, Nixon's secretary of state announced in October that "peace is at hand" in Vietnam.

No one knew what surprises October might bring to this campaign. The columnist Jack Anderson had speculated wildly in August that Carter was planning an invasion of Iran as a deliberate reelection tactic. There was no evidence of any substance to support that speculation. But there was another Iranian possibility—release of the American hostages in Tehran whose capture on November 4, 1979, had reversed Carter's fortunes and propelled him to his party's nomination. As the American election campaign proceeded into October, Iran was engaged in an increasingly desperate struggle with Iraq. Iranian oil fields in the south were besieged and encircled by Iraqi troops who had already occupied vital stretches of territory. The Iranian forces were poorly organized; they lacked spare parts for their American-made military equipment. Their oil revenues had been reduced to a trickle. There were internal uprisings and economic distress. For all these difficulties, there were partial remedies in the United States. Spare military parts could be provided. Billions of dollars in Iranian assets frozen by the United States could be released. Trade sanctions imposed by the United States and its allies could be lifted. All that was required was for Iran to release the hostages. If that occurred before the election it would not only be an October surprise, it would probably determine the outcome.

On October 15, the week of Reagan's discontent, a story appeared on the front page of The *Washington Post* that contained the first solid glimmer of the surprise October might bring. It was written by Michael Getler, the *Post*'s national security analyst. He reported that "some senior U.S. officials . . . now say privately . . . that they would not be surprised if a break in the U.S. embassy hostage crisis comes in the next two or three weeks." It was simultaneously announced that the Iranian Prime Minister, Mohammed Ali Rajai, would make an unexpected visit to the United Nations in New York on October 16. Immediately, President Carter and his national security adviser, Zbigniew Brzezinski, issued conciliatory statements to the effect that the United States supported the "national integrity of Iran" in its war with Iraq. The Rajai visit, reporters were told by the Administration, would bring new opportunities for resolving the hostage question. In the event, nothing tangible—so far as the public was aware—came from Rajai's trip. But each day thereafter, new speculations appeared in the media about the possibility of a "breakthrough." The columnist Joseph Kraft on October 19 went so far as to say that "The Carter Administration has embarked on an all-out effort to win release of the American hostages in Iran. . . . The present scheme bears all the marks of a mad electoral maneuver." He may have overstated the case but there certainly was no doubt that an October surprise had become a distinct possibility.

That, we were told, was a major factor in Reagan's decision

to debate. But there was another and far more intriguing consideration. A face to face debate with Jimmy Carter on the eve of the election, with the presidency of the United States very possibly at stake, would provide Ronald Reagan with a stage for what could be the last great performance of his life. It was an opportunity that would never come again for this man whose whole existence had been sustained by performances, great and small. They had taken him from a small town in Illinois to Hollywood and had taken him, now, to the very doorstep of the White House. As early as August 19, when he enjoyed a substantial lead in the opinion polls, he had confided to Lou Cannon his strong desire for a debate, for an opportunity to perform for an audience that would number in the tens of millions. His staff, however, insisted that there were too many needless risks in such a confrontation and, until October 18, these advisers prevailed. Now, the curtain would rise.

James Earl Carter, the 39th President of the United States, observed his 56th birthday at a town meeting on October 1, held in a high school gymnasium in Flint, Michigan. He had ended his 1976 campaign in this city and a few days later his vaulting ambition for the highest office in the land had been achieved. If fate were more kind or perhaps if he had been a different kind of man in a different kind of world, he would now be enjoying the fruits of the presidency, the joys of office, the praise and affection of his countrymen. Instead, he was a beleaguered and unpopular politician engaged in a desperate, clawing struggle for reelection. His incumbency, in the conventional wisdom, should have given him an insurmountable advantage against an aging Hollywood actor from a minority political party. Instead, it was a burden that threatened to wreck his political career and inflict wounds we could only guess at to his psyche and his fierce pride. He was driven now to barnstorming the country like a Southern circuit rider, defending a record in office that was difficult to defend, flailing out, unfairly, at Ronald Reagan as a "racist" and "warmonger," distributing federal monies like a ward heeler in South Chicago. For Michigan, a state suffering greatly from the recession and the declining fortunes of the automobile industry, he promised to provide $9.3 million for a plant to produce gasohol, $1 million to retrain 1,000 unemployed workers, $29.8 million to Detroit and $1.6 million to Flint to provide summer jobs for young people and $25 million to renovate a Detroit housing project. For Chicago, he brought tidings of a $92 million transportation grant. For Florida there was a plan to relocate Cuban refugees in Puerto Rico, thus removing a social problem. For a Polish-American audience, he had a $640 million commodity credit program for Poland. For New York State there was $240 million to deal with environmental problems. His surrogates in the government were ordered into action. During the month of October, members of his cabinet, including the Secretaries of State and Defense, would spend 110 days campaigning for his reelection.

His rhetoric had become harsh and strident. He used hyperbole and distortion to discredit Reagan and his views. But nothing in early October seemed to work. He came under severe criticism for his tactics and for the "meanness" he displayed. At the end of the first week of this final month of the campaign, his staff was frustrated, dispirited and uncertain what to do next. Edward Walsh, who had been assigned to the White House throughout Carter's term and who had traveled with him from the beginning of the campaign, gave us a memorandum on that period:

> I mark the low point of the Carter campaign . . . the night of October 6 at the Palmer House in Chicago. It was a fund-raising event with several hundred Cook County Democrats led by Mayor Jane Byrne. Carter started talking and in the back of the room dozens of people remained, drinks in hand, chatting away, ignoring the President of the United States.
> Something happened to Carter during that speech. For the first time since the campaign began I heard real emotion in his voice. He talked about the stakes in the election, the little time that was left, the need to do more than just turn out at fund-raisers but to get to work. In the process, he went over the edge again, uttering the line about Reagan dividing "black from white, Jew from Christian, North from South, rural from urban."
> Jody Powell sensed immediately that there would be a new flap. He showed up in the press room of the Palmer House, sniffing for the consensus and doing his best to explain away the remark.

What was most striking about the speech, however, was its emotion. All through September he had seemed to me a politician going through the motions. I became convinced that Carter no longer enjoys campaigning, that more than anything he wants it over so he can get back to Camp David, get back to the lonely business of being president. As with his staff, it isn't fun anymore. It was one thing to pursue a dream of the White House for two and a half years in the first campaign, but now the bureaucrat in his soul was demanding that he get back to the memos in the Oval Office.

A lot of things seemed to fall into place that night. There was the lack of crowds, the absence of any sense of movement; there was Jane Byrne calling for Carter's reelection although everyone in the room knew she had no use for him; there was the noise and indifference in the back of the room. The whole campaign seemed to have fallen stagnant and I thought I detected the first hints of desperation. I wrote about the frustration and the headline of the story said, "Carter Campaign Stalls."

The day the story ran Pat Caddell called me, as he had called other reporters. He was beside himself with frustration, far more emotional than Carter had been in Chicago: "This meanness stuff has gotten way out of hand. It's ridiculous. Reagan is getting a free ride. If Ronald Reagan is elected president you people will have a lot to answer for. . . . Most reporters covering Carter hate his guts but most of them are going to end up voting for him."

Caddell had a point. Hate is his word, and far too strong, but there is no question that Carter has few friends or sympathizers in the press corps. He never has. I don't know of anyone who deliberately is out to get Carter or to slant stories to damage him. But he is the kind of man who seldom or ever gets the benefit of the doubt from the reporters covering him.

That call from Caddell was part of a persistent, or-chestrated effort by the White House to turn the press coverage around, to get people writing stories critical of Reagan which would then be picked up by the tele-vision networks. Eventually the White House succeeded. Kaiser has documented how the coverage turned.

Now it was Reagan on the defensive and Carterites who felt

optimistic and upbeat. Whether they had intimations of an October surprise may never be known. But the timing of the first stories was fortuitous and in the days that followed the Iranian hostage issue once more dominated the news. On October 20, Carter issued a conciliatory statement on the issue, promising that "if Iran should release the hostages, then I will unfreeze the assets in the banks here and in Europe, drop the embargo against trade and work toward resumption of normal commerce with Iran in the future. It is to our advantage to see a strong Iran, a united Iran." Carter's secretary of state, Edmund Muskie, issued his own statement in which he seemed to "tilt" toward Iran in its struggle with Iraq: "We are opposed to the dismemberment of Iran. We believe that the cohesion and stability of Iran is in the interest of the stability of the region as a whole."

Inevitably, there was a smell of politics to the hostage question. Carter had used the hostage issue in the spring as an excuse for not debating Edward Kennedy. He had called an extraordinary press conference at 7 A.M. on the morning of the Wisconsin primary to announce that the release of the hostages was at hand. Now, with little over two weeks until the election, the hostage issue reemerged to his apparent political advantage. Some of the career diplomats in the State Department were incensed and privately accused Carter of "groveling" before the Iranians for personal political gain.

By the week of October 20, Washington was full of stories about the deal that supposedly had been made. By the end of the week expectations had risen to the point that it was widely and incorrectly believed that the issue would be resolved by the Iranian parliament on Sunday, October 26, that most of the hostages would be released that same day and would be flown to Wiesbaden, Germany, in time for Carter to greet them on October 28, the date chosen for the Reagan-Carter debate. David Broder wrote in the *Washington Post* on the 26th: "For almost a year, President Carter has been riding the whirlwind called the hostage issue. And now he is riding it into the final days of his reelection campaign—either to vindication and victory or humiliation and defeat. Among advisers to both Carter and Republican challenger Ronald Reagan, there is little doubt that the safe return of the 52 Americans from Iran before November 4. . . . might give the president the lift he needs to break open a very close contest. But equally, they believe, a dashing of the public's hopes for a resolution of the hostage ordeal might be a blow from which Carter could not recover." The White House was fully aware of the danger and, over the weekend of the 26th, took pains to warn against excessive optimism. There were statements to this effect from Carter, Vice President Mondale and Secretary of State Edmund Muskie. Another statement was issued on the 27th by White House Press Secretary Jody Powell who criticized the media for raising false hopes.

His sensitivity was understandable. Only a week remained until the election and the new polls continued to chart an election in which the candidates remained deadlocked. It could be fatal to Carter if the notion got abroad that he was cynically using the hostage issue for political gain or that in his desperation for a breakthrough he would secretly agree to terms humiliating to the United States. Those suspicions lingered below the surface of events as the candidates arrived in Cleveland for their climactic debate.

Three times in the past 20 years, presidential elections in the United States have been decided by infinitesimal margins in the popular vote. John F. Kennedy in 1960, Richard Nixon in 1968 and Jimmy Carter in 1976 all went to bed on election night uncertain whether they had won or lost. It seemed that election night 1980 would be another such long night, especially in view of the Anderson factor.

John Anderson by late October had no conceivable claim to mass support and no realistic hope of winning the election or even of carrying a single state. His standing in the polls had dropped through the late summer and early fall, and now it was holding steady at about 10 percent. Not only that, what support he had seemed to have lost any real identity. In the summer he was thought of by the Carter camp as a potential "spoiler" who would appeal strongly to liberals who would otherwise vote for the President. By late October, an ABC-Louis Harris survey was showing Anderson drawing support away from the two major candidates almost equally—3 percent from Reagan and 5 percent from Carter. So even if you assumed that Anderson's real motive in the race was a vengeful obsession with taking Carter's presidency away (an accusation Anderson repeatedly denied), he seemed unlikely to be the cause even of that.

October, then, ought to have been a sad month for Anderson. Surprisingly, it wasn't. His aides were telling reporters he didn't have a chance. He was short of funds. His one-on-one debate with Ronald Reagan had clearly done him no good with the electorate. His most prominent supporter, George Ball, jumped ship to Carter. The press was regularly writing him off. And he was happy as a clam.

Bill Peterson of our staff, who was traveling with Anderson, noticed a dramatic change on October 3. After a couple of weeks of hard traveling and unremitting bad news, Anderson was speaking to a group of black Jaycees in Compton, California. He talked at some length and without much passion, and then, as Peterson reported, he "suddenly shifted gears."

Anderson began quoting Theodore Roosevelt. "It is not the critic who counts," he said, "not the one who points out how the strong man stumbles or how the doer of good might have done better. The credit belongs to the man who is actually in the arena, whose face is marred with sweat and dust and blood, who strives valiantly, who dares, and comes up short, again and again."

As Peterson put it in his report that day, "The campaign is no longer a political campaign. It is a human story of a man struggling against impossible odds." Once that was established, Anderson seemed to become progressively more comfortable, and even joyous. "He is more polished," Peterson wrote late in the month. "More forceful. He has learned to shake hands on the stump, kiss babies and wear silly hats and eat sidewalk hot dogs. He has been genuinely touched by the thousands of people who have helped him. And, for their sake, he wants to finish what he began with style and grace."

To understand what was motivating him in October, it's important to understand that Anderson at this point was 58 years old, unemployed, and by nature somewhat preachy. Thus he had no particular incentive to quit. He had cut his ties in life. He had quit the House of Representatives. He had come almost to despise his hometown in Illinois, where he felt people had stopped listening to him as his views had matured; certainly there was nothing there that he wanted to return to. And he had an audience: 10 percent of the electorate isn't much political power, but it is perhaps 10 million people, most of them students and suburbanites and many of them by now accustomed to treating Anderson and his views with rapt attention, if not outright adulation. He had an audience. As the weeks wore on and his attention began inevitably to turn to what would happen after the election, Anderson began to talk increasingly about starting a third party, an idea he had dismissed out of hand several months earlier.

His press secretary, Tom Mathews, was in private life a direct mail specialist, and he had used the mails to create Common Cause and make John Gardner one of the most influential and respected public figures of the seventies. Presumably he could do the same for Anderson, who after all was now better known than Gardner ever had been and who had a well-proven mailing list—217,000 people, who had given $12.4 million to the Anderson cause since January—already in place. A new party would be a way for Anderson to keep doing what he had come to love.

As far as the presidency was concerned, though, Anderson was an unpredictable factor, nothing more. In New York, where he was the Liberal Party nominee, he might pull votes away from Carter but there was little likelihood that such a shift would tip the balance to Reagan.

Anderson was fairly strong in several of the big, close states—New Jersey, Illinois, Pennsylvania, Massachusetts, Wisconsin and Michigan—but it wasn't clear whether he'd pull suburban Republicans away from Reagan or campus Democrats away from Carter. He made a close and complicated race even closer and more complicated.

If the League of Women Voters had included him in the celebrated debate in Cleveland, he might have complicated things even more. But he was not included and, instead, spent the night in Constitution Hall in Washington vainly trying to be plugged in to a cable television network that had hoped to splice his own comments into the Carter-Reagan affair. The electronics didn't work. Tom Mathews, his press secretary, read into all that something devious. "This is more than curious," he said. "Maybe we have a return of the dirty tricks." Anderson, however, was cheerful in the end. He was asked how he would have prepared himself had he been invited to Cleveland. He replied with a smile, "Oh, I think the thing to do is to go out and have a few belts and enjoy yourself."

★

Throughout an autumn of great loveliness, of forests and tree lines bursting into fiery reds and yellows and mahogany browns, there was a palpable sense of political ennui among the people. Ronald Reagan traveled the land declaring that the "Carter record is a litany of despair, of broken promises, of sacred trusts abandoned or forgotten." The President, for his part, repeatedly warned that "the future of our nation is at stake. I doubt if there's ever been a sharper difference between two major candidates than between myself and the Republican nominee. The only possible exception was when Goldwater ran against Lyndon Johnson." This dramatic rhetoric, so far as we could tell in late October, had ignited few fires in the minds of the American electorate. In part that may have been the result of a conscious effort by the candidates to narrow their stated differences, to appear moderate and flexible. In part it may have been a result of the media's preoccupation with style and personality. Whatever the cause, the philosophical gulf between Carter and Reagan was rarely defined as the days wore on. But it existed.

Reaganism, as Harvard Professor James Wilson defined the term, was a counter-revolution against the dominant political, social and governmental trends of the 1960s and 1970s. It was anti-Big Government, anti the new class of intellectuals who had come to prominence and power in Washington and it was inherently and fundamentally anti-"liberal" as that term was popularly understood. At the core of its faith was an unrestrained and often uncritical belief in the capacities of unfettered free enterprise and private initiative, a belief in the "pioneer spirit" which, Reagan and Reaganites believed, had been shackled and diluted by government interventions. Reaganism, in short, challenged the major philosophical premises of the modern Democratic Party and demanded a major turning in the road on which we had come.

Richard Scammon and Ben Wattenberg, right-of-center Democrats who shared some of the premises of the Reaganites, wrote in *Public Opinion* magazine, shortly before the election, that a "political era characterized by a distinct political philosophy has indeed come to an end. We further believe that the philosophy in question—American liberalism—has rendered healthy, vigorous and constructive service to the republic: that its impact will continue to be felt, and that there will be no going back to yesteryear—but, still, it is over." America, they believed, had moved toward the new Republican philosophy which maintained that "economic stagnation and inflation are the real problems. Their major cause is big taxation which feeds big government which, in any event, is not doing well what it is supposed to do. Furthermore the government has been taken over by high-minded elitists who have lost touch with everyday concerns of everyday citizens. Meanwhile, America has grown militarily weak and is being pushed around all over the world."

Jimmy Carter's philosophy was not so easily defined. He had been at heart a small-town businessman from a part of America that we do not associate with excessive modernism, liberalism or elitism. But as president he had inherited the social and political premises of liberal Democrats. He brought to that inheritance the modifying influences of a conservative nature and an engineer's absorption with mechanics, which is to say, how do things really work? His presidency reflected these several tendencies. He could be liberal in the conventional sense in flashes of rhetoric and in programmatic proposals. He could also be conservative in the same sense, as in his genuine concern with balanced budgets, frugality in the White House accounts (he never spent his full entertainment allowance) and in his rejection of a number of initiatives advanced by the left wing of his party—Edward Kennedy's national health care plan, for example. As an engineer he could take a view of government that almost literally might have been replicated on a draftsman's board; it was a bloodless, bookkeeper's vision of government and politics and was naive in its failure to understand the raw and untidy political dynamics of governance. He could behave at times as the most political of men, as the campaign had demonstrated; what he lacked was that broad and profound political understanding that democratic leadership requires. That was a dimension of what was perceived as his great weakness as president—a lack of vision, an inability to comprehend how things fit together in the mosaic of American political life.

If Reaganism, as we have defined it, represented a revolt against the culture and "social issues" that had emerged since 1960—feminism, racial preferences in hiring and schooling, tolerance of homosexuality, drugs, abortion and what can be lumped under the heading of "permissiveness"—then Carter was genuinely the "enemy." He did not, in his personal life, link up to any of these deviations in orthodoxy; he opposed abortion and drug use; he was far too moralistic, in traditional terms, for the more avant-garde elements in the country. But he exhibited a tolerance for diversity and the so-called liberating movements of the era, from race to sex. And while he was in no sense a "knee jerk" liberal in the tradition of Americans for Democratic Action, his democratic orthodoxy clearly was a product of that tradition.

This orthodoxy, as the Reaganites claimed, assigned to the government major roles in the solution of whatever social problems arose and acquired a constituency. This was the source of the Big Government Reagan assailed and Carter, despite the rhetoric of his 1976 campaign, did nothing to diminish the size or influence of the Washington establishment or to dismantle the grand bureaucratic bazaar of special interests that has arisen since the Roosevelt years. Instead of reducing the governmental labyrinth, he enlarged it with the creation of two huge new departments, Energy and Education. He became in his first term, however reluctantly, a Washington man.

On the night of October 28, television sets in 60 million American households were tuned to a program originating in an old convention hall in Cleveland, Ohio. The event was the Reagan-Carter debate. It consumed 90 minutes of prime time and, over the course of it, attracted on the order of 100 million spectators, which was approximately equal to the audience for a Super Bowl football game. Undoubtedly, it was the largest political audience in American history.

The suspense had been building for nearly two weeks. The whole election, we were told, would likely hinge on this event as had been the case (in Carter's view at least) in 1976. Carter was ebullient and cocky as he headed for Cleveland. He had performed with great skill against Gerald Ford four years before. He had honed those skills in dozens of press conferences and town meetings. He had an extraordinary capacity for mastering and memorizing the precise details of virtually every issue. He was quick on his feet, articulate, self-confident and cloaked in the aura of the presidency. Reagan had been through hundreds of difficult performances in his lifetime. He knew how to use the cameras, how to sell and turn on an audience, how to give a polished and professional performance. But he had never played for stakes this high. He had a record of verbal blundering—the wrong word or phrase, the malapropism, the analogy that failed to survive analysis, such as polluting trees. Finally he was nearly 70 years old and the cameras could be harsh, especially in contrast to the younger, well-conditioned president.

So they met in Cleveland as tens of millions looked on in the ultimate act of vicarious politics in the 20th century. As has happened before in moments of intense and high drama, the event itself was, in a sense, less memorable than the anticipation of it. Carter performed brilliantly. His responses to the questions put to him were often irrelevant and off the point. He used them merely as springboards for the political and emotional transactions he wished to consummate with the vast living room audience. He reached out with great skill and cleverness to the old battalions of the old Democratic party— to the blacks, to the labor unions, to the Jews, to the emerging feminist forces, to the South, to the old and the handicapped. He returned repeatedly to the themes of war and peace and to the alleged adventurism of the Reaganites and he did it with none of the "meanness" or heavy-handedness he had shown in campaign speeches:

> I consider myself in the mainstream of my party. I consider myself in the mainstream even of the bipartisan list of presidents who served before me. The United States must be a nation strong. The United States must be a nation secure. We must have a society that's just and fair. And we must extend the benefits of our own commitment to peace, to create a peaceful world. . . . the final judgment about the future of our nation—war, peace, involvement, reticence, thoughtfulness, care, consideration, concern—has to be made by the man in the Oval Office.
>
> It's a lonely job, but with the involvement of the American people in the process, with an open government, the job is a very gratifying one. The American people now are facing next Tuesday a lonely decision. Those listening to my voice will have to make a judgment about the future of this country. And I think they ought to remember that one vote can make a lot of difference.

> *If one vote per precinct had changed in 1960, John
> Kennedy would never have been president of this nation.
> And if a few more people had gone to the polls and voted
> in 1968, Hubert Humphrey would have been president,
> Richard Nixon would not. There is a partnership involved
> in our nation. To stay strong, to stay at peace, to raise
> high the banner of human rights, to set an example for
> the rest of the world, to let our deep beliefs and com-
> mitments be felt by others in other nations, is my plan
> for the future. I ask the American people to join me in
> this partnership.*

We have described earlier in this book the aura of mystery
and unreality that cloaked Ronald Reagan and blurred his image
in the public mind. Was he merely a play actor in a new role
or was he a real political leader, a man who could in truth be
the president of the United States? His encounter with Jimmy
Carter—the real thing—presumably would resolve the question. If he were unreal and incompetent and intellectually unfit,
Carter would expose those frailties. It did not turn out quite
that way. Reagan, in this debate, could not match Carter's
mental agility, his textbook command of the facts, his determination to control the direction and themes of the argument.
But he infused the occasion with a style, a presence, a grand-
fatherly sense of dignity and kindness that evoked sympathy
among millions of Americans who seemed for the first time
to understand what kind of man he really was. His personality
at times overshadowed the intellectual transactions of the encounter and this led many of the network and newspaper commentators to write him off, to declare Carter the clear winner.
They were fixated, as intellectuals have frequently been with
Reagan, on the fact that he was "not with it" in terms of Eastern
sophistication; he was a square; he was not one of them. The
American masses reacted quite differently. The opinion polls
revealed that he had come through quite well, that he had, in
fact, won the encounter in the minds of most Americans.

Reagan achieved something else in Cleveland. No matter
how halting and guarded his words may have been, he left no
doubt that he represented impulses in the American mind and
spirit that were far different than those represented by Jimmy
Carter. His peroration suggested the gulf between them:

*Next Tuesday, all of you will go to the polls, will
stand there in the polling places and make a decision.
I think when you make that decision, it might be well if
you would ask yourself, are you better off than you were
four years ago? Is it easier for you to go and buy things
in the stores than it was four years ago? Is there more
or less unemployment in the country than there was four
years ago? Is America as respected throughout the world
as it was? Do you feel that our security is as safe, that
we're as strong as we were four years ago?*

*And if you answer all of these questions "yes," why
then, I think your choice is very obvious as to whom you
will vote for. If you don't agree, if you don't think that
this course that we've been on for the last four years is
what you would like to see us follow for the next four,
then I could suggest another course that you have. This
country doesn't have to be in the shape that it is in. . . . I
would like to have a crusade today, and I would like to
lead that crusade with your help. And it would be one
to take government off the backs of the great people of
this country, and turn you loose again to do those things
that I know you can do so well, because you did them
and made this country great.*

The issue that was drawn was at the heart of this campaign:
Shall America look to government as the primary referee and
problem solver for society or should there be a return to the
principles of laissez-faire? (See page 359 for the text of the debate.) People like Wattenberg and Scammon thought that the latter choice would be made. Carterites took the other view.

★ November/ ★
Election Day 1980

By Richard Harwood

ON NOVEMBER 2, 1980, before dawn, a message was flashed from Washington to a hotel suite in Chicago, where the President of the United States was asleep. It was 4 A.M. on the last exhausting weekend of his reelection campaign. He was awakened and informed that the Iranian Parliament had at last issued its formal terms for the release of the 52 American hostages who had been seized and placed in captivity almost precisely a year before. Within 90 minutes Jimmy Carter was aboard Air Force One, headed back to Washington for consultations with his advisers. It seemed possible that he was on the brink of a final breakthrough in the hostage impasse. It also seemed possible that what happened in the next 48 hours could determine the outcome of the election.

On this pre-election weekend, Carter was in political trouble. The polls produced by the eminent Dr. George Gallup and others of that fraternity described an election in which Carter and Republican Ronald Reagan were virtually tied in popular support. But the polling trends of the previous few days had been favorable to Reagan; more importantly, the calculations of electoral votes strongly indicated a Reagan victory. There was little more the candidates could do to produce a sea change in the electoral mood. But an unforeseen event—the release of the hostages, for example—could alter the balance. This is what the Reagan people had feared for weeks—the October or November "surprise." It would have been unnatural for Carter not to harbor hopes for such a development, although, in public at least, he had done nothing in the last days of the campaign to exploit the issue for political advantage.

He arrived back in Washington in the pre-dawn darkness of Sunday, November 2, and at 8 A.M. met in the Cabinet Room with Vice President Mondale, Secretary of State Edmund Muskie, Deputy Secretary of State Warren Christopher (who had been chosen to awaken the president that morning), Defense Secretary Harold Brown, National Security Adviser Zbigniew Brzezinski and his deputy, David Aaron; Deputy Treasury Secretary Robert Carswell and Lloyd Cutler, counsel to the president. They talked for two hours and then recessed. At 1 P.M. they gathered again and talked for another hour.

Martin Schram of our staff reported from the White House that "throughout the day...other advisers were pondering matters of politics. The president's pollster, Patrick Caddell, was seen nervously pacing the corridors of the West Wing...moving from one conference to another. The president's closest friend and confidante, Atlanta attorney Charles Kirbo, was also present and conferring with others in the Carter inner circle. Late in the afternoon, a meeting of major political strategists was held in the office of the White House Chief of Staff Jack Watson, with Caddell and campaign chairman Robert S. Strauss among those in attendance. (They were) concerned that even good news in the hostage crisis could offset the hard realities of the latest public polls.

"'It is just too tough to call,' said one of the president's principal campaign advisers. 'On the one hand, it is possible that there can be a positive impact politically where the president's policy of patience and persistence may be shown to have worked in Iran. But there is a down side, too. It may be that cynicism among the public will take hold and that people will come to believe that all of this was in fact engineered for political purposes. I hope that's not the way it turns out to be. But I just don't know.'"

At dusk, the White House asked the television networks for air time for a statement by the president which would interrupt the professional football games. Carter came into the White House press room at 6:23 P.M. and read for four minutes a cautious statement. He described the action of the Iranian Parliament as a "significant development" and as a "positive basis" for a resolution of the long affair. Then he said: "We are within two days of an important national election. Let me assure you that my decisions on this crucial matter will not be affected by the calendar...I wish I could predict when the hostages will return. I cannot. But whether our hostages come home before or after the election, and regardless of the outcome of the election, the Iranian government and the world community will find our country, its people, and the leaders of both political parties united in desiring the early and safe return of the hostages to their homes, but only on a basis that preserves our national honor and our national integrity."

That last pledge—preserving the national honor and integrity—indicated some of the difficulties in the Iranian proposal and implied that a pre-election homecoming was not a realistic prospect. The Iranians had made four demands as their condition for the hostages release. First, the United States must make a "firm commitment" not to interfere politically or militarily in the affairs of the Islamic Republic of Iran. That was a condition to which Carter could easily accede. The remaining three were more difficult. One of them involved the unfreezing and repatriation of between $8 billion and $14 billion of Iranian assets which had been impounded by the U.S. on November 14, 1979, after the hostages were seized. Court claims on much of this money had subsequently been filed by Iran's creditors in the U.S., most of them private commercial companies; an additional 2,700 private claims were filed with the U.S. Treasury.

There was grave doubt in Washington that Sunday that Carter legally could meet the Iranian terms on the prompt disposition of assets. That was likewise true of the demand that any future claims against Iran that might be filed by the hostages or their families must be paid by the United States. Finally, it seemed practically and legally impossible for Carter to return to Iran the "properties of the deceased Shah," as demanded by the Iranian Parliament.

Secretary of State Muskie noted the difficulties in saying that the Iranian proposals "should be viewed as initial steps in a process which will require time, patience and diplomacy." Penne Laingen, the wife of the highest-ranking hostage, likened the negotiations to the haggling in a Persian rug bazaar: "It is very much like rug bargaining... You know that this is only the first price. I believe we must not panic, even though we want that rug very badly. We've waited this long and we know the dealer wants to sell it. But there's a great deal more riding on this carpet besides 52 lives. We must have the courage to walk out of the dealer's store if necessary. We don't want the fringe. We don't want the pieces. We want the whole beautiful thing, with honor."

It was raining in Washington on election day, 1980. The President was out of town. With the hostage impasse still unresolved, he had flown to the Northwest on Monday in a last and somewhat desperate search for votes, pleading again and again for people to abandon the hopeless candidacy of John Anderson and to cast their lot with him just one more time. His face gray and puffy and lined with fatigue, Carter pressed his campaign far into the night, arriving in Portland, Oregon, after the clocks on the East Coast had passed midnight, the dawn of election day. From Portland, he headed for Seattle and the last rally, the last speech, flying over country so different and so far from his native Georgia. He was a long way from home in more ways than one.

Ronald Reagan flew that night to his own home in California and grew reflective as he talked with reporters. He would be disappointed, he said, if he were to lose: "Would you laugh if I told you that I think, maybe, that the people see themselves and that I'm one of them. I've never been able to detach myself or think that I, somehow, am apart from them."

So it was over and now the waiting would begin.

Theodore White has written, "On election day America is Republican until five or six in the evening. It is in the last few hours of the day that working people and their families vote, on their way home from work or after supper; it is then, at evening, that America goes Democratic if it goes Democratic at all. All of this is invisible, for it is the essence of the act that as it happens it is a mystery in which millions of people each fit one fragment of a total secret together, none of them knowing the shape of the whole." (From *The Making of The President, 1960*).

Jimmy Carter knew the shape of the whole as he flew through the night from Seattle to the homeplace in Plains, Georgia. His mood was reflected in the exhaustion and dejection of his staff. Patrick Caddell had informed them that his latest polls revealed something strange happening in the country; there had been a massive shift to Reagan in the past 48 hours.

It was nearly dawn in Georgia when the presidential party arrived. At 8 A.M. Carter went into Plains to vote and to speak to the townspeople from the abandoned train station platform where he had stood four years before, weeping openly as he thanked his neighbors and countrymen for his victory. On this election day far different emotions seized him. "Many people from Plains, from Americus, from Richland, from around this area, have gone all over the nation to speak for me," he said, "and to shake hands with people in other states to tell them that you have confidence in me and that I would not disappoint them if I became president. I've tried to honor your commitment to those other people. In the process, I've tried to honor my commitment . . ." For a moment he couldn't go on. His weary face quivered. Tears filled his eyes. He tried hard to control himself as he finally finished the sentence: ". . . to you." Then he said: "God bless you. Thank you. Don't forget to vote, everybody." His wife, Rosalynn, stood stiffly at his side, her face a study in icy self-control.

They returned to Washington to await the verdict and to learn of a new humiliation in Iran. Thousands of demonstrators paraded through the grounds of the U.S. Embassy, burning American flags, taunting the United States and crying out for Carter's death. It was the first anniversary of the hostage-taking.

The trauma of that November day in 1979 still burned in the national psyche, further complicating and exacerbating the troubled spirit of the American people. As Haynes Johnson traveled the country in the autumn weeks before the election he was struck by the duality of our condition. He saw a nation of quiet towns and peaceful cities, of people with good humor and confidence, of calm judgment and quiet strength. It was true that millions were unemployed, that the inflationary tendencies of the economy were untamed, that great industries were in desperate trouble. But still, he was impressed by how blessed we are in the material dimensions of most of our lives. Everywhere restaurants were crowded, hotels jammed, rental car offices packed, shops filled. But gnawing at the popular consciousness were primordial concerns that we seem to have lost our place in the world, to have lost our nerve or our will or our way. The fear that inflation would erode the social fabric

was profound. So was the fear that we might no longer be able
to compete in world markets, that our ancient pride in Yankee
know-how could no longer be sustained. And there was Iran,
a constant and abrasive symbol of something we had lost, a
symbol of that secret fear nations share with middle-aged men:
the fear of impotence. All these things were churning in the
land and Johnson concluded that the next president would be
unable to tolerate the continued imprisonment of the hostages.
Americans, he reported, wanted an end to it, and they would
favor the use of force. That was a metaphor for the frustrations
churning beneath the surface of our lives, frustrations that
might find an inchoate expression in the voting booths of
America, frustrations that mindlessly found a target that day
in Jackson, Mississippi, where two Saudi Arabian visitors were
set upon and beaten senseless. They had been mistaken for
Iranians.

Ronald Reagan's last appearance of the 1980 campaign was
in San Diego at an old-fashioned patriotic rally Monday night.
It ended with a fireworks display that included the lighting of
a huge American flag and the singing of "God Bless America,"
led by the candidate and his wife. To sophisticated—or jaded—
minds, it was a corny ending for a presidential campaign but
appropriate somehow for Ronald Reagan whose movies and
speeches were of the same genre. It may have been appropriate,
too, for the peculiar circumstances of this election of 1980.
Patrick Caddell, the president's favored pollster, began detecting disturbing vibrations on the weekend before the voting.
Iran was the catalyst, he reported, the frustrating "hinge event"
that was bringing to the surface those churning emotions
Haynes Johnson identified. Caddell's last soundings were completed at 1 A.M. on election day. It was all coming apart for
Jimmy Carter, he concluded, and so informed the president
and his family. That view was shared by the Carter campaign
chairman, Robert Strauss, who told friends at noon on Tuesday—before any votes had been counted—that Reagan might
win it "big." Also at noon that day—possibly as a trivial omen
of what might come—the Democratic party's national chairman, John White, was unable to get a reservation at one of
Washington's popular lunchtime restaurants.

★

Television has come to dominate the leisure aspects of millions of American lives and it has come to dominate in many ways the political information process. The networks have discovered that "news" is an enormously profitable commodity and they invest tens of millions of dollars to provide it. Their finest hours, as William Leonard, the CBS News president has said, are national political conventions and national elections. They employ for elections demographers, opinion analysts, political analysts and thousands of bit players in the supporting casts. They conduct interviews with voters as they leave the polls on election day and extrapolate from that probable outcomes. They collect data, when the polls have closed, from "sample precincts" that are intended to be perfect mirror images of the larger electorate. These data allow instant projections of who has won and who has lost.

On this election day, 1980, the first network projections were made early in the afternoon on the basis of exit polls. The verdict: Reagan. By 6:30 in the evening Indiana had been given—by Walter Cronkite—to Reagan. Virginia, Florida and Ohio soon followed. At 8:15, NBC News declared Reagan the next president of the United States even though millions were still voting in the Western regions. Jimmy Carter had come to a remarkably similar view at that hour and began instructing his aides to cooperate in the transition to a Reagan Administration. Also at that hour, the president placed a call to Ronald Reagan and offered his congratulations. And before 10 P.M.—before the polls had closed in the West—he drove to Washington's Sheraton Washington Hotel to make his formal and public concession of defeat. It was a remarkable decision in view of the fact that fewer than 5 percent of the national vote had been counted. But the television networks had declared a winner and not even the President of the United States would dispute that judgment. The mathematicians and their computers were supreme.

They were generally accurate, too, and well before midnight it was obvious that Ronald Reagan had not merely won an election; he was the beneficiary of an electoral landslide that turned control of the Senate over to the Republicans after 26 years of Democratic rule, added more than 30 Republican House seats, and gave Republicans control of four additional statehouses. Reagan carried 44 of the 50 states and won 489 electoral votes—an epic victory. His margins were sufficiently large that he would have won easily if John Anderson had not been in the race. It was truly a landslide and virtually none of us in the media, the political industry or the polling fraternity had foreseen its dimensions. But the elements for the upheaval had long been present.

★ Epilogue ★

We began our book with an accumulation of evidence that the American people over the past two decades had grown exceedingly critical of the performance and the competence of the great institutions, public and private, that affect our lives. This dissatisfaction stimulated one of the greatest periods of reform in our history. Hundreds of laws were passed to control and improve the behavior of private institutions—environmental regulations, safety and health legislation and countless enactments under the vast umbrella of "consumerism." The legal system adapted itself to this process in recognizing a broad range of new institutional liabilities for defective products and practices. The marketplace itself had been used to discipline and punish the incompetence or bad judgment of entrepreneurs—the American automobile industry, for example. In innumerable ways, the power and discretion of institutions was curtailed because of popular dissatisfactions with the status quo. State and local governmental institutions were not immune. They were compelled to reform police practices, to institute affirmative action programs for women and minorities, to overhaul university admissions and hiring policies, to modify public school enrollment patterns through busing programs. In 1980, this tide of dissatisfaction found a new target in the largest institution of them all—the federal government. Its own competence and behavior were in disrepute and were the targets of the explicit critique of Reaganism: "Get the government off our backs!"

The government in Washington had assumed since World War II a presence in American life that transcended by exponential factors any institutional presence the nation had ever known. It collected and redistributed wealth on an enormous scale. It took on the responsibility for the management of the economy—for wage and price levels, for rates of inflation and interest, for the creation and elimination of jobs, for the stability of whole economic sectors from agriculture to shipbuilding. It financed the largest health care, education and feeding programs in the world. It was the leading patron of the arts and the universities, the leading underwriter of scientific research and development, the leading underwriter of housing, construction, banking, and international trade. It owned and managed more than a third of the land area of the United States. Its regulators and inspectors were involved in almost every aspect of American life including private behavior. Its external interests extended around the globe and into outer space. It employed and otherwise sustained more people than any institution on earth, save the governments of the Soviet Union and China. It consumed or distributed more than a quarter of the gross national product. It was the ultimate Big Mother.

The performance and competence of this vast institution were vigorously and sometimes violently challenged in the 1960s and early 1970s by the American Left. Its interventions in Southeast Asia divided the nation to a degree not experienced since the Civil War. The "imperial presidency," the Federal Bureau of Investigation, the Justice Department, the Central Intelligence Agency and the Defense Department became, to millions of Americans, symbols of a tyrannical—if not "fascist"—centralized state.

At the same time, as the government's internal interventions in the economy and in numberless fields of regulation and areas of social behavior expanded, it was under attack from the American Right for approximately the same intellectual reasons: the diminution of individual liberty, as in the case of school busing, affirmative action programs, minimum wage regulation.

Jimmy Carter in 1976 exploited these diverse perceptions in his campaign for president, promising to rein in the Washington Leviathan, to curb its appetites, to make it leaner and more responsive, to transform it into an institution "as good as the American people." His thesis was that the government was not so much evil as it was incompetent and profligate. That thesis had broad public support, as the political demographers Richard Scammon and Ben Wattenberg, had long argued, beginning with their book *The Real Majority*. In the past 20 years, according to their data, a majority of Americans have become convinced that "big government" itself is the principal cause of inflation; three quarters of all Americans have come to believe that "Washington has become too powerful"; more than 80 percent thought the government "is spending too much." Those public attitudes struck at the very heart of what we call American "liberalism," which is based almost wholly on the concept of a large, powerful and well-financed central state that guides, mediates or arbitrates the nation's social transactions. This was the dominant doctrine of the Democratic Party. That it has been in the postwar years a controversial doctrine is a matter of historical fact. In the nine presidential elections since World War II, the Republicans have won five times and only two Democratic candidates in that period—Lyndon Johnson and Jimmy Carter—received as much as 50 percent of the popular vote. Yet, throughout this period there was a striking political ambivalence in the country. The Democrats remained the majority party in terms of popular loyalties and, with a single exception, retained congressional majorities. The electorate could reject conventional "liberalism" in the choice of its presidents but, through the workings of special interest politics, preserve the economic benefits of that liberalism in the choice of legislators.

This political duality was sustainable so long as the Keynesian economic policies imbedded in liberal doctrine succeeded, as had been largely the case since the 1940s. But in 1980 it was obvious that something had gone wrong. The rate of inflation had briefly reached 20 percent early in the year and remained above 12 percent through the fall. At the same time, the economy was in a recession with eight million people unemployed. The great industries that had been the heart of the American industrial machine—steel and autos—were in desperate condition. The markets were flooded with foreign imports; there were huge deficits in the international balance of trade. Our place in the world economy seemed in real jeopardy for the first time since the end of a world war from which the United States emerged as the supreme economic power on earth.

We had emerged from that war, too, as the supreme military power on earth and as the dominant force in world affairs.

That position also was clearly in jeopardy, if not already lost, in 1980. There was a widespread perception of American impotence in a world of rapid change, a perception that we could no longer influence the course of events, that we were hostages to the whims or designs of other nations, large and small. Iran was the frustrating and infuriating symbol of our impotence. The humiliation of the hostage-taking was brought to the forefront of our consciousness on the very eve of the election with the belligerent demands from the government of Ayatollah Khomeni and a set of conditions for the hostages' release that were difficult, if not impossible, to meet. Nevertheless, expectations were raised that at last the 52 Americans would come home; they were dashed as quickly and by election day it was obvious that another peaceful rescue mission had failed, which meant that Jimmy Carter again had failed.

The American electorate on November 4, 1980, rendered a judgment of incompetence on President Carter, on "liberalism" and on the federal establishment in Washington. Ronald Reagan, in his debate with the president had posed the issues in this way: "Are you better off than you were four years ago? Is it easier for you to go and buy things in the stores than it was four years ago? Is there more or less unemployment in the country than there was four years ago? Is America as respected throughout the world as it was? Do you feel that our security is as safe, that we're as strong as we were four years ago?" The electoral answers to all those questions were negative, not only in terms of the president, but in terms of traditional "liberalism." Virtually every prominent Democratic liberal in the Senate who stood for reelection was defeated—John Culver of Iowa, George McGovern of South Dakota, Warren Magnuson of Washington, Frank Church of Idaho, Birch Bayh of Indiana. There was likewise a slaughter of liberals from the House of Representatives, including John Brademas of Indiana, Al Ullman of Oregon, Lester Wolff of New York, Bob Eckhardt of Texas, Bob Carr of Michigan, James Corman of California, Joe Fisher of Virginia, Thomas Ashley of Ohio, Richardson Preyer of North Carolina. Their defeats followed the defeat in 1978 of five other Senate liberals and the defeat in the Democratic presidential primaries of Edward Kennedy of Massachusetts.

There could be no doubt that the economic and foreign policies of the liberals had been found wanting. And something else may have been at work, which Bill Prochnau of our national staff described:

> *But they were rebelling against more. They were rebelling against the symbol of the federal city, too, the symbol of a city and a government out of control, of decades of federal programs that became so complex and, to many, so ridiculous that the time finally had arrived to call a halt.*
>
> *Traveling the country during this campaign year provided any observer with an abundance of poignant vignettes about grand federal ideas that went awry by the time they reached Peoria:*
>
> - *A little old lady, hands crippled with arthritis, at a druggist's counter in Kansas, struggling with the child-proof container mandated by Washington for her painkillers. She couldn't match arrow to arrow, couldn't use her knobby fingers to push and twist simultaneously. The druggist just mumbled about those "frigging feds."*
> - *A geologist in Montana laughing, without too much humor, about the federal regulation that requires a stretcher at a one-man mine. It reminded him, he said, of the light-bulb Polish joke in reverse.*
> - *People everywhere spending the better part of a decade disengaging auto-emission devices, undoing seatbelt buzzers and lights, wondering when they were going to get the auto safety airbags Washington has been arguing about for more than ten years.*
> - *Workers taking deep breaths of clean air as they walked past closed steel mills toward the unemployment office.*
>
> *The revolt may have been about inflation and unemployment and Jimmy Carter's perceived inadequacies or Ronald Reagan's supposed strength. But what was there, too, was a rejection of the federal city and a lot of what it has come to stand for.*

The revolt to some extent may also have been about "social issues," the code phrase that encompasses those antagonisms in American life arising out of the conflict between traditional values and cultural change. Conflicts of this kind have been with us throughout our history—piety versus licentiousness, class versus class, authority versus permissiveness, town versus gown, black versus white, men versus women, parents versus children, Protestants versus Catholics versus Jews, ethnic versus ethnic. The 1960s and 1970s exacerbated these ancient antagonisms because of the sweep and rapidity of the cultural changes that occurred. We called it a "countercultural revolution," which celebrated sexual freedom and promiscuity, the rejection of authority, the consumption of old and new drugs and hallucinogens, the respectability of homosexuality, the full emancipation of women, radical new styles of music and dress. Hand in hand with those changes was a racial revolution in which black Americans sought an equal place in the sun in every arena of American life.

Reaganism, in one of its dimensions, was a counter-revolution by defenders of traditional values. These were New Right issues, Neo Conservative issues, Right to Life issues and the issues of the Moral Majority legions made up, primarily, of fundamentalist Protestant sects. Evangelist Jerry Falwell spoke their concerns and their political purposes.

> *If nearly half the population is born-again, as pollster George Gallup believes, then why aren't things different? Why is there so much crime, so much poverty, and so much drug abuse? . . . Two and a half centuries ago, at the start of the Great Awakening, there was at least a biblical consensus in what was about to become America. Certainly not everyone believed in God, but there were standards and absolutes that were absolute, that were universally held. Government was not subsidizing abortion, homosexuality was still viewed as a perversion, criminals knew they could expect punishment and not get off lightly if they committed a crime, drug addicts were almost nonexistent, persons who exhibited loose moral behavior were not idealized as they are today. It is because immorality has become entrenched and institutionalized that Christians and other moral people have so much trouble making an impact. How, for example, do you counteract the negative inputs of a public school system that has your child for about six hours a*

*day, five days a week? What you're trying to build into
a child in an hour or two at home is torn down by the
schools with the sex education classes and instruction
about evolution and not the creation of mankind. It is
difficult to cure poverty and reduce unemployment when
we have a government that rewards the nonworker with
welfare checks... What is necessary for the born-again
people of America, the Moral Majority of America, to
have an impact is for us to throw out of office with our
votes those who have made America what it is today.*

The mass media, liberal churchmen and various political
figures were alarmed at the emergence of these political preachers and at the movement they represented. There was some
hypocrisy in that reaction. Preachers and churches and religious
bodies had been actively engaged in American politics throughout our national history, never more prominently than in the
1960s and 1970s in the civil rights and anti-war movements.
The American Rabbinate for years has lobbied assiduously on
behalf of Israel. The Catholic hierarchy has been a political
force of immense influence. Liberal bishops, priests and par-
sons have been heavily engaged in political causes ranging
from Third World liberation to homosexual rights. Nevertheless, the involvement of the Moral Majority was regarded as
a breach of traditional church-state relationships and as a dangerous and intolerant new factor in the American political process. Haynes Johnson, in his travels in the fall of 1980, found
little at which to be alarmed:

*Aside from its effect in certain state elections—and
those are of questionable political value—this (Moral
Majority) attitude does not reflect the country I found.
Americans today are less ideological than in the past.
There is no great swing to the right, as some have feared
recently, just as there wasn't to the left in the 1960s.
People in the country today are far more sophisticated
and far more tolerant, at least in my perspective of 20
years of viewing the country. They see things not in
simplicities, but complexities, and they are not about to
be swayed by the dictates of any group proclaiming to
speak for a "moral majority." The same is true of attitudes about race, sexual mores and other personal val-*

ues. Aside from the vocal single issue interest groups, you simply don't hear the kinds of passion about such questions. Where once drugs, sex and other trappings of a permissive society were issues during election campaigns, now they are largely absent.

Our own polls earlier in the year supported that conclusion. But it was folly to suppose that Reaganism did not have a "social issues" content or to suppose that the Moral Majority had no impact at all. How much impact is conjectural. Jerry Falwell boasted after the election that "these Christian people came out of the pews into the polls and caused this avalanche." Polling data on election day suggested that Reagan got about 60 percent of the white "born again Christian" vote, which was consistent with his share of the overall Protestant vote and his share of votes cast by whites. He received about 45 percent of the Catholic vote and 35 percent of the Jewish vote, which ordinarily is overwhelmingly Democratic. In Brooklyn's normally Democratic Borough Park section—the largest community of Orthodox Jews in the United States—Reagan got 63 percent of the vote.

On election day, 1980, thousands of voters were interviewed as they left the polls. They gave us the mosaic of the election and unraveled that quadrennial democratic mystery by which we choose our presidents, the act, in Teddy White's felicitous words, "in which millions of people each fit one fragment of a total secret together." Ronald Reagan had been chosen by the young, the middle-aged and the old. He outpolled Jimmy Carter among voters over 30 and broke even in the youth vote. He won majorities among both men and women. He was the choice of Republicans, Independents, and of a quarter of the Democrats. He appealed more to the haves than the have-nots, getting 60 percent of the votes of people with family incomes of more than $30,000 a year. But even among the poorest families—those earning less than $10,000 a year—he was the choice of four out of ten. In the middle income groups he outpolled Carter. He won over nearly 30 percent of the self-styled liberals, a majority of the moderates and 70 percent of the conservatives. The Protestants were in his camp; so were a plurality of Catholics. The professional, managerial, clerical and agricultural classes chose him over Carter. He split with the President the blue collar vote and very nearly matched Carter among labor union members. He carried the small cities and towns, suburbia and the farming areas. He won every region of the country, running most strongly in the West and least strongly in the East. Carter's only pluralities were among the poorest and least educated voters, among the Jews and blacks and Hispanics, among big city dwellers, union members, liberals and the unemployed.

The diverse fragments of the electorate who created the Reagan landslide can in no way be lumped together under some glib phrase such as the New Right or the Moral Majority. The Reagan majority was a majority drawn from virtually every class in America, from every political persuasion, from every cultural and ethnic group. Inasmuch as fewer than 30 percent of the electorate and only 36 percent of the actual voters in 1980 consider themselves "conservative" in political philosophy, it would have been impossible to construct the Reagan majority out of that fragment of our people. Indeed, only 11 percent of the Reagan voters said they chose him for being a "real conservative." The overriding reason for their choice, they said, was that "it's time for a change." The second most important factor given was Reagan's image of strong leadership, his ability to get things done.

It is our view, then, that the electorate rendered a judgment of incompetence on Carter, on liberalism, and on the federal establishment in Washington. The result, inevitably, would be a genuinely "conservative" national government. It does not automatically follow, however, that a genuinely "conservative" electorate has emerged. The electorate had only two choices— more of the same or something new. They had been given, in the congressional races as well as in the presidential contest, a choice and not an echo. They will be in a position in elections to come to pass the same harsh judgment on "conservatism" that had been passed on liberalism in 1980. They will apply that most pragmatic of tests: does it work? In their own minds the mandate they gave to the Reaganites was a mandate to control government spending, to control inflation and to create a stronger military force. They were not demanding that the federal government be dismantled, that the United States should enter into foreign adventures or even that taxes should be cut.

They wanted what Americans have always wanted: peace and prosperity; whether they came in a "liberal" or a "conservative" package or a Democratic or Republican package was beside the point.

Many ideologues, many political scientists and many journalists will dispute that view. The votes had barely been counted before a "new era" had been proclaimed, a new era comparable to the New Deal in the immensity of the electoral realignment. Such judgments, in our view, are premature. Everett Ladd, a political scientist at the University of Connecticut, discussed the changing character of the American electorate in an article published in *Public Opinion* magazine prior to the election. What was happening in the country, he wrote, was not a realignment of political parties but a "de-alignment," by which he meant a withdrawal of tribalistic party loyalties in favor of a more pragmatic and detached form of political involvement. The "new era," he argued, is not characterized by mass shifts from one party to another but by the "instability and fluidity" of voters who ask: What works? "For example," Ladd wrote, "the proportion who feel unattached to the Democrats, Republicans, or any other party, is roughly twice today what it was three decades ago . . . (Now) 40 percent called themselves Independents (versus 37 percent for the Democrats and 24 percent for the Republicans)."

As for ideology, he made the argument we have made: "(The) mix of attitudes toward the state—in favor of high levels of government services but troubled by governmental inefficiencies and often ineffective intrusions into complex problems—is neither liberal nor conservative . . . Americans are ambivalent about the contemporary state and this has contributed to an ambivalence about the parties."

Finally, Ladd argued, before a "new era" is declared, before a new "realignment" is realized, three things must occur. The triumphant political leader—the president—will have to achieve these things:

"Advance a series of programs that are, objectively, more effective responses to our national needs than those of the past;

"Secure a set of modest but coherent changes in the way political institutions operate so that they become more responsive and responsible; and

"Convince a clear majority of his fellow citizens that what he has done is sound.

"Were this to happen, it is likely that the realignment . ... would actually take place. But until it happens, the present drift and the vague discontent that distinguish American politics today will continue."

That is Ronald Reagan's problem and his opportunity.

A final note to this book is required. We in journalism sometimes regard the political processes of our country as cynical struggles that ultimately are decided by money, by the hired guns of the political industry and by the biases and predispositions of the media. That is a viewpoint that assumes, as H. L. Mencken insisted, that Americans are boobs, that Joe Six Pack can be manipulated by the Gerald Rafshoons, David Garths and Peter Daileys of the world. Ronald Reagan early in the campaign was regarded, especially in the East, as the ultimate product of the politics of manipulation. He was the ruined old actor with touched-up hair and bad eardrums, a cardboard movie poster. His fate was in the hands of the admen. They would elect him or beat him because there was nothing behind his grin; he was a hollow man whose ghostwritten autobiography, *Where's The Rest of Me*, was the source of innumerable jokes.

These perceptions changed as the campaign unfolded. He seemed real enough in his debate with President Carter. In his speeches and personal contacts with the American people, he conveyed an image of substance. People voted for him, they said, because he would be a strong and intelligent leader who could get things done. Was the image real or a product of the adman's art?

On the available evidence he was a little of both, which probably has been the case with most of our presidents. Lou Cannon, who has followed his political progress for many years, sees strength in the man but sees too that he is "something of a mythic figure. He is an actor and a cowboy identified with a lost America of the past. It is that America, as Reagan has been saying in his speeches for 16 years, that is the 'last best hope of man on earth.'" John Sears, who wrote his speeches and planned his political strategies for several years, had another insight: "Since the primary prerequisite for handling the presidency is to ignore the immensity of it, a president must find the confidence to do so in self knowledge . . . Reagan knows himself better than most presidents and he has kept his identity separate from politics . . . He's proud of having been an actor, and the very fact that he may always be more proud of this accomplishment gives him a fighting chance to be a good president . . . In private conversation he constantly harks back to his life in the movie industry and as a union official and a politician of the Hollywood years. It is his real identity, the self he has neither lost nor abandoned and from which he truly speaks as a man. Reagan knows who he is and therefore he possesses the first prerequisite for being a good president."

The American people, imagery aside, have yet to discover who he is, man or myth. But it has always been so. Democracy is not a fail-safe form of government. It forces us to make choices, to assume the ultimate responsibility for our country. That responsibility has been discharged for more than 200 years and seeing where we have come no one can argue convincingly that it has been discharged by boobs.

★ Appendices ★

PRESIDENTIAL
ELECTORAL VOTES

1980 Electoral Vote

	WASH. 9							4 N.H.
OREGON 6		MONTANA 4	NORTH DAKOTA 3	MINN. 10			3 VT.	ME. 4
	IDAHO 4		SOUTH DAKOTA 4	WIS. 11	MICH. 21		NEW YORK 41	MASS 14
NEVADA 3		WYOMING 3	NEBRASKA 5	IOWA 8		OHIO 25	PA. 27	R.I. 4 CONN. 8
CALIF. 45	UTAH 4	COLORADO 7	KANSAS 7	MO. 12	ILL. 26	IND. 13	W. VA. 6 VA. 12	N.J. 17 DEL. 3 MD. 10 D.C. 3
ARIZONA 6	NEW MEXICO 4	OKLAHOMA 8	ARK. 6		KY. 9	TENN. 10	N.C. 13	
				MISS. 7	ALA. 9	GA. 12	S.C. 8	
ALASKA 3		TEXAS 26	10 LA.				FLA. 17	
	HAWAII 4							

States shown with their number of electoral votes

		Carter	Reagan
STATES + D.C.		7	44
ELECTORAL VOTES		49	489

1976

States shown with their number of electoral votes

	CARTER (Democrat)	FORD (Republican)
STATES	24	27
ELECTORAL VOTES	297	240*

*One Washington State Republican elector voted for Reagan instead of Ford.

1972

☐ Republican

▨ Democrat

Republican

Democrat

Independent

Republican

Democrat

HOW AMERICA VOTED
FIGURES BASED ON ABC EXIT POLL OF 9,341 PEOPLE AT 375 PRECINCTS NATIONWIDE.

■ REAGAN   ▨ CARTER   ☐ ANDERSON

BY PARTY

Group	Reagan	Carter	Anderson
DEMOCRATS (42% OF VOTERS)	25	67%	
REPUBLICANS (29% OF VOTERS)	87	6	5
INDEPENDENTS (29% of VOTERS)	52	30	15

BY AGE

Group	Reagan	Carter	Anderson
18-29 YEARS OLD (28%)	44	42	12
30-49 YEARS OLD (43%)	52	37	9
50+ (28%)	55	38	6

BY RELIGION

Group	Reagan	Carter	Anderson
PROTESTANT (50%)	59	33	6
CATHOLIC (27%)	46	42	9
JEWISH (4%)	35	42	21
OTHER (10%)	39	51	7
NO RELIGION (9%)	38	40	18

Group	Reagan	Carter	Anderson
LABOR UNION FAMILY (30%)	41	49	8
NON-LABOR UNION FAMILY (70%)	55	33	9

BY EDUCATION

Group	Reagan	Carter	Anderson
LESS THAN HIGH SCHOOL GRADUATE (11%)	45	50	3
HIGH SCHOOL GRADUATE (56%)	52	38	8
COLLEGE GRADUATE (33%)	50	35	12

BY SEX

Group	Reagan	Carter	Anderson
MALE (51%)	54	35	9
FEMALE (49%)	47	42	9

BY RACE

Group	Reagan	Carter	Anderson
WHITE (89%)	55	34	9
BLACK (9%)	13	82	4

BY INCOME

Group	Reagan	Carter	Anderson
LESS THAN $10,000 ANNUAL HOUSEHOLD INCOME (16%)	40	50	7
$10,000 — $20,000 ANNUAL HOUSEHOLD INCOME (32%)	47	43	8
$20,000 — $30,000 (26%)	52	37	9
$30,000 +	60	28	10

HOW THEY CAPTURED
THE PRESIDENCY

	CARTER			REAGAN			ANDERSON		
	Popular	%	Electoral	Popular	%	Electoral	Popular	%	Electoral
Alabama	627,808	48	—	641,609	50	9	15,855	1	—
Alaska	33,591	26	—	70,253	55	3	8,564	7	—
Arizona	245,881	28	—	527,935	61	6	76,604	9	—
Arkansas	397,919	48	—	402,946	48	6	21,057	3	—
California	3,040,600	36	—	4,447,266	53	45	727,871	8	—
Colorado	367,966	31	—	650,786	55	7	130,579	11	—
Connecticut	537,407	39	—	672,648	48	8	168,260	12	—
Delaware	106,650	45	—	111,631	47	3	16,344	7	—
D.C.	124,376	76	3	21,765	13	—	14,971	9	—
Florida	1,369,877	39	—	1,945,313	55	17	178,569	5	—
Georgia	892,073	56	12	654,696	41	—	35,896	2	—
Hawaii	135,879	45	4	130,112	43	—	32,021	11	—
Idaho	109,410	25	—	289,789	67	4	27,142	6	—
Illinois	1,951,544	42	—	2,336,391	50	26	344,886	7	—
Indiana	832,213	38	—	1,232,764	56	13	107,729	5	—
Iowa	508,735	39	—	676,556	51	8	114,589	9	—
Kansas	324,974	34	—	562,848	58	7	67,535	7	—
Kentucky	613,389	48	—	630,967	49	9	30,519	2	—
Louisiana	707,981	46	—	796,240	52	10	26,198	2	—
Maine	220,387	42	—	238,156	46	4	53,450	10	—
Maryland	706,327	47	10	656,255	44	—	113,452	8	—
Massachusetts	1,051,104	42	—	1,054,562	42	14	382,044	15	—
Michigan	1,659,208	43	—	1,914,559	49	21	272,948	7	—
Minnesota	924,770	47	10	844,459	43	—	169,960	8	—

								—
								—
								—
								—
								—
								—
								—
								—
								—
								—
								—
								—
								—
								—
								—
								—
								—
								—
								—
								—
								—
								—
								—
								—
								—
								—
								—
								—
Mississippi	429,713	48	—	440,245	50	7	11,826	1
Missouri	917,663	44	—	1,055,355	51	12	76,488	4
Montana	112,961	32	—	197,862	57	4	28,159	8
Nebraska	164,276	26	—	413,401	66	5	44,025	8
Nevada	66,468	27	—	154,570	64	3	17,580	7
New Hampshire	109,080	28	—	221,771	58	4	49,295	13
New Jersey	1,119,576	39	—	1,506,437	52	17	224,173	8
New Mexico	165,186	37	—	245,600	55	4	28,404	6
New York	2,636,963	44	—	2,803,852	47	41	441,341	7
North Carolina	875,776	47	—	913,898	49	13	52,364	3
North Dakota	78,292	26	—	191,273	65	3	22,921	8
Ohio	1,743,829	41	—	2,201,864	52	25	255,521	6
Oklahoma	399,292	35	—	683,807	60	8	38,051	3
Oregon	447,806	39	—	559,589	48	6	109,894	10
Pennsylvania	1,930,719	43	—	2,251,937	50	27	288,588	6
Rhode Island	185,319	48	4	145,576	37	—	56,213	14
South Carolina	422,751	48	—	430,154	49	8	14,114	2
South Dakota	103,909	32	—	198,102	61	4	21,342	6
Tennessee	781,512	49	—	787,244	49	10	35,921	2
Texas	1,845,114	41	—	2,541,519	56	26	109,747	2
Utah	123,691	21	—	436,575	73	4	30,041	5
Vermont	81,421	39	—	93,554	44	3	31,671	15
Virginia	748,673	40	—	983,311	53	12	93,813	5
Washington	581,941	38	—	767,841	49	9	166,180	11
West Virginia	365,205	50	9	331,800	45	—	31,156	4
Wisconsin	988,255	44	—	1,089,750	48	11	159,793	7
Wyoming	49,123	28	—	110,096	62	3	12,350	7
Total	34,968,548	41	49	43,267,462	51	489	5,588,014	7

1976

	Carter			Ford		
	Popular	%	Electoral	Popular	%	Electoral
Alabama	659,171	56.6%	9	504,070	43.4%	—
Alaska	44,055	38.1	—	71,555	61.9	3
Arizona	295,602	41.4	—	418,642	58.6	6
Arkansas	498,604	65.0	6	267,903	35.0	—
California	3,742,284	49.1	—	3,882,244	50.9	45
Colorado	460,801	44.1	—	584,456	55.9	7
Connecticut	647,895	47.4	—	719,261	52.6	8
Delaware	122,559	52.7	3	109,780	47.3	—
D.C.	137,819	83.1	3	27,873	16.9	—
Florida	1,636,000	52.6	17	1,469,531	47.4	—
Georgia	979,409	66.9	12	483,743	33.1	—
Hawaii	147,375	51.2	4	140,003	49.8	—
Idaho	126,549	38.2	—	204,151	61.8	4
Illinois	2,271,295	48.9	—	2,364,269	51.1	26
Indiana	1,014,714	46.1	—	1,185,958	53.9	13
Iowa	619,931	49.4	—	632,863	50.6	8
Kansas	430,421	46.1	—	502,752	53.9	7
Kentucky	615,711	53.6	9	531,852	46.4	—
Louisiana	661,365	52.9	10	587,446	47.1	—
Maine	232,279	49.5	—	236,320	50.5	4
Maryland	759,612	53.0	10	672,661	47.0	—
Massachusetts	1,425,476	58.1	14	1,027,833	41.9	—
Michigan	1,696,714	47.2	—	1,893,742	52.8	21
Minnesota	1,070,440	56.6	10	819,395	43.4	—
Mississippi	381,329	50.9	7	366,846	49.1	—

State	Votes	%		Votes	%	
Missouri	999,163	51.8	12	928,808	48.2	—
Montana	149,259	46.2	—	173,703	53.8	4
Nebraska	233,293	39.3	—	359,219	60.7	5
Nevada	92,479	47.7	—	101,273	52.3	3
New Hampshire	147,645	44.2	—	185,935	55.8	4
New Jersey	1,420,668	49.0	—	1,477,858	51.0	17
New Mexico	199,225	48.9	—	207,718	51.1	4
New York	3,389,558	52.2	41	3,100,791	47.8	—
North Carolina	927,365	55.5	13	741,960	44.5	—
North Dakota	136,078	46.9	—	153,470	53.1	3
Ohio	2,011,621	50.1	25	2,000,595	49.9	—
Oklahoma	532,442	49.3	—	545,708	50.7	8
Oregon	484,643	49.9	—	485,305	50.1	6
Pennsylvania	2,328,677	51.3	27	2,205,604	48.7	—
Rhode Island	227,636	55.6	4	181,249	44.4	—
South Carolina	450,807	59.9	8	346,149	40.1	—
South Dakota	147,068	49.2	—	151,505	50.8	4
Tennessee	825,879	56.5	10	633,969	43.5	—
Texas	2,082,319	51.5	26	1,953,300	48.5	—
Utah	182,110	35.0	—	337,908	65.0	4
Vermont	78,789	43.9	—	100,387	56.1	3
Virginia	813,896	49.3	—	836,554	50.7	12
Washington	717,323	47.9	—	777,732	52.1	9
West Virginia	435,864	58.0	9	314,726	42.0	—
Wisconsin	1,037,056	50.8	11	1,003,039	49.2	—
Wyoming	62,239	40.1	—	92,717	59.9	3
Total	40,626,079	51.0%	297	39,102,291	49.0%	241

1972

	Nixon			McGovern		
	Popular	%	Electoral	Popular	%	Electoral
Alabama	728,701	72.4%	9	256,923	25.5%	—
Alaska	55,349	58.1	3	32,967	34.6	—
Arizona	402,812	61.6	6	198,540	30.4	—
Arkansas	448,541	68.9	6	199,892	30.7	—
California	4,602,096	55.0	45	3,475,847	41.5	—
Colorado	597,189	62.6	7	329,980	34.6	—
Connecticut	810,763	58.6	8	555,498	40.1	—
Delaware	140,357	59.6	3	92,283	39.2	—
D.C.	35,226	21.6	—	127,627	78.1	3
Florida	1,857,759	71.9	17	718,117	27.8	—
Georgia	881,490	75.3	12	289,529	24.7	—
Hawaii	168,933	62.5	4	101,433	37.5	—
Idaho	199,384	64.2	4	80,826	26.0	—
Illinois	2,788,179	59.0	26	1,913,472	40.5	—
Indiana	1,405,154	66.1	13	708,568	33.3	—
Iowa	706,207	57.6	8	496,206	40.5	—
Kansas	619,812	67.7	7	270,287	29.5	—
Kentucky	676,446	63.4	9	371,159	34.8	—
Louisiana	686,852	66.0	10	298,142	28.6	—
Maine	256,458	61.5	4	160,584	38.5	—
Maryland	829,305	61.3	10	505,781	37.4	—
Massachusetts	1,112,078	45.2	—	1,332,540	54.2	14
Michigan	1,961,721	56.2	21	1,459,435	41.8	—
Minnesota	898,269	51.6	10	802,346	46.1	—
Mississippi	505,125	78.2	7	126,782	19.6	—

State					
Missouri	1,154,058	62.3	12	698,531	37.7
Montana	183,976	57.9	4	120,197	37.9
Nebraska	406,298	70.5	5	169,991	29.5
Nevada	115,750	63.7	3	66,016	36.3
New Hampshire	213,724	64.0	4	116,435	34.9
New Jersey	1,845,502	61.6	17	1,102,211	36.8
New Mexico	235,606	61.1	4	141,084	36.6
New York	4,192,778	57.3	41	2,951,084	40.3
North Carolina	1,054,889	69.5	13	438,705	28.9
North Dakota	174,109	62.1	3	100,384	35.8
Ohio	2,441,827	59.6	25	1,558,889	38.1
Oklahoma	759,025	73.7	8	247,147	24.0
Oregon	486,686	52.5	6	392,760	42.3
Pennsylvania	2,714,521	59.1	27	1,796,951	39.1
Rhode Island	220,383	53.0	4	194,645	46.8
South Carolina	477,044	70.8	8	186,824	27.7
South Dakota	166,476	54.2	4	139,945	45.5
Tennessee	813,147	67.7	10	357,293	29.8
Texas	2,298,896	66.2	26	1,154,289	33.3
Utah	323,643	67.6	4	126,284	26.4
Vermont	117,149	62.9	3	68,174	36.6
Virginia	988,493	67.8	11*	438,887	30.1
Washington	837,135	56.9	9	568,334	38.6
West Virginia	484,964	63.6	6	227,435	36.4
Wisconsin	989,430	53.4	11	810,174	43.7
Wyoming	100,464	69.0	3	44,358	30.5
Total	**47,170,179**	**60.7%**	**520***	**29,171,791**	**37.5%**

*A Republican elector voted for John Hospers

1968

	Nixon			Humphrey			Wallace		
	Popular	%	Electoral	Popular	%	Electoral	Popular	%	Electoral
Alabama	146,591	14.0%	—	195,918	18.8%	—	687,664	65.8%	10
Alaska	37,600	45.3	3	35,411	42.7	—	10,024	12.1	—
Arizona	266,721	54.8	5	170,514	35.0	—	46,573	9.6	—
Arkansas	190,759	30.8	—	188,228	30.4	—	240,982	38.9	6
California	3,467,664	47.8	40	3,244,318	44.7	—	487,270	6.7	—
Colorado	409,345	50.5	6	335,174	41.3	—	60,813	7.5	—
Connecticut	556,721	44.3	—	621,561	49.5	8	76,650	6.1	—
Delaware	96,714	45.1	3	89,194	41.6	—	28,459	13.3	—
D.C.	31,012	18.2	—	139,566	81.8	3	—	—	—
Florida	886,804	40.5	14	676,794	30.9	—	624,207	28.5	—
Georgia	380,111	30.4	—	334,440	26.8	—	535,550	42.8	12
Hawaii	91,425	38.7	—	141,324	59.8	4	3,469	1.5	—
Idaho	165,369	56.8	4	89,273	30.7	—	36,541	12.6	—
Illinois	2,174,774	47.1	26	2,039,814	44.2	—	390,958	8.5	—
Indiana	1,067,885	50.3	13	806,659	38.0	—	243,108	11.5	—
Iowa	619,106	53.0	9	476,699	40.8	—	66,422	5.7	—
Kansas	478,674	54.8	7	302,996	34.7	—	88,921	10.2	—
Kentucky	462,411	43.8	9	397,541	37.7	—	193,098	18.3	—
Louisiana	257,535	23.5	—	309,615	28.2	—	530,300	48.3	10
Maine	169,254	43.1	4	217,312	55.3	4	6,370	1.6	—
Maryland	517,995	41.9	10	538,310	43.6	10	178,734	14.5	—
Massachusetts	766,844	32.9	—	1,469,218	63.0	14	87,088	3.7	—
Michigan	1,370,665	41.5	—	1,593,082	48.2	21	331,968	10.0	—
Minnesota	658,643	41.5	—	857,738	54.0	10	68,991	4.3	—
Mississippi	88,516	13.5	—	150,664	23.0	—	415,349	63.5	7

State									
Missouri	811,932	44.9	12	791,444	43.7	—	206,126	11.4	—
Montana	138,835	50.6	4	114,117	41.6	—	20,015	7.3	—
Nebraska	321,163	59.8	5	170,784	31.8	—	44,904	8.4	—
Nevada	73,188	47.5	3	60,598	39.3	—	20,432	13.3	—
New Hampshire	154,903	52.1	4	130,589	43.9	—	11,173	3.8	—
New Jersey	1,325,467	46.1	17	1,264,206	44.0	—	262,187	9.1	—
New Mexico	169,692	51.9	4	130,081	39.8	—	25,737	7.9	—
New York	3,007,932	44.3	—	3,378,470	49.8	43	358,864	5.3	—
North Carolina	627,192	39.5	12	464,113	29.2	—	496,188	31.3	—
North Dakota	138,669	55.9	4	94,769	38.2	—	14,244	5.8	—
Ohio	1,791,014	45.2	26	1,700,586	43.0	—	467,495	11.8	—
Oklahoma	449,697	47.7	8	301,658	32.0	—	191,731	20.3	—
Oregon	408,433	49.8	6	358,866	43.8	—	49,683	6.1	—
Pennsylvania	2,090,017	44.0	—	2,259,403	47.6	29	378,582	8.0	—
Rhode Island	122,359	31.8	—	246,518	64.0	4	15,678	4.1	—
South Carolina	254,062	38.1	8	197,486	29.6	—	215,430	32.3	—
South Dakota	149,841	53.3	4	118,023	42.0	—	13,400	4.8	—
Tennessee	472,592	37.9	11	351,233	28.1	—	424,792	34.0	—
Texas	1,227,844	39.9	—	1,266,804	41.1	25	584,269	19.0	—
Utah	238,728	56.5	4	156,665	41.1	—	26,906	6.4	—
Vermont	85,142	52.8	3	70,255	43.5	—	5,104	3.2	—
Virginia	590,319	43.4	12	442,387	32.5	—	320,272	23.6	—
Washington	588,510	45.2	—	616,037	47.3	9	96,990	7.4	—
West Virginia	307,555	40.8	—	374,091	49.6	7	72,560	9.6	—
Wisconsin	809,940	47.9	12	748,804	44.3	—	127,835	7.6	—
Wyoming	70,927	55.8	3	45,173	35.5	—	11,105	8.7	—
Total	**31,785,148**	**43.4%**	**301**	**31,274,503**	**42.7%**	**191**	**9,901,151**	**13.5%**	**46**

1964

	Johnson			Goldwater		
	Popular	%	Electoral	Popular	%	Electoral
Alabama	0*	0.0%	—	479,085	69.5%	10
Alaska	44,329	65.9	3	22,930	34.1	—
Arizona	237,753	49.5	—	242,535	50.5	5
Arkansas	314,197	56.1	6	243,264	43.4	—
California	4,171,877	59.1	40	2,879,108	40.8	—
Colorado	476,024	61.3	6	296,767	38.2	—
Connecticut	826,269	67.8	8	390,996	32.1	—
Delaware	122,704	61.0	3	78,078	38.8	—
D.C.	169,796	85.5	3	28,801	14.5	—
Florida	948,540	51.2	14	905,941	48.9	—
Georgia	522,163	45.9	—	616,584	54.1	12
Hawaii	163,249	78.8	4	44,022	21.2	—
Idaho	148,920	50.9	4	143,557	49.1	—
Illinois	2,796,833	59.5	26	1,905,946	40.5	—
Indiana	1,170,848	56.0	13	911,118	43.6	—
Iowa	733,030	61.9	9	449,148	37.9	—
Kansas	464,028	54.1	7	386,579	45.1	—
Kentucky	669,659	64.0	9	372,977	35.7	—
Louisiana	387,068	43.2	—	509,225	56.8	10
Maine	262,264	68.8	4	118,701	31.2	—
Maryland	730,912	65.5	10	385,495	34.5	—
Massachusetts	1,786,422	76.2	14	549,727	23.4	—
Michigan	2,136,615	66.7	21	1,060,152	33.1	—
Minnesota	991,117	63.8	10	559,624	36.0	—
Mississippi	52,616	12.9	—	356,512	87.1	7

State						
Missouri	1,164,344	64.1	12	653,535	36.0	—
Montana	164,246	59.0	4	113,032	40.6	—
Nebraska	307,307	52.6	5	276,847	47.4	—
Nevada	79,339	58.6	3	56,094	41.4	—
New Hampshire	182,065	63.6	4	104,029	36.4	—
New Jersey	1,867,671	65.6	17	963,843	33.9	—
New Mexico	194,015	59.0	4	132,838	40.4	—
New York	4,913,156	68.6	43	2,243,559	31.3	—
North Carolina	800,139	56.2	13	624,841	43.9	—
North Dakota	149,784	58.0	4	108,207	41.9	—
Ohio	2,498,331	62.9	26	1,470,865	37.1	—
Oklahoma	519,834	55.8	8	412,665	44.3	—
Oregon	501,017	63.7	6	282,779	36.0	—
Pennsylvania	3,130,954	64.9	29	1,673,657	34.7	—
Rhode Island	315,463	80.9	4	74,615	19.1	—
South Carolina	215,723	41.1	—	309,048	58.9	8
South Dakota	163,010	55.6	4	130,108	44.4	—
Tennessee	635,047	55.5	11	508,965	44.5	—
Texas	1,663,185	63.3	25	958,566	36.5	—
Utah	219,628	54.7	4	181,785	45.3	—
Vermont	108,127	66.3	3	54,942	33.7	—
Virginia	558,038	53.5	12	481,334	46.2	—
Washington	779,699	62.0	9	470,366	37.4	—
West Virginia	538,087	67.9	7	253,953	32.1	—
Wisconsin	1,050,424	62.1	12	638,495	37.7	—
Wyoming	80,718	56.6	3	61,998	43.4	—
Total	**43,126,584**	**61.1%**	**486**	**27,177,838**	**38.4%**	**52**

*Unpledged Democratic electors received 210,732 votes

1960

	Kennedy			Nixon			Byrd	
	Popular	%	Electoral	Popular	%	Electoral	Popular	Electoral
Alabama	318,303	56.8%	5	236,110	42.1%	—	—	6
Alaska	29,809	49.1	—	30,953	50.9	3	—	—
Arizona	176,781	44.4	—	221,241	55.5	4	—	—
Arkansas	215,049	50.2	8	184,508	43.1	—	—	—
California	3,224,099	49.6	—	3,259,722	50.1	32	—	—
Colorado	330,629	44.9	—	402,242	54.6	6	—	—
Connecticut	657,055	53.7	8	565,813	46.3	—	—	—
Delaware	99,590	50.6	3	96,373	49.0	—	—	—
D.C.*	—	—	—	—	—	—	—	—
Florida	748,700	48.5	—	795,476	51.5	10	—	—
Georgia	458,638	62.5	12	274,472	37.4	—	—	—
Hawaii	92,410	50.0	3	92,295	50.0	—	—	—
Idaho	138,853	46.2	—	161,597	53.8	4	—	—
Illinois	2,377,846	50.0	27	2,368,988	49.8	—	—	—
Indiana	952,358	44.6	—	1,175,120	55.0	13	—	—
Iowa	550,565	43.2	—	722,381	56.7	10	—	—
Kansas	363,213	39.1	—	561,474	60.5	8	—	—
Kentucky	521,855	46.4	—	602,607	53.6	10	—	—
Louisiana	407,339	50.4	10	230,980	28.6	—	—	—
Maine	181,159	43.0	—	240,608	57.1	5	—	—
Maryland	565,808	53.6	9	489,538	46.4	—	—	—
Massachusetts	1,487,174	60.2	16	976,750	39.6	—	—	—
Michigan	1,687,269	50.9	20	1,620,428	48.8	—	—	—
Minnesota	779,933	50.6	11	757,915	49.2	—	—	—
Mississippi	108,362	36.3	—	73,561	24.7	—	116,248**	8

State								
Missouri	972,201	50.3	13	962,218	49.7	—	—	—
Montana	134,891	48.6	—	141,841	51.1	4	—	—
Nebraska	232,542	37.9	—	380,553	62.1	6	—	—
Nevada	54,880	51.2	3	52,387	48.8	—	—	—
New Hampshire	137,772	46.6	—	157,989	53.4	4	—	—
New Jersey	1,385,415	50.0	16	1,363,324	49.2	—	—	—
New Mexico	156,027	50.2	4	153,733	49.4	—	—	—
New York	3,830,085	52.5	45	3,446,419	47.3	—	—	—
North Carolina	713,136	52.1	14	655,420	47.9	—	—	—
North Dakota	123,963	44.5	—	154,310	55.4	4	—	—
Ohio	1,944,248	46.7	—	2,217,611	53.3	25	—	—
Oklahoma	370,111	41.0	—	533,039	59.0	7	—	1
Oregon	367,402	47.3	—	408,065	52.6	6	—	—
Pennsylvania	2,556,282	51.1	32	2,439,956	48.7	—	—	—
Rhode Island	258,032	63.6	4	147,502	36.4	—	—	—
South Carolina	198,121	51.2	8	188,558	48.8	—	—	—
South Dakota	128,070	41.8	—	178,417	58.2	4	—	—
Tennessee	481,453	45.8	—	556,577	52.9	11	—	—
Texas	1,167,935	50.5	24	1,121,693	48.5	—	—	—
Utah	169,248	45.2	—	205,361	54.8	4	—	—
Vermont	69,186	41.4	—	98,131	58.7	3	—	—
Virginia	362,327	47.0	—	404,521	52.4	12	—	—
Washington	599,298	48.3	—	629,273	50.7	9	—	—
West Virginia	441,786	52.7	8	395,995	47.3	—	—	—
Wisconsin	830,805	48.1	—	895,175	51.8	12	—	—
Wyoming	63,331	45.0	—	77,451	55.0	3	—	—
Total	**34,221,344**	**49.7%**	**303**	**34,106,671**	**49.6%**	**219**	**116,248**	**15**

*Did not have the vote in 1960
**Unpledged

D = Democrat
R = Republican

DISTRIBUTION OF SENATE SEATS

STATE	PRE-ELECTION D	PRE-ELECTION R	ELECTION '80 D	ELECTION '80 R
Alabama	2		1	1
Alaska	1	1		2
Arizona	1	1	1	1
Arkansas	2		2	
California	1	1	1	1
Colorado	1	1	1	1
Connecticut	1	1	1	1
Delaware	1	1	1	1
Florida	2		1	1
Georgia	2		1	1
Hawaii	2		2	
Idaho	1	1		2
Illinois	1	1	1	1
Indiana	1	1		2
Iowa	1	1		2
Kansas		2		2
Kentucky	2		2	
Louisiana	2		2	
Maine	1	1	1	1
Maryland	1	1	1	1
Massachusetts	2		2	
Michigan	2		2	
Minnesota		2		2
Mississippi	1	1	1	1
Missouri	1	1	1	1
Montana	2		2	
Nebraska	2		2	
Nevada	1	1	1	1
New Hampshire	1	1	1	1
New Jersey	2		2	
New Mexico		2		2
New York	1	1	1	1
North Carolina	1	1		2
North Dakota	1	1	1	1
Ohio	2		2	
Oklahoma	1	1	1	1
Oregon		2		2
Pennsylvania		2		2
Rhode Island	1	1	1	1
South Carolina	1	1	1	1
South Dakota	1	1		2
Tennessee	1	1	1	1
Texas	1	1	1	1
Utah		2		2
Vermont	1	1	1	1
Virginia	1 ind.	1	1 ind.	1
Washington	2		1	1
West Virginia	2		2	
Wisconsin	2		1	1
Wyoming		2		2
Total	**59**	**41**	**48**	**52**

356

D = Democrat
R = Republican

DISTRIBUTION OF HOUSE SEATS

	PRE-ELECTION		ELECTION '80	
STATE	*D*	*R*	*D*	*R*
Alabama	4	3	4	3
Alaska		1		1
Arizona	2	2	2	2
Arkansas	2	2	2	2
California	25	18	22	21
Colorado	3	2	3	2
Connecticut	5	1	4	2
Delaware		1		1
Florida	12	3	11	4
Georgia	9	1	9	1
Hawaii	2		2	
Idaho		2		2
Illinois	10	14	10	14
Indiana	7	4	6	5
Iowa	3	3	3	3
Kansas	1	4	1	4
Kentucky	4	3	4	3
Louisiana	5	3	6	2
Maine		2		2
Maryland	6	2	7	1
Massachusetts	10	2	10	2
Michigan	13	6	12	7
Minnesota	4	4	3	5
Mississippi	3	2	3	2
Missouri	8	2	6	4
Montana	1	1	1	1
Nebraska	1	2		3
Nevada	1		1	
New Hampshire	1	1	1	1
New Jersey	10	5	8	7
New Mexico	1	1		2
New York	26	13	21	18
North Carolina	9	2	7	4
North Dakota		1	1	
Ohio	10	13	10	13
Oklahoma	5	1	5	1
Oregon	4		3	1
Pennsylvania	15	10	13	12
Rhode Island	2		1	1
South Carolina	4	2	2	4
South Dakota	1	1	1	1
Tennessee	5	3	5	3
Texas	20	4	19	5
Utah	1	1		2
Vermont		1		1
Virginia	4	6	1	9
Washington	6	1	5	2
West Virginia	4		2	2
Wisconsin	6	3	5	4
Wyoming		1		1
Total	**275**	**160**	**242**	**193**

'80
PRESIDENTIAL DEBATES

As sponsored by The League of Women
Voters Education Fund
Second Debate
Tuesday, 28 October
Official Transcriptional Record

CLEVELAND, Ohio, 28 October 1980—The following is an
NBIC-verified transcriptional record of the Second Debate of
the series of Presidential Debates sponsored by the League of
Women Voters Education Fund.

Candidates participating (in order of speaking):

GOVERNOR RONALD REAGAN
Republican Party Candidate

PRESIDENT JIMMY CARTER
Democratic Party Candidate

MS. RUTH HINERFELD, League of Women Voters Education Fund: Good evening. I'm Ruth Hinerfeld of the League of Women Voters Education Fund. Next Tuesday is Election Day. Before going to the polls, voters want to understand the issues and know the candidates' positions. Tonight, voters will have an opportunity to see and hear the major party candidates for the presidency state their views on issues that affect us all. The League of Women Voters is proud to present this Presidential Debate. Our moderator is Howard K. Smith.

MR. HOWARD K. SMITH, ABC News: Thank you, Mrs. Hinerfeld. The League of Women Voters is pleased to welcome to the Cleveland Ohio Convention Center Music Hall President Jimmy Carter, the Democratic Party's candidate for reelection to the presidency, and Governor Ronald Reagan of California, the Republican Party's candidate for the presidency. The candidates will debate questions on domestic, economic, foreign policy, and national security issues.

The questions are going to be posed by a panel of distinguished journalists who are here with me. They are: Marvin Stone, the editor of *U.S. News and World Report*; Harry Ellis, national correspondent of the *Christian Science Monitor*; William Hilliard, assistant managing editor of the *Portland Oregonian*; Barbara Walters, correspondent, ABC News.

The ground rules for this, as agreed by you gentlemen, are these: Each panelist down here will ask a question, the same question, to each of the two candidates. After the two candidates have answered, a panelist will ask follow-up questions to try to sharpen the answers. The candidates will then have an opportunity each to make a rebuttal. That will constitute the first half of the debate, and I will state the rules for the second half later on.

Some other rules: The candidates are not permitted to bring prepared notes to the podium, but are permitted to make notes during the debate. If the candidates exceed the allotted time agreed on, I will reluctantly but certainly interrupt. We ask the Convention Center audience here to abide by one ground rule. Please do not applaud or express approval or disapproval during the debate.

Now, based on a toss of the coin, Governor Reagan will respond to the first question from Marvin Stone.

MR. MARVIN STONE, *U.S. News and World Report*: Governor, as you're well aware, the question of war and peace has emerged as a central issue in this campaign in the give and take of recent weeks. President Carter has been criticized for responding late to aggressive Soviet impulses, for insufficient build-up of our armed forces, and a paralysis in dealing with Afghanistan and Iran. You have been criticized for being all too quick to advocate the use of lots of muscle—military action—to deal with foreign crises. Specifically, what are the differences between the two of you on the uses of American military power?

GOVERNOR REAGAN: I don't know what the differences might be, because I don't know what Mr. Carter's policies are. I do know what he has said about mine. And I'm only here to tell you that I believe with all my heart that our first priority must be world peace, and that use of force is always and only a last resort, when everything else has failed, and then only with regard to our national security.

Now, I believe, also, that this meeting . . . this mission, this responsibility for preserving the peace, I believe, is a responsibility peculiar to our country, and that we cannot shirk our responsibility as a leader of the Free World because we're the only ones that can do it. Therefore, the burden of maintaining the peace falls on us. And to maintain that peace requires strength. America has never gotten in a war because we were too strong. We can get into a war by letting events get out of hand, as they have in the last three and a half years under the foreign policies of this Administration of Mr. Carter's, (sic) until we're faced each time with a crisis. And good management in preserving the peace requires that we control the events and try to intercept before they become a crisis.

I have seen four wars in my lifetime. I'm a father of sons; I have a grandson. I don't ever want to see another generation of young Americans bleed their lives into sandy beachheads in the Pacific, or rice paddies and jungles in the . . . in Asia or the muddy battlefields of Europe.

MR. SMITH: Mr. Stone, do you have a follow-up question for the Governor?

MR. STONE: Yes. Governor, we've been hearing that the defense build-up that you would associate yourself with would cost tens of billions of dollars more than is now contemplated. Assuming that the American people are ready to bear this cost, they nevertheless keep asking the following question: How do you reconcile huge increases in military outlays with your promise of substantial tax cuts and of balancing the budget, which in this fiscal year, the one that just ended, ran more than $60 billion in the red?

GOVERNOR REAGAN: Mr. Stone, I have submitted an economic plan that I have worked out in concert with a number of fine economists in this country, all of whom approve it, and believe that over a five-year projection, this plan can permit the extra spending for needed refurbishing of our defensive posture, that it can provide for a balanced budget by 1983 if not earlier, and that we can afford—along with the cuts that I have proposed in government spending—we can afford the tax cuts I have proposed and probably mainly because Mr. Carter's economic policy has built into the next five years, and on beyond that, a tax increase that will be taking $86 billion more out of the people's pockets than was taken this year. And my tax cut does not come close to eliminating that $86 billion increase. I'm only reducing the amount of the increase. In other words, what I'm talking about is not putting government back to getting less money than government's been getting, but simply cutting the increase in . . . in spending.

MR. SMITH: The same question now goes to President Carter. President Carter, would you like to have the question repeated?

MR. STONE: Yes, President Carter, the question of war and peace, a central issue in this campaign. You've been criticized for, in the give and take, for responding late to aggressive Soviet impulses, for an insufficient build-up of our armed forces, and a paralysis in dealing with Afghanistan and Iran. Governor Reagan, on the other hand, has been criticized for being all too quick to advocate the use of lots of muscle— military action—to deal with foreign crises such as I have mentioned. Specifically, what are the differences between the two of you on the uses of American military power?

PRESIDENT CARTER: Mr. Stone, I've had to make thousands of decisions since I've been president, serving in the Oval Office. And with each one of those decisions that affect the future of my country, I have learned in the process. I think I'm a much wiser and more experienced man than I was when I debated four years ago against President Ford. I've also learned that there are no simple answers to complicated questions. H.L. Mencken said that for every problem there's a simple answer. It would be neat and plausible and wrong.

The fact is that this nation, in the eight years before I became president, had its own military strength decreased. Seven out of eight years, the budget commitments for defense went down, 37 percent in all. Since I've been in office, we've had a steady, carefully planned, methodical but very effective increase in our commitment for defense.

But what we've done is use that enormous power and prestige and military strength of the United States to preserve the peace. We've not only kept peace for our own country, but we've been able to extend the benefits of peace to others. In the Middle East, we've worked for a peace treaty between Israel and Egypt, successfully, and have tied ourselves together with Israel and Egypt in a common defense capability. This is a very good step forward for our nation's security, and we'll continue to do as we have done in the past.

I might also add that there are decisions that are made in the Oval Office by every president which are profound in nature. There are always trouble spots in the world, and how those troubled areas are addressed by a president alone in that Oval Office affects our nation directly, the involvement of the United States and also our American interests. That is a basic decision that has to be made so frequently, by every president who serves. That is what I have tried to do successfully by keeping our country at peace.

MR. SMITH: Mr. Stone, do you have a follow-up for...

MR. STONE: Yes. I would like to be a little more specific on the use of military power, and let's talk about one area for a moment. Under what circumstances would you use military forces to deal with, for example, a shut-off of the Persian Oil Gulf, if that should occur, or to counter Russian expansion beyond Afghanistan into either Iran or Pakistan? I ask this question in view of charges that we are woefully unprepared to project sustained—and I emphasize the word sustained— power in that part of the world.

PRESIDENT CARTER: Mr. Stone, in my State of the Union address earlier this year, I pointed out that any threat to the stability or security of the Persian Gulf would be a threat to the security of our own country. In the past, we have not had an adequate military presence in that region. Now we have two major carrier task forces. We have access to facilities in five different areas of that region. And we've made it clear that working with our allies and others, that we are prepared to address any foreseeable eventuality which might interrupt commerce with that crucial area of the world.

But in doing this, we have made sure that we address this question peacefully, not injecting American military forces into combat, but letting the strength of our nation be felt in a beneficial way. This, I believe, has assured that our interests will be protected in the Persian Gulf region, as we have done in the Middle East and throughout the world.

MR. SMITH: Governor Reagan, you have a minute to comment or rebut.

GOVERNOR REAGAN: Well yes, I question the figure about the decline in defense spending under the two previous Administrations in the preceding eight years to this Administration. I would call to your attention that we were in a war that wound down during those eight years, which of course made a change in military spending because of turning from war to peace. I also would like to point out that Republican presidents in those years, faced with a Democratic majority in both houses of the Congress, found that their requests for defense budgets were very often cut.

Now, Gerald Ford left a five-year projected plan for a military build-up to restore our defenses, and President Carter's Administration reduced that by 38 percent, cut 60 ships out of the Navy building program that had been proposed, and stopped the . . . the B-1, delayed the Cruise missile, stopped the production line for the Minuteman missile, stopped the Trident or delayed the Trident submarine, and now is planning a mobile military force that can be delivered to various spots in the world, which does make me question his assaults on whether I am the one who is quick to look for use of force.

MR. SMITH: President Carter, you have the last word on this question.

PRESIDENT CARTER: Well, there are various elements of defense. One is to control nuclear weapons, which I hope we'll get to later on because that is the most important single issue in this campaign. Another one is how to address troubled areas of the world. I think, habitually, Governor Reagan has advocated the injection of military forces into troubled areas, when I and my predecessors—both Democrats and Republicans—have advocated resolving those troubles and those difficult areas of the world peacefully, diplomatically, and through negotiation. In addition to that, the build-up of military forces is good for our country because we've got to have military strength to preserve the peace. But I'll always remember that the best weapons are the ones that are never fired in combat, and the best soldier is one who never has to lay his life down on the field of battle. Strength is imperative for peace, but the two must go hand in hand.

MR. SMITH: Thank you, gentlemen. The next question is from Harry Ellis to President Carter.

MR. HARRY ELLIS, *Christian Science Monitor*: Mr. President, when you were elected in 1976, the Consumer Price Index stood at 4.8 percent. It now stands at more than 12 percent. Perhaps more significantly, the nation's broader, underlying inflation rate has gone up from 7 percent to 9 percent. Now, a part of that was due to external factors beyond U.S. control, notably the more than doubling of oil prices by OPEC last year. Because the United States remains vulnerable to such external shocks, can inflation in fact be controlled? If so, what measures would you pursue in a second term?

PRESIDENT CARTER: Again it's important to put the situation in perspective. In 1974, we had a so-called oil shock, wherein the price of OPEC oil was raised to an extraordinary degree. We had an even worse oil shock in 1979. In 1974, we had the worst recession, the deepest and most penetrating recession since the Second World War. The recession that resulted this time was the briefest since the Second World War.

In addition, we've brought down inflation. Earlier this year, in the first quarter, we did have a very severe inflation pressure brought about by the OPEC price increase. It averaged about 18 percent in the first quarter of this year. In the second quarter, we had dropped it down to about 13 percent. The most recent figures, the last three months, on the third quarter of this year, the inflation rate is 7 percent—still too high, but it illustrates very vividly that in addition to providing an enormous number of jobs—nine million new jobs in the last three and a half years—that the inflationary threat is still urgent on us.

I notice that Governor Reagan recently mentioned the Reagan-Kemp-Roth proposal, which his own running mate, George Bush, described as voodoo economics, and said that it would result in a 30 percent inflation rate. And *Business Week*, which is not a Democratic publication, said that this Reagan-Kemp-Roth proposal—and I quote them, I think—was completely irresponsible and would result in inflationary pressures which would destroy this nation.

So our proposals are very sound and very carefully considered to stimulate jobs, to improve the industrial complex of this country, to create tools for American workers, and at the same time would be anti-inflationary in nature. So to add nine million new jobs, to control inflation, and to plan for the future with an energy policy now intact as a foundation is our plan for the years ahead.

MR. SMITH: Mr. Ellis, do you have a follow-up question for Mr. Carter?

MR. ELLIS: Yes. Mr. President, you have mentioned the creation of nine million new jobs. At the same time, the unemployment rate still hangs high, as does the inflation rate. Now, I wonder, can you tell us what additional policies you would pursue in a second administration in order to try to bring down that inflation rate? And would it be an act of leadership to tell the American people they are going to have to sacrifice to adopt a leaner life-style for some time to come?

PRESIDENT CARTER: Yes. We have demanded that the American people sacrifice, and they have done very well. As a matter of fact, we're importing today about one-third less oil from overseas than we did just a year ago. We've had a 25 percent reduction since the first year I was in office. At the same time, as I have said earlier, we have added about nine million net new jobs in that period of time—a record never before achieved.

Also, the new energy policy has been predicated on two factors: one is conservation, which requires sacrifice, and the other one, increase in production of American energy, which is going along very well—more coal this year than ever before in American history, more oil and gas wells drilled this year than ever before in history.

The new economic revitalization program that we have in mind, which will be implemented next year, would result in tax credits which would let business invest in new tools and new factories to create even more new jobs—about one million in the next two years. And we also have planned a youth employment program which would encompass 600,000 jobs for young people. This has already passed the House, and it has an excellent prospect to pass the Senate.

MR. SMITH: Now, the same question goes to Governor Reagan. Governor Reagan, would you like to have the question repeated?

MR. ELLIS: Governor Reagan, during the past four years, the Consumer Price Index has risen from 4.8 percent to currently over 12 percent. And perhaps more significantly, the nation's broader, underlying rate of inflation has gone up from 7 percent to 9 percent. Now, a part of that has been due to external factors beyond U.S. control, and notably, the more than doubling of OPEC oil prices last year, which leads me to ask you whether, since the United States remains vulnerable to such external shocks, can inflation in fact be controlled? If so, specifically what measures would you pursue?

GOVERNOR REAGAN: Mr. Ellis, I think this idea that has been spawned here in our country, that inflation somehow came upon us like a plague and therefore it's uncontrollable and no one can do anything about it, is entirely spurious and it's dangerous to say this to the people. When Mr. Carter became president, inflation was 4.8 percent, as you said. It had been cut in two by President Gerald Ford. It is now running at 12.7 percent.

President Carter also has spoken of the new jobs created. Well, we always, with the normal growth in our country and increase in population, increase the number of jobs. But that can't hide the fact that there are eight million men and women out of work in America today, and two million of those lost their jobs in just the last few months. Mr. Carter had also promised that he would not use unemployment as a tool to fight against inflation. And yet, his 1980 economic message stated that we would reduce productivity and gross national product and increase unemployment in order to get a handle on inflation, because in January, at the beginning of the year, it was more than 18 percent. Since then, he has blamed the people for inflation, OPEC, he has blamed the Federal Reserve system, he has blamed the lack of productivity of the American people, he has then accused the people of living too well and that we must share in scarcity, we must sacrifice and get used to doing with less. We don't have inflation because the people are living too well. We have inflation because the government is living too well. And the last statement, just a few days ago, was a speech to the effect that we have inflation because government revenues have not kept pace with government spending.

I see my time is running out here. I'll have to get this out very fast. Yes, you can lick inflation by increasing productivity and by decreasing the cost of government to the place that we have balanced budgets, and are no longer grinding out printing press money, flooding the market with it because the government is spending more than it takes in. And my economic plan calls for that. The President's economic plan calls for increasing the taxes to the point that we finally take so much money away from the people that we can balance the budget in that way. But we will have a very poor nation and a very unsound economy if we follow that path.

MR. SMITH: A follow-up, Mr. Ellis?

MR. ELLIS: Yes. You have centered on cutting government spending in what you have just said about your own policies. You have also said that you would increase defense spending. Specifically, where would you cut government spending if you were to increase defense spending and also cut taxes, so that, presumably, federal revenues would shrink?

GOVERNOR REAGAN: Well, most people, when they think about cutting government spending, they think in terms of eliminating necessary programs or wiping out something, some service that government is supposed to perform. I believe that there is enough extravagance and fat in government. As a matter of fact, one of the secretaries of HEW under Mr. Carter testified that he thought there was $7 billion worth of fraud and waste in welfare and in the medical programs associated with it. We've had the General Accounting Office estimate that there are probably tens of billions of dollars that are lost in fraud alone, and they have added that waste adds even more to that.

We have a program for a gradual reduction of government spending based on these theories, and I have a task force now that has been working on where those cuts could be made. I'm confident that it can be done and that it will reduce inflation because I did it in California. And inflation went down below the national average in California when we returned the money to the people and reduced government spending.

MR. SMITH: President Carter.

PRESIDENT CARTER: Governor Reagan's proposal, the Reagan-Kemp-Roth proposal, is one of the most highly inflationary ideas that ever has been presented to the American public. He would actually have to cut government spending by at least $130 billion in order to balance the budget under this ridiculous proposal. I notice that his task force that is working for his future plans had some of their ideas revealed in the *Wall Street Journal* this week. One of those ideas was to repeal the minimum wage, and several times this year, Governor Reagan has said that the major cause of unemployment is the minimum wage. This is a heartless kind of approach to the working families of our country, which is typical of many Republican leaders of the past, but I think has been accentuated under Governor Reagan.

In California—I'm surprised Governor Reagan brought this up—he had the three largest tax increases in the history of that state under his administration. He more than doubled state spending while he was governor—122 percent increase—and had between a 20 percent and 30 percent increase in the number of employees . . .

MR. SMITH: Sorry to interrupt, Mr. Carter.

PRESIDENT CARTER: . . . in California. Thank you, sir.

MR. SMITH: Governor Reagan has the last word on this question.

GOVERNOR REAGAN: Yes. The figures that the President has just used about California is a distortion of the situation there, because while I was Governor of California, our spending in California increased less per capita than the spending in Georgia while Mr. Carter was Governor of Georgia in the same four years. The size of government increased only one sixth in California of what it increased in proportion to the population in Georgia.

And the idea that my tax-cut proposal is inflationary: I would like to ask the President why is it inflationary to let the people keep more of their money and spend it the way that they like, and it isn't inflationary to let him take that money and spend it the way he wants?

MR. SMITH: I wish that question need not be rhetorical, but it must be because we've run out of time on that. Now, the third question to Governor Reagan from William Hilliard.

MR. WILLIAM HILLIARD, *Portland Oregonian*: Yes. Governor Reagan, the decline of our cities has been hastened by the continual rise in crime, strained race relations, the fall in the quality of public education, persistence of abnormal poverty in a rich nation, and a decline in the services to the public. The signs seem to point toward a deterioration that could lead to the establishment of a permanent underclass in the cities. What, specifically, would you do in the next four years to reverse this trend?

GOVERNOR REAGAN: I have been talking to a number of Congressmen who have much the same idea that I have, and that is that in the inner city areas, that in cooperation with the local government and with national government, and using tax incentives and with cooperating with the private sector, that we have development zones. Let the local entity, the city, declare this particular area, based on the standards of the percentage of people on welfare, unemployed, and so forth, in that area. And then, through tax incentives, induce the creation of businesses providing jobs and so forth in those areas. The elements of government through these tax incentives . . . For example, a business that would not have, for a period of time, an increase in the property tax reflecting its development of the unused property that it was making wouldn't be any loss to the city because the city isn't getting any tax from that now. And there would simply be a delay, and on the other hand, many of the people who would then be given jobs are presently wards of the government, and it wouldn't hurt to give them a tax incentive, because they . . . that wouldn't be costing government anything either.

I think there are things to do in this regard. I stood in the South Bronx on the exact spot that President Carter stood on in 1977. You have to see it to believe it. It looks like a bombed-out city—great, gaunt skeletons of buildings, windows smashed out, painted on one of them "Unkept promises," on another, "Despair." And this was the spot at which President Carter had promised that he was going to bring in a vast program to rebuild this department. There are whole . . . or this area . . . there are whole blocks of land that are left bare, just bulldozed down flat. And nothing has been done, and they are now charging to take tourists there to see this terrible desolation. I talked to a man just briefly there who asked me one simple question: "Do I have reason to hope that I can someday take care of my family again? Nothing has been done."

MR. SMITH: Follow-up, Mr. Hilliard?

MR. HILLIARD: Yes, Governor Reagan. Blacks and other non-whites are increasing in numbers in our cities. . Many of them feel that they are facing a hostility from whites that prevents them from joining the economic mainstream of our society. There is racial confrontation in the schools, on jobs, and in housing, as non-whites seek to reap the benefits of a free society. What do you think is the nation's future as a multi-racial society?

GOVERNOR REAGAN: I believe in it. I am eternally optimistic, and I happen to believe that we've made great progress from the days when I was young and when this country didn't even know it had a racial problem. I know those things can grow out of despair in an inner city, when there's hopelessness at home, lack of work, and so forth. But I believe that all of us together, and I believe the presidency is what Teddy Roosevelt said it was. It's a bully pulpit. And I think that something can be done from there, because a goal for all of us should be that one day things will be done neither because of nor in spite of any of the differences between us—ethnic differences or racial differences, whatever they may be—that we will have total equal opportunity for all people. And I would do everything I could in my power to bring that about.

MR. SMITH: Mr. Hilliard, would you repeat your question for President Carter?

MR. HILLIARD: President Carter, the decline of our cities has been hastened by the continual rise in crime, strained race relations, the fall in the quality of public education, persistence of abnormal poverty in a rich nation, and a decline in services to the public. The signs seem to point toward a deterioration that could lead to the establishment of a permanent underclass in the cities. What, specifically, would you do in the next four years to reverse this trend?

PRESIDENT CARTER: Thank you, Mr. Hilliard. When I was campaigning in 1976, everywhere I went, the mayors and local officials were in despair about the rapidly deteriorating central cities of our nation. We initiated a very fine urban renewal program, working with the mayors, the governors, and other interested officials. This has been a very successful effort. That's one of the main reasons that we've had such an increase in the number of people employed. Of the nine million people put to work in new jobs since I've been in office, 1.3 million of those has been among black Americans, and another million among those who speak Spanish.

We now are planning to continue the revitalization program with increased commitments of rapid transit, mass transit. Under the windfall profits tax, we expect to spend about $43 billion in the next ten years to rebuild the transportation systems of our country. We also are pursuing housing programs. We've had a 73 percent increase in the allotment of federal funds for improved education. These are the kinds of efforts worked on a joint basis with community leaders, particularly in the minority areas of the central cities that have been deteriorating so rapidly in the past.

It's very important to us that this be done with the full involvement of minority citizens. I have brought into the top level, top levels of government, into the White House, into administrative offices of the Executive branch, into the judicial system, highly qualified black and Spanish citizens and women who in the past had been excluded.

I noticed that Governor Reagan said that when he was a young man that there was no knowledge of a racial problem in this country. Those who suffered from discrimination because of race or sex certainly knew we had a racial problem. We have gone a long way toward correcting these problems, but we still have a long way to go.

MR. SMITH: Follow-up question?

MR. HILLIARD: Yes. President Carter, I would like to repeat the same follow-up to you. Blacks and other non-whites are increasing in numbers in our cities. Many of them feel that they are facing a hostility from whites that prevents them from joining the economic mainstream of our society. There is racial confrontation in the schools, on jobs, and in housing, as non-whites seek to reap the benefits of a free society. What is your assessment of the nation's future as a multi-racial society?

PRESIDENT CARTER: Ours is a nation of refugees, a nation of immigrants. Almost all of our citizens came here from other lands and now have hopes, which are being realized, for a better life, preserving their ethnic commitments, their family structures, their religious beliefs, preserving their relationships with their relatives in foreign countries, but still holding themselves together in a very coherent society, which gives our nation its strength.

In the past, those minority groups have often been excluded from participation in the affairs of government. Since I've been president, I've appointed, for instance, more than twice as many black federal judges as all previous presidents in the history of this country. I've done the same thing in the appointment of women, and also Spanish-speaking Americans. To involve them in the administration of government and the feeling that they belong to the societal structure that makes decisions in the judiciary and in the executive branch is a very important commitment which I am trying to realize and will continue to do so in the future.

MR. SMITH: Governor Reagan, you have a minute for rebuttal.

GOVERNOR REAGAN. Yes. The President talks of government programs, and they have their place. But as governor, when I was at that end of the line and receiving some of these grants for government programs, I saw that so many of them were dead-end. They were public employment for these people who really want to get out into the private job market where there are jobs with a future.

Now, the President spoke a moment ago about . . . that I was against the minimum wage. I wish he could have been with me when I sat with a group of teenagers who were black, and who were telling me about their unemployment problems, and that it was the minimum wage that had done away with the jobs that they once could get. And indeed, every time it has increased you will find there is an increase in minority unemployment among young people. And therefore, I have been in favor of a separate minimum for them.

With regard to the great progress that has been made with this government spending, the rate of black unemployment in Detroit, Michigan, is 56 percent.

MR. SMITH: President Carter, you have the last word on this question.

PRESIDENT CARTER: It's obvious that we still have a long way to go in fully incorporating the minority groups into the mainstream of American life. We have made good progress, and there is no doubt in my mind that the commitment to unemployment compensation, the minimum wage, welfare, national health insurance, those kinds of commitments that have typified the Democratic party since ancient history in this country's political life are a very important element of the future. In all those elements, Governor Reagan has repeatedly spoken out against them, which, to me, shows a very great insensitivity to giving deprived families a better chance in life. This, to me, is a very important difference between him and me in this election, and I believe the American people will judge accordingly.

There is no doubt in my mind that in the downtown central cities, with the, with the new commitment on an energy policy, with a chance to revitalize homes and to make them more fuel efficient, with a chance for our synthetic fuels program, solar power, this will give us an additional opportunity for jobs which will pay rich dividends.

MR. SMITH: Now, a question from Barbara Walters.

MS. WALTERS: Mr. President, the eyes of the country tonight are on the hostages in Iran. I realize this is a sensitive area, but the question of how we respond to acts of terrorism goes beyond this current crisis. Other countries have policies that determine how they will respond. Israel, for example, considers hostages like soldiers and will not negotiate with terrorists. For the future, Mr. President, the country has a right to know, do you have a policy for dealing with terrorism wherever it might happen, and, what have we learned from this experience in Iran that might cause us to do things differently if this, or something similar, happens again?

PRESIDENT CARTER: Barbara, one of the blights on this world is the threat and the activities of terrorists. At one of the recent economic summit conferences between myself and the other leaders of the Western world, we committed ourselves to take strong action against terrorism. Airplane hijacking was one of the elements of that commitment. There is no doubt that we have seen in recent years—in recent months—additional acts of violence against Jews in France and, of course, against those who live in Israel, by the PLO and other terrorist organizations.

Ultimately, the most serious terrorist threat is if one of those radical nations, who believe in terrorism as a policy, should have atomic weapons. Both I and all my predecessors have had a deep commitment to controlling the proliferation of nuclear weapons. In countries like Libya, or Iraq, we have even alienated some of our closest trade partners because we have insisted upon the control of the spread of nuclear weapons to those potentially terrorist countries.

When Governor Reagan has been asked about that, he makes the very disturbing comment that non-proliferation, or the control of the spread of nuclear weapons, is none of our business. And recently when he was asked specifically about Iraq, he said there is nothing we can do about it.

This ultimate terrorist threat is the most fearsome of all, and it's part of a pattern where our country must stand firm to control terrorism of all kinds.

MR. SMITH: Ms. Walters, a follow up?

MS. WALTERS: While we are discussing policy, had Iran not taken American hostages, I assume that, in order to preserve our neutrality, we would have stopped the flow of spare parts and vital war materials once war broke out between Iraq and Iran. Now we're offering to lift the ban on such goods if they let our people come home. Doesn't this reward terrorism, compromise our neutrality, and possibly antagonize nations now friendly to us in the Middle East?

PRESIDENT CARTER: We will maintain our position of neutrality in the Iran and Iraq war. We have no plans to sell additional materiel or goods to Iran, that might be of a warlike nature. When I made my decision to stop all trade with Iran as a result of the taking of our hostages, I announced then, and have consistently maintained since then, that if the hostages are released safely, we would make delivery on those items which Iran owns—which they have bought and paid for—also, that the frozen Iranian assets would be released. That's been a consistent policy, one I intend to carry out.

MR. SMITH: Would you repeat the question now for Governor Reagan, please, Ms. Walters?

MS. WALTERS: Yes. Governor, the eyes of the country tonight remain on the hostages in Iran, but the question of how we respond to acts of terrorism goes beyond this current crisis.

There are other countries that have policies that determine how they will respond. Israel, for example, considers hostages like soldiers and will not negotiate with terrorists.

For the future, the country has the right to know, do you have a policy for dealing with terrorism wherever it might happen, and what have we learned from this experience in Iran that might cause us to do things differently if this, or something similar, should happen again?

GOVERNOR REAGAN: Barbara, you've asked that question twice. I think you ought to have at least one answer to it. I have been accused lately of having a secret plan with regard to the hostages. Now, this comes from an answer that I've made at least 50 times during this campaign to the press, when I am asked have you any ideas of what you would do if you were there? And I said, well, yes. And I think that anyone that's seeking this position, as well as other people, probably, have thought to themselves, what about this, what about that? These are just ideas of what I would think of if I were in that position and had access to the information, and which I would know all the options that were open to me.

I have never answered the question, however, second; the one that says, well, tell me, what are some of those ideas? First of all, I would be fearful that I might say something that was presently under way or in negotiations, and thus expose it and endanger the hostages, and sometimes, I think some of my ideas might require quiet diplomacy where you don't say in advance, or say to anyone, what it is you're thinking of doing.

Your question is difficult to answer, because, in the situation right now, no one wants to say anything that would inadvertently delay, in any way, the return of those hostages if there . . . if there is a chance that they're coming home soon, or that (it) might cause them harm. What I do think should be done, once they are safely here with their families, and that tragedy is over—we've endured this humiliation for just lacking one week of a year now—then, I think, it is time for us to have a complete investigation as to the diplomatic efforts that were made in the beginning, why they have been there so long, and when they come home, what did we have to do in order to bring that about—what arrangements were made? And I would suggest that Congress should hold such an investigation. In the meantime, I'm going to continue praying that they'll come home.

MR. SMITH: Follow-up question.

MS. WALTERS. I would like to say that neither candidate answered specifically the question of a specific policy for dealing with terrorism, but I will ask Governor Reagan a different follow-up question. You have suggested that there would be no Iranian crisis had you been president, because we would have given firmer support to the Shah. But Iran is a country of 37 million people who were resisting a government that they regarded as dictatorial.

My question is not whether the Shah's regime was preferable to the Ayatollah's, but whether the United States has the power or the right to try to determine what form of government any country will have, and do we back unpopular regimes whose major merit is that they are friendly to the United States?

GOVERNOR REAGAN: The degree of unpopularity of a regime when the choice is total authoritarianism . . . totalitarianism, I should say, in the alternative government . . . makes one wonder whether you are being helpful to the people. And we've been guilty of that. Because someone didn't meet exactly our standards of human rights, even though they were an ally of ours, instead of trying patiently to persuade them to change their ways, we have, in a number of instances, aided a revolutionary overthrow which results in complete totalitarianism, instead, for those people. I think that this is a kind of a hypocritical policy when, at the same time, we're maintaining a detente with the one nation in the world where there are no human rights at all—the Soviet Union.

Now, there was a second phase in the Iranian affair in which we had something to do with that. And that was, we had adequate warning that there was a threat to our embassy, and we could have done what other embassies did—either strengthen our security there, or remove our personnel before the kidnap and the takeover took place.

MR. SMITH: Governor, I'm sorry, I must interrupt. President Carter, you have a minute for rebuttal.

PRESIDENT CARTER: I didn't hear any comment from Governor Reagan about what he would do to stop or reduce terrorism in the future. What the Western allies did decide to do is to stop all air flights—commercial air flights—to any nation involved in terrorism or the hijacking of airplanes, or the harboring of hijackers. Secondly, we all committed ourselves, as have all my predecessors in the Oval Office, not to permit the spread of nuclear weapons to a terrorist nation, or to any other nation that does not presently have those weapons or capabilities for explosives. Third, not to make any sales of materiel or weapons to a nation which is involved in terrorist activities. And, lastly, not to deal with the PLO until and unless the PLO recognizes Israel's right to exist and recognizes U.N. Resolution 242 as a basis for Middle East peace.

These are a few of the things to which our nation is committed, and we will continue with these commitments.

MR. SMITH: Governor Reagan, you have the last word on that question.

GOVERNOR REAGAN: Yes. I have no quarrel whatsoever with the things that have been done, because I believe it is high time that the civilized countries of the world made it plain that there is no room worldwide for terrorism; there will be no negotiation with terrorists of any kind. And while I have a last word here, I would like to correct a misstatement of fact by the President. I have never made the statement that he suggested about nuclear proliferation and nuclear proliferation, or the trying to halt it, would be a major part of a foreign policy of mine.

MR. SMITH: Thank you, gentlemen. That is the first half of the debate. Now, the rules for the second half are quite simple. They're only complicated when I explain them. In the second half, the panelists with me will have no follow-up questions. Instead, after the panelists have asked a question, and the candidates have answered, each of the candidates will have two opportunities to follow up, to question, to rebut, or just to comment on his opponent's statement.

Governor Reagan will respond, in this section, to the first question from Marvin Stone.

MR. STONE: Governor Reagan—arms control: The President said it was the single most important issue. Both of you have expressed the desire to end the nuclear arms race with Russia, but by methods that are vastly different. You suggest that we scrap the Salt II treaty already negotiated, and intensify the build-up of American power to induce the Soviets to sign a new treaty—one more favorable to us. President Carter, on the other hand, says he will again try to convince a reluctant Congress to ratify the present treaty on the grounds it's the best we can hope to get.

Now, both of you cannot be right. Will you tell us why you think you are?

GOVERNOR REAGAN: Yes. I think I'm right because I believe that we must have a consistent foreign policy, a strong America, and a strong economy. And then, as we build up our national security, to restore our margin of safety, we at the same time try to restrain the Soviet build-up, which has been going forward at a rapid pace, and for quite some time.

The Salt II treaty was the result of negotiations that Mr. Carter's team entered into after he had asked the Soviet Union for a discussion of actual reduction of nuclear strategic weapons. And his emissary, I think, came home in 12 hours having heard a very definite nyet. But taking that one no from the Soviet Union, we then went back into negotiations on their terms, because Mr. Carter had cancelled the B-1 bomber, delayed the MX, delayed the Trident submarine, delayed the Cruise missile, shut down the Missile Man—the three—the Minute Man missile production line, and whatever other things that might have been done. The Soviet Union sat at the table knowing that we had gone forward with unilateral concessions without any reciprocation from them whatsoever.

Now, I have not blocked the Salt II treaty, as Mr. Carter and Mr. Mondale suggest that I have. It has been blocked by a Senate in which there is a Democratic majority. Indeed, the Senate Armed Services Committee voted 10 to 0, with seven abstentions, against the Salt II treaty, and declared that it was not in the national security interests of the United States. Besides which, it is illegal, because the law of the land, passed by Congress, says that we cannot accept a treaty in which we are not equal. And we are not equal in this treaty for one reason alone—our B-52 bombers are considered to be strategic weapons; their Backfire bombers are not.

MR. SMITH: Governor, I have to interrupt you at that point. The time is up for that. But the same question now to President Carter.

MR. STONE: Yes. President Carter, both of you have expressed the desire to end the nuclear arms race with Russia, but through vastly different methods. The Governor suggests we scrap the Salt II treaty which you negotiated in Vienna . . . or signed in Vienna, intensify the build-up of American power to induce the Soviets to sign a new treaty, one more favorable to us. You, on the other hand, say you will again try to convince a reluctant Congress to ratify the present treaty on the grounds it is the best we can hope to get from the Russians.

You cannot both be right. Will you tell us why you think you are?

PRESIDENT CARTER: Yes, I'd be glad to. Inflation, unemployment, the cities are all very important issues, but they pale into insignificance in the life and duties of a president when compared with the control of nuclear weapons. Every president who has served in the Oval Office since Harry Truman has been dedicated to the proposition of controlling nuclear weapons.

To negotiate with the Soviet Union a balanced, controlled, observable, and then reducing levels of atomic weaponry, there is a disturbing pattern in the attitude of Governor Reagan. He has never supported any of those arms control agreements—the limited test ban, Salt I, nor the Antiballistic Missile Treaty, nor the Vladivostok Treaty negotiated with the Soviet Union by President Ford—and now he wants to throw into the wastebasket a treaty to control nuclear weapons on a balanced and equal basis between ourselves and the Soviet Union, negotiated over a seven-year period, by myself and my two Republican predecessors.

The Senate has not voted yet on the Strategic Arms Limitation Treaty. There have been preliminary skirmishings in the committees of the Senate, but the Treaty has never come to the floor of the Senate for either a debate or a vote. It's understandable that a senator in the preliminary debates can make an irresponsible statement, or, maybe, an ill-advised statement. You've got 99 other senators to correct that mistake, if it is a mistake. But when a man who hopes to be president says, take this treaty, discard it, do not vote, do not debate, do not explore the issues, do not finally capitalize on this long negotiation—that is a very dangerous and disturbing thing.

MR. SMITH: Governor Reagan, you have an opportunity to rebut that.

GOVERNOR REAGAN: Yes, I'd like to respond very much. First of all, the Soviet Union . . . if I have been critical of some of the previous agreements, it's because we've been out-negotiated for quite a long time. And they have managed, in spite of all of our attempts at arms limitation, to go forward with the biggest military build-up in the history of man.

Now, to suggest that because two Republican presidents tried to pass the Salt treaty—that puts them on its side—I would like to say that President Ford, who was within 90 percent of a treaty that we could be in agreement with when he left office, is emphatically against this Salt treaty. I would like to point out also that senators like Henry Jackson and Hollings of South Carolina—they are taking the lead in the fight against this particular treaty.

I am not talking of scrapping. I am talking of taking the treaty back, and going back into negotiations. And I would say to the Soviet Union, we will sit and negotiate with you as long as it takes, to have not only legitimate arms limitation, but to have a reduction of these nuclear weapons to the point that neither one of us represents a threat to the other. That is hardly throwing away a treaty and being opposed to arms limitation.

MR. SMITH: President Carter?

PRESIDENT CARTER: Yes. Governor Reagan is making some very misleading and disturbing statements. He not only advocates the scrapping of this treaty—and I don't know that these men that he quotes are against the treaty in its final form—but he also advocates the possibility, he said it's been a missing element, of playing a trump card against the Soviet

Union of a nuclear arms race, and is insisting upon nuclear superiority by our own nation, as a predication for negotiation in the future with the Soviet Union.

If President Brezhnev said, we will scrap this treaty, negotiated under three American presidents over a seven-year period of time, we insist upon nuclear superiority as a basis for future negotiations, and we believe that the launching of a nuclear arms race is a good basis for future negotiations, it's obvious that I, as president, and all Americans, would reject such a proposition. This would mean the resumption of a very dangerous nuclear arms race. It would be very disturbing to American people. It would change the basic tone and commitment that our nation has experienced ever since the Second World War, with all presidents, Democratic and Republican. And it would also be very disturbing to our allies, all of whom support this nuclear arms treaty. In addition to that, the adversarial relationship between ourselves and the Soviet Union would undoubtedly deteriorate very rapidly.

This attitude is extremely dangerous and belligerent in its tone, although it's said with a quiet voice.

MR. SMITH: Governor Reagan?

GOVERNOR REAGAN: I know the President's supposed to be replying to me, but sometimes, I have a hard time in connecting what he's saying with what I have said or what my positions are. I sometimes think he's like the witch doctor that gets mad when a good doctor comes along with a cure that'll work.

My point I have made already, Mr. President, with regard to negotiating: it does not call for nuclear superiority on the part of the United States. It calls for a mutual reduction of these weapons, as I say, that neither of us can represent a threat to the other. And to suggest that the Salt II treaty that your negotiators negotiated was just a continuation, and based on all of the preceding efforts by two previous presidents, is just not true. It was a new negotiation because, as I say, President Ford was within about 10 percent of having a solution that could be acceptable. And I think our allies would be very happy to go along with a fair and verifiable Salt agreement.

MR. SMITH: President Carter, you have the last word on this question.

PRESIDENT CARTER: I think, to close out this discussion, it would be better to put into perspective what we're talking about. I had a discussion with my daughter, Amy, the other day, before I came here, to ask her what the most important issue was. She said she thought nuclear weaponry—and the control of nuclear arms.

This is a formidable force. Some of these weapons have ten megatons of explosion. If you put 50 tons of TNT in each one of railroad cars, you would have a carload of TNT—a trainload of TNT stretching across this nation. That's one major war explosion in a warhead. We have thousands, equivalent of megaton, or million tons, of TNT warheads. The control of these weapons is the single major responsibility of a president, and to cast out this commitment of all presidents, because of some slight technicalities that can be corrected, is a very dangerous approach.

MR. SMITH: We have to go to another question now, from Harry Ellis to President Carter.

MR. ELLIS: Mr. President, as you have said, Americans, through conservation, are importing much less oil today than we were even a year ago. Yet U.S. dependence on Arab oil as a percentage of total imports is today much higher than it was at the time of the 1973 Arab oil embargo, and for some time to come, the loss of substantial amounts of Arab oil could plunge the U.S. into depression.

This means that a bridge must be built out of this dependence. Can the United States develop synthetic fuels and other alternative energy sources without damage to the environment, and will this process mean steadily higher fuel bills for American families?

PRESIDENT CARTER: I don't think there's any doubt that, in the future, the cost of oil is going to go up. What I've had as a basic commitment since I've been president is to reduce our dependence on foreign oil. It can only be done in two ways: one, to conserve energy—to stop the waste of energy—

and, secondly, to produce more American energy. We've been very successful in both cases. We've now reduced the importing of foreign oil in the last year alone by one third. We imported today two million barrels of oil less than we did the same date just a year ago.

This commitment has been opening up a very bright vista for our nation in the future, because with the windfall profits tax as a base, we now have an opportunity to use American technology and American ability and American natural resources to expand rapidly the production of synthetic fuels, yes; to expand rapidly the production of solar energy, yes; and also to produce the traditional kinds of American energy. We will drill more oil and gas wells this year than any year in history. We'll produce more coal this year than any year in history. We are exporting more coal this year than any year in history.

And we have an opportunity now, with improved transportation systems and improved loading facilities in our ports, to see a very good opportunity on a world international market, to replace OPEC oil with American coal as a basic energy source. This exciting future will not only give us more energy security, but will also open up vast opportunities for Americans to live a better life and to have millions of new jobs associated with this new and very dynamic industry now in prospect because of the new energy policy that we've put into effect.

MR. SMITH: Would you repeat the question now for Governor Reagan?

MR. ELLIS: Governor Reagan, Americans, through conservation, are importing much less oil today than we were even a year ago. And yet, U.S. reliance on Arab oil as a percentage of total imports is much higher today than it was during the 1973 Arab oil embargo. And the substantial loss of Arab oil could plunge the United States into depression.

The question is whether the development of alternative energy sources, in order to reduce this dependence, can be done without damaging the environment, and will it mean for American families steadily higher fuel bills?

GOVERNOR REAGAN: I'm not so sure that it means steadily higher fuel costs, but I do believe that this nation has been portrayed for too long a time to the people as being energy-poor when it is energy-rich. The coal that the President mentioned—yes, we have it—and yet one eighth of our total coal resources is not being utilized at all right now. The mines are closed down; there are 22,000 miners out of work. Most of this is due to regulations which either interfere with the mining of it or prevent the burning of it. With our modern technology, yes, we can burn our coal within the limits of the Clean Air Act. I think, as technology improves, we'll be able to do even better with that.

The other thing is that we have only leased out—begun to explore—2 percent of our outer continental shelf for oil, where it is believed, by everyone familiar with that fuel and that source of energy, that there are vast supplies yet to be found. Our government has, in the last year or so, taken out of multiple use millions of acres of public lands that once were—well, they were public lands subject to multiple use—exploration for minerals and so forth. It is believed that probably 70 percent of the potential oil in the United States is probably hidden in those lands, and no one is allowed to even go and explore to find out if it is there. This is particularly true of the recent efforts to shut down part of Alaska.

Nuclear power: There were 36 power plants planned in this country. And let me add the word safety; it must be done with the utmost of safety. But 32 of those have given up and cancelled their plans to build, and again, because government regulations and permits, and so forth, take—make it take—more than twice as long to build a nuclear plant in the United States as it does to build one in Japan or in Western Europe.

We have the sources here. We are energy rich, and coal is one of the great potentials we have.

MR. SMITH: President Carter, your comment?

PRESIDENT CARTER: To repeat myself, we have this year the opportunity, which we'll realize, to produce 800 million tons of coal—an unequalled record in the history of our country. Governor Reagan says that this is not a good achievement, and he blames restraints on coal production on regulations—regulations that affect the life and the health and safety of miners, and also regulations that protect the purity of our air and the quality of our water and our land. We cannot cast aside those regulations. We have a chance in the next 15 years, insisting upon the health and safety of workers in the mines, and also preserving the same high air and water pollution standards, to triple the amount of coal we produce.

Governor Reagan's approach to our energy policy, which has already proven its effectiveness, is to repeal, or to change substantially, the windfall profits tax—to return a major portion of $227 billion back to the oil companies; to do away with the Department of Energy; to short-circuit our synthetic fuels program; to put a minimal emphasis on solar power; to emphasize strongly nuclear power plants as a major source of energy in the future. He wants to put all our eggs in one basket and give that basket to the major oil companies.

MR. SMITH: Governor Reagan.

GOVERNOR REAGAN: That is a misstatement, of course, of my position. I just happen to believe that free enterprise can do a better job of producing the things that people need than government can. The Department of Energy has a multi-billion-dollar budget in excess of $10 billion. It hasn't produced a quart of oil or a lump of coal, or anything else in the line of energy. And for Mr. Carter to suggest that I want to do away with the safety laws and with the laws that pertain to clean water and clean air, and so forth: as Governor of California, I took charge of passing the strictest air pollution laws in the United States—the strictest air quality law that has ever been adopted in the United States. And we created an OSHA—an Occupational Safety and Health Agency—for the protection of employees before the federal government had one in place. And to this day, not one of its decisions or rulings has ever been challenged.

So, I think some of those charges are missing the point. I am suggesting that there are literally thousands of unnecessary regulations that invade every facet of business, and indeed, very much of our personal lives, that are unnecessary; that government can do without; that have added $130 billion to the cost of production in this country; and that are contributing their part to inflation. And I would like to see us a little more free, as we once were.

MR. SMITH: President Carter, another crack at that?

PRESIDENT CARTER: Sure. As a matter of fact, the air pollution standard laws that were passed in California were passed over the objections of Governor Reagan, and this is a very well-known fact. Also, recently, when someone suggested that the Occupational Safety and Health Act should be abolished, Governor Reagan responded, amen.

The offshore drilling rights is a question that Governor Reagan raises often. As a matter of fact, in the proposal for the Alaska lands legislation, 100 percent of all the offshore lands would be open for exploration, and 95 percent of all the Alaska lands, where it is suspected or believed that minerals might exist. We have, with our five-year plan for the leasing of offshore lands, proposed more land to be drilled than has been opened up for drilling since this program first started in 1954. So we're not putting restraints on American exploration, we're encouraging it in every way we can.

MR. SMITH: Governor Reagan, you have the last word on this question.

GOVERNOR REAGAN: Yes. If it is a well-known fact that I opposed air pollution laws in California, the only thing I can possibly think of is that the President must be suggesting the law that the federal government tried to impose on the State of California—not a law, but regulations—that would have made it impossible to drive an automobile within the city limits of any California city, or to have a place to put it if you did drive it against their regulations. It would have destroyed the economy of California, and, I must say, we had the support of Congress when we pointed out how ridiculous this attempt was by the Environmental Protection Agency. We still have the strictest air control, or air pollution laws in the country.

As for offshore oiling, only 2 percent now is so leased and is producing oil. The rest, as to whether the lands are going to be opened in the next five years or so—we're already five years behind in what we should be doing. There is more oil now, in the wells that have been drilled, than has been taken out in 121 years that they've been drilled.

MR. SMITH: Thank you, Governor. Thank you, Mr. President. The next question goes to Governor Reagan from William Hilliard.

MR. HILLIARD: Governor Reagan, wage earners in this country—especially the young—are supporting a Social Security system that continues to affect their income drastically. The system is fostering a struggle between the young and the old, and is drifting the country toward a polarization of these two groups. How much longer can the young wage earner expect to bear the ever-increasing burden of the Social Security system?

GOVERNOR REAGAN: The Social Security system was based on a false premise, with regard to how fast the number of workers would increase and how fast the number of retirees would increase. It is actuarially out of balance, and this first became evident about 16 years ago, and some of us were voicing warnings then. Now, it is trillions of dollars out of balance, and the only answer that has come so far is the biggest single tax increase in our nation's history—the payroll tax increase for Social Security—which will only put a bandaid on this and postpone the day of reckoning by a few years at most.

What is needed is a study that I have proposed by a task force of experts to look into this entire problem as to how it can be reformed and made actuarially sound, but with the premise that no one presently dependent on Social Security is going to have the rug pulled out from under them and not get their check. We cannot frighten, as we have with the threats and the campaign rhetoric that has gone on in this campaign, our senior citizens—leave them thinking that in some way they're endangered and they would have no place to turn. They must continue to get those checks, and I believe that the system can be put on a sound actuarial basis. But it's going to take some study and some work, and not just passing a tax increase to let the load—or the roof—fall in on the next administration.

MR. SMITH: Would you repeat that question for President Carter?

MR. HILLIARD: Yes. President Carter, Wage earners in this country, especially the young, are supporting a Social Security system that continues to affect their income drastically. The system is fostering a struggle between young and old and is drifting the country toward a polarization of these two groups.

How much longer can the young wage earner expect to bear the ever-increasing burden of the Social Security System?

PRESIDENT CARTER: As long as there is a Democratic president in the White House, we will have a strong and viable Social Security system, free of the threat of bankruptcy. Although Governor Reagan has changed his position lately, on four different occasions, he has advocated making Social Security a voluntary system, which would, in effect, very quickly bankrupt it. I noticed also in the *Wall Street Journal* early this week that a preliminary report of his task force advocates making Social Security more sound by reducing the adjustments in Social Security for the retired people to compensate for the impact of inflation.

These kinds of approaches are very dangerous to the security, the well-being and the peace of mind of the retired people of this country and those approaching retirement age. But no matter what it takes in the future to keep Social Security sound, it must be kept that way. And although there was a serious threat to the Social Security system and its integrity during the 1976 Campaign and when I became president, the action of the Democratic Congress working with me has been to put Social Security back on a sound financial basis. That is the way it will stay.

MR. SMITH: Governor Reagan?

GOVERNOR REAGAN: Well, that just isn't true. It has, as I said, delayed the actuarial imbalance falling on us for just a few years with that increase in taxes, and I don't believe we can go on increasing the tax, because the problem for the young people today is that they are paying in far more than they can ever expect to get out. Now, again this statement that somehow I wanted to destroy it and I just changed my tune, that I am for voluntary Social Security, which would mean the ruin of it.

Mr. President, the voluntary thing that I suggested many years ago was that with a young man orphaned and raised by an aunt who died, his aunt was ineligible for Social Security insurance because she was not his mother. And I suggested that if this is an insurance program, certainly the person who is paying in should be able to name his own beneficiary. That is the closest I have ever come to anything voluntary with Social Security. I, too, am pledged to a Social Security program that will reassure these senior citizens of ours that they are going to continue to get their money.

There are some changes that I would like to make. I would like to make a change in the regulation that discriminates against a wife who works and finds that she then is faced with a choice between her father's or her husband's benefits, if he dies first, or what she has paid in, but it does not recognize that she has also been paying in herself, and she is entitled to more than she presently can get. I'd like to change that.

MR. SMITH: President Carter's rebuttal now.

PRESIDENT CARTER: These constant suggestions that the basic Social Security system should be changed does call for concern and consternation among the aged of our country. It is obvious that we should have a commitment to them, that Social Security benefits should not be taxed and that there would be no peremptory change in the standards by which Social Security payments are made to retired people. We also need to continue to index Social Security payments, so that if inflation rises, the Social Security payments would rise a commensurate degree to let the buying power of a Social Security check continue intact.

In the past, the relationship between Social Security and Medicare has been very important to providing some modicum of aid for senior citizens in the retention of health benefits. Governor Reagan, as a matter of fact, began his political career campaigning around this nation against Medicare. Now, we have an opportunity to move toward national health insurance, with an emphasis on the prevention of disease; an emphasis on out-patient care, not in-patient care; an emphasis on hospital cost containment to hold down the cost of hospital care for those who are ill; an emphasis on catastrophic health insurance, so that if a family is threatened with being wiped out economically because of a very high medical bill, then the insurance would help pay for it. These are the kinds of elements of a national health insurance, important to the American people. Governor Reagan, again, typically is against such a proposal.

MR. SMITH: Governor?

GOVERNOR REAGAN: When I opposed Medicare, there was another piece of legislation meeting the same problem before the Congress. I happened to favor the other piece of legislation and thought that it would be better for the senior citizens and provide better care than the one that was finally passed. I was not opposing the principle of providing care for them. I was opposing one piece of legislation versus another.

There is something else about Social Security. Of course, it doesn't come out of the payroll tax. It comes out of a general fund, but something should be done about it. I think it is disgraceful that the Disability Insurance Fund in Social Security finds checks going every month to tens of thousands of people who are locked up in our institutions for crime or for mental illness, and they are receiving disability checks from Social Security every month while a state institution provides for all of their needs and their care.

MR. SMITH: President Carter, you have the last word on this question.

PRESIDENT CARTER: I think this debate on Social Security, Medicare, national health insurance typifies, as vividly any other subject tonight, the basic historical differences between the Democratic party and Republican party. The allusions to basic changes in the minimum wage is another, and the deleterious comments that Governor Reagan has made about unemployment compensation. These commitments that the Democratic party has historically made to the working families of this nation have been extremely important to the growth in their stature and in a better quality of life for them.

I noticed recently that Governor Reagan frequently quotes Democratic presidents in his acceptance address. I have never heard a candidate for president, who is a Republican, quote a Republican president, but when they get in office, they try to govern like Republicans. So, it is good for the American people to remember that there is a sharp basic historical difference between Governor Reagan and me on these crucial issues—also, between the two parties that we represent.

MR. SMITH: Thank you, Mr. President, Governor Reagan. We now go to another question—a question to President Carter by Barbara Walters.

MS. WALTERS: Thank you. You have addressed some of the major issues tonight, but the biggest issue in the minds of American voters is yourselves—your ability to lead this country. When many voters go into that booth just a week from today, they will be voting their gut instinct about you men. You have already given us your reasons why people should vote for you, now would you please tell us for this, your final question, why they should not vote for your opponent, why his presidency could be harmful to the nation and, having examined both your opponents record and the man himself, tell us his greatest weakness.

PRESIDENT CARTER: Barbara, reluctant as I am to say anything critical about Governor Reagan, I will try to answer your question. First of all, there is the historical perspective that I just described. This is a contest between a Democrat in the mainstream of my party, as exemplified by the actions that I have taken in the Oval Office the last four years, as contrasted with Governor Reagan, who in most cases does typify his party, but in some cases, there is a radical departure by him from the heritage of Eisenhower and others. The most important crucial difference in this election campaign, in my judgment, is the approach to the control of nuclear weaponry and the inclination to control or not to control the spread of atomic weapons to other nations who don't presently have it, particularly terrorist nations.

The inclination that Governor Reagan has exemplified in many troubled times since he has been running for president— I think since 1968—to inject American military forces in places like North Korea, to put a blockade around Cuba this year, or in some instances, to project American forces into a fishing dispute against the small nation of Ecuador on the west coast of South America. This is typical of his long-standing inclination, on the use of American power, not to resolve disputes diplomatically and peacefully, but to show that the exercise of military power is best proven by the actual use of it.

Obviously, no president wants war, and I certainly do not

believe that Governor Reagan, if he were president, would want war, but a president in the Oval Office has to make a judgment on almost a daily basis about how to exercise the enormous power of our country for peace, through diplomacy, or in a careless way in a belligerent attitude which has exemplified his attitudes in the past.

MR. SMITH: Barbara, would you repeat the question for Governor Reagan?

MS. WALTERS: Yes, thank you. Realizing that you may be equally reluctant to speak ill of your opponent, may I ask why people should not vote for your opponent, why his presidency could be harmful to the nation, and having examined both your opponent's record and the man himself, could you tell us his greatest weakness?

GOVERNOR REAGAN: Well, Barbara, I believe that there is a fundamental difference—and I think it has been evident in most of the answers that Mr. Carter has given tonight—that he seeks the solution to anything as another opportunity for a federal government program. I happen to believe that the federal government has usurped powers of autonomy and authority that belong back at the state and local level. It has imposed on the individual freedoms of the people, and there are more of these things that could be solved by the people themselves, if they were given a chance, or by the levels of government that were closer to them.

Now, as to why I should be and he shouldn't be; when he was a candidate in 1976, President Carter invented a thing he called the misery index. He added the rate of unemployment and the rate of inflation, and it came, at that time, to 12.5 percent under President Ford. He said that no man with that size misery index had a right to seek reelection to the presidency. Today, by his own decision, the misery index is in excess of 20 percent, and I think this must suggest something.

But, when I had quoted a Democratic president, as the President says, I was a Democrat. I said many foolish things back in those days. But the president that I quoted had made a promise, a Democrat promise, and I quoted him because it was never kept. And today, you would find that that promise is at the very heart of what Republicanism represents in this country today. That's why I believe there are going to be millions of Democrats that are going to vote with us this time around, because they too want that promise kept. It was a promise for less government and less taxes and more freedom for the people.

MR. SMITH: President Carter?

PRESIDENT CARTER: I mentioned the radical departure of Governor Reagan from the principles or ideals of historical perspective of his own party. I don't think this can be better illustrated than in the case of guaranteeing women equal rights under the Constitution of our nation. For 40 years, the Republican party platforms called for guaranteeing women equal rights with a constitutional amendment. Six predecessors of mine who served in the Oval Office called for this guarantee of women's rights. Governor Reagan and his new Republican party have departed from this commitment—a very severe blow to the opportunity for women to finally correct discrimination under which they have suffered.

When a man and a woman do the same amount of work, a man gets paid $1.00, a woman only gets paid 59 cents. And the Equal Rights Amendment only says that equality of rights shall not be abridged for women by the federal government or by the state governments. That is all it says—a simple guarantee of equality of opportunity which typifies the Democratic party, and which is a very important commitment of mine, as contrasted with Governor Reagan's radical departure from the long-standing policy of his own party.

MR. SMITH: Governor Reagan?

GOVERNOR REAGAN: Yes. Mr. President, once again, I happen to be against the amendment, because I think the amendment will take this problem out of the hands of elected legislators and put it in the hands of unelected judges. I am for equal rights, and while you have been in office for four years and not one single state—and most of them have a majority of Democratic legislators—has added to the ratification or voted to ratify the Equal Rights Amendment. While I was governor, more than eight years ago, I found 14 separate instances where women were discriminated against in the body of California law, and I had passed and signed into law 14 statutes that eliminated those discriminations, including the economic ones that you have just mentioned—equal pay and so forth.

I believe that if in all these years that we have spent trying to get the amendment, that we had spent as much time correcting these laws, as we did in California—and we were the first to do it. If I were president, I would also now take a look at the hundreds of federal regulations which discriminate against women and which go right on while everyone is looking for an amendment. I would have someone ride herd on those regulations, and we would start eliminating those discriminations in the federal government against women.

MR. SMITH: President Carter?

PRESIDENT CARTER: Howard, I'm a Southerner, and I share the basic beliefs of my region about an excessive government intrusion into the private affairs of American citizens and also into the private affairs of the free enterprise system. One of the commitments that I made was to deregulate the major industries of this country. We've been remarkably successful, with the help of a Democratic Congress. We have deregulated the air industry, the rail industry, the trucking industry, financial institutions. We're now working on the communications industry.

In addition to that, I believe that this element of discrimination is something that the South has seen so vividly as a blight on our region of the country which has now been corrected—not only racial discrimination but discrimination against people that have to work for a living—because we have been trying to pick ourselves up by our bootstraps, since the long depression years, and lead a full and useful life in the affairs of this country. We have made remarkable success. It is part of my consciousness and of my commitment to continue this progress.

So, my heritage as a Southerner, my experience in the Oval Office, convinces me that what I have just described is a proper course for the future.

MR. SMITH: Governor Reagan, yours is the last word.

GOVERNOR REAGAN: Well, my last word is again to say this: we were talking about this very simple amendment and women's rights. And I make it plain again: I am for women's rights. But I would like to call the attention of the people to the fact that that so-called simple amendment could be used by mischievous men to destroy discriminations that properly belong, by law, to women respecting the physical differences between the two sexes, labor laws that protect them against things that would be physically harmful to them. Those would all, could all be challenged by men. And the same would be true with regard to combat service in the military and so forth.

I thought that was the subject we were supposed to be on. But, if we're talking about how much we think about the working people and so forth, I'm the only fellow who ever ran for this job who was six times president of his own union and still has a lifetime membership in that union.

MR. SMITH: Gentlemen, each of you now has three minutes for a closing statement. President Carter, you're first.

PRESIDENT CARTER: First of all, I'd like to thank the League of Women Voters for making this debate possible. I think it's been a very constructive debate and I hope it's helped to acquaint the American people with the sharp differences between myself and Governor Reagan. Also, I want to thank the people of Cleveland and Ohio for being such hospitable hosts during these last few hours in my life.

I've been president now for almost four years. I've had to make thousands of decisions, and each one of those decisions has been a learning process. I've seen the strength of my nation, and I've seen the crises it approached in a tentative way. And I've had to deal with those crises as best I could.

As I've studied the record between myself and Governor Reagan, I've been impressed with the stark differences that exist between us. I think the result of this debate indicates that that fact is true. I consider myself in the mainstream of my party. I consider myself in the mainstream even of the bipartisan list of presidents who served before me. The United States must be a nation strong. The United States must be a nation secure. We must have a society that's just and fair. And we must extend the benefits of our own commitment to peace, to create a peaceful world.

I believe that since I've been in office, there have been six or eight areas of combat evolved in other parts of the world. In each case, I alone have had to determine the interests of my country and the degree of involvement of my country. I've done that with moderation, with care, with thoughtfulness; sometimes consulting experts. But, I've learned in this last three and a half years that when an issue is extremely difficult, when the call is very close, the chances are the experts will be divided almost 50-50. And the final judgment about the future of the nation—war, peace, involvement, reticence, thoughtfulness, care, consideration, concern—has to be made by the man in the Oval Office. It's a lonely job, but with the involvement of the American people in the process, with an open Government, the job is a very gratifying one.

The American people now are facing, next Tuesday, a lonely decision. Those listening to my voice will have to make a judgment about the future of this country. And I think they ought to remember that one vote can make a lot of difference. If one vote per precinct had changed in 1960, John Kennedy would never have been president of this nation. And if a few more people had gone to the polls and voted in 1968, Hubert Humphrey would have been president, Richard Nixon would not.

There is a partnership involved in our nation. To stay strong, to stay at peace, to raise high the banner of human rights, to set an example for the rest of the world, to let our deep beliefs and commitments be felt by others in other nations, is my plan for the future. I ask the American people to join me in this partnership.

MR. SMITH: Governor Reagan?

GOVERNOR REAGAN: Yes, I would like to add my words of thanks, too, to the ladies of the League of Women Voters for making these debates possible. I'm sorry that we couldn't persuade the bringing in of the third candidate, so that he could have been seen also in these debates. But still, it's good that at least once, all three of us were heard by the people of this country.

Next Tuesday is Election Day. Next Tuesday all of you will

go to the polls, will stand there in the polling place and make a decision. I think when you make that decision, it might be well if you would ask yourself, are you better off than you were four years ago? Is it easier for you to go and buy things in the stores than it was four years ago? Is there more or less unemployment in the country than there was four years ago? Is America as respected throughout the world as it was? Do you feel that our security is as safe, that we're as strong as we were four years ago? And if you answer all of those questions "yes," why then, I think your choice is very obvious as to whom you will vote for. If you don't agree, if you don't think that this course that we've been on for the last four years is what you would like to see us follow for the next four, then I could suggest another choice that you have.

This country doesn't have to be in the shape that it is in. We do not have to go on sharing in scarcity with the country getting worse off, with unemployment growing. We talk about the unemployment lines. If all of the unemployed today were in a single line allowing two feet for each of them, that line would reach from New York City to Los Angeles, California. All of this can be cured and all of it can be solved.

I have not had the experience the President has had in holding that office, but I think in being Governor of California, the most populous state in the Union—if it were a nation, it would be the seventh-ranking economic power in the world— I, too, had some lonely moments and decisions to make. I know that the economic program that I have proposed for this nation in the next few years can resolve many of the problems that trouble us today. I know because we did it there. We cut the cost—the increased cost of government—in half over the eight years. We returned $5.7 billion in tax rebates, credits and cuts to our people. We, as I have said earlier, fell below the national average in inflation when we did that. And I know that we did give back authority and autonomy to the people.

I would like to have a crusade today, and I would like to lead that crusade with your help. And it would be one to take government off the backs of the great people of this country, and turn you loose again to do those things that I know you can do so well, because you did them and made this country great. Thank you.

MR. SMITH: Gentlemen, ladies and gentlemen, for 60 years the League of Women Voters has been committed to citizen education and effective participation of Americans in governmental and political affairs. The most critical element of all in that process is an informed citizen who goes to the polls and who votes. On behalf of the League of Women Voters, now, I would like to thank President Carter and Governor Reagan for being with us in Cleveland tonight. And, ladies and gentlemen, thank you and good night.

ACCEPTANCE SPEECH
BY
PRESIDENT JIMMY CARTER
DEMOCRATIC NATIONAL CONVENTION
NEW YORK, NEW YORK
AUGUST 14, 1980

FELLOW DEMOCRATS, fellow citizens:

I thank you for the nomination you've offered me. And I especially thank you for choosing as my running mate the best partner any president ever had—Fritz Mondale.

With gratitude and with determination, I accept your nomination.

And I am proud to run on a progressive and sound platform that you have hammered out at this convention.

Fritz and I will mount a campaign that defines the real issues—a campaign that responds to the intelligence of the American people—a campaign that talks sense—and we're going to beat, whip the Republicans in November.

We'll win because we are the party of a great president who knew how to get reelected—Franklin D. Roosevelt. And we're the party of a courageous fighter who knew how to "give 'em hell"—Harry Truman. And as Truman said, he just told the truth and they thought it was hell.

And we're the party of a gallant man of spirit—John Fitzgerald Kennedy. And we're the party of a great leader of compassion—Lyndon Baines Johnson.

And the party of a great man who should have been president and would have been one of the greatest presidents in history— Hubert Horatio Hornblower Humphrey. I have appreciated what this convention has said about Senator Humphrey, a great man who epitomized the spirit of the Democratic Party, and I would like to say that we're also the party of Governor Jerry Brown and Senator Edward M. Kennedy.

I'd like to say a personal word to Senator Kennedy. Ted, you're a tough competitor and a superb campaigner and I can attest to that. Your speech before this convention was a magnificent statement of what the Democratic Party is and what it means to the people of this country—and why a Democratic victory is so important this year. I reach out to you tonight and I reach out to all those who have supported you in your valiant and passionate campaign.

Ted, your party needs—and I need—you and your idealism and dedication working for us. There is no doubt that even greater service lies ahead of you—and we are grateful to you and to have your strong partnership now in the larger cause to which your own life has been dedicated.

I thank you for your support. We'll make great partners this fall in whipping the Republicans.

We're Democrats and we have had our differences, but we share a bright vision of America's future—a vision of good life for all our people—a vision of a secure nation, a just society, a peaceful world, a strong America—confident and proud and united.

And we have a memory of Franklin Roosevelt forty years ago when he said that there are times in our history when concerns over our personal lives are overshadowed by concern for "what will happen to the country we have known." This is such a time—and I can tell you that the choice to be made this year can transform our own personal lives and the life of our country as well.

During the last presidential campaign, I crisscrossed this country and I listened to thousands and thousands of people— housewives and farmers, teachers and small-business leaders, workers and students, the elderly and the poor—people of every race and every background and every walk of life. It was a powerful experience—a total immersion in the human reality of America.

And I have now had another kind of total immersion—being president of the United States of America. Let me talk for a moment about what that job is like—and what I have learned from it.

I've learned that only the most complex and difficult tasks come before me in the Oval Office. No easy answers are found there—because no easy questions come there.

I've learned that for a president, experience is the best guide to the right decisions. I'm wiser tonight than I was four years ago.

And I have learned that the presidency is a place of compassion. My own heart is burdened for the troubled Americans. The poor and the jobless and the afflicted—they've become part of me. My thoughts and my prayers for our hostages in Iran are as though they were my own sons and daughters.

The life of every human being on Earth can depend on the experience and judgment and vigilance of the person in the Oval Office. The president's power for building and his power for destruction are awesome. And the power is greatest exactly where the stakes are highest—in matters of war and peace.

And I have learned something else—something that I have come to see with extraordinary clarity. Above all, I must look ahead—because the president of the United States is the steward of the nation's destiny.

He must protect our children—and the children they will have—and the children of generations to follow. He must speak and act for them. That is his burden—and his glory.

And that is why a president cannot yield to the short-sighted demands, no matter how rich or powerful the special interests might be that make those demands. And that is why the president cannot bend to the passions of the moment, however popular they might be. And that is why the president must sometimes ask for sacrifice when his listeners would rather hear the promise of comfort.

The president is a servant of today. But his true constituency is the future. That is why the election of 1980 is so important.

Some have said it makes no difference who wins this election. They are wrong.

This election is a stark choice between two men, two parties, two sharply different pictures of what America is and what the world is. But it is more than that.

It is a choice between two futures. The year 2000 is just less than 20 years away—just four presidential elections after this one. Children born this year will come of age in the 21st century.

The time to shape the world of the year 2000 is now. The decisions of the next few years will set our course, perhaps an irreversible course—and the most important of all choices will be made by the American people at the polls less than three months from tonight.

The choice could not be more clear—nor the consequences more crucial.

In one of the futures we can choose—the future that you and I have been building together—I see security and justice and peace.

I see a future of economic security—security that will come from tapping our own great resources of oil and gas, coal and sunlight—and from building the tools, the technology and factories for a revitalized economy based on jobs and stable prices for everyone.

I see a future of justice—the justice of good jobs, decent health care, quality education, and the full opportunity for all people, regardless of color or language or religion: the simple human justice of equal rights for all men—and for all women, guaranteed equal rights at last—under the Constitution of the United States of America.

And I see a future of peace—a peace born of wisdom and based on the fairness toward all countries of the world—a peace guaranteed both by American military strength and by American moral strength as well.

That is the future I want for all people—a future of confidence and hope and a good life. It is the future America must choose—and with your help and with your commitment, it is the future America will choose.

But there is another possible future.

In that other future, I see despair—the despair of millions who would struggle for equal opportunity and a better life—and struggle alone.

And I see surrender—the surrender of our energy future to the merchants of oil, the surrender of our economic future to a bizarre program of massive tax cuts for the rich, service cuts for the poor and massive inflation for everyone.

And I see risk—the risk of international confrontation: the risk of an uncontrollable, unaffordable, and unwinnable nuclear arms race.

No one, Democrat or Republican leader, consciously seeks such a future. And I do not claim that my opponent does. But I do question the disturbing commitments and policies already made by him and by those with him who have now captured control of the Republican Party.

The consequences of those commitments and policies would drive us down the wrong road. It's up to all of us to make sure America rejects this alarming, and even perilous, destiny.

The only way to build a better future is to start with realities of the present. But while we Democrats grapple with the real challenges of a real world, others talk about a world of tinsel and make-believe.

Let's look for a moment at their make-believe world.

In their fantasy America, inner-city people and farm workers and laborers do not exist. Women, like children, are to be seen but not heard. The problems of working women are simply ignored. The elderly do not need Medicare. The young do not need more help in getting a better education. Workers do not require the guarantee of a healthy and a safe place to work.

In their fantasy world, all the complex global changes of the world since World War II have never happened. In their fantasy America, all problems have simple solutions. Simple—and wrong.

It is a make-believe world. A world of good guys and bad guys, where some politicians shoot first and ask questions later.

No hard choices. No sacrifice. No tough decisions. It sounds too good to be true—and it is.

The path of fantasy leads to irresponsibility. The path of reality leads to hope and peace. The two paths could not be more different. Nor could the futures to which they lead.

Let's take a hard look at the consequences of our choice.

You and I have been working toward a secure future by rebuilding our military strength—steadily, carefully and responsibly. The Republicans talk about military strength—but they were in office for eight out of the last 11 years—and in the face of a growing Soviet threat they steadily cut real defense spending by more than a third.

We've reversed the Republican decline in defense. Every year since I've been president, we've had real increases in our commitment to a stronger nation—increases which are prudent and rational. There is no doubt that the United States of America can meet any threat from the Soviet Union.

Our modernized strategic forces, a revitalized NATO, the Trident submarine, the cruise missile, Rapid Deployment Force—all these guarantee that we will never be second to any nation. Deeds, not words—fact, not fiction.

We must and we will continue to build our own defenses. We must and we will continue to seek balanced reductions in nuclear arms.

The new leaders of the Republican Party, in order to close the gap between their rhetoric and their record, have now promised to launch an all-out nuclear arms race. This would negate any further effort to negotiate a strategic arms limitation agreement.

There can be no winners in such an arms race—and all the people of the Earth can be the losers.

The Republican nominee advocates abandoning arms control policies which have been important and supported by every Democratic president since Harry Truman and also by every Republican president since Dwight D. Eisenhower. This radical and irresponsible course would threaten our security—and could put the whole world in peril.

You and I must never let this come to pass.

It's simple to call for a new arms race. But when armed aggression threatens world peace, tough-sounding talk like that is not enough. A president must act—responsibly. When Soviet troops invaded Afghanistan, we moved quickly to take action. I suspended some grain sales to the Soviet Union. I called for draft registration. We joined wholeheartedly with the Congress. And I joined wholeheartedly with the Congress and with the U.S. Olympics Committee and led more than 60 other nations in boycotting the big propaganda show in Russia—the Moscow Olympics.

The Republican leader opposed two of these forceful but peaceful actions and he waffled on the third. But when we asked him what he would do about aggression in Southwest Asia, he suggested blockading Cuba. Even his running mate wouldn't go along with that.

He doesn't seem to know what to do with the Russians. He's not sure if he wants to feed them or play with them or fight with them.

As I look back on my first term, I'm grateful that we've had a country with a full four years of peace. And that's what we're going to have for the next four years—peace.

It's only common sense that if America is to stay secure and at peace, we must encourage others to be peaceful as well.

As you know, we've helped in Zimbabwe-Rhodesia, where we stood firm for racial justice and democracy. And we have also helped in the Middle East. Some have criticized the Camp David accords and they've criticized some delays in the implementation of the Middle East peace treaty.

Well, before I became president there was no Camp David accord and there was no Middle East peace treaty. Before Camp David, Israel and Egypt were poised across barbed wire, confronting each other with guns and tanks and planes. But afterward, they talked face-to-face with each other across a peace table—and they also communicated through their own ambassadors in Cairo and Tel Aviv.

Now that's the kind of future we're offering—of peace to the Middle East if the Democrats are reelected in the fall.

I am very proud that nearly half the aid that our country has ever given to Israel in the 32 years of her existence has come during my administration. Unlike our Republican predecessors, we have never stopped nor slowed that aid to Israel. And as long as I am president, we will never do so. Our commitment is clear: security and peace for Israel: peace for all the peoples of the Middle East.

But if the world is to have a future of freedom as well as peace, America must continue to defend human rights.

Now listen to this: The new Republican leaders oppose our human rights policy. They want to scrap it. They seem to think it's naive for America to stand up to freedom and—for freedom and democracy. Just what do they think we should stand up for?

Ask the former political prisoners who now live in freedom if we should abandon our stand on human rights.

Ask the dissidents in the Soviet Union about our commitment to human rights.

Ask the Hungarian-Americans, ask the Polish-Americans.

Listen to Pope John Paul II.

Ask those who are suffering for the sake of justice and liberty around the world.

Ask the millions who've fled tyranny if America should stop speaking out for human principles.

Ask the American people. I tell you that as long as I am president, we will hold high the banner of human rights, and you can depend on it.

Here at home the choice between the two futures is equally important.

In the long run, nothing is more crucial to the future of America than energy—nothing was so disastrously neglected in the past.

Long after the 1973 Arab oil embargo, the Republicans in the White House had still done nothing to meet the threat to national security of our nation. Then, as now, their policy was dictated by the big oil companies.

We Democrats fought hard to rally our nation behind a comprehensive energy program and a good program—a new foundation for challenging and exciting progress. Now, after three years of struggle, we have that program.

The battle to secure America's energy future has been fully and finally joined. Americans have cooperated with dramatic results.

We've reversed decades of dangerous and growing dependence on foreign oil. We are now importing 20 percent less oil. That is one and a half million barrels of oil every day less than the day I took office.

And with our new energy policy now in place, we can discover more, produce more, create more, and conserve more energy—and we will use American resources, American technology, and millions of American workers to do it with.

Now what do the Republicans propose?

Basically their energy program has two parts.

The first part is to get rid of almost everything that we've done for the American public in the last three years.

They want to reduce or abolish the synthetic fuels program. They want to slash the solar energy incentives, the conservation programs, aid to mass transit, aid to the elderly Americans to help pay their fuel bills.

They want to eliminate the fifty-five mile speed limit. And while they're at it, the Republicans would like to gut the Clean

Air Act. They never liked it to begin with.

That's one part of the program.

The other part is worse.

To replace what we have built, this is what they propose: to destroy the windfall profits tax, and to "unleash" the oil companies and let them solve the energy problem for us.

That's it. That's the whole program. There is no more.

Can this nation accept such an outrageous program? No! We Democrats will fight it every step of the way, and we'll begin tomorrow morning with the campaign for reelection in November.

When I took office, I inherited a heavy load of serious economic problems besides energy—and we've met them all head-on. We've slashed government regulation and put free enterprise back into the airlines, the trucking and the financial systems of our country—and we're now doing the same thing for the railroads. This is the greatest change in the relationship between government and business since the New Deal.

We've increased our exports dramatically. We've reversed the decline in the basic research and development. And we have created more than 8 million new jobs—the biggest increase in the history of our country.

But the road's bumpy, and last year's skyrocketing OPEC price increases have helped to trigger a worldwide inflation crisis.

We took forceful action, and interest rates have now fallen, the dollar is stable and, although we still have a battle on our hands, we are struggling to bring inflation under control.

We are now at a critical turning point in our economic history. Because we made the hard decisions—because we guided our economy through a rough but essential period of transition—we have laid the groundwork for a new economic age.

Our economic renewal program for the 1980s will meet our immediate need for jobs by attacking the very same long-term problems that caused unemployment and inflation in the first place. It will move America simultaneously towards our five great economic goals—lower inflation, better productivity, revitalization of American industry, energy security and jobs.

It is time to put all America back to work—not in make work, but in real work.

There is real work in modernizing American industry and

creating new industries for America.

Here are just a few things we will build together:

New industries to turn our coal and shale and farm products into fuel for our cars and trucks, and to turn the light of the sun into heat and electricity for our homes; A modern transportation system for railbeds and ports to make American coal into a powerful rival of OPEC oil;

Industries that will provide the convenience of communications and futuristic computer technology to serve millions of American homes, offices and factories;

Job training for workers displaced by economic changes;

New investment pinpointed in regions and communities where jobs are needed most;

Better mass transit in our cities and between cities;

And a whole new generation of American jobs to make homes and vehicles and buildings that will house us and move us in comfort—with a lot less energy.

This is important, too: I have no doubt that the ingenuity and dedication of the American people can make every single one of these things happen. We are talking about the United States of America—and those who count this country out as an economic superpower are going to find out just how wrong they are.

We are going to share in the exciting enterprise of making the 1980s a time of growth for America.

The Republican alternative is the biggest tax giveaway in history. They call it "Reagan-Kemp-Roth." I call it a free lunch Americans cannot afford.

The Republican tax program offers rebates to the rich, deprivation for the poor and fierce inflation for all of us. Their party's own vice presidential nominee said that "Reagan-Kemp-Roth" would result in an inflation rate of more than 30 percent. He called it "voodoo economics." He suddenly changed his mind toward the end of the Republican convention, but he was right the first time.

Along with this gigantic tax cut, the new Republican leaders promise to protect retirement and health programs, and to have massive increases in defense spending.

And they claim they can balance the budget.

If they are serious about these promises—and they say they are—then a close analysis shows that the entire rest of the government would have to be abolished—everything from education to farm programs, from the G.I. Bill to the night watchman at the Lincoln Memorial. And the budget would still be in the red.

The only alternative would be to build more printing presses to print cheap money. Either way the American people lose. But the American people will not stand for it.

The Democratic Party has always embodied the hope of our people for justice, opportunity and a better life. And we've worked in every way possible to strengthen the American family, to encourage self-reliance, and to follow the Old Testament admonition: "Defend the poor and fatherless: give justice to the afflicted and needy." (Psalms 82:3)

We have struggled to assure that no child in America ever goes to bed hungry, that no elderly couple in America has to live in a substandard home, and that no young person in America is excluded from college because the family is poor.

What have the Republicans proposed? Just an attack on everything we have done in the achievement in social justice and decency that we've won in the last 50 years—ever since Franklin Delano Roosevelt's first term. They would make Social Security voluntary. They would reverse our progress on the minimum wage, full employment laws, safety in the work place and a healthy environment.

Lately, as you know, the Republicans have been quoting Democratic presidents, but who can blame them? Would you rather quote Herbert Hoover or Franklin Delano Roosevelt? Would you rather quote Richard Nixon or John Fitzgerald Kennedy?

The Republicans have always been the party of privilege, but this year their leaders have gone even further. In their platform, they have repudiated the best traditions of their own party.

Where is the conscience of Lincoln in the party of Lincoln? What's become of that traditional Republican commitment to fiscal responsibility? What's happened to their commitment to a safe and sane arms control?

Now I don't claim perfection for the Democratic Party. I don't claim that every decision that we have made has been right or popular. Certainly they've not all been easy. But I will say this:

We've been tested under fire. We've neither ducked nor hidden. And we've tackled the great, central issues in our time, the historic challenges of peace and energy which had been ignored for years.

We've made tough decisions and we've taken the heat for them. We've made mistakes and we've learned from them. So we have built the foundation now for a better future.

We've done something else—perhaps even more important. In good times and bad, in the valleys and on the peaks, we've told people the truth—the hard truth—the truth that sometimes hurts.

One truth that we Americans have learned is that our dream has been earned for progress and for peace. Look what our land has been through within our own memory—a great depression, a world war, the technological explosion, the civil rights revolution, the bitterness of Vietnam, the shame of Watergate, the twilight peace of nuclear terror.

Through each of these momentous experiences we've learned the hard way about the world and about ourselves. For we've matured and we've grown as a nation. And we've grown stronger.

We've learned the uses and the limitations of power. We've learned the beauty and responsibility of freedom. We've learned the value and the obligation of justice—and we have learned the necessity of peace.

Some would argue that to master these lessons is somehow to limit our potential. That is not so. A nation which knows its true strengths, which sees its true challenges, which understands legitimate constraints—that nation, our nation—is far stronger than one which takes refuge in wishful thinking or nostalgia.

The Democratic Party—the American people—have understood these fundamental truths.

All of us can sympathize with the desire for easy answers. There's often the temptation to substitute idle dreams for hard reality.

The new Republican leaders are hoping that our nation will succumb to that temptation this year. But they profoundly misunderstand and underestimate the character of the American people.

Three weeks after Pearl Harbor, Winston Churchill came to North America—and he said:

"We've not journeyed all this way across the centuries,

across the oceans, across the mountains, across the prairies because we are made of sugar candy."

We Americans have courage.

Americans have always been on the cutting edge of change. We've always looked forward with anticipation and confidence. I still want the same thing that all of you want—a self-reliant neighborhood and strong families: work for the able-bodied and good medical care for the sick, opportunity for our youth and dignity for our old, equal rights and justice for all people.

I want teachers eager to explain what a civilization really is—and I want students to understand their own needs and their own aims, but also the needs and yearnings of their neighbors. I want women free to pursue without limit the full life of what they want for themselves.

I want our farmers growing crops to feed our nation and the world, secure in the knowledge that the family farm will thrive and with a fair return on the good work they do for all of us. I want workers to see meaning in the labor they perform—and work enough to guarantee a job for every worker in this country.

And I want the people in business free to pursue with boldness and freedom new ideas. And I want minority citizens fully to join the mainstream of American life, and I want from the bottom of my heart to remove the blight of racial and other discrimination from the face of our nation, and I'm determined to do it.

I need for all of you to join me in fulfilling that vision. The choice—the choice between the two futures—could not be more clear. If we succumb to a dream world, then we'll wake up to a nightmare. But if we start with reality and fight to make our dreams a reality—then Americans will have a good life, a life of meaning and purpose in a nation that's strong and secure.

Above all, I want us to be what the founders of our nation meant us to become—the land of freedom, the land of peace, and the land of hope.

Thank you very much.

ACCEPTANCE SPEECH
BY
GOVERNOR RONALD REAGAN
REPUBLICAN NATIONAL CONVENTION
DETROIT, MICHIGAN
JULY 17, 1980

MR. CHAIRMAN, delegates to this convention, my fellow citizens of this great nation:

With a deep awareness of the responsibility conferred by your trust, I accept your nomination for the Presidency of the United States. I do so with deep gratitude.

I am very proud of our party tonight. This convention has shown to all America a party united, with positive programs for solving the nation's problems; a party ready to build a new consensus with all those across the land who share a community of values embodied in these words: family, work, neighborhood, peace and freedom.

I know we have had a quarrel or two in our party, but only as to the method of attaining a goal. There was no argument about the goal. As President, I will establish a liaison with the fifty Governors to encourage them to eliminate, wherever it exists, discrimination against women. I will monitor Federal laws to insure their implementation and to add statutes if they are needed.

More than anything else, I want my candidacy to unify our country, to renew the American spirit and sense of purpose. I want to carry our message to every American, regardless of party affiliation, who is a member of this community of shared values.

Never before in our history have Americans been called upon to face three grave threats to our very existence, any one of which could destroy us. We face a disintegrating economy, a weakened defense and an energy policy based on the sharing of scarcity.

The major issue of this campaign is the direct political, personal, and moral responsibility of Democratic Party leadership—in the White House and in Congress—for this unprecedented calamity which has befallen us. They tell us they have done the most that humanly could be done. They say that the United States has had its days in the sun, that our nation has passed its zenith. They expect you to tell your children that the American people no longer have the will to cope with their problems, that the future will be one of sacrifice and few opportunities.

My fellow citizens, I utterly reject that view. The American people, the most generous on earth, who created the highest standard of living, are not going to accept the notion that we can only make a better world for others by moving backwards ourselves. Those who believe we *can* have no business leading the nation.

I will not stand by and watch this great country destroy itself under mediocre leadership that drifts from one crisis to the next, eroding our national will and purpose. We have come together here because the American people deserve better from those to whom they entrust our nation's highest offices, and we stand united in our resolve to do something about it.

We need a rebirth of the American tradition of leadership at *every* level of government and in private life as well. The United States of America is unique in world history because it has a genius for leaders—many leaders—on many levels. But, back in 1976, Mr. Carter said, "Trust *me*." And a lot of people did. Now, many of those people are out of work. Many have seen their savings eaten away by inflation. Many others on fixed incomes, especially the elderly, have watched helplessly as the cruel tax of inflation wasted away their purchasing power. And, today, a great many who trusted Mr. Carter wonder if we can survive the Carter policies of national defense.

"Trust me" government asks that we concentrate our hopes and dreams on one man, that we trust him to do what's best for us. My view of government places trust not in one person or one party, but in those values that transcend persons and parties. The trust is where it belongs—in the people. The responsibility to live up to that trust is where *it* belongs, in their elected leaders. That kind of relationship, between the people and their elected leaders, is a special kind of *compact*, an agreement among themselves to build a community and abide by its laws.

Three hundred and sixty years ago, in 1620, a group of families dared to cross a mighty ocean to build a future for themselves in a new world. When they arrived at Plymouth, Massachusetts, they formed what they called a "compact," an agreement among themselves to build a community and abide by its laws.

The single act—the voluntary binding together of free people to live under the law—set the pattern for what was to come.

A century and a half later, the descendants of those people pledged their lives, their fortunes and their sacred honor to found this nation. Some forfeited their fortunes and their lives; none sacrificed honor.

Four score and seven years later, Abraham Lincoln called upon the people of all America to renew their dedication and their commitment to a government of, for and by the people.

Isn't it once again time to renew our compact of freedom, to pledge to each other all that is best in our lives, all that gives meaning to them—for the sake of this, our beloved and blessed land?

Together, let us make this a new beginning. Let us make a commitment to care for the needy, to teach our children the values and the virtues handed down to us by our families, to have the courage to defend those values and the willingness to sacrifice for them.

Let us pledge to restore, in our time, the American spirit of voluntary service, of cooperation, of private and community initiative, a spirit that flows like a deep and mighty river through the history of our nation.

As your nominee, I pledge to restore to the federal government the capacity to do the people's work without dominating their lives. I pledge to you a government that will not only work well, but wisely, its ability to act tempered by prudence, and its willingness to do good balanced by the knowledge that government is never more dangerous than when our desire to have it help us blinds us to its great power to harm us.

The first Republican President once said, "While the people retain their virtue and their vigilance, no Administration by any extreme of wickedness or folly can seriously injure the government in the short space of four years."

If Mr. Lincoln could see what's happened in these last three and a half years, he might hedge a little on that statement. But, with the virtues that are our legacy as a free people and with the vigilance that sustains liberty, we still have time to use our renewed compact to overcome the injuries that have been done to America these past three and a half years.

First, we must overcome something the present Administration has cooked up: a new and altogether indigestible economic stew, one part inflation, one part high unemployment, one part recession, one part runaway taxes, one part deficit spending and seasoned by an energy crisis. It's an economic stew that has turned the national stomach. It is as if Mr. Carter had set out to prove, once and for all, that economics is indeed a "dismal science."

Ours are not problems of abstract economic theory. These are problems of flesh and blood, problems that cause pain and destroy the moral fiber of real people who should not suffer the further indignity of being told by the White House that it is all somehow their fault. We do not have inflation because— as Mr. Carter says—we have lived too well.

The head of a government which has utterly refused to live within *its* means and which has, in the last few days, told us that this year's deficit will be $60 billion, dares to point the finger of blame at business and labor, both of which have been engaged in a losing struggle just trying to stay even.

High taxes, we are told, are somehow good for us, as if, when government spends our money it isn't inflationary, but when we spend it, it is.

Those who preside over the worst energy shortage in our history tell us to use less, so that we will run out of oil, gasoline and natural gas a little more slowly. Conservation is desirable, of course, for we must not waste energy. But conservation is not the sole answer to our energy needs.

America must get to work producing more energy. The Republican program for solving economic problems is based on growth and productivity.

Large amounts of oil and natural gas lay beneath our land and off our shores, untouched because the present Administration seems to believe the American people would rather see more regulation, taxes and controls than more energy.

Coal offers great potential. So does nuclear energy produced under rigorous safety standards. It could supply electricity for thousands of industries and millions of jobs and homes. It must not be thwarted by a tiny minority opposed to economic growth which often finds friendly ears in regulatory agencies for its obstructionist campaigns.

Make no mistake. We will not permit the safety of our people or our environmental heritage to be jeopardized, but we are going to reaffirm that the economic *prosperity* of our people is a fundamental part of our environment.

Our problems are both acute and chronic, yet all we hear from those in positions of leadership are the same tired proposals for more government tinkering, more meddling and more control—all of which led us to this state in the first place.

Can anyone look at the record of this Administration and say, "Well done"? Can anyone compare the state of our economy when the Carter administration took office with where we are today and say, "Keep up the good work"? Can anyone look at our reduced standing in the world today and say, "Let's have four more years of this"?

I believe the American people are going to answer these questions the first week of November and their answer will be, "No—we've had enough." And, when the American people *have* spoken, it will be up to us—beginning next January 20th—to offer an Administration and Congressional leadership of competence and more than a little courage.

We must have the clarity of vision to see the difference between what is essential and what is merely desirable, and then the courage to use this insight to bring our government back under control and make it acceptable to the people.

We Republicans believe it is essential that we maintain both the forward momentum of economic growth and the strength of the safety net beneath those in society who need help. We also believe it is essential that the integrity of all aspects of Social Security be preserved.

Beyond these essentials, I believe it is clear our federal

government is overgrown and overweight. Indeed, it is time for our government to go on a diet. Therefore, my first act as Chief Executive will be to impose an immediate and thorough freeze on federal hiring. Then, we are going to enlist the very best minds from business, labor and whatever quarter to conduct a detailed review of every department, bureau and agency that lives by federal appropriation. We are also going to enlist the help and ideas of many dedicated and hard-working government employees at all levels who want a more efficient government as much as the rest of us do. I know that many are demoralized by the confusion and waste they confront in their work as a result of failed and failing policies.

Our instructions to the groups we enlist will be simple and direct. We will remind them that government programs exist at the sufferance of the American taxpayer and are paid for with money earned by working men and women. Any program that represents a waste of their money—a theft from their pocketbooks—must have that waste eliminated or the program must go—by Executive Order where possible, by Congressional action where necessary. Everything that can be run more effectively by state and local government we shall turn over to state and local government, along with the funding sources to pay for it. We are going to put an end to the money merry-go-round where our money becomes Washington's money, to be spent by the states and cities only if they spend it exactly the way the federal bureaucrats tell them to.

I will not accept the excuse that the federal government has grown so big and powerful that it is beyond the control of any President, any Administration or Congress. We are going to put an end to the notion that the American taxpayer exists to fund the federal government. The federal government exists to *serve* the American people and to be accountable to the American people. On January 20th, we are going to reestablish that truth.

Also on that date we are going to initiate action to get substantial relief for our taxpaying citizens and action to put people back to work. None of this will be based on any new form of monetary tinkering or fiscal sleight of hand. We will simply apply to government the common sense we all use in our daily lives.

Work and family are at the center of our lives, the foundation of our dignity as a free people. When we deprive people of what they have earned, or take away their jobs, we destroy their dignity and undermine their families. We cannot support our families unless there are jobs, and we cannot have jobs unless people have both money to invest and the faith to invest it.

These are concepts that stem from the foundation of an economic system that for more than two hundred years has helped us master a continent, create a previously undreamed of prosperity for our people and has fed millions of others around the globe. That system will continue to serve us in the future if our government will stop ignoring the basic values on which it was built and stop betraying the trust and good will of the American workers who keep it going.

The American people are carrying the heaviest peacetime tax burden in our nation's history—and it will grow even heavier, under present law, next January. This burden is crushing our ability and incentive to save, invest and produce. We are taxing ourselves into economic exhaustion and stagnation.

This must stop. We *must* halt this fiscal self-destruction and restore sanity to our economic system.

I have long advocated a 30 percent reduction in income tax rates over a period of three years. This phased tax reduction would begin with a 10 percent "down payment" tax cut in 1981, which the Republicans in Congress and I have already proposed.

A phased reduction of tax rates would go a long way toward easing the heavy burden on the American people. But, we should not stop here.

Within the context of economic conditions and appropriate budget priorities during each fiscal year of my Presidency, I would strive to go further. This would include improvement in business depreciation taxes so we can stimulate investment in order to get plants and equipment replaced, put more Americans back to work and put our nation back on the road to being competitive in world commerce. We will also work to reduce the cost of government as a percentage of our Gross National Product.

The first task of national leadership is to set honest and realistic priorities in our policies and our budget and I pledge that my Administration will do that.

When I talk of tax cuts, I am reminded that every major tax cut in this century has strengthened the economy, generated renewed productivity and ended up yielding new revenues for the government by creating new investment, new jobs and more commerce among our people.

The present Administration has been forced by us Republicans to play follow-the-leader with regard to a tax cut. But, we must take with the proverbial "grain of salt" any tax cut proposed by those who have given us the greatest tax *increase* in our history. When those in leadership give us tax increases and tell us we must also do with less, have they thought about those who have always had less—especially the minorities? This is like telling them that just as they step on the first rung of the ladder of opportunity, the ladder is being pulled up. That may be the Democratic leadership's message to the minorities, but it won't be ours. Our message will be: we have to move ahead, but we're not going to leave *anyone* behind.

Thanks to the economic policies of the Democratic Party, millions of Americans find themselves out of work. Millions more have never even had a fair chance to learn new skills, hold a decent job, seize the opportunity to climb the ladder and secure for themselves and their families a share in the prosperity of this nation.

It is time to put America back to work, to make our cities and towns resound with the confident voices of men and women of all races, nationalities and faiths bringing home to their families a decent paycheck they can cash for honest money.

For those without skills, we'll find a way to help them get skills.

For those without job opportunities we'll stimulate new opportunities, particularly in the inner cities where they live.

For those who have abandoned hope, we'll restore hope and we'll welcome them into a great national crusade to make America great again!

When we move from domestic affairs and cast our eyes abroad, we see an equally sorry chapter in the record of the present Administration.

—A Soviet combat brigade trains in Cuba, just 90 miles from our shores.

—A Soviet army of invasion occupies Afghanistan, further threatening our vital interests in the Middle East.

—America's defense strength is at its lowest ebb in a generation, while the Soviet Union is vastly outspending us in both strategic and conventional arms.

—Our European allies, looking nervously at the growing menace from the East, turn to us for leadership and fail to find it.

—And, incredibly more than 50 of our fellow Americans have been held captive for over eight months by a dictatorial foreign power that holds us up to ridicule before the world.

Adversaries large and small test our will and seek to confound our resolve, but the Carter Administration gives us weakness when we need strength, vacillation when the times demand firmness.

Why? Because the Carter Administration lives in the world of make-believe. Every day, it dreams up a response to that day's troubles, regardless of what happened yesterday and what will happen tomorrow. The Administration lives in a world where mistakes, even very big ones, have no consequence.

The rest of us, however, live in the real world. It is here that disasters are overtaking our nation without any real response from the White House.

I condemn the Administration's make-believe, its self-deceit and—above all—its transparent hypocrisy.

For example, Mr. Carter says he supports the volunteer army, but he lets military pay and benefits slip so low that many of our enlisted personnel are actually eligible for food stamps. Re-enlistment rates drop and, just recently, after he fought all week *against* a proposal to increase the pay of our men and women in uniform, he helicoptered out to our carrier the *U.S.S. Nimitz,* which was returning from long months of duty. He told the crew that he advocated better pay for them and their comrades! Where does he really stand, now that he's back on shore?

I'll tell you where *I* stand. I do *not* favor a peacetime draft or registration, but I do favor pay and benefit levels that will attract and keep highly motivated men and women in our volunteer forces and an active reserve trained and ready for an instant call in case of an emergency.

An Annapolis graduate may be at the helm of the ship of state, but the ship has no rudder. Critical decisions are made at times almost in Marx Brothers fashion, but who can laugh? Who was not embarrassed when the Administration handed a major propaganda victory in the United Nations to the enemies of Israel, our staunch Middle East ally for three decades, and then claimed that the American vote was a "mistake," the result of a "failure of communication" between the President, his Secretary of State and his U.N. Ambassador?

Who does not feel a growing sense of unease as our allies, facing repeated instances of an amateurish and confused Administration, reluctantly conclude that America is unwilling or unable to fulfill its obligations as leader of the free world?

Who does not feel rising alarm when the question in any discussion of foreign policy is no longer, "Should we do something?", but "Do we have the capacity to do *anything*"

The Administration which has brought us to this state is seeking your endorsement for four more years of weakness, indecision, mediocrity and incompetence. No American should vote until he or she has asked, "Is the United States stronger and more respected now than it was three and a half years ago? Is the world today a safer place in which to live?"

It is the responsibility of the President of the United States, in working for peace, to insure that the safety of our people cannot successfully be threatened by a hostile foreign power. As President, fulfilling that responsibility will be my Number One priority.

We are not a warlike people. Quite the opposite. We always seek to live in peace. We resort to force infrequently and with great reluctance—and only after we have determined that it is absolutely necessary. We are awed—and rightly so—by the forces of destruction at loose in the world in this nuclear era. But neither can we be naive or foolish. Four times in my lifetime America has gone to war, bleeding the lives of its young men into the sands of beachheads, the fields of Europe and the jungles and rice paddies of Asia. We know only too well that war comes not when the forces of freedom are strong, but when they are weak. It is then that tyrants are tempted.

We simply cannot learn these lessons the hard way again without risking our destruction.

Of all the objectives we seek, first and foremost is the establishment of lasting world peace. We must always stand ready to negotiate in good faith, ready to pursue any reasonable avenue that holds forth the promise of lessening tensions and furthering the prospects of peace. But let our friends and those who may wish us ill take note: the United States has an obligation to its citizens and to the people of the world never to let those who would destroy freedom dictate the future course of human life on this planet. I would regard my election as proof that we have renewed our resolve to preserve world peace and freedom. This nation will once again be strong enough to do that.

This evening marks the last step—save one—of a campaign that has taken Nancy and me from one end of this great land to the other, over many months and thousands and thousands of miles. There are those who question the way we choose a President, who say that our process imposes difficult and exhausting burdens on those who seek the office. I have not found it so.

It is impossible to capture in words the splendor of this vast continent which God has granted as our portion of his creation. There are no words to express the extraordinary strength and character of this breed of people we call Americans.

Everywhere we have met thousands of Democrats, Independents and Republicans from all economic conditions and walks of life bound together in that community of shared values of family, work, neighborhood, peace and freedom. They are concerned, yes, but they are not frightened. They are disturbed, but not dismayed. They are the kind of men and women Tom Paine had in mind when he wrote—during the darkest days of the American Revolution—"We have it in our power to begin the world over again."

Nearly one hundred and fifty years after Tom Paine wrote those words, an American President told the generation of the Great Depression that it had a "rendezvous with destiny." I believe *this* generation of Americans today also has a rendezvous with destiny.

Tonight, let us dedicate ourselves to renewing the American Compact. I ask you not simply to "Trust *me*," but to trust your values—our values—and to hold me responsible for living up to them. I ask you to trust that American spirit which knows no ethnic, religious, social, political, regional or economic boundaries, the spirit that burned with zeal in the hearts of millions of immigrants from every corner of the earth who came here in search of freedom.

Some say that spirit no longer exists. But I have seen it— I have felt it—all across the land, in the big cities, the small towns and in rural America. The American spirit is still there, ready to blaze into life if you and I are willing to do what has to be done, the practical, down-to-earth things that will stimulate our economy, increase productivity and put America back to work.

The time is *now* to limit federal spending, to insist on a stable monetary reform and to free ourselves from imported oil.

The time is *now* to resolve that the basis of a firm and principled foreign policy is one that takes the world as it is and seeks to change it by leadership and example, not by lecture and harangue.

The time is *now* to say that while we shall seek new friendships and expand and improve others, we shall not do so by breaking our word or casting aside old friends and allies.

And, the time is *now* to redeem promises once made to the American people by another candidate, in another time and another place. He said,

"...For three long years I have been going up and down this country preaching that government—federal, state and local—costs too much. I shall not stop that preaching. As an immediate program of action, we must abolish useless offices. We must eliminate unnecessary functions of government....

"...we must consolidate subdivisions of government and, like the private citizen, give up luxuries which we can no longer afford.

"I propose to you, my friends, and through you that government of all kinds, big and little be made solvent and that the example be set by the President of the United States and his cabinet."

So said Franklin Delano Roosevelt in his acceptance speech to the Democratic National Convention in July, 1932.

The time is *now*, my fellow Americans, to recapture our destiny, to take it into our own hands. But, to do this will take many of us, working together. I ask you tonight to volunteer your help in this cause so we can carry our message throughout the land.

Yes, isn't *now* the time that we, the people, carried out these unkept promises? Let us pledge to each other and to all America on *this* July day forty-eight years later, we intend to do *just that*.

I've thought of something that is not part of my speech and I'm worried over whether I should do it.

Can we doubt that only a Divine Providence placed this

land, this island of freedom, here as a refuge for all those people in the world who yearn to breathe freely: Jews and Christians enduring persecution behind the Iron Curtain, the boat people of Southeast Asia, of Cuba and Haiti, the victims of the drought in Africa, the freedom fighters of Afghanistan and our own countrymen held in savage captivity?

I'll confess that I've been a little afraid to suggest what I'm going to suggest—I'm more afraid not to—that we begin our crusade joined together in a moment of silent prayer. God bless America.

About the Authors

DAN BALZ, currently political editor on the national desk, will be going to Texas after the elections to become The *Post*'s Southwest bureau chief. Before coming to The *Post* in 1978, he worked at *National Journal* magazine in Washington as deputy editor and as a reporter.

DAVID S. BRODER is The *Post*'s chief political correspondent and also writes a twice-weekly column that is carried by more than 255 newspapers across the nation. In 1973, he received a Pulitzer Prize for distinguished commentary. He has covered every national campaign and convention since 1956, traveling up to 100,000 miles a year to interview voters and report on the candidates. His most recent book is *Changing of the Guard: Power and Leadership in America*.

LOU CANNON has been chief of The *Post*'s news bureau in Los Angeles since July 1977. He joined the paper in 1972 as a reporter on the national news staff, covering politics and the Nixon administration. Prior to that, he was a Washington correspondent for the Ridder newspaper chain.

WILLIAM H. GREIDER is assistant managing editor/national news of The *Post*. He came to The *Post* from the *Louisville Courier-Journal* as a national correspondent in 1969.

RICHARD HARWOOD is deputy managing editor of The *Post*. He came to the paper in 1966 from the *Louisville Courier-Journal* and since then has had a number of assignments including national politics and public affairs reporting, correspondent in Vietnam, national editor and assistant managing editor/national news. He was responsible for coordinating editorial matter for this book, and did much of the writing for it. He is the co-author of several other books.

HAYNES JOHNSON is a columnist on the national staff of the *Washington Post*. In 1966, he won the Pulitzer Prize for his reporting of the civil rights struggle in Selma, Ala. He has edited, authored or co-authored nine books, most recently *In the Absence of Power: Governing America*.

FRANK JOHNSTON, whose photographs of the campaign form a section of this book, traveled for five years with UPI, including 13 months as staff combat photographer in Vietnam, before joining The *Post* in 1968. He is twice winner of the White House News Photographers award. His graphic photos of the Jonestown, Guyana, mass deaths in November 1978 were included in the Berkley instant paperback book, *Guyana Massacre*.

NICHOLAS LEMANN was born and raised in New Orleans. He has worked as an editor and writer for The *Washington Monthly* and *Texas Monthly*, and came to The *Post* in 1979 as a staff writer.

BILL PETERSON has written about politics, education, world poverty, lifestyles and a tobacco spitting contest since he came to The *Post* from The *Louisville Courier-Journal* in 1975. He is author of *Coaltown Revisited: An Appalachian Notebook*, and co-author of two other books on rural America.

T. R. REID joined the national news staff of The *Post* in 1977 as a reporter specializing in Congress and political affairs. Prior to his arrival at The *Post* he had been Washington bureau chief of the *Trenton* (N.J.) *Times*.

MARTIN SCHRAM, as a writer on the presidency, has been observing and analyzing the action of those who occupy the Oval Office, and those who seek to work there, since 1968. The author of *Running for President 1976*, he joined The *Post* in 1979, after having served for six years as Washington bureau chief of *Newsday*.

EDWARD J. WALSH is White House correspondent for The *Post*, and is due to become a national reporter after the election. In 1979 he received the Merriman Smith Memorial Award for distinguished presidential news coverage. Before coming to the paper in 1971, Walsh had been a reporter for the *Houston Chronicle*.